# ROMANTICISM

by Jean Clay

with a foreword by Robert Rosenblum

CHARTWELL BOOKS INC.

# CONTENTS

Published by Chartwell Books Inc.
A Division of Book Sales Inc.
110 Enterprise Avenue
Secaucus, New Jersey 07094

This book was produced by the editors of Réalités-Hachette
under the direction of Jean Clay

Layout by Jean-Louis Germain

Translation from the French by Daniel Wheeler and Craig Owen
Editorial assistance by Anne Hoy, Margaret Aspenwald,
Linda Bradford, and Michael Rinehart

Originally published in French under the title *Le Romantisme*
Copyright © 1980 Hachette, Paris
English language copyright © 1981 by Hachette-Vendome
All rights reserved
This book, or parts thereof, must not be reproduced in any form
without permission of the publisher

**Library of Congress Cataloging in Publication Data**
Clay, Jean
    Romanticism.

    Translation of: Romantisme
    Bibliography: p.
    1. Romanticism in Art.    2. Painting, Modern—17th–18th
    centuries.    3. Painting, Modern—19th century.
    I. Title
    ND   188.   R64C5913          759.05'2          81–7555
                                                    AACR2
**ISBN:** 0-89009-588-4
Printed and bound in Italy
by Grafiche Editoriali Ambrosiana S.p.A., Milan

# Foreword

by Robert Rosenblum

In thinking and writing about the period of vast upheaval and reconstruction that is roughly bracketed between the years 1760 and 1850, art historians have been regimented by two stubborn "isms": Neoclassicism and Romanticism. To be sure, the subtlest of recent views tend to blur the edges of these ostensibly antagonistic categories, often making the Neoclassic a part of the Romantic whole; but nobody until Jean Clay has attacked the entire period with a set of questions and answers so fresh and so illuminating that we feel a total liberation from our earlier prejudices. Rather than shaking his head at the obvious diversity of style and subject that bewilders the spectator in search of tidy historical order, Clay has sought out new means of disclosing the underlying patterns of emotional and visual structure that can unite the most seemingly unlike artists—Greuze and Fuseli, Copley and Goya, West and Girodet, Ingres and Géricault, Millet and Friedrich. His approach is at once abstract and particular. The skeleton of his argument is a series of essay-analyses that focus on the period's new insistence upon working with the abstract stuff of which two-dimensional images are made—the objectification, as it were, of such things as pure line, disembodied color, fluid atmosphere, emphatically flat surfaces—namely, the kind of thing that we have often assumed to be the exclusive domain of modern painting since Manet. In discussing these matters, Clay often employs the structuralist theories of such weighty thinkers as Saussure, Derrida, and Lévi-Strauss, and the going is not always easy. But for more empirical readers, these philosophical bones are instantly fleshed out by what is not only the most dazzling visual anthology I know of the full range of Romantic art, but also by a sequence of comparisons so provocative that even the most jaded art historian will sit up and shout Eureka!

Shattering all familiar compartments, Clay, for instance, can juxtapose Ingres's 1814 view of Pope Pius VII holding mass in the Sistine Chapel with Goya's almost exactly contemporaneous record of Ferdinand VII presiding over the Philippine *Junta,* making us realize how both artists are newly concerned with ways of conveying the awesome distance that separates us, the spectators, from these supremely powerful rulers who are almost lost in a remote and sanctified space. Similarly, he can cross the cultural boundaries of Nordic versus Mediterranean landscape traditions by demonstrating how the fogbound mountain views of both Friedrich, working in Germany, and Valenciennes,

working in Rome, annihilate traditional perspective constructions by prying the spectator loose from a secure footing in the foreground and immersing him in a framed immensity that implicitly continues in all directions. Rejecting other *idées reçues,* he can hasten to demonstrate the variety and importance of color in Ingres's work, whether used as an almost objectified, abstract component silhouetted against a black ground or as a warm, vibrant glow that fuses separate objects. Or studying the language of gesture, he can realign major and minor works by considering the emotional and structural meaning of arms rigidly extended in heroic conviction, as in the work of David, or of female bodies that undulate in abstract arabesques, as in that of Prud'hon. Throughout, in fact, Clay insists on the fusion of form and meaning, so that astute comments on, say, the period's frequent structural assertion of the framed image's rectilinear shape do not exist isolated in the vacuum-packed world of mid-20th-century formalist criticism, but have immediate reverberations in the experience of everything from the mortuary limpness of a David corpse to the cruciform mysteries suggested by the mullions of a Friedrich window. Clay may begin with the abstract internal structure of art, but he immediately converts it into vivid emotional and historical realities, whether considering the period's fascination with animal metaphors, psychosexual exploration, or the evocations prompted by Gothic architecture.

It should be said, too, that the richness of Clay's achievement is increased immeasurably by the vast international scope of his illustrations, which totally and happily destroy the traditionally xenophobic viewpoint of most earlier French writers on Romantic art. His belief that the changes he explores are a pan-European phenomenon means that he can move freely from France to England, from Germany to Spain, from Denmark to Switzerland, from Italy to Austria. And his equally wide erudition means that the yawns which might be produced by yet another illustration of a textbook classic by David or Géricault are instantly stifled by an abundance of unfamiliar material culled from the latest art-historical research. There is not only Guardi, but Servandoni; not only David, but Broc; not only Friedrich, but Oehme; not only Goya, but Paret; not only Fuseli, but Jefferys; not only Ingres, but Lehmann. And even such esoteric material as the anatomical fantasies of Gamelin and Gautier d'Agoty or the physiognomical *bizarreries* of Lequeu and Messerschmidt are woven into this dense fabric. In short, Clay has compiled a cornucopian bounty that may nourish the most diverse audiences. Philosophers, cultural historians, art historians, and, not least, the casual bibliophile who wishes to savor with images, rather than words, the visual fruits of the Romantic era—all should gather here.

# Introduction

"Ah! Couture, if only you were older, we could crush these abominable Romantics." Thus spoke Baron Gros, generally regarded as the father of French Romanticism. Since this *cri du coeur*, such confusion has never ceased to gather about the new art that emerged after 1760 and continued to flourish until midway through the following century. What does "Romanticism" mean? A.O. Lovejoy, in his *Essays in the History of Ideas*, relates how in 1824 two scholars, Messieurs Dupuis and Cotonet, set out to define the term, only to give up in total despair after twelve months of suffering. A century later (in 1925), Vermeylen managed to compile some 150 accepted definitions, all of which seemed pertinent. "We have babbled on about this endless subject for the last two years," wrote the critic Delécluze in his journal for 1827, "without being able even to determine what the romantic genre consists of. Opinions proved much more numerous than those who spoke on the subject, since each of us changed his mind not only within the same month or week, but even in the course of the same meeting." Hailed as the "Victor Hugo of painting," Delacroix declared: "Sir, I am a pure classicist." For Baudelaire, "Romanticism lies not at all in the choice of subject or in exact truth, but rather in a way of feeling." Earlier, in 1829, Goethe had written: "I call classic what is healthy and romantic what is sick." Finally, in the second half of the 19th century, Degas added: "A classicist is a romantic who has arrived." In our own time, Walter Friedlander has stated: "We can certainly speak of a *romantic classicism* in regard to certain pictures by Ingres or Girodet, or of *classical romanticism* in the instance of Delacroix's *Medea*."

To find direction through all these indirections, we have taken our point of departure from an observation made by Walter Benjamin in 1918: "Only since the Romantic age has it been thought that the true nature of an art work could be grasped once the work has been considered for itself, independently of its relation to theory or morality, and that such consideration would be sufficient." Here, of course, Benjamin spoke of literature, and by doing so in this way he revived an attitude that had been initially formulated by the Jena group centered upon the Schlegel brothers at the beginning of the 19th century. Theirs was a philosophical Romanticism, which saw literature as an independent, self-generating form, a form that breeds its own theory, at the same time that it materializes itself as a work of art. And in our understanding of the approach, we have gained fresh insight from two recent books, Todorov's *Théories du symbole* and Lacoue-Labarthe and Nancy's *L'Absolu littéraire*. "One could say, " writes Todorov, "that in classical doctrine, art and discourse are subject to an objective outside themselves, whereas with the Romantics [art and discourse] constitute an autonomous realm." Thus, the principle of imitation "is incompatible with the Romantic point of view, in that it subjects the work to something that is exterior (anterior, superior), to it: nature."

Although literary in their early 19th-century origins, these notions appear no less valid when applied to the painting of the period. They call for examining the work as *intransitive* form, that is, form whose meaning resides in the structure of the picture and not in its reference to some religious, political, or ideological program. Before referring elsewhere, the painting refers to itself. Given this, the work should no longer be perceived as a *document* (the trace or evidence of something other than itself) but rather as a *monument*, whose construction and disposition must be investigated and whose unity and internal relationships must be revealed[1]. Consequently, our task in this book has been to organize a series of chapters each of which is devoted to a formal issue, whose fundamental relevance for painting permits us to illuminate one component or another of the individual work's significant or expressive structure. In offering these analyses and interpretations, however, we have made no attempt to be exhaustive or definitive but only to indicate the possibilities for reading certain remarkable pictures anew.

"Romanticism" is difficult to define for the very reason that the term characterizes the historic moment when painting, like literature, emerged in its modern form, a self-contained reality. As a result, any attempt to classify Romantic painting according to thematic or stylistic criteria risks losing sight of what distinguishes it from earlier developments—precisely that internal focus which the art places upon its own material and formal constituents, a focus that locates Romantic pictures squarely within modernism. It might be claimed, as Friedrich Schlegel did, that Romanticism is modernity itself, since for the first time, often in an explicit manner, the chief effort lay in investigating (and thus revitalizing) form. "The Romantic genre of poetry," wrote Schlegel, "is still in the process of becoming; it is its very nature to be capable of nothing but a process of always becoming."

Certain contemporary observations point to this advent of the expressive formalism that for present purposes we have called *pictoriality*. Schiller, for instance, wrote in 1797: "Diderot is too preoccupied for my taste with matters that are outside art and pays too little attention to the object itself and its execution." To which Goethe replied: "Diderot has not seen fit to rise high enough to understand that the culture flowing from art must go its own way." Concerning Stendhal, Mérimée commented in 1850: "He admired the masters in a French way, that is, from a literary point of view, examining the pictures of the Italian school as if they were dramas. This is still the critical approach in France, where no one has any feeling for form or any innate love of color." For Baudelaire, writing in 1861, "both line and color make one think and dream; the pleasures they produce are of different orders, but perfectly equal and absolutely independent of the picture's subject." Thus, Fritz Novotny is quite correct when, in characterizing the most innovative work of the age, he called the art of Goya and Delacroix *painterly painting*.

Needless to say, however, a formalist conception of Romantic painting in no way reduces the art to its material components: the painting surface, the rectilinear shape of that surface, its grain,

1. Mantoux ahd Cheyère. *The Romantic.*

2. Ferdinand von Rayski. *Suicide in the Artist's Studio.* c. 1840.

4. Joseph Anton Koch.
*The Painter at the Crossroads*
(between the Baroque and Neoclassicism). 1791.

5. *The Great Battle between the Romantic
and the Classic at the Door to the Museum*, 1827.

6. Joseph Vigné.
*Romanticism, or the Literary Monster*. 1824.

the painter's gesture, and pigment. What the approach does is reveal the discrepancy that developed between the representational or narrative demands placed upon painting and the process through which those demands were met in materials that proved resistant to them. It discloses how the picture was realized, how its physical elements conformed *relatively* to artistic intentions, and how those intentions were modified in the very moment they assumed plastic form. In this way we gain access to and can appreciate a source of the art's magnetic greatness: the tension or precarious play between the rival needs of mimesis and those of materials whose compelling presence progressively changed the whole mimetic purpose of painting. The questions the formalist commentator asks resemble the problems confronted in the studio: To what extent should one figure or another evince the action of the hand that draws or paints it? How can a landscape image suggest illusionistic depth once it has been realized in strokes that are as flat and opaque as the surface that supports them? What degree of deformation can human physiognomy tolerate for the sake of a perfect arabesque line? In posing such questions about the pictures reproduced in this book, our goal has been to maintain a balance between two positions:

• The *materials-oriented*, modernist position, which sees the manifest destiny of painting in a complete equivalence of image and surface (that is, a single color spread over the canvas or paper edge to edge).
• The *idealist* position, which considers the picture already created in the mind of the artist, who has only to project it upon the insignificant, physical support.

But our greatest error in all this would be to ignore the figurative or representational aspect of Romantic painting, to sin by anachronism and overvalue those aspects of a picture that "anticipate" 20th-century abstraction. Our ambition has not been to prove that Romney or Delacroix achieved the aims of Kandinsky, or Turner those of Rothko. Wherever we refer to modern masters in this discussion, it is for the purpose of exposing line and touch, for instance, *in their gradual movement away from figural données:* This, by definition, means that one can never forget the commitment to recognizable subject matter that remained firmly in place throughout the entire period called "Romantic."

Thus, in view of the continuing, though shifting, balance between art and the figuration imposed on it from without, we should inquire just what was the relation of painting to the "Gothic" and sentimental literature—"Romantic," as the age would soon specify—that began to proliferate throughout Europe after the middle of the 18th century? The relation is at once both real and nonliteral. But it exists at a different level—indirect and unconscious—from that of the iconographic theme. And it is precisely this indirect relationship between literature and painting that we are most concerned about here, leaving to a subsequent but parallel volume a study of those artists who, from Chardin to Corot, claimed to find their primary inspiration

in an immediate, face-to-face encounter with the external world.

However faithful to detail Girodet may have been in his *Atala* (1808), nothing about this symmetrical, ordered, Neoclassic composition, other than its anecdote or plot, bears any relation to Chateaubriand's text—that is, to its "grain" or texture, its form. On this occasion, Girodet allowed himself and his work to be dominated by literature. The same artist, however, discovered in the Ossian legend (Fig. 357)—as did Ingres (Fig. 358)—the potential for genuinely *pictorial effects:* juxtaposed heterogeneous spaces, transparency, diffused light, blurred contours, all serving to echo what Hélène Toussaint has called "prose set to slightly breathless rhythms, stringing together dry metaphors in a sequence devoid of all system . . . [and leading] toward an estrangement then thought to be delicious." The *roman noir*, satanism, and "Gothic" ballads yielded other "indirect" sources for painting, sources, moreover, whose intuitive qualities, having been lifted directly from dreams, now seemed to call for a mutated imagery. Before writing *The Castle of Otranto*, Horace Walpole experienced a vision that he later incorporated into the novel: "I had thought myself in an ancient castle . . . and that, on the upper banister of a great staircase I saw a gigantic hand in armour. In the evening I sat down and began to write, without knowing in the least what I intended to say."

We know that the *Poems of Ossian*, published in 1760–63 as translations of ancient Gaelic ballads, were in fact composed almost entirely by an 18th-century Scots schoolmaster, James Macpherson, who thereby perpetrated one of the most celebrated hoaxes in the history of literature. Still, it must be admitted that "Ossianism" had preceded *Ossian*. Indeed, a number of works, such as Young's "Night Thoughts" (1742–45), Hervey's "Meditations among the Tombs" (1746), and Gray's "Elegy Written in a Country Churchyard" (1751) prefigured the nebulous, nocturnal, melancholic atmosphere evoked by the "Northern Homer." And the Ossianic craze persisted well after the fraud had been exposed, for the simple reason that the mood or climate captured by the so-called "Gaelic" bard responded to a deep aesthetic need. It was not a matter of literature having a mechanical effect upon painting but rather of a theme that proved conducive, in literature as well as in painting, to the decomposition of the rhetorical or plastic spaces inherited from the Renaissance.

Thus, we do not look for illustrations of Schelling's nature philosophy in the paintings of Friedrich, but try, rather, to understand how that philosophy encouraged, by a process of active transformation, new plastic departures, such as the destabilization of the centralized vantage point and the deceleration or acceleration of atmospheric perspective (Figs. 373, 374). By the same token, it is not the effect of Burke's observations on the sublime that we must seek out in English Romantic painting, but how that painting suggests immensity by means of close cropping, which makes the Alps (Figs. 206–207) seem both limitless and fragmentary—limitless *because* fragmentary.

If we must trace the reputed influence on painting of Burke and his *Philosophical Enquiry into the Origin of Our Ideas of the Sublime and Beautiful* (1757), we would measure it not in the thematic detail of works but in the conceptual orientation of individual artists. A century before Burke, Pascal had defined the imagination thus: "It is that deceiving element in man, that mistress of error and falsehood, and all the more deceitful for not always being so." Far from treating the imagination negatively, Burke saw "deceit" as the privileged mode of aesthetic expression. He even urged that all literalist reconstitution of things be suppressed—the better to make the imagination soar. Only the vague and the imprecise could fuel visionary flights, but when Burke looked at painting, he found it too precise, too finicking in its depiction of objects to permit "a grand and commanding conception." This was because reason, with all its insistence upon measure, proportion, limitation, and control, dominated the art then available to Burke. Only by overcoming reason could the identity of things be suspended. Burke therefore sought out the immeasurable and the incoercible—emptiness, darkness, solitude, silence, death—because in their very imponderability they provided a springboard to the "tranquility shadowed with horror" that he called "delight" and saw as the proper climate of the sublime. And the sublime induces not reflection but effusion, rapture, transport. "Far from being produced by them, [the sublime]," wrote Burke, "anticipates our reasonings, and hurries us on by an irresistible force." As the painter loses control and begins to float, he finds himself plunged into aesthetic turmoil. Emotion then breaks down all defenses and propels the artist outside himself, causing him to break the rules and exceed the limits of artistic practice. The sublime is always transgressive and aggressive, for the effect of compulsion and anxiety is the subversion of law. It resists all norms, all conformity, and promotes contradiction, rupture, lawlessness—hence innovation. On this level, philosophical thought functions less as a catalogue of themes than as a redefinition of the status of the creative individual in relation to the world.

Once the autonomy of the pictorial process comes to seem equal in importance to the notion of Romantic painting as a challenge to its own tradition, we find ourselves dispensing with certain of those classifications so often invoked for this period, such as national identity, genres, pre- and post-revolutionary art. We can also dismiss the long-nurtured opposition of Neoclassicism and Romanticism. Whatever its metaphysical and moralizing intentions, the idealist program called for by Winckelmann in the 18th century and by Quatremère de Quincy at the beginning of the following century prepared the way for a formalist advance. These writers extolled the severity, the regularity, "the noble simplicity and serene grandeur" of Greek art, all the while that they inveighed against naturalistic detail and illusionism. From this came restrained depth, frontality, pur-

ified contours, the affirmation of the arabesque upon the naked surface of paper or canvas. As a result, Neoclassicism poses a paradox, for the more the work became "ideal," the more it tends to reveal and validate its material components. Eventually we realize that such a program, even though imposed by powerful authority, succeeded in "taking hold" only because it offered an implicit response to the aspiration toward pictoriality, whose development flourished the more the concept of imitation met with overt challenge.

Given the seeming inevitability of polarities, we have preferred, on this occasion, to substitute for the Neoclassic/Romantic dichotomy another structural opposition:

• Painting as the product of an *organic* conception and process, wherein the work, as Baudelaire phrased it, "comes into being like a world," whole, complete, and integral throughout all its parts, this organic "holism" generated through an active, feverish engagement of the artist's body submitting utterly to compulsion. When a work thus realized evinces the hand and activity that produced it, the viewer's response cannot but be both sympathetic and empathetic. Chapters II and III address themselves to these issues.

• The notion of painting as the product of *assemblage*, an additive, serial process that could hardly be more different from the organic. Here the age abandoned the old academic unity—composition—and structured pictures by selecting fragments left from that shattered coherence, combining, joining, and juxtaposing them until some "stage" in the process gained the status of a "final," signed work. Such concerns will dominate the analyses in Chapters I and V.

This leaves Chapter IV, on color, to become the common ground where the two currents meet and fuse.

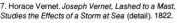
7. Horace Vernet. *Joseph Vernet, Lashed to a Mast, Studies the Effects of a Storm at Sea* (detail). 1822.

## Darkness, hallucination, madness . . .

"Always alone among people, I return home to dream by myself, and submit to the liveliness of my own melancholy. What turn will it take today? Toward death." This was not Goethe's Werther but Napoleon Bonaparte writing in 1786. Melancholy—the vague soulfulness that would soon nurture the *Rêveries* of Senancourt (1799) and sap the energies of Chateaubriand's René spared neither the future conqueror of Europe nor even those mid-18th-century rational pragmatists, the creators of the great *Encyclopédie*. "I admit that there is a secret covenant between death and night, which touches us without our suspecting it," wrote Diderot in *Pensées détachées sur la peinture* (1775). Meanwhile, a truth as old as antique wisdom, reactivated by the implications of modern science, runs through *Le Rêve d'Alembert*. "Everything changes, everything passes away," wrote Diderot. "Nothing remains but the Sum. The world endlessly begins and ends. . . . Alive, I act and react *en masse*. . . . Dead, I act and react in molecules." Unity no longer meant the individual person, since man was now seen as "an infinity of animalcules the metamorphoses of which could not be predicted."

The Newtonian conception of the world as a mechanism, which dominated 18th-century thought, was itself a source of the period's melancholy. The science historian A.E. Burtt tells us that wherever the theory of universal gravitation was taught as fact there arose the suspicion that man was no more than a weak and localized spectator, a relatively unimportant by-product of an infinite, automatic machine that had existed since all eternity and would continue to exist throughout all eternity. In 1799 Laplace published his *Traité de mécanique céleste*. "This time," writes G. Gusdorf, "the God of Newton is reduced to the condition of a 'do-nothing king'; thus, when General Bonaparte, a member of the Institute, asked Laplace what function he assigned to God in his system, the answer was: 'I don't need that hypothesis.'"

*(continued on page 11)*

8. The tranquilizing chair invented c. 1810 by the American physician Benjamin Rush.

top right: 9. Francisco Goya. *The Road to Hell*. 1819.

above 10. Francisco Goya. *Courtyard at the Madhouse*. 1794.

right: 11. Francisco Goya. *Madness Run Amok*. c. 1815–24.

12. Magician at work under the Empire.

13. Henry Fuseli. *Screech-Owl on the Body of a Woman.* c. 1820.

15. Caspar David Friedrich. *Screech-Owl on a Cross over a Grave.* 1836–37.

14. Francisco Goya. *"Who Will Deliver Us?"* 1797–98.

16. Louis Boulanger. *The Witches' Sabbath.* 1828.

17. Gustave Doré. *The Forest of the Damned.* 1861. Illustration for Dante's *Inferno.*

18. Victor Hugo. *The Dream.*

19. Louis Boulanger. *The Phantoms.*

20. Henry Fuseli. *The Nightmare.* c. 1790.

21. *The Monster of Gévaudon.* "This beast is the size of a young bull and is given to attacking women and children. It drinks their blood, then cuts off and carries away their heads. A reward of 27,000 *livres* awaits anyone who kills the animal." Text and engraving of 1770.

22. Henry Fuseli. *Woman Confronting the Laocoön.* 1801–05.

23. James Barry. *Satan, Sin, and Death.* c. 1790. Sin separates Death and Satan by revealing to them that they are father and son.

24. Francisco Goya. *The Disasters of War.* c. 1810–11.

25. Victor Hugo. *Laces and Specters.*

26. George Cruikshank. *The Drunkard's Children.* 1848.

(continued from page 8)

Some, like Benjamin Constant in 1790, suggested that "God . . . died before finishing his work. . . . We are like clocks without hands, clocks whose mechanisms, endowed with intelligence, continue to work until worn out."

This anxiety, with its link to human finiteness and a sense of the absurd, found an almost unbearable expression in the prosaic violence of Géricault's pictures and in the engravings of Goya (Fig. 28). From 1775 onward the macabre increasingly gained presence at the Paris Salon, displacing even the nocturnes and ruins pictures that had emerged just before midcentury.

Progressively, as certain sectors of 18th-century society escaped the universalist and normative will so characteristic of the Enlightenment, (the desire to "standardize men and beliefs," as A.O. Lovejoy phrased it), Romantic individualism asserted itself and evinced a sense of the difference—the tragic singularity—in the destiny of each human being. For Michel Foucault, the lyrical experience that began with Hölderlin was "related to the disclosure of the various forms of finitude." The German poet saw the age's clinical and anatomical rationality, with its positivist attitude toward death derived from the study of cadavers, and the concurrent emergence of poets singing of emptiness and the absence of God as one and the same thing.

The anxiety of the age found in sexuality (Sade, Goya, Fuseli), in magic (Marcel Brion has called the 18th century "the golden age of magicians and charlatans"), in drugs (deQuincey, Baudelaire, Gautier), and in art the means to objectify, distance, and expell feelings of abandonment, misery, and dereliction—and then to turn those feelings back upon themselves in order to transform them into the materials of aesthetic enjoyment. In 1757 Burke asserted that whenever fear and danger press too close, they are quite simply dreadful and can yield no pleasure. At a certain remove, however, he found that both fear and danger offer the possibility of delightful experience.

28. Francisco Goya. *"Nothing. That's what he'll say."* from *The Disasters of War.* 1812–20.

27. Jacques Gamelin. *The Last Judgment,* from *Nouveau recueil d'ostéologie et de myologie.* 1779.

29. Jean-Baptiste Carpeaux. *Guillotined Head* (after Géricault). See page 292.

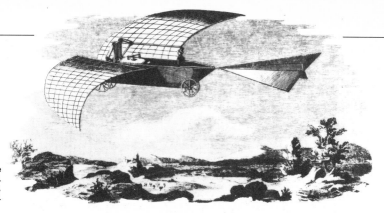

30. Project for a flying machine powered by pyroxylin combustion. *Leipziger Illustrierte,* January 30, 1847.

far left: 31. Étienne Louis Boullée. Project for the Newton Cenotaph. c. 1789–99.

left: 32. Étienne Louis Boullée. Overall view of the interior of the Newton Cenotaph (Fig. 31). The effect of stars would have been produced by holes in the vault.

33. Karl Friedrich Schinkel. Design for Mozart's *The Magic Flute.* 1815.

34. Claude Nicolas Ledoux. *Meditation on the Birth of the World,* for the cemetery of the town of Chaux. 1804.

35. John Russell. *The Face of the Moon.* 1795. Painted, according to the artist, "from nature."

# Dreams of outer space . . . and gardens of illusion

In the middle of the 18th century, the "whirlwinds of fine matter" in which Descartes had sought the origins of the universe were definitively replaced by the impeccable and inalterable clockwork posited by Newton. Now the English physicist would inspire Boullée to conceive one of his most beautiful creations (Figs. 31, 32) and Ledoux to meditate on the genesis of the world (Fig. 34).

A painter smitten with astronomy, John Russell, invented a new genre of nature painting—the moonscape (Fig. 35)—pretending that he was serving both science, by the accuracy of his observation, and art, by the beauty of his chiaroscuro modeling of the relief surface.

The 18th century was also the time when the park *à la française*—that image of man's dominance over the world—was replaced by the "Anglo-Chinese" garden, with all its variety, asymmetry, and surprise. William Chambers considered gardening the highest of all the arts and, in honor of this conviction, made three visits to China. In 1772 he wrote that the Chinese had attained perfection in their gardens. He also reported that the Chinese attributed to gardens a capacity for arousing passions far superior to that of any other art. He declared their gardeners to be not only botanists but painters and philosophers as well. An inventive group, they seemed never to repeat a composition. As A.O. Lovejoy has noted, this was when originality, a conception unacceptable to Neoclassicism and, moreover, inimical to the whole idea of imitating nature, made a massive entry into the period's arguments and debates.

The garden sprang from nostalgia and constituted a *trompe l'oeil.* It appeared in the midst of an agricultural revolution, which, begun in England at the end of the previous century, the garden was intended to make one forget. Supposedly the country was the realm of "natural" life, at a time when cities, with all their commerce and trade, were being denounced as dens of iniquity.

36. J. J. Grandville. *"He plays with the worlds."* 1845.

37. Rousseau botanizing.

39. James Hall. Reconstruction of a Gothic nave with poles, ash, and willow. 1797. The author wanted to demonstrate the vegetal origins of Gothic architecture.

38. A. T. Brongniart. Installation plan for the park at Berny. 1786. The irregular part was meant for dreaming; the geometrical part for producing.

IDÉES
Pour la Construction des
Rochers dans les Jardins
Anglais.

Dessinées d'après Nature dans
la Forest de Fontainebleau en
1784 par le Rouge alors Ingén.
Géographe de S. A. S. M. le Comte
de Clermont.

40. Le Rouge. Ideas for the construction of rocks in "Anglo-Chinese" gardens. 1734.

41. Marc-Antoine Laugier. *The Primitive Hut* (the origin of the builder's art). Frontispiece to *Traité d'architecture*, 1753.

42. Sham ruin suitable for habitation in the "Anglo-Chinese" garden of M. de Monville at Retz. 1780–81.

43. Hubert Robert. *Imaginary View of the Louvre's Grande Galerie in Ruins.* c. 1799.

44. Jacques Louis David. *Marie-Antoinette on Her Way to the Guillotine*. 1793.

45. Execution of Marie-Antoinette, October 16, 1793.

46. The Faubourg Saint-Antoine during the revolution of 1830.

47. Insurrection of February 24, 1848.

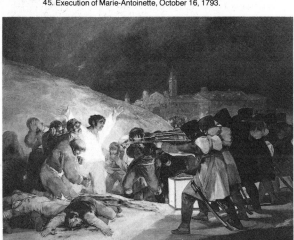

48. Francisco Goya. *The Third of May, 1808*.

49. Anne Louis Girodet. *Napoleon I*. 1812–14.

50. Jacques Louis David. *Napoleon Bonaparte Crossing the Alps, May 20, 1800*.

51. Anne Louis Girodet. *Napoleon at Saint-Cloud*. 1812.

52. François Rude. *Napoleon Awakening to Immortality*. 1845.

## The acceleration of history and the industrial revolution

From 1780 to 1850 industrial revolution and political upheaval went hand in hand. David and his friends became intimately involved in the events of 1789–94. A tireless supporter of Robespierre, David himself barely escaped the guillotine in 1794. Fifty years later, in 1848, Hugo, Lamartine, and David d'Angers would figure among those responsible for the February revolution, which made Paris' Hôtel de Ville the last of the Romantic salons. (" 'Ah! my friend,' cried Lamartine, 'how heavy this burden of power!' " Hugo wrote in *Choses vues*.) When the working-class insurrection broke out in June, the revolutionary movement split into "those who were content with Robespierre and those who went as far as Babeuf [a late-18th-century proto-Marxist]," whereupon most writers and artists sided with the provisionary government and its protector, General Cavaignac.

Meanwhile, there had been the charismatic figure of Napoleon. "The life of Napoleon is the event of the century for all the arts," wrote the twenty-eight-year-old Delacroix. It was the Corsican General-cum-Emperor who inspired the grand sweep of Gros' immense idealizations of the hero's progress. But David, the Le Brun of the Bonapartist regime, had already achieved his principal masterpieces before the time of the Empire. In the opinion of Delécluze, the vast quantity of commissions let by David, all in the service of propaganda, would produce nothing but a decade of stale narrations "offered to the multitude like some kind of 'visible' *Moniteur* [then Paris' most widely read newspaper] in which the acts depicted would capture all attention, leaving nothing for the artists' work. . . . From 1810 to 1813, the genre resulted in countless bad pictures."

When it comes to the industrial revolution and its effects on mores and landscape, English painters proved considerably more alert than their Continental counterparts. A work like the iron bridge at Coalbrookdale, the first of its kind (Fig. 57), and the neighboring foundries of Shropshire inspired, around the turn of the 19th century, some fifty pictures painted in either a topographical or a picturesque style. Loutherbourg (Fig. 390), Turner, Paul Sandby, Cotman, and John Linnell all took up industrial themes. French Romantics, on the other hand, preferred for the most part to ignore industrialization. Delacroix felt only dismay that "strips of iron should be aligned over great spaces, [making] an expeditious route that draws places together and saves time." He denigrated "those English steamboats whose form is so shabby. Great indignation against those races that know nothing but *aller vite*. May they go to the devil and faster yet in their machines and improvements, which turn man into another machine."

The tone adopted by the great French Romantic painter was also that of Friedrich, Baudelaire, and Gautier, who wrote in 1843: "Everything is so regulated, geared, and labeled that chance and accident are no longer possible. Another century of improvement and each person will be able to foresee at birth what will happen to him all the way to the day he dies."

55. The Queen's crystal factory at Creusot. c. 1785.

above left: 53. William Hogarth. *The Two Apprentices*. 1747.

left: 54. T. Allom. *Printing on Calico*. 1830.

From 1780 to 1850 British textile production increased from 40 to 2,025 million yards.

56. View of the old forge for the manufacture of rails at Creusot. c. 1850.

57. Thomas Farnolls Pritchard. Iron Bridge at Coalbrookdale, England. c. 1779.

59. An 1829 locomotive designed by George and Robert Stephenson.

58. Joseph Paxton. Crystal Palace. 1853.

60. Original steam-powered road vehicle designed by Cugnot in 1770.

## The rise of the middle class and the high price of progress

61. J. J. Grandville.
*The French Painted by Themselves.* 1840.

62. J. J. Grandville. *Money.* c. 1845.

When the twenty-four-year-old Lord Byron rose in the House of Lords in 1812 and declared that the economic welfare of impoverished workers held greater consequence for the community at large than the enrichment of a few monopolists, he spoke in terms that would seldom be heard again until that year of pan-European revolution: 1848. The first generation of Romantics reconciled their high contempt for the bourgeoisie with an immense ignorance of the new working conditions brought by industrialization.

"Commerce, by enriching the citizens of England, has helped to make them free, and liberty has in turn expanded commerce. This accounts for the greatness of the State," wrote Voltaire in 1734. A century later Balzac would speak of "the aristocracy of the strongbox" and of "our civilization that since 1815 has replaced the honor principle with the money principle." "What pleasure," asked Delacroix in 1853, "could you find among rich merchants who today compose most of the upper classes? The narrow minds of the counting house striving to appear distinguished makes a contrast of the most absurd sort."

Soon Flaubert would divide history into three eras: "Paganism, Christianism, and Vulgarism." East of the Rhine the nostalgic landscapes of Friedrich were understood less and less, and when their author died in 1840 he had been almost completely forgotten. The public wanted an art with precise and tangible qualities, which the Düsseldorf painters would provide.

But the taste for realism would not go so far as to favor a description of the living conditions suffered by the nascent working class: ruptured family unity; dislocation; specialization that reduced tasks to a few automatic gestures governed by the rhythm of the machine; police surveillance of the whole enterprise; 12-to-15-hour work days (until 1860); and widespread child labor. In 1834, 13 percent of all those employed in the British textile industry were children under 13. By 1847 the French industrial force, in factories employing 10 or more, consisted of 670,000 men, 254,000 women, and 130,000 children. In a famous report published in 1840, Dr. Villermé described the arrival of workers at a cotton mill, "pale, thin women walking barefoot through the mud; dirty children dressed in rags and smeared with machine oil, carrying in their hands the bit of bread that was to nourish them."

The African slave trade, abolished in 1794 and legalized anew by Napoleon in 1802, would not stop until around 1850, when economic developments rendered it useless. Meanwhile, some 15 to 50 million Africans are estimated to have been transported to the Americas, with approximately 15 percent of them perishing along the way. A city like Liverpool had as many as 15 ships committed full time to the slave traffic in 1730— and 132 in 1792! The subject would inspire Turner to create one of his most powerful works (Fig. 430).

63. Children working in the coal mines of Britain.

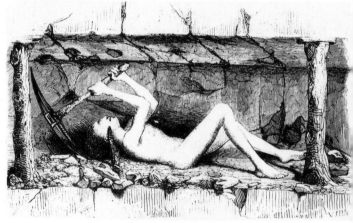

64. Youth mining coal in Britain.

65. William Blake. Illustration for John Gabriel Stedman's *Narrative of a Five Year's Expedition against the Negroes of Surinam.* 1796.

66. Child labor in British cotton mills. 1839.

67. Jean Honoré Fragonard. *The Curious.* c. 1765.

68. Gavarni. *A Loge at the Italians.* c. 1840.

69. Louis Boilly.
*An Assembly of
Thirty-five Expressive Heads.*
c. 1825.

70. Gavarni. *Behind the Scene.* 1838.

The neutrality of the spectator is questioned. In the painting by Fragonard (Fig. 67) the viewer becomes the subject of the subject that he examines. This reversability of looks—this permutation of roles—has an unsettling effect. In the drawing by Gavarni (Fig. 70) a curtain prevents our seeing the theatre auditorium. We see only figures looking out at the hall, but we cannot see what they see. The space created by the artist cannot but induce frustration.

Now the viewing public has become the picture. Captured frontally and inscribed within a strict geometrical structure (Fig. 68), filling the visual field by accumulation edge to edge (Fig. 69), or disposed around a banquet table like a frame (Fig. 72), the bourgeois—the ordinary man—acquired the status of a motif at the very moment that he became the principal consumer of art.

71. William Blake. *The Laocoön.* c. 1820.

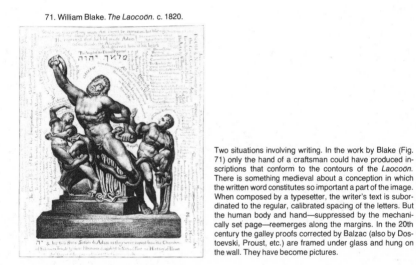

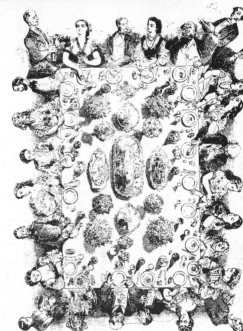

Two situations involving writing. In the work by Blake (Fig. 71) only the hand of a craftsman could have produced inscriptions that conform to the contours of the *Laocoön*. There is something medieval about a conception in which the written word constitutes so important a part of the image. When composed by a typesetter, the writer's text is subordinated to the regular, calibrated spacing of the letters. But the human body and hand—suppressed by the mechanically set page—reemerges along the margins. In the 20th century the galley proofs corrected by Balzac (also by Dostoevski, Proust, etc.) are framed under glass and hung on the wall. They have become pictures.

72. *A Banquet,*
illustration for *La Vie parisienne.* 1853.

73. Benjamin Roubaud.
*Caricature of
Honoré de Balzac.* 1838.

75. Benjamin Roubaud.
*Hugo and Paris.* 1841.

74. Honoré de Balzac.
Printer's proof. 1838.

The 19th century invented these macrocephalic heads. Such art reflected two developments: the familiarity of the image of a star personality, and the sanctification of the intellectual hero.

Speed became a pleasure. Beginning in 1816, "Russian mountains" and "French mountains" attracted huge crowds in Paris. The medical profession believed them to be therapeutic. According to Dr. Cotterel, "300 feet are covered in 8 seconds on the ascent, and more than 700 on the descent. . . . Each round of three ascents and as many descents, in less than a minute, makes a journey of 300 feet at about 37.5 miles an hour. . . ." (1817).

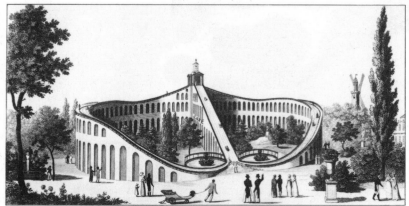

76. Roller coaster ("French mountains") at Beaujon Park. 1817.

# The age of "revivals"

Beginning in the mid-18th century, a new attitude developed in regard to history, a movement that would receive reinforcement from the French Revolution. Throughout Europe this traumatic event was experienced as a sudden mutation in the process of social evolution. What Turgot in 1751 called the "successive progress of the human species" led to a view of the future as a perspective, a march toward a known objective: happiness, reason, and positive science.

But once history was believed to have direction and development, it also had to have a past—divided up in distinct segments. It is this "periodization" that accounts for the "revivals" designed to bear contemporaries back to one portion or another of humanity's linear evolution. Thus, we have the archaic and cyclopian style of Ledoux (Fig. 83); the Egypto-Syrian fantasies of Boullée, Schinkel, and Lequeu (Figs. 80, 81, 84); the Hellenistic graces of Canova (Fig. 79); the heroic Rome of David (Fig. 82); the 18th century's "Gothicomania" (Figs. 77, 78); and, finally, the eclecticism of Lequeu, who combined classical and medieval features in his Rendez-vous de Bellevue (Fig. 85), an early manifestation of the "pavilion" style.

77. James Wyatt. Fonthill, the neo-Gothic "abbey" built for William Beckford. 1796–1806.

78. The stairway in Horace Walpole's neo-Gothic country house, "Strawberry Hill." 1754.

79. Antonio Canova. *Pauline Borghese.* 1804–08.

80. Étienne Louis Boullée. Project for a cenotaph in the Egyptian manner. c. 1789–99.

81. Karl Friedrich Schinkel. Design for Mozart's *The Magic Flute.* 1815.

82. Jacques Louis David. *Oath of the Horatii* (detail). 1784.

84. Jean-Jacques Lequeu. Project for a cowshed. Early 19th century.

83. Claude Nicolas Ledoux. Project for the prison at Aix-en-Provence. c. 1785.

85. Jean-Jacques Lequeu. Le Rendez-vous de Bellevue, project for an observatory. Early 19th century.

86. Physionotrace portrait.
c. 1790.

87. The physionotrace device
invented by G. L. Chrétien. 1786.

89. Jacques Daguerre. *The Atelier of the Artist.* 1837.

88. Jean-Baptiste
Sabatier-Blot.
*Mme Sabatier-Blot*
(detail). c. 1844.
Daguerreotype.

90. Nicéphore Niepce.
*View Through a Window at Grasse. 1826.*

91. Jacques Daguerre. *A Paris Boulevard.* c. 1838.

92. Château de Chambord. 1843. Daguerreotype.

## From representation to re-presentation: photography

Photography came about as one of the many attempts to achieve absolute verisimilitude—to represent to the eye precisely what could be found in the factual world. Daguerre boasted that his process was "eminently suited to render the subtleties of nature." Within a few years, daguerreotypy would spread throughout the entire world, the first manifestation of the mass, universal culture so characteristic of the 20th century. And what accelerated its dissemination was precisely the magic of verisimilitude. In 1859 Baudelaire denounced the specious reasoning of *la multitude:* "Since photography gives us every possible guarantee of exactitude (and the fools believe it!), art must mean photography." According to this point of view, painting—an imperfect process because dependent upon the subjectivity of the painter—could only disappear.

The mimetic preoccupations of Europe continued throughout the 18th century, in, for example, the increased use of the *camera oscura* (mentioned by Leonardo da Vinci in the 15th century), a device that made it possible to obtain a direct reflection of nature upon the interior wall of a box. At the end of the period came the *silhouette* craze, quickly succeeded by the general delight in Chrétien's *physionotrace* (Figs. 86, 87), which permitted a profile to be drawn on a glass plate and, by means of a mechanical arm, simultaneously engraved on copper. The image could be printed and thus multiplied. Chrétien had considerable success from 1786 to 1830, counting Marat, Saint-Just, Bonaparte, and Louis XVIII among his clients. But it was the rising bourgeoisie that wanted to be portrayed at any price. Gisèle Freund tells us that the Salon of 1793 included a hundred physionotrace portraits, while at the next exhibition a dozen rooms, each containing some fifty works, were reserved for that art.

All these processes share with photography its supposedly *direct* (contiguous) relationship between the object described and its image. Omitting interpretation, the technique simply provided an objective record of a profile or of light reflected from some segment of nature. The same interest gave rise to the wax museums, which had great popular success in the final quarter of the 18th century. In order to reproduce Mme du Barry, Curtius (the Grévin of his time) "followed Sanson [France's public executioner] and his cart all the way to the cemetery. Despite the December cold, he installed himself with his wax and brushes on the edge of the burial pit, propping the head up with a pair of stones."

The photograph gathered and condensed all such effects. Dauthendey, an early photographer, wrote about the first plates made by Daguerre: "At the outset we did not dare look long at the images he produced. We were intimidated by the clarity of the men [portrayed], believing that these small, even tiny faces fixed upon a plate could themselves look back at us." It took awhile to grasp the fact that photography was not "reality." Painting, now liberated from the need for mimetic illusionism, could move on to redefine its own proper realm.

## The status of the artist: from professional painter . . .

From the end of the Renaissance to the turn of the 19th century, the artistic profession entered a critical stage. The growing instability of the artist's relations with the seats of power, as well as with a public that itself was undergoing great change, simply accelerated the more artists responded with progressively extreme forms of originality or even singularity. Isolated, believing himself misunderstood, indeed persecuted, the artist bit by bit sought refuge in a rhetoric of genius, proclaiming himself to be the beacon and prophet, but also the victim, of an age given up totally to material values. Lenormant, in his 1847 biography of Gérard, tells us that "the social shifts that occurred over a period of two centuries made the condition of artists more difficult than it had once been. Then, the choice of subjects to treat was, so to speak, ready-made. . . . The mind-set of painters tended toward the traditional, and the absence of major problems in such important areas permitted [them] to apply the whole of their faculties to the process of execution."

This was the general theme that Delécluze developed in his 1855 history of French Neoclassicism: "David lacked, as did his pupils and all their contemporaries, a governing idea that, like a star, would have guided them in the journey they had to make. As a result of the terrible revolutions that their age witnessed in religion, morals, and politics, they found themselves forced to obey a multiplicity of different systems that succeeded one another in beliefs, tastes, and habits."

Now, in a parallel development, beginning with Shaftesbury at the outset of the 18th century, we see the spread of a theory whose tendency was to identify human creations with those of divine origin. Such a notion endowed the artist with Promethean power. His mission was not to imitate things but rather to create a world. The artist did not copy the world; he rendered it legible. By the end of the 18th century the theme had become a source of constant preoccupation. The genius-creator, Wittkower tells us, "began to be thought of as the most elevated of all human types." Given such a destiny, the artist had no choice but to hurl himself body and soul into a search for the new. To Bernardin de Saint-Pierre, Girodet said: "Why shouldn't one be allowed a chance to stretch still further [than Raphael and Poussin] the effects and boundaries that these great men knew? But one wanders in space; one no longer follows a sure path. . . . Ah well! When one goes astray, it's marvelous to fall from the heavens. Icarus could not stay aloft, but he did give his name to the Icarian Sea, and his fall became almost a triumph."

Caught between a demiurgic ambition and social necessity (indeed, the exigencies of a powerful force) the artist maneuvered, became isolated, and rebelled. Goya painted an allegory of Madrid in honor of Joseph Bonaparte, the "intruder King" of Spain. After the liberation of the Spanish capital in 1812, he replaced the head of Joseph with the word *Constitución*, then restored Joseph's image when the French returned, only to reimpose *Constitución* in 1813, which in 1814 gave way to the head of Ferndinand VII.

*(continued on page 23)*

93. Nathaniel Dance. *Fuseli in the Study Hall at the Royal Academy.*

94. J. S. Deville. Plaster mask of the face of William Blake. 1823.

95. Henry Fuseli. *Self-Portrait.* 1780

96. Anton Raphael Mengs. *Self-Portrait* (detail). 1774.

97. John Flaxman. *Self-Portrait.* 1778–79.

98. Jean-Baptiste Isabey. *Hubert Robert* (detail).

99. James Barry. *Self-Portrait* (detail). 1767.

20

100. Antoine Jean Gros.
*Self-Portrait* (detail)..

101. Anne Louis Girodet.
*Self-Portrait* (detail).

102. J. S. Cless. *The Atelier of David.*

103. Jacques Louis David.
*Self-Portrait.* 1794.

104. J. M. Langlois.
*Jacques Louis David.*
c. 1825.

105. Fleury-Richard.
*Ingres Posing
in the Studio
of David.*

106. Benjamin Roubaud.
"A la couleur grise,
Monsieur le successeur
de la maison Raphael,
Michel-Ange et Cie."
Caricature of Ingres. 1842.

107. Francisco Goya. *Self-Portrait*. 1815.

108. Francisco Goya. *Self-Portrait*. 1795.

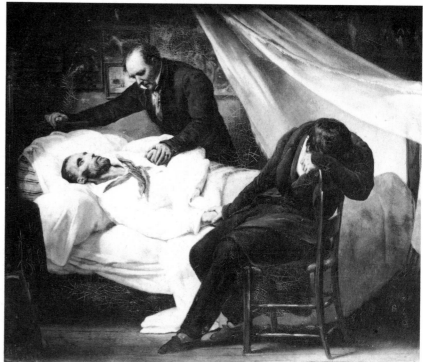

109. Ary Scheffer.
*The Death of Gericault*.
1824.

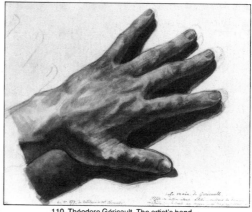

110. Théodore Géricault. The artist's hand
sketched on his deathbed. 1824.

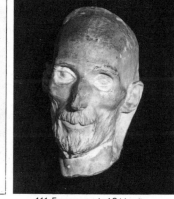

111. Funerary mask of Géricault.

112. Eugène Delacroix.
*Study for the Raft of the Medusa*. c. 1824.
Delacroix himself had posed for this figure,
which he later copied
from the painting by Géricault
the year of the latter's untimely death.

113. A. M. Colin.
*Delacroix at Age Twenty-six*.
c. 1824.

114. Eugène Delacroix.
Caricature made
for *Charivari*.

115. Delacroix in 1842. Daguerreotype.

116. Cornelius Varley. *J. M. W. Turner.* 1820.

121, 122. Caspar David Friedrich.
*Self-Portraits.*
below: c. 1800; bottom: c. 1810.

123. Phillipp Otto Runge.
*Self-Portrait* (detail). c. 1802.

117. T. Fernley.
*J. M. W. Turner
on Varnishing Day.*
1837.

119. Ramsay R. Reinagle.
*John Constable*
(detail). c. 1799.

120. G. Richmond. *Samuel Palmer.* 1829.

124. Georg Friedrich Kersting. *Friedrich in His Studio.* 1811.

118. *Turner at Work.*
Caricature for
*The Almanach of the Month.*
June, 1846.

## . . . to the melancholy and Promethean genius

*(continued from page 20)*

Long distrusted in academic circles, Ingres suddenly found himself acknowledged in 1824 (the year of Delacroix's *Massacre at Chios*) and elected as *chef d'école* charged with the responsibility for rolling back the Romantic wave. Thereafter his life would become a long, uninterrupted sequence of official honors and important appointments. For Théophile Silvestre, writing in 1856, the creator of *Jupiter and Thetis* (Fig. 167) had become "the little bourgeois elephant, built of misshapen stumps." "We can see him yet," he added, "during those June days in 1848, impassively finishing his *Venus Anadyomede* to the sound of the tocsin of civil war, when the victims' blood ran in streams along the streets of Paris. Happy insensitivity!"

Turner, born into the sawdust of a barbershop, was shrewd enough to carry out a brilliant public career as part of England's artistic establishment, while also living a secret, clandestine existence devoted totally to the strangest, and least commercial, kinds of experimentation. Ruskin describes him as stubborn, obstinate, concerned only for the dictates of his own spirit, and as silent as a block of granite. A friend of Louis-Philippe, even visiting the "July Monarch" at the Château d'Eu in 1845, Turner nonetheless lived mainly on the margins of society, a "bear" of a figure whose untidy appearance shocked the elegant Delacroix: "He lived avariciously with an old servant woman. I recall receiving him once only when I lived on the Quai Voltaire. He made a mediocre impression. He looked like an English farmer, dressed in a black suit, a rather thickset man in heavy shoes, his face hard and cold."

It may have been French Romanticism, the last of Europe's Romanticisms to emerge, that found the most moving accents in which to speak of painting as a "passion," as something absolute. Throughout his life, Delacroix would remain true to the feverish profession of faith that he had made at the age of twenty-six: "Beautiful painting, so insulted, so misunderstood, delivered up to idiots who exploit her; but there are those who will still take her to heart with religious fervor." This was the context in which we must consider Géricault, a partisan, if ever there was one, of the genius theory. His death at the early age of thirty-four made him seem Christ-like, the incarnation of the Romantic fate. His funerary mask could often be found hung like an icon on studio walls during the 1830s and '40s. Delacroix wrote: "I have seen the death mask of my poor Géricault. A monument worthy of veneration! I was tempted to kiss it. . . . Poor Géricault, I shall often think of you! I imagine that your spirit will often hover over my work. . . . *Adieu*, poor young man!"

# CHAPTER I

# The Rediscovery of the Picture Surface

125. H. Fuseli (1741–1825).
*Marius and the Cimbrian Soldier.* 1768–70.

126. B. Gagneraux (1756–95).
*The Punishment of Cupid.* 1792.

127. J. Flaxman (1755–1826).
*Illustration for the Iliad.* 1793.

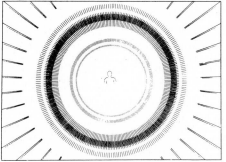

128. J. Flaxman. *Beatific Vision*
(Dante, *Paradiso* XXXIII).

A decisive influence, engraving by its very nature tended to reduce figures to simple contour lines and to cancel all perspective. This in turn favored alignment parallel to the frontal plane. Shadows, when indicated, appear as a screen of parallel lines, which themselves reinforce the surface. To depict the infinite extent of Paradise, Flaxman used the simplest of means, mechanically drawing in a series of small identical marks.

Renaissance painting had its very inception in the denial of its physical support. As Erwin Panofsky observed: "The painting surface has lost that materiality which it had possessed in high-mediaeval art. It has ceased to be an opaque and impervious working surface—either supplied by a wall, a panel, a piece of canvas, a leaf of vellum, a sheet of paper or manufactured by the techniques peculiar to the tapestry weaver or the *peintre-verrier*—and has become a window through which we look out into a section of the visible world."

This conception of the support as immaterial evinced itself not only in the analogies made by Renaissance theoreticians but also in the technical procedures they recommended. Both Alberti and Leonardo da Vinci described the painting surface as a pane of glass interposed between the artist and his subject. "The only thing painters seek to accomplish," wrote Alberti, "is that the forms of the things seen appear upon this plane as if it were made of transparent glass." Then for Leonardo, "perspective is nothing more than an object viewed through a smooth, transparent glass, on whose surface everything located behind the glass can be traced."

Such was the conception that it inspired Alberti's famous window metaphor, which remained an irresistible image right up to Diderot in the mid-18th century. "I describe a rectangle of whatever size I please," wrote Alberti, "which I imagine to be an open window through which I view whatever is to be depicted there." The "veil," or "intersector," that the 15th-century theoretician also proposed in this passage arose, like Dürer's slightly later perspective apparatus, from the same logic. Either directly or indirectly, the objective was to set aside or even to nullify the palpable reality of the painting surface, which would be reduced to the status of a *support*, a focal plane upon which the image would be *projected*. "I believe nothing more convenient can be found," Alberti declared, "than the veil . . . whose usage I was the first to discover. It is like this: a veil loosely woven of fine thread, dyed whatever color you please, divided up by thicker threads into as many parallel square sections as you like, and stretched on a frame. I set this up between the eye and the object to be represented, so that the visual pyramid passes through the loose weave of the veil."

In the Romantic period painters acted as if they had ceased to look through the veil or pane of glass and had determined, consciously or not, to acknowledge its existence, whether in the form of a wall, a panel, a canvas, or a sheet. It was as if transparency had begun to opacify, the screen to consolidate, the veil to tighten its mesh—to *resist*. The impenetrable flatness of the working surface would seem to have reasserted itself and thus come to influence the painter in every aspect of his art. Now it would control the delineation of figures and also reduce perspectival illusion, by advancing the background—a simplified and geometricized "ground"—*toward* the picture plane.

Consider, for example, the series of drawings and prints that Robert Rosenblum has grouped under the rubric of "the international style of 1800." In the works of Fuseli, Gagneraux, and Flaxman reproduced here (Figs. 125–128) every suggestion of sculptural relief has been abolished. Volume is expressed only by means of pure line. The rare bits of shadow—indicated by a pattern of parallel lines—

actually serve less to excavate the surface than to reinforce its frontality. Objects appear only in their purest form, abstracted away from all weight, immanence, and materiality. The outline figure (along with the minimalist conception of the image this presupposes) constituted one of the era's most profound aspirations, explored and defined in the great profusion of engravings produced during the second half of the 18th century. Some of these prints documented Egyptian, Etruscan, and Greco-Roman antiquities (an activity fueled by the discovery of Herculaneum and Pompeii in 1738 and 1748, which would excite not only antiquarians and archaeologists but artists too, including Piranesi, Vien, Gavin Hamilton, and James Barry). Others reproduced and thus spread knowledge of the Florentine "primitives": Giotto, Masaccio, etc. For painters, the common appeal of these graphics, despite the supposed antagonism of the styles they treated, was, as Robert Rosenblum has observed, the same studied simplicity and linearity, restricted depth, and friezelike disposition that they all shared—characteristics accentuated by the engraving process itself.

Engraving played a crucial and definitive role in the art of this time. Tomaso Piroli, who engraved the plates for Flaxman's illustrations of Homer, Aeschylus, and Dante (Figs. 127, 128), also prepared engravings after Masaccio and in 1789 supervised a new edition of *Antiquities of Herculaneum* (1757–62). Other craftsmen engraved both antiquities and the contemporary works of West and Canova. In the instance of Flaxman, a comparison of the original drawings and the plates made after them reveals how much the incised line enhanced the clarity and crispness of the works, as well as how much it equalized and thus frontalized near and far. The Flaxman engravings resulted from a paradoxical combination of Platonic inspiration (the work of art as ideal form, purged of all contingency) and industrial expediency. The model drawings, for instance, had to resemble bas-reliefs and also be suitable for engraving, both of which demanded a simplicity that could be easily, rapidly, and economically transposed into other materials. (The artist, moreover, had little interest in the execution of his engravings, which he left to subordinates.)

The great aesthetic value placed upon these plates, by a universally fascinated Europe (Figs. 134, 135), surprised and embarrassed Flaxman. Whereas he had wanted merely to provide themes and motifs capable of inspiring artists, Ingres and many others proclaimed them to be the manifesto of a new art, the culmination and even transcendence of the Greek style, as this had been evinced in the graphic linearity of antique vases. Beginning in 1799, A.W. Schlegel, writing in the review *Athenaeum*, demonstrated that Flaxman had not been content simply to copy the silhouettes on Greek vessels. These rarely displayed scenes of action; in addition, their figures were generally painted solid and thus not reduced to the simple contours used by the English master, who tended to synthesize in one purified line the Greeks' richly detailed descriptions of rites and costumes. Then, while the ancients had aligned their figures in friezelike formations, Flaxman did not hesitate to locate his on several different planes, even though he endowed all the bounding contours with a comparable, if not identical, thickness. Such contradictory means produced an effect of depth and yet denied it, thereby creating a ten-

129. J.B. Piranesi (1720–78). *Capriccio*.

Piranesi treated stone like an epidermus and decorative architectural ruins like wounds or sores.

130. E.L. Boullée (1728–99). *Cenotaph*.

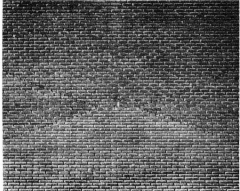

131. E.L. Boullée. Detail of Fig. 130.

Fascinated by the grain of a wall, Boullée drew not only gigantic architecture but also the brick-by-brick detail of its wall surfaces.

132. N. de Largillière (1656–1746). *Portrait of Marie Anne Victoire de Bourbon.* 1724.

Largillière anticipated Neoclassical murality. The low placement of the figure liberated a vast zone above, where frontality is reinforced by pilasters.

sion that lies at the very heart of the period and its art.

Flaxman, of course, was not the only one to derive the means of a new art from the linearism of the Greek vase painters. As Girodet wrote to Gérard in 1790: "[David] will tell you that a clever man can profit from copying Etruscan jugs." Delécluze, who mingled with a small group of David's pupils known as the *Penseurs* and *Primitifs*—a radical sect intent upon restoring painting to the purity of its origins—tells us that "the only book we would consult was Stuart's *Antiquities of Athens*; it promptly caused us to favor the simplest composition taken from an Etruscan vase over the [Renaissance] works recently imported from Italy."

But what neither Flaxman, nor the Penseurs, nor any other artist of the time could articulate—except in their works—was how this conception of flatness and linearity fostered a new definition of the working surface. The moment that drawing is divorced from perspective and volume, then ceases to indicate anything but the essence of things, we have passed from an economy of a scenic space to the economy of a planar space. The line flows freely over the whiteness of the page, filling it from edge to edge. Line takes complete command of a two-dimensional realm whose every part comes alive under the generative effect of a curving, arabesque line, the function of which is to validate the white of the support—"the touching whiteness of paper" that Matisse spoke of in the early 20th century. This whiteness would work—actively—as surface, eliminating all dead zones and empty, inert "skies." The entire page begins to "breathe." In this way, idealism is turned completely upside down, since what results is the affirmation and activation of the work's material, immediate, and tangible components. No longer does drawing mean the projection of a figure upon a surface; rather, it is the vitalization of the white—thus the space—of the page and its realization as a plastic element. Henceforth it would matter little whether the "reserves," or untouched areas of white surface, belonged to the figure or to the ground, since both partake equally of the same organism. Here was a lesson learned by the entire generation of 1800, from Ingres to Runge.

This revived interest in the visibility of the surface as such leads us, as if by a process of stratification, from the level of white to that of grain. The grain or texture of the work, of skin, of walls—here is a paradigm the elucidation of which can be had from a pair of anecdotes whose opposition reveals a great deal about the heightened visual and tactile relations between painting and skin. First, there was the passion that Ingres indulged for smoothness and finish, which expressed itself in a contrary emotion: a horror of open wounds and sores. Thus in Rome, the master's pupil Amaury-Duval tells us, "whenever M. Ingres directed his daily walk along [the road to Tivoli] and came near an unfortunate [beggar who regularly stationed himself there to expose his lesions to the sympathy of passersby], Mme Ingres hastened to throw her shawl over the head of her husband and lead him by the hand until they had left the poor wretch well behind." But such behavior proved totally contrary to that of Piranesi, who in his youth, so the illustrious engraver Bianconi tells us, "set out to draw the cripples and hunchbacks that he saw everyday in Rome, the refuge of the most choice specimens of this sort that Europe then produced.

He also loved to draw ulcerated legs, broken arms—all forms of illness—and whenever he found a new case in one of the churches, it was as if he had discovered a new *Apollo Belvedere* or a *Laocoön*, so quick was he to begin drawing it" (1779).

Once free to deal with the grain of the painting, drawing, or print surface, the artist also gained freedom to evoke the grain of other surfaces—stone and skin—as if in this period a subliminal chain linked together, whatever the figural elements given, everything dermal, mural, or textural. Piranesi could slip, almost by hallucination, from ulcerated flesh to the metal plate in which he gouged out images of eroded monuments and gaping ruins (Fig. 129). A comparable manifestation was the tactility sought by the architect Ledoux, who thought that stone should "arouse new feelings and develop its own intrinsic properties." Then came Boullée, the obsessive designer of immense ramparts that he rendered brick by brick (Figs. 130, 131), the handling suggestive of a new kind of close-up sensuous vision. ("The skeleton of architecture," wrote Boullée, "is a wall stripped absolutely bare.") Murality also found its affirmation in the painting of David, who in a letter to his supplier stipulated: "Because it is for a history painting, we would just as soon the canvas had some grain, not polished with pumice." And, again, it appears in the basket metaphor devised by Ingres, for whom nature was a sealed wall: "Lines break up very frequently in nature in order to rejoin and interweave, like, so to speak, willows whose interlacement makes a basket." Finally, Matisse picked up the image, unconciously displacing it to the only field where it has any meaning, that of the work of art: "Ingres said . . . that drawing is like a basket from which one cannot take a willow without making a hole."

At another "stratum" or level, the ground or support found itself reasserted by watercolor, most especially in the effects of transparency and "reserve" that it encouraged. Developed significantly in Great Britain at the end of the 18th century, the medium had a lasting effect on art in general, with influences traceable from J.R. Cozens to Corot and Cézanne, or, as Henri Lemaître has shown, from Cotman (Fig. 133) to Gauguin. Watercolor accelerated innovation in the 19th century, by permitting the underlying paper to modulate hues and by favoring flat, frontal strokes spread like water in small or large monochromatic zones over the surface of the sheet. Through the reserve, watercolor *represents* at the same that it *materializes* the support, which therefore causes the untouched ground to become an element of drawing. A virgin zone, a patch with nothing below it, an expression costing nothing, the "reserve" (a "saving," a "thrift," a *lacuna*) constitutes at once both depth and flatness, sign and substance. Unlike the object it denotes, the reserve form derives not from construction or production, but rather from abstention. The difference discloses just how much the *tache* ("color patch"), before ever it refers to something outside the picture, partakes of a differential system of textures, colors, and lines that together make up the surface.

For the whole movement belatedly called Neoclassic, the challenge of inventing a concrete pictorial ground became a determining factor. It could even be said that this is what distinguishes the movement from other currents, and that, for Neoclassicism, investigating the status of the support

133. J.S. Cotman (1782–1842).
*Behold Yon Oak.* 1804.

"Reserve" appears everywhere in the watercolors of Cotman. Here, the medium radiating outward from large empty zones reflects influence from Chinese painting.

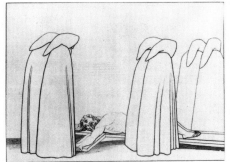

134. J. Flaxman (1755–1826). *Hypocrites.* 1793.

135. F. Goya (1746–1828).
*Procession of Hooded Figures.* c. 1795.

Goya adopted the linear technique formulated by Flaxman, but the bits of tone he added suffice to reintroduce depth, shadow, atmosphere, and thus illusion.

136. A.R. Mengs (1728–79).
*Jupiter and Ganymede.* 1758–59.

To deceive his friend Winckelmann, the great theoretician of Neoclassicism, Mengs, executed this fake Roman fresco.

and that of the wall signifying it amounted to one and the same thing. The wall emerged as the sign standing for the substance, the revetment that would guarantee the Neoclassical ground its solidity, its equivalence with the white space of the canvas.

This issue of the wall is as complex as painting itself. The solidity and resistance of the "ground" are all the more difficult to analyze by virtue of the fact that they derive from an indissoluble combination of factors, among which texture, color, and structure are all equally important. There is no texture without color, and no color that does not imply a structural decision: expansion of the same color, opposition and contrast, gradations of value and intensity, etc. The artist could reinforce the presence of the ground by a methodical application of a grid or screen, which, for instance, becomes manifest through the pronounced cut and join of stones in a structural wall (Fig. 151). Or he could call attention to the working surface by representing such regular geometric forms as pilasters, panels, and ribs that reiterate the parallels of the picture's own format (Figs. 132, 148, 168), or yet by covering it with the kind of regular brushwork that David, as we shall see, exemplified with his *frottis* or "scumbling" (Figs. 270–273).

In the Middle Ages, reflective materials (gilt, mosaic) served to emphasize the flatness of the surface. The 15th-century "primitives" achieved the same end by representing spreads of brocade or other types of patterned fabric (Conrad Witz), repetitive decorations such as garlands and foliage, and marbling (Fra Angelico, Andrea del Castagno), or by covering the field with large monochromatic planes of contrasting red, green, and rose (Sassetta, Domenico Veneziano). Meanwhile, Giotto's handling of walls and skies had been irregular, creating a patchwork effect that tends to accentuate the frontality of the overall conception. In the *Last Judgment* at Padua, two angels roll out the sky like a tarpaulin, as if to show us its consistency.

In the Romantic era other techniques would emerge, thanks to the passion for classical antiquity. (But it could just as well be said that this passion was the child of the age's own plastic needs.) Four major influences were at work, all issuing from the same source: Greek vase painting (already mentioned); the tabular or frieze disposition found on sarcophagi; abstract architectural ornament, with its pilasters and geometric reliefs; and finally the pictorial flatness of the frescoes uncovered at Pompeii.

It was Vien whose interest in the Pompeiian paintings initiated French Neoclassicism, which David would bring to full flower. ("I opened the door," said the older master, "David rushed through it.") And there survives a drawing by David made after a print of Vien's *Selling of Cupids.* Despite the supposed archness of the anecdote, Vien's picture, painted in 1763 (Fig. 150), was actually very radical in its chromatic simplification, shallow depth, and frieze composition, where the figures are spaced to leave the wall fully evident. But even before adopting Pompeiian themes, Vien had taken a keen interest in Roman materials and techniques. Under the influence of the antiquarian Comte de Caylus, then engaged in publishing his seven-volume *Recueil d'antiquités égyptiennes, étrusques, grecques et romaines* (1752–67), Vien began experimenting in 1754 with encaustic, a wax medium he found described in Pliny. That year he exhibited a helmeted

head of Minerva painted on wood. "This was," writes Locquin, "the main curiosity of the season, a sensation among artist and collectors."

At precisely the same moment, other painters—Hallé, Bachelier, and, above all, Le Lorrain—were devoting themselves to similar experiments. And in 1759 Mengs executed a superb pastiche (Fig. 136) for the express purpose of deceiving his learned friend, the historian Winckelmann. The fact that the latter was indeed taken in suggests the degree to which Mengs had come to know Roman frescoes.

Such period curiosities can be interpreted on three different levels: technical, aesthetic, and moral:

● From the *technical* point of view, painters disclosed a revived interest in the materials of painting. They became implicitly aware, even before getting into figuration, of the fact that the matness, cloudiness, and density of wax produces certain specific effects. They even considered the kind of surface texture the medium might offer, thereby going against their training, which had subordinated everything to the mimetic reproduction of relief and modeling. This openness to the potential expressivity of techniques is reflected in the heterodox interest in tempera shown by Ingres (whose own pupils would soon revive fresco painting). It was also echoed in contemporary England, where Blake refused to employ oil because by its very nature the medium seemed to connote a materialism altogether at odds with this artist's spiritual aspirations. But such an attitude simply confirmed that the notion of technical categories had begun to lose meaning. Already, expression would invariably be implied in the choice of materials.

● In the *aesthetic* realm, painters took up exactly what art lovers nourished on Renaissance classicism found shocking in the vast, uniform, frontal surfaces of Roman painting. Travelers and experts generally described the Pompeiian frescoes as vulgar, unfinished, and inept. After visiting the barely excavated underground chambers of Herculaneum, Président de Brosse singled out "three figures grouped on a uniform reddish ground, as if painted on colored paper." About two of the frescoes he observed: "Neither of the pictures, it must be confessed, has any perspective." This was precisely what began to intrigue painters. Mural affirmation and the equation of painting with its support became assimilated—perhaps unconsciously—as positive elements conducive to a regeneration of official art, then given over completely to the illusionistic feast that was the Rococo.

● On the *moral* level, antique "murality," its candor, its denial of optical trickery proved satisfying to the thoughtful of a period—that of the Diderot-d'Alembert *Encylopédié*—groping for ethics in the painting profession. This, of course, had to be translated primarily in terms of the mimetic imperative, which meant being as "true" as nature itself. Beginning in 1750, artists were exhorted to represent "virtuous and heroic actions . . . a passionate zeal for the honor and well-being of the nation and, above all, the defense of its religion."

But this taste for morality, this propensity for demonstrations of virtue in a realm (art) where they have no relevance could also be accompanied by the scrupulous craftsmanship and technical probity thought to be present in the frontalized conception of Roman fresco painting. It is significant that at

137. J. van Ruisdael (1628–82). *Landscape with Woman and Child.* 1649.

138. J. Crome (1768–1821). *Landscape with Cottages.* Early 19th century.

139. P. Cézanne (1839–1906). *Village Church.* 1866–70.

From Ruisdael to Cézanne, the tendency in landscape painting was toward a flattened space, the demands of the support proving more urgent than those of depth.

140. J.A. Watteau (1684–1721). *The Perspective.* c. 1715.

*The Perspective* derived simultaneously from landscape architecture, theatre, and painting. Nostalgic in mood, Watteau revealed the old perspective system to be threatened by a lateral invasion of paired curtains of trees. The garden suggests the theatre with the three-dimensionality of the scene assuming the facticity of a stage set.

Herculaneum and Pompeii artists had eyes only for the broad, richly saturate monochrome planes, even though intimately mixed with these was an abundance of veritable *folies perspectives,* whose *trompe l'oeil* extravagance could match even the most sophisticated constructions of Veronese and Tiepolo. But illusionism—optical jugglery—could hardly appeal to a generation henceforth intent upon embracing, and no longer contradicting, the logic of material.

Here was a commitment that the Davidian age shared with 17th-century French classicism (that is, with Jansenism). The works of Champaigne, Poussin, Stella, Lemaire, and Le Sueur served as a general stimulus, but the pictures that truly counted were those in which the articulation of solid and void, of wall and window (the *veduta*) was suppressed in favor of the first part of this dialectic, even where the ground—the solid wall—completely filled and blocked the canvas, as in Champaigne's *Ex-voto* and Poussin's *Judgment of Solomon* and *Self-Portrait.* It could also occur through the reduced number of openings seen in Poussin's *Testament of Eudamidas,* as well as through the insistent use of architectural motifs aligned parallel to the picture plane, with screens, pillars, and especially pilasters often preferred to columns. In several of the pictures in Le Sueur's series on the Life of Saint Bruno (1645–48; accessioned by the royal collections in 1776) the boxed-in wall segments that tend to block the horizon and the rigor of the geometric grid squaring up the different scenes prefigured Neoclassical experiments and thus explain the revived interest in Le Sueur that developed in the late 18th century. "A sign of the times," Locquin tells us (meaning 1770), "is the recrudescence of devotion to Le Sueur and Poussin. . . . The neo-Poussinist movement continued to flourish right up to the end of the century. It attained its apogee in 1782, when the apotheosis of the great artist was solemnly celebrated in the Roman Pantheon, a homage to his genius that brought forth a host of panegyrics."

This so-called "neo-Poussinism" should, however, be approached with care. Beyond the occasional similarity of pose and the shared propensity toward geometricization, there is a fundamental stylistic difference between the new art and its prototypes, a discrepancy that can actually help us grasp the essential characteristics of Neoclassicism. When Locquin, in his still remarkable history of French painting from 1747 to 1785, wrote in 1912 that "David re-created in his *Andromache* the bare, severe ground of the *Testament of Eudamidas,*" he would appear to have overlooked a fundamental aspect of Poussin's art. Here the *fond,* or "ground," cannot be dissociated from the figuration inasmuch as it is the underpainting, or *fond,* that from one edge to the other provides the very substance of the forms and objects represented. This underpainting emerges, or surfaces, in "slabs" or planes, and the figures, instead of breaking free of the ground, seem to arise out of it, as if extruded, an effect that induces a slow reading of the picture. Unity is something broader than the individual figure; it is the patch where a few accents and highlights help to evoke from the common connective tissue a silhouette or a torso, without rupturing the ocher preparation that lies under everything and breaks through from below in patches. Thus, Locquin's term "ground" loses meaning since the underpainting constantly rises to the surface and becomes image, denoting a face, a rock, a garment, a harness, or even a bunch of grapes. The form was already there once the ocher preparation had been put down, and had only to be brought to light from this textural substratum—not projected upon a neutral ground from a preliminary study.

Style or technique has its consequences in the kind of narrative offered by Poussin's picture. Grandiloquent gesture is resisted, slowly eroded, and eventually negated by the gradual surfacing of the underlying color. Consubstantial with the raised arm or erect body, it tends to absorb forms and confound them with the patch that surrounds, overflows, and traverses them. Here, classicism is to be discovered less in compositional rigor than in a kind of pictorial economy, which allows a scene to become visible only on condition that its assertive (phatic) character be restrained, which holds back through pigment what it gives through narrative, and which expresses only by simultaneously muffling its rhetorical and mimetic effects.

This explains the unstable nature of a pictorial fabric that fluctuates in and out of depth, depending on the appearance and disappearance of a color that partakes of both textural ground and the surface of depicted objects. (Equally destabilizing is the way in which distances, cloud streaks, and patches of sky between trees are often rendered with the thickest strokes, added at the end as if to generate a countermovement wherein the most distant and immaterial part of the image is rendered by the picture's nearest and most palpable component.)

The manner developed by Poussin could hardly have been more remote from Neoclassical conceptions, since twice over it eludes the definition of painting as the representation of objects within the fictive depth of a scene. Color, for instance, works against three-dimensionality, however restricted this may be, and the delineation of objects is subordinated to the differential economy of an array of color patches that together constitute the surface. As a result, the dependence of painting on the nomination or description of objects, and thus on linguistic or rhetorical presuppositions, is reduced. The picture derives not from the logic of language but from its own specific coherence.

For two centuries adulated as a draftsman and composer, Poussin was always regarded as a poor colorist. Mengs even suggested that his pictures were merely sketches and studies. Meanwhile, Reynolds reproached the 17th-century master for his "dryness" and Delacroix assumed his "systematic abandonment of color" to be not only a fact but also deliberate. It required a Cézanne, at the dawn of the 20th century, to take up and radicalize the whole issue of color-surface at the point where the genius of Poussin had left it a quarter of a millennium earlier (Figs. 139, 142).

We need only compare the *Germanicus* of 1628 with Greuze's *Caracalla* (Fig. 149), with Vien's *Selling of Cupids* (Fig. 150), or with David's *Oath of the Horatii* (Fig. 82) to understand how the thematic similarities, significant as these may be, threaten to obscure the essential differences. When David claimed to revive "the immortal Poussin drawing on canvas the sublime lessons of philosophy," he boasted an ancestry to which he had no right, because Neoclassicism reversed the Poussinesque conception of the "ground," the wall, the surface.

141. E. Delacroix (1798–1863).
*Bouquet of Flowers.* c. 1848.

142. P. Cézanne (1839–1906).
*Bouquet of Flowers.* c. 1902.

The frontality of Delacroix's *Bouquet* ("flowers arranged against a gray ground" as the artist described the picture) is reinforced in Cézanne's copy. By adding a horizontal band along the bottom (denoting a table or an easel), the younger master indicated that he was painting not flowers but a surface, not a slice of nature but a picture.

143. J. Constable (1776–1837).
*Spring, East Bergholt Common.* 1814.

144. T. Rousseau (1812–67). *Rain Effect.*

In Fig. 143 the wood support shows through in a number of places; in Fig. 144 the grain of the panel, often heightened with a dark line, participates directly in the definition of the image.

The only thing the wall in David's art has in common with that of Poussin's is its frontalized disposition parallel to the picture plane. Far from absorbing the figure as in Poussin, the ground is a screen—a plain, hard, resistant surface—that functions like a "counter-repoussoir" to impel the figures toward us and increase the legibility of the gestures. This projective method (as opposed to the inductive method of Poussin) resulted in a friezelike arrangement of figures profiled against the ground, figures whose modeling seems to owe as much to sculpture and antique reliefs as to fresco painting. And David's *frottis* or "scumbling" (a fluctuating brushiness so different from Poussin's "slabs" of color) proves to be an extremely effective means of producing that resistant surface. Whether obvious (Figs. 270, 273) or dissembled under a thin layer of paint (Fig. 163), the regular, repetitive strokes, applied edge to edge, guarantee by their continuity and consistency the tangible, tactile presence of the wall. Delacroix, who tried the technique (Fig. 271), observed that "touch properly used serves as a suitable means of emphasizing the various planes of objects. A strong, emphatic stroke makes them advance, a weak one makes them withdraw."

Neoclassicism needed a contracted, hermetic space—the wall-screen—once it set out, as we have seen, to create a legible, didactic space capable of displaying its moralistic, sentimental themes, its "Roman" and pathetic poses. Little wonder, then, that Neoclassical painting became so intimately involved with theatre, either by seeking its models there or, even more, by providing them for the stage. If, as we are told, David discovered the theme of his *Oath of the Horatii* in a ballet-pantomine by Noverre, the reverse occurred in the instance of Greuze's *Village Bride*, which the *comédiens-italiens* transformed into a *tableau vivant*. Still other paintings were "staged" for the revolutionary pageants. David designed costumes and armor for the theatre and served as advisor to the actor-director Talma. And, according to Hautecoeur, he even undertook to produce some of the tragedies by Marie-Joseph Chénier.

Theatricality was the driving force of Neoclassicism. "The interpretation of painting as tragedy," writes James H. Rubin, "is consubstantial with 18th-century thought." History painting was supposed to have a *cathartic* effect, to arouse "terror and pity." It was a matter of inventing *types* in which each person could recognize the universality that he bore within himself, in the same way that, as A.O. Lovejoy has indicated in his *Essays in the History of Ideas*, the univeralist rationalism of the 18th century insisted upon, at the expense of diversity and deviation, the identity and profound equality of individuals at the center of the very same nature that created them all alike.

This was the age that rediscovered and republished (newly engraved by Morel d'Aleux) the typological drawings that Le Brun in 1678 had devoted to characters and temperaments. In them Louis XIV's court painter reduced the complexities of the human soul to a set of constant features that could be directly copied in the studios. Other plates by the same engraver disseminated the famous "comparative physiognomies" in which Le Brun attempted to classify different human types in relation to the animal kingdom (camel-men, sheep-men, etc.).

The period also brought forth Lavater's *Essay of Physiognomy*, which had a remarkable success throughout Europe and many editions—even popularized ones. The Swiss author believed he had invented an exact science making it possible to establish a quasi-mechanical relationship between the character (the interior) and the morphology (the exterior) of the individual human being. The thesis was taken up by Dr. Gall, the inventor of phrenology, who claimed to have located "the organ of kindness" in "a long protuberance of the frontal bone." These psycho-physiological theories, articulated through a limited number of virtues and vices (vanity, guile, etc.) joined with the theories of gesture, like that of Paillot de Montabert, who at the turn of the 19th century claimed to have developed a visual vocabulary of "the great agitations of the soul." This too propounded a catalogue of distinctive features and proposed it, in the form of a hieroglyphic chart, as the constant base upon which to construct pictures that would also be like Tables—figural forms—of Law.

Indeed, Europe at the end of the 18th century—the time of Revolution and Empire—gave itself over entirely to attitudinizing and mimicking. According to Jean Starobinski, "the hand raised in oath, the tension experienced by a body that sets the future in a moment of exaltation, conforms to an archaic model. If in one respect it initiates a new departure, in another it reenacts a very old contractual archetype."

Neoclassicism, therefore, means legibility, linearity, the aesthetic of the contour line, the profile, the cursive and the discursive. It aspired to consensus in a moment of social crystallization during which painting borrowed its models from—but also imposed them upon—history in the making. However, it did not do so without generating along its margins or in its legacy a regrouping of forces around the issue of the individual subject—from which a wholly different movement would develop.

## As artists chasten their drawing, figures begin to echo the rectangular shape of the support

If Neoclassicism can be distinguished by its special concern for the physical characteristics of the support (the flatness of the painting surface, the rectilinear geometry of its shape)—characteristics that impose themselves upon the structure of the figures and dictate their square-shouldered stability and frontality—we must view Subleyras as a precursor of the School of David. Born near Avignon and winner of the Grand Prix in 1727, Subleyras established himself in Rome and would die there of tuberculosis at age fifty. He made his reputation mainly with several large religious compositions, but it is the Louvre's *Charon* (Fig. 147) that clearly discloses the artist to have been a transitional figure, active at a moment when the Baroque style was undergoing reinterpretation and even rejection. The free-flowing, thoroughly Baroque volumes of the foreground shades are, for instance, contravened by the structural rigor present almost everywhere else in the picture. In order to evoke a sense of profundity—and what could be more profound than the passage from life to death?—Subleyras blurred his distances, scaled his Charon the full height of the picture, and made the painting's main vertical axis coincide with the sole of a foot aligned parallel to the picture plane. As for the barque, it conforms to a strict horizontal that is perpendicular to the frame.

Geometry is also at work, albeit more discreetly, in Subleyras' *Nude* (Fig. 145), especially when seen in relation to a work like the celebrated *Rokeby Venus* of Velázquez (National Gallery, London), or the nudes of such French contemporaries as Boucher, De Troy, Natoire, Trémolières, etc., where nothing links the structure of the figures to the materiality of the object-picture. The blocked recession and the regular, even obvious brushwork also partake, as Pierre Rosenberg has remarked, of the new spirit. David, according to his pupil Couder, admired Subleyras, which, however, does not tell us just what aspect of this master's production most appealed to the younger artist. *Patroclus* (Fig. 146), which David executed when he had almost concluded his study in Rome, already reveals the tendency toward geometricization that would distinguish French painting as it evolved in the Davidian circle.

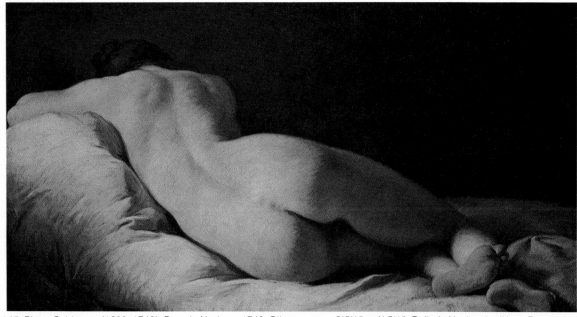

145. Pierre Subleyras (1699–1749). *Female Nude.* c. 1740. Oil on canvas, 2′5¼″ × 4′ 5½″. Galleria Nazionale d'Arte, Rome.

146. Jacques Louis David (1748–1825). *Academy (Male Nude), or Patroclus.* c. 1780. Oil on canvas, 4′ 1¼″ × 5′ 7″. Musée Thomas-Henry, Cherbourg.

147. Pierre Subleyras.
*Charon Passing the Shades.*
Before 1734.
Oil on canvas,
4'5¼" × 2'8¾".
Louvre.

# Pilasters *declare* and reinforce the painting surface

As early as the reign of Louis XV, Vien and Greuze were proposing radical departures that would lead to Neoclassicism. "One speaks of the 'Davidian Revolution,'" Locquin wrote in 1912 concerning pictorial art in the third quarter of the 18th century. ". . . We should like to show that the triumph of David in 1785 was simply the outcome of a slow evolution." Clearly evident in the two canvases reproduced on this page are: 1) the reduction of illusionistic depth until "usable" space is limited to no more than a few feet beyond the picture plane; 2) a strict parallelism of the background wall and the painting surface; and 3) a reinforcement of the rear plane by means of the vertical lines inscribed upon it (fluted pilasters, for instance). For his *Selling of Cupids* (Fig. 150) Vien took inspiration from an antique fresco uncovered in 1759 at Pompeii and published in an engraving of 1762. But Roman art also interested Vien for its material processes, and some eight years before the *Selling of Cupids* he had caused a great stir with his experiments in encaustic (using hot wax, instead of oil, as the medium). Ultimately, however, what he retained from Pompeiian painting, other than its themes, was his insistence upon flat, smooth surfaces. As a consequence, the severity of Vien's new manner has been placed in the service of anecdotes that remain resolutely Rococo and "futile." "It is a pity," wrote Diderot, "that this composition should be somewhat spoiled by an indecent gesture on the part of the little butterfly Love that the slave holds by his wings. The Love has placed a hand over the bend of his left arm, which rises to indicate in a highly suggestive manner the measure of the delight he promises."

It was quite otherwise in Greuze's picture (Fig. 149), the complete title of which is: *The Emperor Septimius Severus reproaches his son, Caracalla, for having wanted to assassinate him in the gorges and says to him: "If you desire my death, order Papinius to effect it with this sword."* The artist has flattened and geometricized a compositional scheme employed by Poussin for his *Death of Germanicus* and *Death of Eudamidas*. A frame within the frame, the wall hanging, with its deeper tonality, isolates the body and outstretched arm of the Emperor; color in general tends toward a monochromatic gray; and the space occupied by the figures is so shallow that the background plane becomes an essential actor in the pictorial drama. Called a "bas-relief" by Boucher, Greuze's canvas scandalized the critics, beginning with Diderot: "The rear wall of the painting touches the very drapery on the Emperor's bed, and this drapery touches the other figures. There is no depth in all this, no magic."

What Diderot could not grasp at this time was the affirmation of a deliberately contracted space that tends

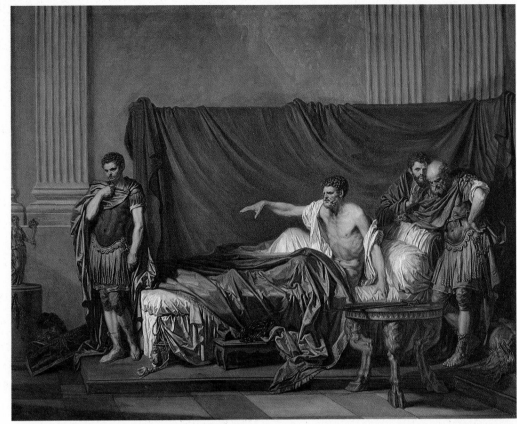

149. Jean-Baptiste Greuze (1725–1805). *Septimius Severus Reproaching Caracalla*. 1769. Oil on canvas, 4'¾"×5'3". Louvre.

150. Joseph Marie Vien (1716–1809). *Selling of Cupids*. 1763. Oil on canvas, 3'1½"×3'10¾". Musée National, Fontainebleau.

to recapitulate the two-dimensionality of the support. Just as he could not perceive how the actors—even more than in Vien's art—have been subordinated to the matrix of verticals and horizontals that structure the work and govern its rhythms (see the arm of Severus, which anticipated that in David's *Socrates* [Fig. 151]). Greuze himself, even as he maintained the shallowness of his pictorial space,

would abandon the equivalence of figure and setting. In this regard, David's *Lavoisier and His Wife* (Fig. 148), executed *after* the *Horatii* and the *Socrates*, represents a retreat from Greuze's painting, although the younger master did adopt the structural and iconographical theme of the pilaster, while also narrowly restricting visual depth. For the rest, David's picture, with its portrait of the illustrious chemist

and his wife among their instruments is a transitional and rather nostalgic work, offering a succulent contrast between the frontal opacity of the background wall and the aerial transparency of the research instruments, as in the balloon-flask in the lower right foreground, rendered with a *trompe l'oeil* precision that allows an invisible window to be reflected twice, once upright and once inverted!

151. Jacques Louis David (1748–1825). *Death of Socrates.* 1787. Oil on canvas, 4'3¼"×6'5¼".
Metropolitan Museum of Art, New York.

An underlying web of vertical
and horizontal lines
assures the rectitude of figures

152. Jacques Louis David. *Study for Death of Socrates*. 1787.
Charcoal heightened in white on gray-brown paper, 20½×17″. Musée Bonnat, Bayonne.

"In that very moment, the inane genre of painting was dealt a fatal blow," wrote Stendhal to acknowledge the triumph of David's *Oath of the Horatii* and *Death of Socrates* (Fig. 151), paintings in which the didactic mode had at last found a form equal to its moralizing ambitions. Often treated in the second half of the 18th century—even put on stage in 1763—the theme of Socrates drinking hemlock provided David with an opportunity to succeed, as no one else had, in realizing "the expression of a great maxim, a lesson for the spectator," thereby honoring the program that Diderot had recommended for painting.

It was in antique Roman bas-reliefs that David discovered the friezelike conception of his picture. Expressive of the *exemplum virtutis* are the clear spatial distribution of the contents, the legibility of everything, and the enhanced scale of the figures whose poses and gestures discharge the picture's responsibility for providing a moral lesson. These qualities can be seen in Socrates who, superbly silhouetted against the stone wall, makes his own death the occasion for a philosophical exhortation; in the despair of the disciples and the servant; and in Xanthippe's farewell made from the stairs. Then closely allied to all the sublime attitudes is the realism of the details; the blue undertones and veining of the flesh; the rippling muscles; the traces of blood caused by ankle irons; the clamp of Critias' hand upon Socrates' leg; the servant's raised left foot, etc. The very pathos of the painting derives from the minute care of the iconographical research and the crispness of the facture. We are in the paradoxical world of classical antiquities, among figures drawn from Greco-Roman sarcophagi and statuary (such as a bust of Socrates) but brought to life, "clothed" in flesh, and rendered with a precision worthy of Jan van Eyck.

Moreover, the structure and disposition of the figures are controlled by the invisible web of the squaring seen in the study reproduced in Fig. 152. With David, squaring was not simply a device for transferring a preliminary drawing to a larger canvas. Rather, *by anticipating* the transfer, the artist allowed the grid to intervene and guide his hand in the preparation of the painting. *Even before its inscription* upon the sheet, the regular network of verticals and horizontals predetermined the placement of the academies (nude studies). David drew with this skeleton of interlocking coordinates already integrated into his gesture, imposing its axes upon the figures and thus *reinforcing* them (as concrete is reinforced with an armature of iron rods).

The figures are not, of course, composed exclusively of parallels and perpendiculars, but the latent presence of a structural matrix contributes to the arrangement of objects and figures as if they were variations upon the intersecting lines, with all their rectilinear rigor (whose planar geometry echoes the picture's framing edge). The imaginary squaring that anticipated the compositional study functions somewhat as does Matisse's plumb line, which "by determining the vertical direction, forms in combination with its opposite, the horizontal, the draftsman's compass. . . . Around this fictive line evolves the arabesque."

In *Socrates,* three networks—two of which are invisible—underlie and control the image: the perspective grid, which determines the spatial recession and the respective sizes of the figures in relation to their position in depth; the squaring of the two-dimensional plane just discussed; and finally the join of the dressed stones in the wall, which stands forth like an iconographical transposition of the first two, invisible webs.

153. Pierre Narcisse Guérin (1774–1833). *The Return of Marcus Sextus.* 1797–99. Oil on canvas, 7′1½″×8′. Louvre.

154. Honoré Dufau (1770–1821). *Death of Ugolino.* 1800. Oil on canvas, 3′9″×4′9¾″.
Musée des Beaux-Arts, Valence.

# Figures align themselves along the axes and angles of a frontalized cross

The students and admirers of David followed his lead and created endless compositions based upon crosses, squares, and T-squares. Geometry is simply presupposed in the way they organized their groups along straight lines and right angles. In the Guérin painting reproduced in Fig. 153, Focillon saw "that sort of large cross formed by the prone, luminously livid body of the dead woman and the standing, back-lighted figure of the man." Escholier observed that "this striking composition is reduced to two great lines, one horizontal, the other vertical, whose rigid effect is calculated." Here we have a predisposition that would survive even in the teaching of Thomas Couture, the pupil of David's pupil Gros, who in 1867 recommended "establishing, by imagination or by reality, a horizontal line and a vertical line in front of the objects that are to be reproduced. This procedure provides an excellent guide that should always be retained."

"Guérin, a pupil of Régnault certainly, but I have a suspicion that he listened at the door to my studio," David said concerning *Marcus Sextus* (Fig. 153). In this work Guérin adopted ideas from the painter of the *Horatii*, but, ironically, it was done for the purpose of reversing the political effect of that earlier masterpiece. Thus, the "Roman" and "republican" style of David served to pictorialize the story (a story actually invented by the artist) of an émigré who returned home after his banishment by Sulla, only to find his wife dead and his daughter in despair. But it is in the painting by Harriet (Fig. 155), a student of David and a rare artist who died at an early age in Rome, that the rectilinear structuring of the composition assumes full force. In "a somewhat desolate landscape," reflecting "the wide and rather new impact of the Pre-Romanticism nourished by English or Germanic sources,"[1] a heavy architectural motif, which extends beyond the frame on three sides, reinforces the static quality of the figures. These, in consequence, become like so many variations upon a preexisting orthogonal scheme.

For his evocation of Dante's story of Count Ugolino (Fig. 154)—immured along with his children by Bishop Ruggieri and condemned to die of starvation—Dufau, while still a pupil in David's studio, placed his figures at the center of the composition and so arranged them that, paradoxically, they seem controlled, like actors on a stage, by the presence of the spectator. As in David's *Socrates* (Fig. 151), a matrix of cut and joined stones, its abstract character reinforced by the right angle of the blocked door (right), echoes the rectitude of the main protagonist.

155. Fulchran Jean Harriet (1778–1805). *Oedipus at Colonnus*. 1796. Oil on canvas, 5'1½" × 4'4¼". Private collection.

''The day after Marat's death,'' Delécluze tells us, ''a deputation appeared at the Convention to express the pretended regrets of the people. A certain Guirault carried the word, saying: 'What a crime! A parricidal hand has robbed us of the people's most intrepid defender, who died for liberty. Our eyes seek him still among you, our representatives. Oh, frightful spectacle! This man on his deathbed! Where are you, David? You have given posterity the image of Lepeletier dying for the Fatherland, but now you have another picture to paint.' . . . 'Yes, I will undertake it,' cried David, his voice choked with emotion.''

Writing a half-century later, Delécluze commented: ''It was while carried away by the most violent political passions that David produced [the portrait of Marat assassinated in his tub], whose full merit David himself failed to recognize until, in a calmer moment, he had forgotten his miserable idol and could consider the terrible image as a work of art.''

''A Jacobin pietà'' (Fig. 156), the canvas dedicated to Marat represents the ''Friend of the People'' just as David had found him on the eve of his murder, trying to relieve the torments of his skin disease. With incomparable authority, the artist divided his canvas into two generally equal parts. Below, smooth and brilliant handling, with powerful modeling provided by highlights, takes account of every detail (the gaping wound, the imperfections of the wood, the patching on the bathsheet, the inkpot, etc.). Above, a modulated range of strokes evincing the brush's progress across the canvas (from left to right) succeeds touch by touch in giving substance and consistency to the wall that encloses the scene.

But so emphatic are the verticals and horizontals of the lower half (in the packing crate, the writing board, and top edge of the tub) that they project over and govern the entire surface, *including the amorphous zone above.* By virtue of its imperious firmness, the rectilinearity can be sensed even in the upper part, which contains no drawing whatever. Thus, the question raised by David's picture, for those viewing it from a modernist perspective, might be formulated as follows: How far could the artist have gone in expanding the generalized zones while still controlling *Marat* with an armature of plane geometry? What helps guarantee such control in the present picture is the almost isomorphic relationship between the frontal plane of the box and the overall painting surface.

Twenty-five years after David had completed *Marat,* the same ''rectitude'' operates in *Virgil Reading from the Aeneid* (Fig. 157), the only painting by Ingres that is truly tied to the aesthetic of his master, David. When, as was

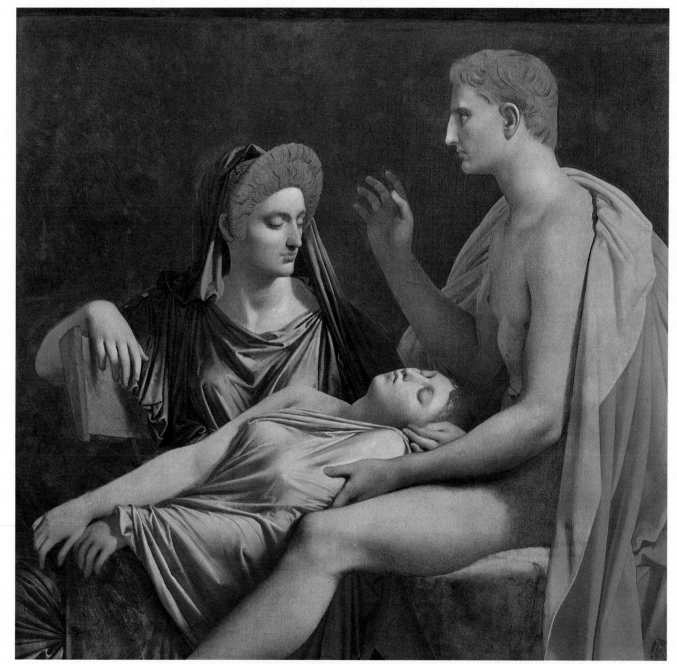

157. Jean Auguste Dominique Ingres (1780–1867). *Virgil Reading from the Aeneid.* c. 1819. Oil on canvas, 4′6¼″×4′8″. Musées Royaux des Beaux-Arts, Brussels.

probable, he cut this fragment from a larger canvas, Ingres—who never allowed the picture to leave his studio—eliminated the contradictions that in the large version at Toulouse obscure the linear web in the ornamental floor and wall and the static quality of the figures. In the picture reproduced here, the drama has been intensified, concentrated as it is upon the three principal actors caught in the same square matrix, in the same netlike trap. It is the moment when Octavia, the sister of Augustus, faints upon hearing Virgil (from beyond the frame) mention

her son Marcellus, who in all likelihood had been poisoned by Livia for the benefit of her son Agrippa. Meanwhile, the Empress Livia remains impassive under the gaze of Augustus, whose rarefied passion also, according to the artist's notes, interested Ingres.

Delaborde, in his biography of Ingres, characterized *Virgil Reading from the Aeneid* ''as a fragment detached from the walls of Pompeii.'' And the Roman ''frontality'' that it assumes is further enhanced by the rather dry and harsh texture of the pigment.

156. Jacques Louis David (1748–1825). *Death of Marat.* 1793. Oil on canvas, 5′11¾″×5′5″. Musées Royaux des Beaux-Arts, Brussels.

158. Jean Germain Drouais (1763–88). *Marius at Minturnae.* 1786. Oil on canvas, 8′10¾″×11′11¾″. Louvre.

159. Pierre Narcisse Guérin (1774–1833). *Sacrifice to Asclepius.* 1803. Oil on canvas, 9′6½″×8′6″. Musée des Beaux-Arts, Arras.

## Gestures fit to hurl thunderbolts dramatize the Neoclassical matrix of interlocking coordinates

160. Auguste Alphonse Gaudar de La Verdine (1780–1804). *Manlius Tarquatus Sentencing His Son to Die.* 1799. Oil on canvas, 3′9″×4′9″. École Nationale Supérieure des Beaux-Arts, Paris.

Neoclassical moralism (see Fig. 151) generated among the pupils and followers of David a veritable plethora of declamatory pantomimes. Drouais, David's favorite disciple, provided the first manifestation in *Marius at Minturnae* (Fig. 158), a work directly inspired by *The Oath of the Horatii* (Fig. 82). (To this masterpiece the young artist was said to have contributed the painting of one of the outstretched arms and the Sabine tunic.) "It was two years ago that France lost Talma," wrote Stendhal in 1818, "and at the Louvre it would have been difficult to count ten large canvases in which this great actor's solemn gestures or something of his head movements had not been imitated."

The raised arm of the soldier swearing vengeance reflects not only David and Talma, and through them Poussin's *Germanicus,* but also Caravaggio, whose dual principle has here been adopted and even accentuated. This required that the arm be sharply defined and made to stand clear of the somber ground; also that it be endowed with a dynamic power capable of activating the surface—

somewhat like Paul Klee's arrows, which are not only lines but also directional forces pulling all other forms in their wake.

At the beginning of the 19th century, postures tended to become codified, a process verified by such writings as *La Théorie du geste* by Paillot de Montabert (1813), who attempted to catalogue "the great agitations of the soul." In 1805 Quatremère de Quincy, a defender of the *Beau idéal,* called for a "hieroglyphic" style of writing in which the idea, symbolized once and for all, would become substituted in painting for the empirical observation of physical facts. Such were the issues that occupied painters like Gaudar de La Verdine, in his Prix de Rome painting (Fig. 160), and the Lille artist Serrur, whose submission to the 1820 Beaux-Arts competition (Fig. 161) shows Ajax defying Athena, in the aftermath of a shipwreck that he survived despite the goddess. If the nudity of the hero remains a product of the Davidian legacy, the dramatic amplitude of the surrounding sky signals new influences, at the same time that it recalls the storms of Joseph Vernet and Loutherbourg.

161. Henri Serrur (1794–1865). *Ajax.* 1820. Oil on canvas, 4′2″×3′1½″. Musée des Beaux-Arts, Lille.

162. Jean-Louis Laneuville (1748–1826). *Portrait of Barère de Vieuzac.* c. 1793. Oil on canvas, 4'3¼"×3'2½". Kunsthalle, Bremen.

## Like a sudden eruption, the human image surges up from the bottom of the canvas

blazing note of the vest. "David, the proud Cimabue of the genre called Classic," wrote Baudelaire, thereby pinpointing with one word what the artist had drawn from his study of the Florentine "primitives" (Giotto and Fra Angelico) for the placement of a single figure like that in *Madame de Verninac,* where frontality of an impeccably tectonic order looks forward to the Fernand Léger of *Nu sur fond rouge* (Hirschorn Museum).

The reductive aesthetic this expresses can be found actually articulated as early as 1769 by the *philosophe* Hemsterhuis (1720–90) in his *Letter on Sculpture* (a treatise recently examined by Starobinski). "The spirit," wrote Hemsterhuis, "finds the greatest beauty in that which it can form an idea of in the briefest span of time. . . . [The spirit] wants to receive a great many ideas in the shortest time possible . . . It seems incontestable that there is something in us which rejects everything related to what we call succession and duration. . . . I think that [sculpture] should go further, through the ease and excellence of its contours, toward *minimizing* the time that I spend in forming an idea of the object, to the end that a perfect expression of actions and passions may *maximize* the number of ideas received, and with that achieved, it should follow that the effect would be a sense of calm and majesty."

If acted upon, such a conception would, quite obviously, lead to a dominance of the whole over the detail, of contours over texture, and of immediate impact over progressive revelation. Hemsterhuis wanted to apprehend art apart from issues of *iconography* (history, myth) and even those of *form* (composition, color, texture, etc.) so as to formulate an *economics* of aesthetic vision, which would grant full value to perceptual processes—to the experience of the spectator. Here was an aesthetic of *instantaneity* corresponding to the advent—at a much later date—of the instantaneity that photography would allow, in the sense that the new technology provided a means of selecting and transcribing, with all the speed of a shutter click, a record of a certain aspect of the empirical world.

The imperious figure opposite (Fig. 163), surging up like a monolithic mass powerful enough to break free of the frame that sections it along the bottom, could be taken for an apparition, but one whose presence is palpable and very real.

Isolated upon a monochrome ground, adroitly placed off center (like Philippe de Champaigne's *Mère Angélique Arnauld* in the Louvre), wound about with a saffron scarf bordered in palmettes, seated upon a mahogany and gilt-bronze chair styled *à l'antique,* Mme de Verninac seems, before anything else, to be a light-toned, cleanly contoured form that the eye can easily encompass at first glance.

"Everything is equal [in this picture]," complains Delacroix in his journal, "there is no more interest in the head than in the draperies or in the chair."

Delacroix (the brother of Mme de Verninac) could have said as much about Convention delegate Barère in his portrait by Laneuville (Fig. 162), a David pupil whose manner so resembled that of the older master that as late as 1966 the picture seen here was still attributed to him. Comparing *Barère* with *Madame de Verninac,* we find the same unified ground, the same emphatic contour, the same brusque projection of the body (in this instance from behind the horizontal of a tribune), an effect made even more pronounced by the

163. Jacques Louis David (1748–1825). *Portrait of Madame de Verninac.* 1799. Oil on canvas, 4'9"×3'8". Louvre.

164. Jean Auguste Dominique Ingres. *Napoleon on His Throne* (detail of Fig. 165).

A *kitsch*-like brilliance accentuates the frontality
of a figure borrowed from Asian theocracies

"Relief is unworthy of the majesty of history," declared Ingres, whose portrait of Napoleon is symmetrical, monumental, glacial, and menacing (Fig. 165). In it the artist lavished the most minute and hyperrealist care upon every detail (Fig. 164): the carpet with its imperial eagle; the downiness of the ermine flecked with black tails; the scepter of Charles V "shoed" in jewels and an acanthus corolla; Charlemagne's "hand of justice"; the bees embroidered upon the crimson velvet mantle, the laces; the golden crown of laurel, etc. Such unselective precision tends to produce a solemn, petrified icon whose overall, pervasive brilliance reinforces the absolute frontality of the image. Commissioned in 1806 for the French Legislature (which sat in the Palais-Bourbon) and executed in the same year (that of Prussia's collapse at Jena), Ingres' painting is a political work. Its purpose was to envelop the former Corsican General in Roman and medieval references and by this means to invest him with symbols of a legitimacy even older than that of the Bourbons; to give an air of permanence to Napoleon's reign (which was destined to last only eleven years); and, still more, to endow the Emperor with a haunting and charismatic nature. This accounts, as Robert Rosenblum notes,[2] for the evocation of two older models, one antique and the other Christian: the *Jupiter* of Phidias and Jan van Eyck's *God the Father*. Modern propaganda, a Napoleonic invention, has here made use of very old and well-known themes that together yielded an efficacious mix of theocratic and patriarchal implications. What ensued, however, was a poor reception by the Parisian public at the Salon of 1806 (where Ingres also showed his *Self-Portrait* and the portraits of the Rivière family). The picture was called "gothic," meaning "primitive," archaic, medievalizing and even Oriental—everything that was not classic. Enemies spoke of the *empereur mal-ingre* (a pun upon the painter's name meaning the "sickly Emperor"), while *Pausanias français* explained that "M. Ingres wants nothing less than to roll French art back four hundred years, to restore our art to its infancy."

Ingres turned quite bitter over the negative response to his formidable ambitions. For the year 1806 the painter's correspondence from Rome gives us this record of his feelings: "What horrors have I just heard? I know everything that happens in Paris concerning me. And so the Salon is the theatre of my shame. I am the victim of ignorance, dishonesty, and calumny . . . I suffer insults day and night; I am pestered to death; never have I been so unhappy. . . ."

165. Jean Auguste Dominique Ingres (1780–1867). *Napoleon on His Throne*. 1806.
Oil on canvas, 8'6"×5'3¾". Musée de L'Armée, Paris.

INGRES. P<sup>xit</sup>

ANNO 180

# Arabesque sensuality
## flattened against mythological heavens

166. Jean Auguste Dominique Ingres (1780–1867). *Venus Wounded by Diomedes*. c. 1803. Oil on canvas, 10¼ × 13". Kunstmuseum, Basel.

Ingres quickly broke away from the style of his master, David, with its fundamental commitment to the proportions of actual human anatomy. David, of course, was not indifferent to the allure of the arabesque, as this could be found inscribed upon Greek vases. Delécluze tells us that he even recommended such sources to his pupils: "He particularly praised the naturalness and elegance in the handling of figures on so-called Etruscan vases." But David never sought to assimilate this radically flat, linear style into his painting. Despite his proclaimed desire to "achieve pure Greek" (*faire du grec pur*), David remained attached to modeling of the sort represented by Roman bas-reliefs. The "Greek" of his *Sabines*, as well as of his *Leonidas*, is restricted to the nudity of the heroes. Ingres reversed this approach and abandoned anatomical truth in order to assure the autonomy of the contour line. For Ingres, line in its relation to the surface would have primacy over subject matter and its representation.

But why did this artist assume and nourish the legacy of the *Barbus* ("Bearded Ones") and the *Penseurs* ("Thinkers"), that small group of reformers who, in the very studio of David, attempted to bend the master's teaching toward an archaism of the greatest purity? The *Venus* reproduced in Fig. 166 constitutes a veritable manifesto of the new painting. This can be seen in the picture's diminished depth; in the perspective canceled by means of an impenetrable cushion of clouds; in the willfully hard contours (making the horses seem made of wood); in the gold leaf applied to the manes and chariot so as to emphasize the materiality of the painting surface; in the proliferation of curves outlining the figure of Venus, her outstretched arm, her abdomen, her thigh and then reverberating throughout the entire composition (in the horses' cruppers and breaststraps, the carriage wheel, the shield, etc.). This is not to say, however, that the arabesques unfurl over a composition that is perfectly flat

(in the manner of Flaxman [Figs. 125–128], whom Ingres admired). In his close analysis of the picture, Robert Rosenblum has noted that "although the horses, chariot, and figure are restricted to almost Egyptian profile and frontal views, and are arranged in layers of nearly eggshell thinness, they nevertheless have gently swelling surfaces of flesh, armor and drapery that create a sensuous ripple across the ostensible flatness of the picture plane. The minute deviation from strict parallelism in the angle of Mars' javelin, which casts a fine shadow against the flank of the foremost horse, is characteristic of these subtle irregularities and pressures, as in the slight turn of Venus' head from a rigorous profile view."[3] What matters is not whether Ingres created flat painting but that he engaged in the *process of flattening* pictorial space. Illusionistic depth reveals itself *by reason of its very suppression* (which Ingres did not ever fully attain). But we sense the artist's reductive effort, which could never be

felt in an image strictly limited to two dimensions, such as a playing card. This lesson would not be lost on Matisse, whose most frontalized and decorative panels always retain—as if to salute the old perspective system—a line or a simple stroke suggestive of three-dimensional space. In the *Venus*, as well as in *Jupiter and Thetis* (Fig. 167), the lascivious bodies of the female protagonists—sinuous and invertebrate—are those of two mothers trying to intervene on behalf of their sons, Achilles in the first instance and Aeneas in the second. Rosenblum speaks of "a highly charged eroticism, as if the edges and surfaces of the female form were being expanded and contracted in an active, caressing way." And Kenneth Clark, in regard to the "troubling" figure, mentions "her extraordinary hand, half octopus, half tropical flower."

The huge picture in the Musée Granet (Fig. 167) constitutes one of the century's most extravagant productions. Here, Ingres would seem to have returned to the pose he employed for the 1806 *Napoleon*, but if Delécluze is to be believed, the *Jupiter* had been conceived first. A giant vignette, the Olympian is simultaneously without depth (see the radical foreshortening of the thighs) and infinitely volumetric, since one of his elbows rests upon a distant, scaleless cloud. Juno (on the left) also floats outside any system of measure. Thetis, all supplication, cleaves to the King of the gods' side like a membrane, as if by suction, and it is perhaps the "bourgeois" detail of the two joined toes that says the most for the artist's own erotic involvement.

The temerity of the young *pensionnaire* at the French Academy in Rome sending this painted phantasm to the Académie des Beaux-Arts in Paris in fulfillment of his educational requirements! It elicited nothing but sorrowful comments. The picture "generally lacks volume and depth; there are no masses; the color is weak and flat. The blue sky is of a uniform and hard tonality. . . . The head of Thetis is forced back; nor is there any way to tell which leg belongs to the right thigh," etc. Ingres was admonished because he "used his talent only to stoop beneath himself." Twenty-five years later, the creator of *Thetis*, now much sobered, would return to that early phase of his career in the course of correcting a portrait by his pupil Amaury-Duval: "It is a bit flat. . . . it lacks halftones. . . . I have painted like that. . . . Now I make things turn. . . . Everyone wants it to turn. . . . I couldn't care less if it turns. . . . However! . . . Beware! . . . No one will understand it. . . . Decidedly, more relief. . . ."

167. Jean Auguste Dominique Ingres. *Jupiter and Thetis*. 1811. Oil on canvas, 10'6½" × 7'9¼". Musée Granet, Aix-en-Provence.

## Mirror reflection, squaring, and the repetition of motifs —three ways of bonding the image to the frontal plane

168. Jean Auguste Dominique Ingres (1780–1867). *Study for Madame Moitessier.* c. 1856. Oil and pencil on linen, 1'6"×1'3". Musée Ingres, Montauban.

169. Jean Auguste Dominique Ingres. *Madame Moitessier* (detail of Fig. 170).

While pursuing the conventional art of society portraiture, the elderly Ingres— seventy years of age—renewed and cultivated the formal and theoretical interests of his youth. If the pose in *Madame Moitessier* (Fig. 170) is borrowed from a fresco found at Herculaneum—even to the arrangement of the figure's right hand, ''as pliable as a starfish''[4]—this work, the product of some twelve years of thought and effort, harbors an altogether modern complexity. Thus, the vertical frame that, on the right of Mme Moitessier, encloses her profile image does not belong to the mirror in which the reflection occurs, a fact confirmed by the continuity of the red ribbon and ornamental comb. Indeed, the mirror extends over almost the whole of the visible background wall. What it shows is what Mme Moitessier sees in front of her. The mirror—which shares with figurative painting the property of being at once both surface and depth—here reflects a sequence of verticals that join with the rectilinear frame to create an armature of right angles. This strongly frontalized matrix—for which an initial study (Fig. 168) divulges all the underlying rigor of the composition—is realized in values of gray and yellow (which evoke the subdued tonalities of Poussin). Such regular geometry stands in striking contrast to the brilliant pattern spread over the picture by the flowered dress. But the garment has been represented with so little shading and relief that it gives no hint of the model's anatomy beneath. And the more this area of color tends to lose its quality as clothing, the more it assumes a kind of autonomy as pure painting. What the detail in Fig. 169 suggests is a screen of color patches whose insistent verticality and obsessive precision recall the brocade dresses of the Mannerist Bronzino (a 16th-century painter whose art Ingres came to know during his four-year sojourn in Florence). Thus, the picture as a whole seems less an example of unified frontality than a juxtaposition of three different processes of frontalization: mirror reflection, systematic parallelism, and the explicit two-dimensionality of the foreground plane.

170. Jean Auguste Dominique Ingres. *Madame Moitessier.* 1856. Oil on canvas, 3'11¼"×3'1¼". National Gallery (courtesy of the Trustees), London.

# Clothing
of a uniform black
silhouetted against
a bare, planar background

At sixteen years of age, Chassériau painted a remarkably authoritative picture displaying all the characteristics of a program (Fig. 172). The color is isolated and even presented on a palette (in the upper left corner), and line, by representing nothing but itself (along the right margin), declares and reinforces the picture surface—as in a modern work by Barnett Newman. The frock coat—almost monochrome (except for a burst of dark strokes signifying the elbow and a ''fringe'' of lighter-toned brushwork in the subject's right arm)— would be little more than a Chinese shadow without the pair of white touches that, by contrast, bring out the richness of the black. Modeling has been used only for the face, the hand clutching the book, and the table it rests on. Not even Ingres, Chassériau's master, took French painting so close to reductive flatness. Perhaps for this very reason, the older artist saw Chassériau as his most promising disciple (''Come see,'' Ingres had said to his class, ''this child will be the Napoleon of painting'') until the influence of Delacroix bore the prodigy off in a different direction. In 1840, when he was twenty-one, Chassériau rejoined Ingres, who in 1834 had become director of the French Academy in Rome. This permitted the young artist to take account of everything that already separated him from his mentor. For the latter, Rome was the city of Raphael, ''who is not a man, who is a god come down to earth,'' and he sent his pupils to take on, under his supervision, the colossal task of copying the fifty-two compositions of the Vatican's Loggia frescoes. Chassériau, for his part, saw Rome ''as the earthly place where sublime things are the most numerous. . . . but also as a tomb. . . . In a long conversation with M. Ingres, I saw that on many issues we could never have a meeting of minds.'' By 1845 Chassériau had been definitively claimed by Romanticism. About the rupture, Ingres announced: ''Never speak to me again of that child!''

Quite a different case was that of Lehmann, who entered Ingres' studio in 1832. In the portrait here (Fig. 171), which Liszt sat for in 1839 at Lucca and which Lehmann then finished in Rome under the eyes of his teacher, the thoroughly simplified silhouette has been set off against paneling whose rectilinearity assures the stability of the picture and its subject.

171. Henri Lehmann (1814–1882). *Portrait of Franz Liszt*. c. 1839. Oil on canvas, 2'5¼"×1'11½". Musée Carnavalet, Paris.

172. Théodore Chassériau (1819–56). *Self-Portrait*. 1835.
Oil on canvas, 3′3¼″×2′8¼″. Louvre.

Bonington and Delacroix made effective use of *reserve* as a means of setting young female silhouettes into relief. The paradox of the reserve—that bit of support left untouched by pigment—consists in the effect of physical volume created through a process of deliberate nonintervention. What seems a stroke or a form—what "stands forward" or advances—is nothing more (in watercolor) than the paper itself, which because unsullied (or prepared with a monochrome wash) is actually less thick than the painted part of the surface. And the ostensible presence of the "ground" as a constituent element of the figure cannot fail to call attention to the mechanism by which the illusion has been created. The moment a surface comes forth as *both* virgin support and volume it is the process itself which is revealed, right along with the evidence of the figure it gives form to. We grasp at once *both* the image and the artifice that makes it possible. Bonington drew the silhouette first, then surrounded it with wash and sepia (Fig. 173). Next, he used graphite for the details of face and clothing. In the art of his friend Delacroix (Fig. 174), working twenty years later, the delineation is less insistent and the play of strokes much freer. Eager biographers have been able to link the pianist with the bare breasts and disheveled hair to a tender but brief liaison mentioned by Delacroix in his journal for March 20, 1849. At Chopin's place, "Mme Kalergi . . . played, but with little feeling. On the other hand, she is very beautiful when, while playing, she raises her eyes in the manner of the Magdalenes of Guido Reni or Rubens.''

174. Eugène Delacroix (1798–1863). *Marie Kalergis at the Piano.* c. 1849. Sepia on paper, 8½×6¾". Collection of Mme Vaudoyer.

From the "reserve," or untouched, flat surface, emerges a sense of full, solid form

173. Richard Parkes Bonington (1801–28). *Girl Seated in a Romantic Gorge.* c. 1825. Charcoal, wash, sepia on paper, 15¼×11¾". Musée des Beaux-Arts, Besançon.

175. Michel François Dandré-Bardon (1700–83). *The Adoration of the Skulls.* c. 1730?
Oil on canvas, 1′8¾″×2′¾″. National Gallery of Art, Washington.

By a system of boxes and parallels, columns and entablatures, the orthogonal structure of the frame invades the picture whose shape the frame defines. In a structure where the "squaring" and "nesting" are clearly related to the frontality of the surface, the planes settle in alongside one another as much as they progressively step back into depth. The converging lines are either conjured away (Fig. 175) or weakened by shadow (Fig. 177), and the blocked distance prevents the eye from becoming lost in infinity. More than Poussin's work with its internal rectangles, Dandré-Bardon's picture (Fig. 175) makes one think of the porticoes painted by the Tiepolos, as

well as of the *Scene of a Murder at the Foot of a Statue* by the Venetian artist Bencovitch (Clamecy). Winner of the second Prix de Rome in 1725, Dandré-Bardon spent five years in Italy, six months of them in the city of the Doges. An eclectic generally forgotten today who became director of the Marseilles Academy in 1754, he was also professor of history at the École Royale and the author of numerous texts on painting. Pierre Rosenberg has found the theme of the painting reproduced here rather difficult to make out (no doubt it involves an order of mendicant monks praying in the presence of relics), but he compares the artist's style to that of Magnasco.

Whatever the architectural order— Doric, Ionic, or Corinthian—the structure remains the same in these three pictures separated by some sixty-six years. But in the later works, by David (Fig. 177) and Robert (Fig. 176), the figures are more completely integrated into the linear grid that governs the surface, whereas in the Dandré-Bardon the penitents have been disposed as if in counterpoint to the rectilinearity of the colonnade.

In *Brutus,* as in the other works of David, a veritable picture within the picture is formed, here by the weeping women set off against the background drapery, the shaft of light serving to isolate them even further.

# The picture frame reduced and multiplied within the interior of the picture

176. Hubert Robert (1733–1808). *Salle des Saisons*. 1802–03. Oil on canvas, 15×18″. Louvre.

177. Jacques Louis David (1748–1825). *The Lictors Returning to Brutus the Bodies of His Sons*. 1789.
Oil on canvas, 10′8″×13′11¼″. Louvre.

## Ceilings tilt toward the picture's own vertical plane and there become mass

178. Francesco Guardi (1712–93).
*The Doge at Saint Mark's.* c. 1770.
Oil on canvas, 2'2½"×3'3¼".
Musées Royaux des Beaux-Arts, Brussels.

179. Antonio Canal, called Canaletto (1697–1768). *London: Interior of the Rotunda at Ranelagh.* c. 1754.
Oil on canvas, 1'6½"×2'6". National Gallery (courtesy of the Trustees), London.

180. Francesco Guardi. *The Doge Thanks the Grand Council.* c. 1770.
Oil on canvas, 2′2½″×3′2½″. Musée des Beaux-Arts, Nantes.

Venetian optical experiments, aided by the *camera oscura,* caused new interest to be focused on architectural superstructures. The panoramic conception of the pictorial space grew until it embraced the ceiling, which itself, in several canvases of Guardi's so-called *fêtes vénitiennes* series, became the principal feature of the scene depicted. Here (Fig. 180), the hall of the Great Council seems almost crushed by the weight of the gilded molding overhead. Enhancing the powerful crustlike medium that spreads over two-thirds of the painting's upper region are thin, curvilinear strokes of light yellow, which have the effect of further intensifying the sense of materiality, all the while that the weight

of the superstructure is strongly accentuated by a flattened perspective that advances the central tondo toward the foreground plane. The sheer verticality of this yellow field stands in marked contrast to the allusive lightness of the paintings represented on the room's walls. (Recognizable among the pictures within this picture is Tintoretto's *Paradise,* which fills the back wall above the enthroned Doge.)

Guardi took care to make the left and right edges of the ceiling intersect the corners of the canvas (Fig. 178), which further augments the coherence and authority of the spatial conception.

This structural reinforcement (along the outer perimeters of the format) would be less effective had it been

applied by Canaletto to the circular projection of the Ranelagh Rotunda (Fig. 179). There the artist compensated by means of a slight perspectival distortion that tilts the vault upward and an illumination that emphasizes the upper reaches of the image.

181. Hubert Robert (1733–1808). *Interior of the Temple of Diana at Nîmes.* 1787. Oil on canvas, 7'11¼"×7'11¼". Louvre.

## The lacy edges of ruins seem to tear the very canvas upon which they are painted

Projected into the interior of these two ruins—one antique, the other modern—by the absence of receding depth and the close cropping, the viewer of Robert's pictures collides with the largely frontal presence of an architecture whose lateral dimensions align with the frame (especially evident in *Burning of the Opéra* [Fig. 182], where the side walls, with their flat brushwork, hang like a ribbon fringe from the top of the building). For a brief moment, the crenelated stones profiled against the sky could be read as a rip or tear dividing a flat image into two pieces. Imperiously extending across the entire work, this tear evinces the relationship often found in Robert's painting

between its plastic or formal elements (line, contour, shape) and the tangible reality of the painting surface. Line, far from floating freely, adheres to edges and takes over the whole of the planar space. In many of his works, Robert succeeded in repeating, paraphrasing, contradicting, and "commenting upon" the geometry of the format, which, by virtue of such treatment, becomes overtly integrated into the pictorial scheme (Figs. 235, 236).

In the two pictures shown here, reduced depth is compensated for in the numerous cells, cavities, and setbacks, which together serve to evoke a space that is at once both closed and penetrated. These architectural

carcasses and skeletons reflect Robert's love of ruins, at the same time that they also reflect the rubbish of modern times—a love that encouraged the 18th century not to "miss" the urban disasters of the age.

182. Hubert Robert. *Burning of the Opéra in the Palais Royal.* 1781. Oil on canvas, 5'7¼"×4'1½". Louvre.

# The regularity of a foreground portico
# validates the surface and sets off the distant scene

184. Francesco Guardi (1712–93). *Imaginary View*. c. 1775. Oil on canvas, 13×20″. Museo del Castelvecchio, Verona.

In the final quarter of the 18th century, while systematizing the intuitions of Marco Ricci and, especially, Canaletto, the Venetian Francesco Guardi produced a great many works in which the foreground is occupied by a portico aligned parallel to the picture's surface. This portico, whose rhythms dominate the image, is deliberately positioned, or oriented, so as to echo the actual shape of the canvas, while also suggesting the continuation of the colonnade beyond the visual field. The objective here is not to focus our attention upon some detail or other in space; indeed, one could say that, on the contrary, a sort of "indifference" has suspended the relationship between foreground and distance. The portico, at the same time that it lateralizes the image, tends to shift from the painting to the seeing eye. Thus, before it becomes a spectacle to be seen—a "view" or *veduta*—the

picture is a viewing apparatus, an enlarged sight or viewfinder, a slide projector that has not yet "framed" the image and for this very reason becomes all the more present to the eye. Many of the "caprices" painted by Guardi in his late career contain structures ostensibly extended to the left or right of the pictorial field, their arches abutting the frame as if to buttress it and emphasize its role in the selection process.

In the painting reproduced above (Fig. 184) Guardi added a supplementary refinement: The portico has been reduced to a single column, whose imaginary prolongation toward the right occurs by virtue of our memory and consciousness of the arabesque line. At the same time that the eye completes the movement initiated by the arcade fragment, the viewer's sense of archaeology reconstitutes the ruined monument.

Guardi's critical intelligence may be the child of his reflection upon the large Baroque *trompe l'oeil* compositions of J. B. Tiepolo, whose foregrounds abound in columns that serve to flank and set off the doings of opulent crowds or nude goddesses. But while transposing this two-plane spatial disposition into the prosaic realm of everyday life, Guardi also reversed the effect of his illusionistic technique. By dissociating the first and second planes—separating the foreground from the midground—he affirmed perspective for what it is: an artifice.

183. Francesco Guardi. *A Portico*. c. 1780. Gouache on paper, 1′9¾″×1′3″.
Musée Jacquemart-André, Paris.

185. Hubert Robert (1733–1808). *Falls under a Ruined Bridge.* 1791.
Oil on canvas, 2'5½" × 1'11½". Musée des Beaux-Arts, Tours.

# A wall erected at mid-distance both blocks and channels the spectator's view

186. Hubert Robert. *View of the Acqueducts to Nero's Palace in Rome.* n.d.
Oil on canvas, 8'¾" × 5'¾". Musée National du Château, Versailles.

The massive perpendicularity of a deep-toned wall occupies the greater part of these pictures and intercepts the eye, thereby blocking recession and brutally restricting the *veduta* ("view"). But the invasion of the surface by the wall (whether parallel to the canvas, as in Fig. 186, or set at an angle to it, as in Fig. 185) is counterbalanced by a gap—a "diaphragm"—which at the heart of the obstacle gives us a framed bit of sky or water, whose color allies itself with that of the picture's upper portion. This opposition of solid and void, of the closed and the open, of the heavy and the impalpable dramatizes the landscape, and Hubert Robert made great use of it in certain formulations, the most radical of which is the portico or the triumphal arch that seals off distance from the top to the bottom of a picture while also allowing a narrow passage into depth. A later, vegetal translation of the technique can be found in the forest thickets of Théodore Rousseau, where a dense and bituminous screen of branches and

leaves fills the foreground—pierced only by bits of daylight.

Until 1933, when it was reattributed to Fragonard, *Waterfalls at Tivoli* (Fig. 187), had been considered a work by Robert. Such confusions can be accounted for by the great friendship of the two painters, who, beginning in 1759, drew regularly side by side at the Villa d'Este and in the Roman environs.

187. Jean-Honoré Fragonard (1732–1806).
*Waterfalls at Tivoli.* c. 1760.
Oil on canvas, 2'4¼" × 1'11½". Louvre.

188. Caspar David Friedrich (1774–1840). *Ruin*. c. 1824.
Watercolor, 7×4¾″. Staatliche Kunstsammlungen, Kupferstichkabinett, Dresden.

## With space choked off, attention falls upon the grain of both stone and pigment

189. Pierre Henri de Valenciennes (1750–1819).
*Ruined Arcade*. c. 1782–84.
Oil on paper, 16½×10″. Louvre.

The separation maintained between the picture plane and the almost frontal alignment of the wall activates and sensitizes the painted surface. In Friedrich's picture (Fig. 188), the nonparallelism of the two planes is rectified by the brushwork, which validates the right portion of the design and advances it toward us. The same slight distortion can also be found in Valenciennes' *Ruined Arcade* (Fig. 189), where the thickness of the strokes and the freshness of the accents increase the ambiguity of the depth. The immediacy of these continuous, unbroken walls, covering the whole or the greater portion of the surface, compels us to read them as texture. Thus, we apprehend not so much the monument as the stones that make it up.

The eye is fascinated less by thematic detail than by the painter's handling. This occurs because proximity prevents intellectual mastery and thus all attempts to estimate the time or place of the object described. "Time," wrote Chateaubriand in his *Memories from Beyond the Tomb,* "does for men what space does for buildings. Neither can be judged except from a distance and in perspective. When too close, they cannot be seen. When too far, they are no longer visible." But perspective, after having been suppressed along the margins, returned to the heart of the work through the apertures introduced there. Hubert Robert excelled at this dialectic of near and far (Figs. 185, 186). His oblique view of St. Peter's in Rome (Fig. 190) contains an almost ideological countermovement, for while Christianity's most illustrious monument has been pressed into the vice of a narrow format, attention is drawn away from it by the decorative element in the foreground, where some idlers lie about vaguely intent upon a preaching monk.

190. Hubert Robert (1733–1808). *Group near a Window at Saint Peter's in Rome.* c. 1762–63. Oil on wood, 19×14¼″. Private collection.

# A cross expresses both form and content

192. Caspar David Friedrich. *View Through a Window*. 1806.
Sepia wash on paper, 12¼×9½".
Kunsthistorisches Museum, Vienna.

191. Caspar David Friedrich (1774–1840). *Woman at the Window*. 1822. Oil on canvas, 17¼×14½".
Nationalgalerie Staatliche Museen, Berlin.

The theme of the single, open window is an invention of the 19th century. After Friedrich introduced it in an ink drawing of 1806 (Fig. 192), his pupil Dahl took up the subject seventeen years later (Fig. 193), simultaneously emphasizing its symmetry, its frontality, and the sense of actuality it provides. But whereas in the Friedrich the wall is defined sufficiently to disclose the various objects hanging on it (scissors, the edges of a pair of small pictures), in the Dahl the embrasure coincides generally with the painting's own width, which tends to draw the viewer close, there inviting him to contemplate the precisely rendered landscape (the Elbe and the King of Saxony's summer castle), isolated, framed, and set off by the aperture.

The hyperprecision of the landscape image—which contrasts with the blurred reflections in the windows—reminds the modern spectator of the famous analogy made by the Renaissance theoretician Alberti (see p. 266) between a view (a landscape seen through a window) and a picture within a picture. Friedrich's work produces somewhat less the impression of a hole cut in the wall, mainly because of the luminary transition the artist effected between interior and exterior spaces. Then too Friedrich's landscape is more fluid and generalized—less precise— than Dahl's. Still, in all three instances, the more or less clear opposition of inside and outside finds reinforcement in a rectilinearity that screens and structures the surface. And the gridlike coordinates constitute a play of perpendiculars that becomes increasingly dominant the more the upper portion of the picture is given over to them. As for *Woman at the Window* (Fig. 191), it has even been said that the slender cross traced against the sky—with its deliberately irregular drawing and its possible religious connotations—is the true theme of the picture, symptomatic of an urge to endow art with transcendental meaning.

193. Johan Christian Clausen Dahl (1788–1857). *Window*. 1823.
Oil on canvas, 2'3½"×1'5¾". Museum Folkwang, Essen.

194. Caspar David Friedrich (1774–1840). *Skeletons in the Stalactite Cave.* c. 1834.
Pencil and sepia on paper, 7½ × 10¾″. Kunsthalle, Hamburg.

# A fractured surface yields up the enigma of art and life

195. Caspar David Friedrich. *Cavern.* 1813. Oil on canvas, 19¼ × 17¼″. Kunsthalle, Bremen.

196. Caspar David Friedrich. *Ravine*. 1821.
Oil on canvas, 15×17¼". Stiftung Pommern, Kiel.

In *Ravine* (Fig. 196) as in *Cavern* (Fig. 195), painted eight years later, Friedrich depicted a fractured surface and made it yield up the enigma of a black hole—a fault, a crevice—whose latent meaning is perhaps to be discovered in a drawing (Fig. 194), which with its jagged edges framing two skeletons provides the ''negative'' of the first two images.

Their space closed on all sides, organized around a gaping wound, these pictures come forth in strong contrast to the vast, spiritualized landscapes that made Friedrich's reputation. Writing in 1830, the artist argued for naturalism and made use of a metaphor whose polemical purpose seems less interesting than a certain unconscious import that it conveys: ''The painter should not paint merely what he sees before him, but also what he sees within him. If he sees nothing within himself, he should give up trying to paint what he sees without. Otherwise, his pictures will resemble screens behind which one expects to find only sick people, or even dead ones.'' The works reproduced on these two pages are like two perforated ''screens,'' and Friedrich's oeuvre offers numerous ridges, windows, portals, ranks of trees, and monastic ruins that suggest the same opposition between a ''blocked'' surface and an opening onto the unknown.

Born in Pomerania on the Baltic coast, Friedrich would be haunted by this Northern countryside, especially the island called Rügen, where he kept returning all his life. The painter was thirteen when he suffered a particularly tragic experience. During a skating party, the ice broke under his feet, and after having been rescued by his brother, he watched the latter disappear into the freezing water. From this may have come the deep melancholy that would afflict Friedrich until 1840, when he died in a state of mental alienation.

# In the Alps, Caspar Wolf discovers an abstract play of solids and voids

197. Caspar Wolf (1735–83). *Lake Thun and Mt. Niesen Viewed from the Grotto of Saint Beatus.* 1776. Oil on canvas, 1′9¼″×2′6″. Kunstmuseum, Basel.

198. Caspar Wolf. *Arch of the Saint Beatus Grotto.* 1776. Oil on canvas, 1′9¼″×2′6″. Aargauer Kunsthaus, Aarau.

The Swiss artist Caspar Wolf was the great pioneer of mountainscape painting. Attempting neither the picturesque nor the sublime, he sought documentary truth and a methodical exploration of sites that still remained inaccessible to all but true Alpinists. His purpose was to satisfy the curiosity of a growing number of Europeans crossing the Alps on the Grand Tour. Like his contemporary the naturalist Horace Bénédict de Saussure, who left several remarkable accounts of his conquest of Mont Blanc, Wolf offered his impressions through the ultimate medium of book publication. In the prospectus to the 1779 edition of *Description detaillée des vues remarquables de la Suisse,* we find this statement: ''Foreigners arrive in droves to contemplate [the peaks and natural phenomena of Switzerland]; now being published are descriptions that are often prepared with too little care and are only the fruit of an all-too-hasty trip. . . . [Thanks to the engravings made from Wolf's paintings], each reader can make a tour in his own study, at his leisure considering the miracles of creation, yet gaining an exact and true idea of them.''

The scientific concerns of Wolf simply make his feeling for pure form—the equilibrium of his solids and voids, the importance of his frontal, foreground zones—all the more striking. The serene amplitude of the curves—whether defining a vault or the edge of a stone mass profiled against the sky—has been calculated in relation to the rectangle of the painting surface. It is this relationship that distinguishes Wolf's art from so many purely documentary illustrations in which the ''picturesque'' site is merely transcribed upon a neutral ground, producing a plastically inert image. Also present—as Barbara Stafford has noted in her

70

study of 18th- and early-19th-century records of *voyages pittoresques*—is the pictorial realization of a poetic theme often taken up following Shaftesbury's introduction of it in 1709: the world viewed as a work of art and nature as a masterpiece infinitely more accomplished than actual artifacts.[5] By revealing the structural coherence of material, the microscope also revealed the imperfections of human work, for a crystal was found to be better "conceived" than an obelisk and a muscle better designed than a motor. After all, art had its source in nature, since nature gave art its most beautiful effects. Buffon, as Hubert Damisch has pointed out, "used the word 'figuration' to mean a specific mode of organizing matter that is characteristic of minerals."

Now the whole of the Alps assumed the character of one colossal sculpture. Sébastien Mercier, a "voyager" writing in his diary in 1785, described the extreme pleasure that he experienced in viewing a scale model of the Alpine chain, a work measuring 7 meters long to which a Swiss officer had devoted twenty years of effort. After three hours with this creation, Mercier found himself fascinated by its "rugged and gigantic nature, its bold design, its majestic forms." He spoke of it as a work of art.

For Wolf, the hollows counted for as much as the solid volumes. Thus, the grotto subject gave him the opportunity to demonstrate (Fig. 199) his will to organize surface in terms of abstract masses and strokes of color before adding (Fig. 200) the precision necessary to transform a few green accents into a slender tree and rapid brushwork into the murky depths of the earth. And he did not forget to indicate scale by introducing one or two figures (Fig. 197).

199. Caspar Wolf. *Study for the Grotto of Saint Beatus Viewed from the West.* 1776. Oil on cardboard, 9½×15¼". Aargauer Kunsthaus, Aarau.

200. Caspar Wolf. *Grotto of Saint Beatus Viewed from the West.* 1776. Oil on canvas, 1'9¼"×2'4¾". Aargauer Kunsthaus, Aarau.

An altitudinous landscape
becomes identified
with the painting surface

203. Caspar Wolf. *Geltenbach Waterfalls in Winter.* 1774. Oil on canvas, 2'8" × 1'9¼". Collection Oskar Reinhart. Winterthur.

202. Caspar Wolf (1735–83). *Alpine Landscape with a Rainbow.* 1778. Oil on canvas, 2'8¼" × 1'9¼". Kunstmuseum, Basel.

By allowing their mountains to fill the picture all the way to its upper edge, painters considerably reduced the importance of the sky. They also transformed perspective recession into a wall whose verticality tends to coincide with the painting surface.

It was this disposition—close up and frontal—that Turner adopted in 1802 when the Peace of Amiens permitted him to leave England (then some twelve years cut off from the Continent by the French Revolution and Napoleonic wars) and at last to behold the Alps, thereby fulfilling a desire first conceived from viewing the watercolors of John Robert Cozens (Figs. 207, 208). What Turner discovered, on a grand scale,

was the epic and monumental dimension he had sought in Wales and on the Isle of Wight. Two months of passionate exploration in Switzerland would have multiple echoes in his subsequent work (Fig. 525), and he returned home full of enthusiasm for "fragments and precipices . . . strikingly grand." Encountering the painter-diarist Joseph Farington in the Louvre on his way back, Turner declared that he had found the Alps "very romantic" and that he had witnessed "very fine thunderstorms among the mountains." The meticulously executed view of Reichenbach (Fig. 201), with its dead trees, its goats (on the right), and its shepherds around a fire (on the left),

forms part of a series of large watercolors prepared by the artist for exhibition. For his foreground Turner borrowed a plunging view that he would often adopt in his paintings of the Alps and of Italy, as if responding to an observation made by Edmund Burke in his deliberations on the sublime: "I am apt to imagine, likewise, that height is less grand than depth; and that we are more struck at looking down from a precipice, than looking up at an object of equal height."

Thirty years before Turner, the Swiss Caspar Wolf (Fig. 202) had experimented with the same kind of view—frontal and parallel to the picture plane—adding to it a spatial ambiguity

that makes the foreground seem unstable and floating. It is as if this part of the landscape were obeying its own independent laws of perspective, a daring effect that threatens the coherence of the whole.

The grandiose character of the Alps drew allusive prose from Wolf's contemporaries. On the sixteenth day of an expedition to the "Giant's Collar," Horace Bénédict de Saussure, the Geneva professor who "discovered" Mont Blanc, exclaimed in 1788: "The soul ascends, the vision of the spirit tends to expand, and in the midst of this majestic silence one seems to hear the voice of nature and to become certain of its most secret operations."

201. Joseph Mallord William Turner (1775–1851). *The Great Fall of the Reichenbach.* 1804. Watercolor, 3'3¾" × 2'3¼". Trustees of the Cecil Higgins Art Gallery, Bedford.

## Landscapes become screens reducing three-dimensional recession to almost nothing

204. Francis Towne (1740–1816). *The Source of the Aveyron*. 1781.
Watercolor on cream-laid paper, 12¼ × 8¾". Collection D. Oppé, London.

In the broadly brushed Alpine landscape (Fig. 204), the modulation of the blues, both in the sky and in the mountains, does nothing to help us estimate the depth of the space. The darker zone that suddenly and without transition abuts the large light-toned area on its left could just as well be read as closer (to see this, we have only to reverse the image), provided we could suspend our a priori conception of the phenomenal world. Henri Lemaître, in his book on English landscape painting in watercolor (1951), explains that Towne was "the first, in 1777, to upset the rapport between the tonality of the foreground and that of the background, a rapport that in fact was respected by all of Towne's predecessors and many of his successors. It derived from a rule that treatises had long held to be inviolable, to the effect that color should progressively lighten the greater the depth depicted." In Towne, therefore, color works against both empirical experience and artistic tradition. By ignoring the value gradations called *sfumato,* it brings distance forward. As a result, the picture surface becomes a scene of ambiguity, in which what we know about space is confounded by what the color gives us.

Lemaître also points out the curious technique employed by the English artist for denoting contours. "He applies colored ink of a reddish cast; the line is then scratched in by knife, with an admirable delicacy." This accounts for "the metallic radiance" of the high ridges (on the left), the febrility of the ocher veining, and the fissures that seem simultaneously to penetrate both the paper and the steep masses.

Francis Towne was a provincial from Devonshire, a marginal figure who in 1780 made the journey to Rome, where he became the companion of Thomas Jones (Figs. 489, 490). On the way home he sojourned for a month in Switzerland, there executing the several watercolors of mountain scenes that, in Lemaître's opinion, "figure among the most original landscapes painted in the late 18th century." Forgotten after his death and rediscovered a century later, Towne's work moved equally far from picturesqueness, from topography, and from Romantic effusiveness. Thus, it could be appreciated only by later generations who meanwhile had assimilated Japanese woodcuts and the art of Cézanne.

Beyond the repoussoir (a dead tree or a bit of snow-covered terrain), Francis Towne erected a vertical screen wherein three-dimensional recession has been reduced to almost nothing. Abruptly surging up behind the zoomorphic trunk in the foreground, the trees in Hyde Park (Fig. 205) seem flattened out like leaves—their branches assuming the character of veins. The perspective withdrawal of the walkway is canceled by a dense, frontal thicket of foliage. Moreover, the nearly manic precision of the botanical details accentuates the effect of presence, transforming the passage into a patchwork of gray-green touches.

205. Francis Towne.
*Trees in Hyde Park*. 1797.
Watercolor on paper, 17¾ × 14¼".
Toledo Museum of Art.

# Colossal stone ramparts make a lateral invasion of the planar space

206. Joseph Mallord William Turner (1775–1851). *The Upper Fall of the Reichenbach.* c. 1818. Watercolor over pencil heightened with white, 11×15¼″.
Yale Center for British Art (Paul Mellon Collection), New Haven.

207. John Robert Cozens (1752–97). *Entrance to the Valley of the Grande Chartreuse in Dauphiné.*
1783. Watercolor, 10¼×14½″. Ashmolean Museum, Oxford.

Mountains, with their enormous, bruising masses, made a lateral invasion of the picture's two-dimensional space. For Cozens as well as for Turner, the Alps provided an occasion for demonstrating the expressiveness of raw volume. Challenging the balanced, harmonious solutions offered by classical landscape painting (that of Claude Lorrain and Gaspard Dughet, for instance), the English masters painted less the forms of nature than their weight, the roughness of matter, the intrinsic power of minerals, the scaleless telluric fragments devoid of proportion and spatial content, all battered, broken, and thrown about by forces beyond every human capability. Quite simply, mountains constituted an immensity that excluded man and defied submission to his aesthetic eye (Figs. 206, 208).

Beginning in 1688, the poet John Dennis spoke of mountains as "Ruins upon Ruins in monstrous Heaps, and Heaven and Earth confounded," and as "Rocks that were void of all form, but what they had receiv'd from Ruine." The idea then spread that "the life of the earth is stamped upon its monuments." Rocks and abrupt outcroppings were felt to be sentient—as if they could recount the history of matter, of the geological erosion of a world in which the human race made a late and furtive appearance. If for Dennis the Alps were ruins, the contemplation of which produced "a delightful Horrour, a terrible Joy," they also came forth as witnesses to the antediluvian age, as the shattered remains of a universal cataclysm. This identification of mountains with ruins would persist throughout the 18th century. In 1776 a traveler spoke of "these vast monuments to the decay of the universe," and in 1784 Bernardin de Saint-Pierre, author of the Rousseauesque novel *Paul et Virginie,* observed: "A mere pebble in our rivers is older than the pyramids of Egypt."

It is this quality of immanence within geology that Cozens and Turner expressed in their watercolors, which reflect, just as concurrent writings do, the ambivalence signaled by Barbara Stafford—that nature seemed to be both "tomb and organism."[6] Witness to a distant past, nature was also perceived as "geologically and biologically alive." The same sentiment can be found expressed in a 1785 diary note made by Cozens' contemporary Sébastien Mercier: "We must not regard the earth's mass as a piece of inanimate mud, a coarse pile of stagnant elements. . . . Everything is alive in this great body. Nature is at work in the depths of dark abysses and subterranean passages, just as she smiles and turns green on her surface. Minerals breed; rocks grow; and a generative property penetrates deep into the hardest rocks."

208. John Robert Cozens. *Near Chiavenna in the Grisons.* c. 1781. Watercolor and pencil, 1'4½"×2'½". Yale Center for British Art, New Haven.

209. Caspar David Friedrich (1774–1840). *View of the Hedelstein, near Rathen, on the Rhine.* c. 1828. Watercolor on paper, 10¼×9″. Germanisches Nationalmuseun, Nürnberg.

## Rocky outcroppings loom up like projections of personal solitude

Thomas Girtin constructed his large watercolor of Bamburg Castle (Fig. 210)—with its luminous double hearth—by means of broad, flat strokes, heightened with a series of small, curvilinear touches of rich brown. It makes a monumental image—immediate and tangible—of a compact, almost tactile presence.

Before his premature death at the beginning of the century, Girtin seemed destined to have a career as brilliant as that actually achieved by his friend Turner, who was also his rival during the formative years when together the two artists sought to expand upon the precedent set by John Robert Cozens (Figs. 207, 208).

A comparable spirit dictated the approach taken by Friedrich (Fig. 209), but the German artist cultivated subtle contrasts, liquid light, and a discreet handling of gray and yellow. Even the rocky outcropping softly silhouetted against the sky is a value variation upon the theme of gray.

The solitary rock formation appears to be a leitmotiv of the travel accounts written in the 18th century. Barbara Stafford, in her study of the genesis of romantic sentiment, has found that a reversal of roles occurred in the descriptions and engravings of *voyages pittoresques.*[7] While the observer is diminished to the point of insignificance, a boulder becomes the main image. If this object fascinates the traveler, it is less by reason of its strange, fantastic, anthropomorphic forms than for its sheer size and presence. "Loss of identity," "empathy," and "passionate identification"—these are the themes that Girtin and Friedrich endowed with pictorial amplitude. They show us, by means of a low vantage point, a peak that is simultaneously distant and accessible, a summit toward which we are borne by the moderated slope of the terrain.

Girtin's watercolor reproduced in Fig. 210 belongs to what Barbara Stafford calls "ambiguous monuments": vague ruins whose stones are closely integrated with the vestiges of human constructions. This period theme would have its maximum fulfillment in Victor Hugo, who was fascinated by time's power to confound, little by little, man's work with that of God. Bernardin de Saint-Pierre had already entertained the concept, in somewhat inverse order, when he concluded *Études de la nature* (1784) by associating the memory of great men with the durability of megaliths: "Thus, I encompass both past and future in my present vision of a bare boulder, and, by dedicating it to virtue with a simple inscription, I render the rough form more venerable than if I had decorated it with the five orders of architecture."

210. Thomas Girtin (1775–1802). *"The Rocking Stone."* c. 1797. Watercolor, 21¾×17¾″. Tate Gallery, London.

211. John Sell Cotman (1782–1842). *The Baggage Wagon.* c. 1835. Oil on wood, 17×12¾". Castle Museum, Norwich.

## Curtains of foliage seal off the visual field

212. John Sell Cotman. *In the Bishop's Garden.* c. 1835. Oil on cardboard, 9¾×7½". Castle Museum, Norwich.

Allowing the picture surface to be obstructed by an invasion of frontally aligned vegetation yielded a formal theme that, from Paul Huet to Théodore Rousseau, became increasingly important in the 19th century. Already in the 18th century, artists like Watteau, Fragonard, Hubert Robert, and Louis Moreau had erected imposing curtains of foliage that function to block off perspective (Fig. 140), but no one had presented the almost mineral impasto that spreads like "dung" or polypary over the canvases of John Sell Cotman (Figs. 211, 212). A self-taught artist born in Norfolk, Cotman is best known for the astonishing concision of his watercolors, with their mingled influences from Thomas Girtin (Fig. 210) and Chinese painting. An extensive and daring use of reserves (Fig. 133) enabled Cotman to construct his image by integrating into it broad zones of virgin paper whose flatness is that of the support itself. But in certain of his works, the artist maintained this frontality while completely changing his

material and process. Thus, in the *Baggage Wagon*, (Fig. 211), as well as in the *Bishop's Garden* (Fig. 212), he realized his formal objective by covering the surface with a surcharge of "spongy," granular medium.

Impasto is not to be found in the painting of Johan Christian Dahl (Fig. 213), who enlivened the ample branches of his birch tree by salting it with a multitude of tiny white highlights. A former pupil of Caspar David Friedrich, whose house and studio he began sharing in 1823 (see pp. 66–67), Dahl—a Norwegian with close ties to Carus (Figs. 291, 292) and the poet Tieck—achieved a secure place in the Romanticism of Northern Germany, assimilating its special qualities—obsessive precision and the mystical implications of an "inhabited" nature, a nature suffused with divine spirit.

The appeal of the work reproduced here derives in great part from the double overhang that structures it. The overhang from which we view the scene allows us not only to take in the vegetal

mass from above, but also to confront it head-on like a great sail or a stain that spreads in every direction, all the way to the picture's edges. Then there is the tree whose arched trunk projects over an abyss in a way that destabilizes the form and contradicts its supposed durability. No doubt the artist was to a certain extent playing upon the human power of empathy by offering the spectator, in the precariously canted object, an image with which he can identify his own vertigo and fear of falling.

213. Johan Christian Clausen Dahl (1788–1857). *Birch Tree in a Storm.* 1849. Oil on canvas, 3'1¼"×2'4¼". Billedgalleri, Bergen.

# Perspective collapses as if viewed through a telephoto lens

214. Théodore Géricault (1791–1824). *Four Jockeys Riding at a Gallop.* c. 1820. Oil on canvas, 10¼ × 15″. Musée Bonnat, Bayonne.

Géricault painted the accelerated speed of modern vision, doing so with a synthesizing approach that grasped the density of things—that which declares *tache* ("color patch") and surface—before specifying depth.

In Géricault's *Cart* (Fig. 215)—the Napoleonic epic seen from the troops' point of view—the wounded man in the foreground has been positioned at an angle (like Christ in the Deposition) designed to prevent the image from projecting forward in space. In addition, the grain of the canvas is evident throughout the ocher areas, while the highlights emerge from thick applications of medium that are almost devoid of modeling.

The same kind of "telephoto" effect (a true anticipation of race-track photography) brings everything toward the picture plane in Géricault's *Four Jockeys* (Fig. 214). The plunging view, the overlapping silhouettes, the monochrome passages (a quality accentuated by the broad unfinished area under the horses) foretell Manet, and no painting before this master would give such an impression of speed, along with all that such an approach implies:

absence of detail, deliberate "instantaneity" of execution, and dynamic poses evincing the greatest possible concentration of energy.

Representing speed was one of the major concerns of Géricault, whose works often convey nothing so much as dissatisfaction with the material limitations of painting. Had he lived longer, instead of dying prematurely in 1824 at age thirty-three, this artist would certainly have been interested in photography (Daguerre was an almost exact contemporary). Meanwhile, Géricault became one of France's first lithographers. He also wanted to treat the same subject in several different pictures. Passionate about dioramas and panoramas, Géricault exclaimed before his own *Raft of the Medusa* (Fig. 218): "A painting in the grand manner? No, it is an easel picture!" He demanded "painting [done] with buckets of color on walls a hundred feet long." Fascinated, so his friend Théodore Lebrun tells us, by a coach that passed in front of his inn, Géricault tried to capture live "the rapidly turning wheels, the blurred spokes all fused by the rapidity of the movement and

transformed into an uninterrupted series of brilliant strokes."

No less modern is his attitude toward the traditional principles of painting. He abandoned the kind of stylistic unity so characteristic of David or Guérin, Géricault's master, who nonetheless said that the younger artist had "the stuff of three or four painters." Géricault cut across schools and aesthetic ideologies, but utilized them as if the end of painting were not a masterpiece (which it remained for Gros or Girodet), but an experiment.

Of the 220 pictures painted by Géricault, only 3 were exhibited in his lifetime and no more than a dozen for a century thereafter (when the famous *Medusa* claimed most of the attention). All the rest were regarded as sketches or unfinished canvases. Géricault was not really discovered until 1924 at the time of the centennial retrospective held in the Hôtel Charpentier. Meanwhile, what seemed a lack of consistency in his work began to make sense or assume "direction" once modern art made its own commitment to experiment and rupture with the past, thereby clarifying the extent of Géricault's reach.

215. Théodore Géricault. *Cart Bearing Wounded Soldiers*. c. 1818.
Oil on canvas, 12¼ × 11½″. Fitzwilliam Museum, Cambridge.

216. Théodore Géricault (1791–1824). *Sketch for the Raft of the Medusa.* 1818. Gouache on paper, 15¾×20″. Fogg Art Museum (bequest of Grenville L. Winthrop), Harvard University, Cambridge.

Exhaustively prepared with numerous studies and through interrogation of the ship's survivors, *The Raft of the Medusa* did not receive its final form until a variety of different arrangements had been tried for the principal group. The well-known story involved the foundering of the frigate *Medusa* in 1816, when 150 persons scrambled aboard a makeshift raft, only 15 of whom would survive after 12 days of horror and despair. According to the naval officer who rescued them, "these unhappy people had been obliged to fight a great number of their comrades who staged a revolt in the hope of taking over the remaining provisions. The others had been swept out to sea, had died of hunger, or gone mad. The ones I saved had been feeding on human flesh for several days, and when I found

them, the ropes serving as mast stays were loaded with pieces of such meat, hung there for drying."

The study in the Fogg Art Museum (Fig. 216) presents a frontal group whose compactness serves well to evoke a sense of claustrophobic crowding on the open sea, where the shipwreck victims cling to the raft, piled one on top of the other or dragging half-submerged in water. The morphology of the bodies in the foreground and the restricted depth of the ensemble recall certain passages in Michelangelo's *Last Judgment,* which Géricault had recently admired in Rome. It also evokes the central group in Rubens' *Fall of the Damned* (Munich), a work that, as Lorenz Eitner has shown, directly inspired the French master through the medium of an engraving.

Soon, however, Géricault managed to pivot his composition (Fig. 217) and replace the imploding, amorphous mass of bodies, devoid of center or hierarchy, with a sequence of elements that unfold along a diagonal picked out by highlights and dramatically impelled toward a point well beyond the foreground scene: the rescue boat.

The torsioned grace of the dying, the expressive gestures, the Caravaggesque luminism of the final version (Fig. 218); the steep and close-up perspective upon the slightly tilted "platform"; the omnipresence of the light, which seems to originate simultaneously from the background, from the left, and from a point behind the viewer; and, finally, the contrast between the raft and the threatening verticality of the wave on the left—all seem to suggest an

elaborate stage set, for a theatre or even a wax museum. The paradoxical combination of art-historical references and concrete "life studies" (for the cadavers) results in something ambiguous, halfway between reportage and a piece of academic bravura. In Géricault's *Raft of the Medusa,* the Davidian tradition, which sought to render an actual event by means of studies from both nature and the classical heritage, reached the point of maximum tension.

The work shocked conservatives, who saw it as nothing but an exercise in baseness offering no hero of a positive nature. "Everything is hideously passive . . . not fit for a moral society. The work could be said to have been done for the pleasure of vultures," complained the *Gazette de France* in

217. Théodore Géricault. *Sketch for the Raft of the Medusa.* 1818. Oil on canvas, 2′1½″×2′8¾″. Louvre.

1819. The Restoration government was wary of purchasing a picture that denounced the incompetence of its maritime personnel. Thus, it offered the artist six thousand francs to execute a painting on the subject of the Sacred Heart of Jesus.

Two conceptions of the *Raft of the Medusa:* compact and centrifugal

218. Théodore Géricault. *The Raft of the Medusa.* 1819.
Oil on canvas, 16′1¼″×23′6″. Louvre.

219. Eugène Delacroix (1798–1863). *Bouquet of Flowers*. 1848.
Oil on cardboard, 1′5¾″ × 1′11¼″. Kunsthalle, Bremen.

# Composition is suspended as flowers spread across and gradually fill the picture surface

For three centuries the familiar motif of a flower bouquet has never failed to provide an irresistible opportunity for formal innovation. From Rigaud to Caillebotte, from Monnoyer to Redon, this genre demands tabletop juxtaposition and a polycentric, egalitarian distribution of discrete elements disposed side by side in a shallow space, altogether making an arrangement guaranteed to "dedramatize" the composition. The bold cropping of Delacroix's *Bouquet* in Fig. 219 partakes of this experience. Here, the flowers are packed in so closely that they virtually cover the painting surface. With the top of the vase barely indicated, we could almost view the work upside-down, or even on its side, just as we might certain of the antigravitational paintings of Paul Klee. In the work on the right (Fig. 220), Delacroix took up a subject that allowed him to build a structure in which the relationship among the elements (a cumulative and nonhierarchical relationship) counts for more than their equivalence with the exterior world. The theme also gave him license to risk a separation of the object (petals) from the brushstrokes that render it. As would soon happen in Courbet and the Impressionists, the touches of color exceed the physical limits of the flowers (Fig. 221). In its comments on a Northern painter, made in an 1831 article, *Le Moniteur universel* went on to exalt "the truth of imitation . . . the downy texture of the leaves, their striations, the variations in their thickness, the notches chewed out by insects." It was this subordination to imagery and local color that Delacroix challenged, which made him the great transitional figure linking Chardin and Monet.

Beaudelaire compared the palette of the painter of *Sardanapalus* (Fig. 321) to a "cleverly assorted bouquet of flowers." The metaphor could also be reversed so as to see Delacroix as having organized his bouquets with the same freedom that he took with his palette. As in Cézanne's apples at a later date, the attraction that a flower motif held for painters derived in large measure from its malleability. Unlike the human face and figure, it lent itself to plastic manipulation and thus stimulated the artist to ever-greater surface experiment.

220. Eugène Delacroix. *Flowers*. 1848. Oil on canvas, 2'½"×2'10¼". Musée des Beaux-Arts, Lille.

221. Eugène Delacroix. *Flowers* (detail of Fig. 220).

# In every fold of pigment the obsessive swarm of a scaleless world

222. Richard Dadd (1817–86). *The Fairy Feller's Master Stroke.* 1857–64.
Oil on canvas, 21¼ × 15¾". Tate Gallery, London.

journey on the Continent and to Syria and Egypt. On August 28, 1843, the twenty-six-year-old Dadd stabbed his father to death, after having tried to strangle him. Interned at Bethlem and then at Broadmoor, the artist continued to work productively for the next half-century.

The *Fairy Feller's Master Stroke* (Fig. 222), Dadd's most important painting, was done for the director of the asylum and required several years to complete. It represented a woodcutter applying the whole of his erect volume to the task of breaking open a chestnut, closely watched by a population of fairies, gnomes, elves, Spanish dancers, etc.

Dadd painted with the microscopic skill of a miniaturist (recalling the obsessive meticulousness of Altdorfer). Something strange emerges from the contrast between his thick, heavy, layered surface and the morphological distortions of his figures and objects (daisies, chestnuts), which have a "warped" look as if perceived through a magnifying glass moved from point to point across the entire canvas. Dozens of figures are half-encrusted in the texture from which they seem to emanate (Fig. 223). Crisscrossed with huge plants, the whole surface resembles nothing so much as a visual trap, consisting of an unstable, threatening substance in which characters are juxtaposed in such diverse scales that the eye must refocus for each of them (see, for instance, the detail of the magician at the center, with his immense arm extended).

Unable to summon his imagination at will, Dadd (so he said) adopted a method whereby he stood before the canvas thinking of nothing until his vague, amorphous, random marks began to assume form and become figures before his eyes. And these, notes Patricia Allderidge in her monographic catalogue (Tate, 1974), seem indeed to have been evoked less by conscious decision than "hallucinated" one after the other through the movement of the brush.

Rediscovered in the 1950s, Dadd is evidently a borderline case in 19th-century painting. The recluse of Bethlem Hospital—like his contemporaries Edward Lear or Lewis Carroll, who described the subjective elasticity of space and the traps of both language and logic—captured the neurotic, inverse side of rationalistic, puritanical Victorian society, with its domestic values and aesthetic niceties. For the modern viewer, *Master Stroke* seems a therapeutic exercise in which the painter, by the "fussed" juxtaposition of his figures, tried as best he could to cover an elusive surface that tended to break up and escape his control. On a field that he could not unify *rationally,* Dadd finally prevailed by means of juxtaposition, manic accumulation, and a saturation of hyperrealist detail.

The tragic fate of Richard Dadd has made him a marginal figure in the artistic history of his time. The son of a wealthy Kentish pharmacist (four of whose seven children would die in psychiatric hospitals), Dadd began his career under the best auspices. At age nineteen he was already established—

the winner of three medals at the Royal Academy—when he achieved great public success with his fantasies inspired by Shakespeare's ever-popular *Midsummer Night's Dream.* In 1842–43, however, the first symptoms of schizophrenia began to appear, in the wake of an exhausting six-month

223. Richard Dadd. *The Fairy Feller's Master Stroke* (detail of Fig. 222).

224. Jean-François Millet (1814–75). *Crows in Winter*. 1862. Oil on canvas, 1'11½" × 2'4¾".
Kunsthistorisches Museum, Vienna.

# Soil and texture: *terra mater*

225. Caspar David Friedrich (1774–1840). *Cemetery by Moonlight*. c. 1834.
Sepia wash over pencil, 5½ × 7½″. Cabinet des Dessins, Louvre

Commenting on *Crows in Winter* (Fig. 224), Robert Herbert wrote that ''there are few precedents in Western art for a landscape so flat and so lacking in pictorial incident, particularly on the edges of the composition, where the eye instinctively seeks elements that enframe an open space.''[8] It is significant that several writers have compared this bare, boundless earth to the battlefield in Gros' *Eylau* (Fig. 510), as if every stippled plane referred back to some historic, melancholy, wintry land, to the humus where the dead are buried, to Michelet's *terra mater*. In refusing to arrest the gaze, to engage the eye in compositional games, Millet projects, even precipitates, the viewer right up against the surface texture—sod and pigment—that stretches from edge to edge. The great art here lay in maintaining equilibrium between

telluric reverie (''the sweet magnetism of the viscous'' spoken of by Bachelard) and physical involvement in sensuous material, with this evoked by gestural, broken touches and scattered, light-toned accents.

What remains implicit in Millet, despite his clouds of crows, becomes manifest in Friedrich's sepia sketch (Fig. 225), where the dark gash of a gaping tomb is hovered over by an owl perched upon a shovel, altogether making a more literal image than Millet's tilted plow, with its blade half-buried. (See also the tumulus motif common to both pictures.) But Friedrich too has realized his landscape by means of tiny, patient strokes, with the result that each tuft of grass and each stone is reconstituted through the minute stippling of ink on paper, this intensified vision ripe with religious feeling.

# Waves and clouds: two rolling forces in competition for the frontal plane

226. Gustave Courbet (1819–77). *The Wave*. 1870. Oil on canvas, 2'7½"×3'3¼". Collection Oskar Reinhart "Am Romerholz," Winterthur.

Two bands of equal height divide the space of the picture reproduced in Fig. 227, the two parts separated by an absolutely straight line indicating the horizon. Water and sky occupy parallel spaces, but far from flowing into or interpenetrating one another, they stand apart as rivals in density and power. But if the upper zone, a heavy, dark, convex cushion of clouds, has been realized in gradations of blended and rather mat values, which together *describe* a stormy atmosphere, the opposite obtains in the lower zone, where the pigment itself has weight, the result of thick applications of white medium distributed over the entire width. Here, it is a matter of texture, grain, mass, and brilliant handling, all of which suggests a heightened concern for the tactile and

the material. The canvas is cleaved in half by the rivalry of the two systems, each of which comes forward in turn, depending on whether the viewer responds to illusionistic shading (the clouds) or to the physical presence of rich pigment (the waves).

Although not quite so systematic a work, the picture in Fig. 226 offers the same textural opposition. But the frontal effect is less insistent, since the wave, driven by a whirlpool, curls up to create a trough or hollow that recalls one of Courbet's favorite themes: the grotto or cavern through which the artist could give effect to his pantheistic vision.

The art historian Henri Focillon, writing in 1928, mentions Courbet's "large buttery strokes loaded with medium, softly married one to the

other," and it is also medium and textural density that Cézanne found so important in the Ornans master: "A constructor. A rude mixer of plaster. A grinder of colors. He masons like a Roman. . . . No one else in this century can beat him. . . . The big wave pictures, the one in Berlin [right], prodigious, one of the century's strokes of luck, much more palpitating, fuller, with a foamier green, a nastier orange [than the version in the Louvre], with its frothy dishevelment, its tide that comes from the depths of the ages, its sky all in tatters and its livid roughness. It hits one straight in the stomach. . . ."

227. Gustave Courbet. *The Wave*. 1870. Oil on canvas, 3′8″×4′8¾″.
Nationalgalerie Staatliche Museen Preussischer Kulturbesitz, Berlin.

## Drama on the high seas projected like frames from a "disaster" film

228. Théodore Gudin (1802–80). *The Devotion of Captain Desse.* 1831.
Oil on canvas, 6′10¾″×9′8¼″. Musée des Beaux-Arts, Bordeaux.

For all the pathos of their grand marines, neither Gudin, a pupil of Girodet, nor Eugène Isabey, the son of a miniaturist in the time of the Empire, could match the crepuscular tragedies of Turner (Fig. 430) or even the sense of an overall cosmic brew that the English artist managed to achieve with paint, as much by the scrapings of his palette knife as by the shrill discords of his color (which seem at one with the spirit of Melville's *Moby Dick,* published in 1851). Instead, both Gudin and Isabey offered a crowd-pleasing precision of detail. Whatever the subject—the edifying heroism of Captain Desse sailing to the aid of a Dutch ship (Fig. 228) or a melodramatic shipwreck (Isabey's revisualization [Fig. 229] of a fire aboard the *Austria* that on 13 September, 1858, took the lives of more than five hundred people)—the public wanted to know everything. In regard to

Gudin's picture, for example, *Le Moniteur universel* observed that "the event would have held still greater interest if the figure of Captain Desse had stood out more, had he been easier to identify."

But if this type of painting was dominated by social imperatives—to the point where dioramas and panoramas seem to have influenced the format—it also evinced a free, even "athletic"

sense of pictorial design that would have been inconceivable before Romanticism (cf. Joseph Vernet's sea-storm paintings).

In both canvases, the drama, seized at its climactic moment, has been brought forward and frontalized, whether the point of view is an elevated one, which has the viewer hanging right over the bridge of the distressed ship, or from the trough of the waves. As used by Isabey,

229. Eugène Isabey (1804–86). *Burning of the Steamer* Austria. 1858.
Oil on canvas, 7′11¼″×14′1¼″. Musée des Beaux-Arts, Bordeaux.

the arrangement serves to send the poor shipwreck victims rolling toward us in clusters, all the way from the bulwarks.

Cropping as close as possible into the vast areas of dark or light (smoke or storm) that give the spectacles their lyric sweep, the artists emphasized proximity and thus heightened the viewer's feelings of shock. In this way, they anticipated by a full century the ''disaster'' films of our own time.

# CHAPTER II

# The Liberation of Line

230. J.D. Ingres (1780–1867). *Study for La Source.*

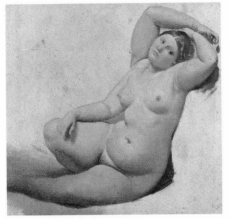

231. J.D. Ingres. *Study for the Turkish Bath.*

Ingres sought the arabesque line throughout many fraught sessions with the model, whom he asked to strike one pose after another. "He often erased, was never satisfied, and cried like a baby before his canvas . . ." (Amaury-Duval, *L'Atelier d'Ingres).*

232. H. Fuseli (1741–1825). *The Embrace.* 1813.

Form produced not by a pre-established scheme but by a gestural reassessment of the surface.

To his journal, Delacroix confided: "Some lines are monstrous, the straight, the serpentine, and, above all, the parallel." In Baudelaire's opinion, "a well-drawn figure fills you with a pleasure that has nothing to do with the subject. Whether voluptuous or terrifying, this figure owes all its charm to the arabesque it cuts in space." By the mid-19th century, the expressive autonomy of line, independent of the object it denotes, had become an established principle—even when it was denounced as wrong. In 1848 Champfleury could write sarcastically of Ingres as "the priest of line," while in 1857 Théophile Silvestre felt scandalized at what he viewed as the same master's reduction of art "to the cult of form, by the abolition of ideas, [and his] pursuit, through the agency of straight and curved lines, of some plastic absolute, taken as the principle and purpose of all things."

A century earlier, in his defense of the serpentine, Hogarth had energetically embraced the autonomy of line, like that known from 16th-century Mannerist art, and acknowledged the pleasure such a form generates by its visual activation of the spectator and by its seduction of the eye into "a wanton kind of chace." This emphasis on the autonomous expressivity of line can also be found, at least as implicit, in the Platonic ideas of Winckelmann, the 18th century's Neoclassical theoretician, who held that the trivial details and imperfections of ordinary nature should be absorbed into "the noble contour," "the beautiful line," "the undulating line," which efface accidents, bulges, and everything else of a prosaic or anecdotal character. And Lessing, in his *Laocoön* (1767), went further, stating that even *expression* (psychology, body language, allegory) must give way to beauty of form.

Ingres, in speaking about his art, adopted almost word for word the arguments of Winckelmann ("the Greeks, so well served by the climate and customs of their beautiful country, which always allowed them to study beauty in the nude, . . ."). For the painter of *Venus Wounded by Diomedes* (Fig. 166), the reference to classical Greece, which seemed all the more peremptory for being vague ("The Greeks, Monsieur, the Greeks! Raphael himself pales by comparison . . ."), provided a fiction justifying the liberation of line. And Degas too understood this when he declared to Valéry that "the great merit of M. Ingres is his reaction on behalf of arabesque form against drawing based exclusively on proportion, then practiced by the school of David." In other words, Ingres reversed the supposed hierarchy in the pictorial process. It was not "nature"—empirical reality—that should determine the proportions of figures—but rather the contrary: a curving line sought and finally discovered—resolved—among some one or more of the postures assumed by the model (Figs. 230, 231). What took primacy over all else was the deployment of that line—its relation to the flat surface (Fig. 232). The object is not effaced, but simply subordinated to the demands of form. And that this meant as much to Delacroix as to Ingres—despite all the polemics of the time—would be understood by Matisse in the 20th century: "Both expressed themselves in *arabesque* and *color.* . . . They forged the same links in the chain. Only nuances prevent our confusing them."

Delacroix admired Raphael who, he said, "raised to the highest level of perfection that brilliant creation of Italian genius: *the linear arabesque.*" And,

like Ingres, he made abundant use of the musical metaphor whenever he wanted to emphasize the abstract qualities of painting. The journal kept by Delacroix offers not only a detailed account of his investigations, but also the most basic theoretical statement on 19th-century French painting, a text that assembles under one cover all the great aesthetic debates of the artist's time. Inevitably, it is a point of frequent reference for any consideration of modern art.

As for the internal coherence of the picture, Delacroix was fully conscious of what set his synchronic method—the method of Veronese, Rubens, and Gros—apart from the "montage" technique practiced by David and his school. The painter of the *Sabines* (Louvre)—at least in his multifigure canvases—liked to develop his works in stages, from successive studies of details to a final arrangement of them, one by one, on the large surface, squared to make this possible (Figs. 151, 152). And a picture created in this fashion requires a diachronic, or sequential, reading. Even David realized this, since Delécluze tells us that he "conceived the notion that, in order to return contemporary art to antique simplicity, he should engage the spectator, not by sacrificing everything to a dramatic effect, as had been done in painting since the 17th century, but, on the contrary, by fixing [the viewer's] attention serially on each figure, with this accomplished through the perfection of the handling."

What Delacroix deplored in David he also regretted in Michelangelo. For the Romantic master, the *Last Judgment* offered nothing but "striking details, striking like a blow with the fist; when it comes to interest, unity, and interconnections, all that is missing. . . . It seems that in making an arm or a leg, [Michelangelo] thought only in terms of this arm or that leg, [and] absolutely nothing about its relationship . . . either with the action of the picture or with that of the figure to which it belongs."

Finally, however, Delacroix made Géricault the true focus of his criticism: "I have reexamined Géricault's lithographs—even the horses and lions—all of it cold, despite the excellence of the details. There is no wholeness in any of it. Not one of those horses is without its affectation, or something too small or poorly joined. Never is there a background that has anything to do with the subject." And for the *Raft of the Medusa* (Figs. 216–218) Géricault did indeed employ an additive rather than a synthetic order in building his pictorial structure. "His procedure was that of the Davidian school," wrote Géricault's biographer. And according to Batissier, a contemporary of the artist: "He did not, like most painters, begin a picture with a total conception, as in a large study for which he would have prepared each part in a preliminary work. On the contrary, he would choose a head or an entire figure and then paint it without worrying about the rest until the detail had been finished."

For the most part, the works by Géricault that have come down to us are studies, fragments loosely related to a final piece (*Raft of the Medusa*) or some project never carried through (*Race of the Barberi Horses*). He went on indulging himself in study after study, as if he wanted to defer synthesis—as if the end purpose of the process did not interest him.

Delacroix, however, took a totally different approach. As his large sketches (Figs. 428, 429) and even his preparatory drawings reveal, he tended

top: 233. J.B. Piranesi (1720–78). *Colosseum, Rome.* 1776.
Here the shape of the support governed the design. Thus, while viewed from above like a crater, the Colosseum does not display perspective foreshortening. The objective was to square up the image and fill the pictorial field.

above: 234. J.B. Piranesi. *Pyramid of Cestus, Rome.* 1755. The upper and lower extremities of the pyramid point out and *declare* the shape of the support, thereby challenging the illusionism present in the image.

235. H. Robert (1733–1808).
*Ruins in the Baths of Julian in Paris.*

236. H. Robert. *Entrance, Palace of the Conservators.*

Rounded or rectangular, the shape of the support is echoed or parodied within the pictorial design.

from the very start to take account of the picture's overall economy. As we have seen, this master could scarcely find words strong enough to denounce paintings "composed successively like a puzzle, its individual pieces carefully prepared and fitted together one by one." In other words, he hated "the general absence of *sacrifice.*" Delacroix subscribed—if he did not inspire—to Baudelaire's assertion that "a good picture, faithful and equal to the dream that begot it, should be produced like a world." For the painter, as for the poet, "a harmoniously realized picture consists of a series of pictures superimposed one upon the other."

The need to proceed by layers and strata—not by the agglomeration of fragments—had already been espoused by Gainsborough, who, according to Reynolds, wanted "the whole going on at the same time, in the same manner as nature creates her works." And Reynolds himself, upon the unveiling of his *Infant Hercules*, exclaimed: "There are ten under it!" Gros recommended to his pupils that they "bring out every part simultaneously" (Figs. 420, 421). And from Ingres we have this: "In constructing a figure, do not proceed by bits and pieces. Carry everything forward at the same time, and, as it has been so well put, draw the *ensemble.*" This advice, however, counted only for isolated figures and had no relevance to Ingres' own painting except where it concerned sketches for individual figures (Fig. 283) or portraits (Figs. 168–170). In his large multifigure compositions, Ingres applied quite a different principle, the additive one seen in *Saint Symphorian* (Figs. 533–535), over which—despite his apprenticeship in David's studio—he had little mastery.

That painting should be constituted as "a whole," as Reynolds termed it, and function like a single body, with internal coherence, was demonstrated a bit later by Carus (Figs. 291, 292) in the comparison he made between painting and mirror reflection. Certainly, the German artist said, a painting cannot compete with a mirror in its ability to reproduce the image of nature—its forms and colors. But the reflection is obviously no more than a fragment artificially detached from a much greater whole, whereas a painting "strikes us as a microcosm, as something worthy in or of itself. . . . It is a creation full of intellectual energy."

For Delacroix it was at all levels of pictorial production, and all closely integrated, that the work should be realized as an organic totality. Chromatic unity, compositional, morphological, rhythmic unity, textural unity—this was what Delacroix found lacking in Poussin: "His figures are planted one next to the other like statues. . . . They resemble cutouts." On the other hand, Le Sueur, a younger contemporary of Poussin, achieved it, in Delacroix's opinion: "He had the skill, which Poussin lacked altogether, to endow everything he depicted with unity. The figure itself became a perfect ensemble of lines and effects, and the picture, an assembly of all the figures, is harmonized throughout." What Delacroix found challenging was "that accord between accessories and the principal subject, which seems to me to be one of the most important of things, if not the most important." Rembrandt remained the unsurpassable model: "In Rembrandt himself—and here is perfection—figure and ground are one." In Courbet, however, Delacroix saw just the opposite: "The landscape is of an extraordinary vigor, but Courbet merely enlarged a study that can be seen

there next to this canvas. Thus, the figures were put in later and without any relationship with what surrounds them."

This much-desired unity exacted what Delacroix called "sacrifices." It even justified "flaws," for pictorial coherence must prevail, even at the expense of the object represented. Once again the bad example proved to be Poussin, whom Delacroix reproached for having subordinated everything to "correctness carried to the nth degree. . . . Never a slip or a sacrifice made for the sake of linkage, of a soft effect or the overall sweep of the composition." The 19th-century master saw the power of painting not in its truth to detail but in the amplitude of its creative momentum. It was not possible to have at one and the same time both documentary precision (which implies a close-up, fragmented vision) and a broad principle capable of mobilizing at first glance not only the viewer's attention but also his body. The canvas could be considered as a totality only by suppressing the specific identity of individual objects." "What he seeks," wrote Théophile Silvestre after talking with Delacroix in his studio, "is the expressive drama of the whole, the currents of action that draw in the spectator. If you examine each of these figures individually, you will be struck by the exaggerated, sometimes monstrous development of his active forms, a development that the artist has deemed essential to the energy of movement and the intensity of expression."

Of course, classical doctrine itself had already articulated the principle of the autonomous pictorial apparatus in which all plastic components are interdependent and essential. Panofsky went all the way back to the Stoics for a definition of beauty as "harmony of the parts in relation to one another and of the parts to the whole." It was a definition that Alberti in the 15th century established as an axiom, one that would persist right into the 18th century, albeit under various names. Thus, Diderot could be certain that *pleasure* came from "the perception of relationships," at the same time that Quatremère de Quincy, 18th-century France's theoretician of the ideal, characterized the conditions of *grandeur* in the following manner: "In order for the effect of largeness to be produced, the object through which it is realized must be simple enough to strike us in a single blow, that is, as a whole, while also striking us by reason of the relations among its constituent parts."

But a change occurred at the beginning of the 19th century when this old theory of the work as an internal unity intersected with a new conception wherein the picture became an arena evincing the corporeal engagement of the painter. The harmony of relationships would not be denied but rather displaced, absorbed into another level of the work—that of gesture. The picture was no longer to be *executed;* it would be *invested*—invaded, filled up, occupied. Instead of the artist's ideal thought, the surface would bear the inscription of a gesturing hand at work with material—that is, working the material and being worked by it. Once achieved, the canvas becomes the field where nothing of the struggle has been effaced—the struggle of a body shaping a medium and a medium shaping (managing, channeling) a body. The concept of "mechanical form" elaborated by A. W. Schlegel at the turn of the 19th century helps to clarify precisely what Romantic painting would henceforth reject: "Form is mechan-

top: 237. J. Constable (1776–1837).
*Sketch for Hadleigh Castle*. 1828–29.
above: 238. John Constable. Detail of Fig. 237.

Constable executed his preparatory oil "sketches" on the same scale as the final works, a procedure that allowed him to give full rein to his most "troweled" and painterly manner. Here he could liberate his stroke from strict adherence to the shape of the objects represented.

239. A. Magnasco (1681–1747).
*Nuns Spinning Lace* (detail).

240. J.H. Fragonard (1732–1806). *Imaginary Figure* (detail).

However free, the stroke of 18th-century artists—slashing or filamented—remained subordinate to the object it described. Such handling served mainly to display the artist's technical mastery, until Goya, Turner, and Constable abandoned "point by point" denotation of objects and sought to realize equivalences and displacements.

ical when it is conferred upon a certain material by an external action, such as a purely accidental intervention, having nothing to do with the composition of that material, as, for example, when one gives some sort of shape [*Gestalt*] to a soft mass so that, when dry, it will retain that shape." In opposition to mechanical form, Schlegel offered "organic form," generated within the thing (or the work) and determined by the materiality, the *fond* or substance, of that thing (that work).[1]

Prior to Romanticism, the evidence of gesture on the canvas often aroused suspicion. It even brought condemnation for reasons of both taste and morals. In 1730 the Comte de Caylus warned the academicians against the draftsmanly license taken by young painters, then succumbing to the "flattering charm of quickly jotting their ideas down on paper. . . . There is something libertine about it that should be censured." In 1755 Greuze would be taken to task for his *pinceau torché* ("hasty brush"), which immediately restored him to a smooth manner (except in drawing [Fig. 248]). Sixty-six years later, Delécluze, David's pupil and the advocate of Neoclassicism in the *Journal des débats*, continued to consider self-asserting brushwork slipshod and symptomatic of immorality. Constable, after executing full-scale but sketchy versions of his large paintings (Figs. 237, 238), copied them in a more conventional manner for official exhibition.

Still, facture, brio, overt brushiness, *fa presto* had been a Venetian tradition since the time of Titian, a tradition perpetuated in the 17th century by Vignon, Vouet, Velázquez, Hals, and Rembrandt, among others. But their works were made to be viewed from a distance, which permitted the broad, separate touches to melt together in the spectator's eye. (Rembrandt declared: "My pictures are not for sniffing.") And however liberated the painterly technique, it always remained at the service of a *realistic effect*, firmly established in the mainstream of *mimesis* (Figs. 239–241). As for what Vasari had characterized as "those sketches that, suddenly brought forth in the heat of inspiration, express an idea in a few strokes," they were, until the 18th century, limited to use within the studio. A *bozzetto* ("preparatory study") by the 17th-century master Luca Giordano—whose friends nicknamed him *Luca fa presto*—discloses a facture almost as *lâchée* ("loose" or "free") as that of Delacroix (Fig. 242), but it would never have occurred to the Neopolitan painter to exhibit such an exercise as a self-sufficient work. Now, however, Delacroix would do precisely that: "One must . . . create painting-sketches that will have the freedom and candor of *croquis*."

Progressively, as loose, free handling replaced tight, smooth brushwork in the early 19th century, a perceptible change in meaning also occurred. Fuseli revealed what was at stake when he wrote that the less an art work divulges the means of its production the more those means resemble the operations of nature. To disclose and even cultivate touch, to render it irreducible to the effect of reality was to introduce a "corrupting" element into the principle of imitation, something that within the very texture of the painting surface fights against the whole scheme of illusionism. "Many masters," observed Delacroix, "have avoided drawing attention to [the painter's touch], no doubt with the idea of getting closer to nature, which indeed does not divulge [its creator's hand]. The stroke is a means like any other

to transform thought into painting." More and more, however, the whole principle of re-presentation came to be questioned. Allowing overt gesture and covering the canvas with a series of marks that transgress upon the evident structure of the depicted object meant admitting to the arbitrariness of the pictorial enterprise, thus accepting in principle its autonomy—its character as a set of conventions. Whether or not a picture may be finished no longer depended upon the degree of its "finish," but rather upon its internal coherence, which only the artist could determine (Fig. 243). Now one heard an old dictum attributed to Rembrandt: "A picture is finished when the artist has stopped working on it." And Delacroix asserted: "There are a good many pictures with no painterly texture whatever that are, however, far from being finished." He went so far as to consider sketchiness as the fundamental attribute of painting—that which distinguishes painting from the other arts. He even spoke of the impossibility of sketching in either literature or music: "There approximation is intolerable; that is, what in painting we call *indication*—or *croquis*—is impossible. In painting, however, a beautiful indication or a deeply felt sketch can, in expression, equal the most finished of works."

Toward the middle of the 18th century, several writers began noticing a shift in attitude toward *aesthetic* satisfaction (at about the same time that this word was invented in Germany). Abbé Dubos in 1733 and Burke in his 1757 essay on the "sublime" called attention to the phenomenon wherein the pleasure felt by the spectator does not always derive from the object (which might even be threatening or repellent) but rather from the representational *act* itself. "When we look carefully at such pictures [those that depict ordinary or unpleasant objects], our main interest," wrote Dubos, "does not focus upon the imitated object but, of course, upon the art of the imitator. It is less the object that holds our eye than the craftsmanly skill."

What mattered, therefore, was not the *effect* of the representation (the image produced), but the physical process that brought it about. Increasingly, as the century progressed, the emphasis fell simultaneously on distinctive technique and on the painter's corporeal investment of himself in the painting—his manner and his pleasure. (According to Burke, "we have a pleasure in imitating.") For Dezallier d'Argenville, writing in 1745, "a stroke of the brush . . . one touch of a tree in a picture reveals its author to have a picturesque [e.g., an individual] handwriting." This two-fold—individual and physical—orientation would continue its ascendency for the next two centuries, finally culminating in Jackson Pollock and the "action painting" of the 1950s. Every mark became a trace or deposit of energy, and every sign the product of a moment in the life of a body (Fig. 244). (In 1908 Matisse wrote: "Drawing is like making an expressive gesture, but with the advantage of permanence.") European artists discovered the old Chinese proverb which held that "to copy is to enter into the movement of the artist's body."[2]

The sensitivity to handling and the shift of interest toward process would eventually penetrate even those circles most hostile to such factors. From the time of Géricault onward, the teaching establishment accepted the principal of two types of copy: that in which the student produced a virtual replica

99

241. T. Gainsborough (1727–88).
*Portrait of the Duchess of Beaufort* (detail). c. 1780.

In his treatment of faces, Gainsborough observed the conventions of smooth handling. Garments and monumental piles of powdered hair, however, gave the painter the opportunity to endow medium with an incomparable transparency.

242. E. Delacroix (1798–1863).
*Nereid,* after Rubens. c. 1822.

In his copy after Rubens, Delacroix isolated a vigorously rhythmic sequence of curves that traverse and activate the surface. A quarter of a century later he would write in his journal: "Rubens is very *free* in his Nereids, so as not to lose his light and color."

243. H. Daumier (1808–79).
*The Print Collectors.* 1870–73.

With light evoked in long "ribbons" of thick pigment, the old Baroque sketch has now achieved the status of an actual picture.

of a masterwork, and then an exercise wherein the artist had the right to try reconstituting, in the manner of a sketch, the master's original movement (Fig. 242). It was from this intrusion of touch and corporeal energy, of handwriting and gesture, into painting—always resisted but finally victorious—that would flow into one of the mainstreams of 19th-century art, all the way through Impressionism. (It even became official: witness Monet's large *Nymphéas* in the Orangerie.) Here the art historian Meyer Schapiro sees an expression of the period, an unconscious protest against and recoil from industrial society, mechanization, and the division of labor that eliminated the relationship between the producer and his product.[3] The flowering of gesture would constitute an exemplary, altogether marginal, almost exotic affirmation of personal craftsmanship, of collaboration between the artist and his work carried out from beginning to end. This line of thought can be related to Freud, for whom "the artist is basically someone who turns away from reality, since he cannot adjust to the renunciation of instinctual satisfaction that reality immediately requires of him and [who] allows his erotic and ambitious desires to play freely in his fantasy life. But he finds a way back from the fantasy world to reality to the degree that, by virtue of his gifts, he extracts from his fantasies the form of a new category of real things that for humanity assumes the value of precious images of reality." For Freud, it is "reality" that, through reaction, stimulates the artist to create, whereas for Schapiro, it is the organization of the means of production. Hence, two arguments that parallel one another, but with a change of factors. In both cases, however, the work of art—always supplementary—is endowed with social or didactic worth. Freud saw it as the generator of "a new category of real things," while Schapiro perceives the possibility of a less fragmented human being.

The shift from object to creator, from the denoted to the productive act of denotation is corroborated in other areas of culture, such as linguistics. According to Wilhelm von Humboldt, writing around 1830, "language should be considered less as a finished product and more as a production." Tzvetan Todorov quotes this statement from *Théories du symbole* and comments thus: for Humboldt, "the object of the science of language should not be empirically observable linguistic forms but the activity whose product they are. This faculty *is* language much more than uttered words and phrases. . . . One of the most important consequences of this change in perspective is the emphasis placed on the process of expression, at the expense of that of imitation or, more broadly, of representation and designation; thus also [the emphasis placed] on the process of action upon others or, to use a symmetrical term, of impression. Words are not the image of things but of that which speaks; the expressive function takes precedence over the representational function."

It is the same preeminently expressive function that we attribute to the probing gesture of Delacroix in his drawings, where the line unwinds like a ball of string, as if the artist's hand were unconsciously seeking to untie a form, to liberate the hand's graphic energy, to disengage some unforeseeable motif inextricably caught in the lingering grid of classical composition (Fig. 322). It is drawing that expands "from within," the pencil seeming to follow as much as to trace the filament of line that traverses

the open space of the sheet, returning several times to one zone or another, there multiplying the ovoid marks until a body or head appears. Even before they represent anything, these lines in the process of inventing themselves, of venturing onto the white surface, are the image of the engagement of a hand in its work. The work of the surface, since in Delacroix, drawing is made to *produce* the surface. For February 13, 1847, the artist made this entry in his journal: "Worked on the composition for the *Foscari.* Tried an 80 canvas. I think that is the way it will go." Then two days later: "Tried *Foscari* on the 80 canvas. Definitely, that swamps it. I shall try a 60." Here the support has ceased to be prepared space on which a design would be inscribed. Clearly, Delacroix's procedure had nothing to do with squaring a canvas for the transfer of a preestablished composition. But the drawing is no longer intangible. It "seeks itself" on different canvases. And it was this probed or "tested" convergence, this *play* within the dialectical articulation of plastic or formal components that signaled the *formalist* (not the mimetic or realist) approach taken by many Romantic painters.

Through the aesthetics of gesture and its trace, a new explicit awareness developed—not only in Delacroix but also in Goya and Turner—representing a radical change in the Aristotelian and humanist conception of art as it had prevailed up to the 19th century. Aristotle, as summarized by Robert Klein, considered "the work of art to be the practical realization of an idea preconceived and then imposed with 'violence,' as the school said, upon external matter. This was a radical, methodical process, and the only subjective conditions were, as far as the artist was concerned, knowledge and received temperament." In the 15th century Alberti would reiterate the theory exactly when he demanded "that the painter never touch his work with brush or chalk without having first fixed perfectly in his mind what he should undertake. . . . We will endeavor to have thought everything through so that there may be nothing in our work that we do not know precisely where we should place it." Four centuries later, Ingres sounded a true echo: "When one has mastered one's craft and truly learned how to imitate nature, the more one should think about the whole picture, and have it, so to speak, 'in one's head,' the better to be able to execute it with ardor and consistency." Such a statement is in total accord with the Cartesian conception of the subject. "I can discover within us," wrote Descartes, "only one thing that could justify our self-esteem, which is knowing how to exercise our free will, and the dominion that we have over our desires."

The dominance of the painter over his production and the projection of the painter's intention upon the neutrality of the support—these are two sides of the same coin. But right away, it must be added that in the instance of Ingres, the Aristotelian position raises ideological and polemical issues. The man who wept with rage before his unfinished pictures and who spent twelve years on the placement of a single figure (Figs. 168–170) clearly demonstrated himself incapable of bringing to life on the canvas—in one stroke—an image already fully formed "in his head." But even the most perfectly realized paintings by this master were prepared in hundreds of studies (sometimes a hundred drawings just for an arm) in the course of which the final state gradually

244. G. Romney (1734–1802). *The Weird Sisters.*

It took the whole arm to give this curve its amplitude.

245. A. L. Barye (1796–1802).
*Lion Lying in Wait for His Prey.*

The sculptor sought a vibrant line that could make stone throb with life.

246. R. Töpffer (1799–1846).
*The Voyages and Adventures of Dr. Festus.* 1840.

The quiver of the drawing reflects the quaking of the spirit. Thanks to an expressive line, the whole image shakes with uncertainty.

247. T. Bewick (1753–1828). *Snowman.*

In his woodcuts engraved across the grain, Bewick ignored the shape of the support, thereby causing the image to float on the page.

took form (to whatever extent, that is, we may speak of a final state in the art of a painter who never stopped revising his pictures as long as he retained possession of them).

Even so, the 18th century saw the birth of an "effusionist" conception of pictorial production. Greuze, after a particularly violent domestic scene, in which he had to parry blows with both his wife and her lover, went running out of the house: "Stunned by what I had seen, I returned trembling to my studio. I took a pencil and made a sketch of that horrible scene. It is one of the most beautiful that I have ever done." This was an extreme case, but we should note what Diderot recommended in his 1761 *Salon*: "Before he takes up his brush, it is necessary for the painter to shiver twenty times over his subject, he must have lost sleep, got up during the night and run, in nightshirt and bare feet, to dash off sketches by the glimmer of a lamp."

The question of technical mastery would assume a different dimension when taken up by Schelling in his *Philosophy of Nature.* Now the emphasis fell on the unconscious energy of "living creative nature," which courses through, nourishes, and universalizes the artistic act, transcending the will of the painter and—despite him—producing beauty. "The work of art," wrote Schelling, "will appear excellent to the degree that it shows a sketch of the pure, creative, active power of nature."[4]

This intervention of cosmic energies—whose pantheistic and spiritualist connotations would well up in the Romanticism of such painters as Friedrich and Carus—was from the start seen by French artists as linked to inner compulsion. Delacroix declared: "I have no liking whatever for rational painting. . . . If I can't get as worked up as a serpent in the hands of a witch, I am cold. I must recognize this and submit to it, and it is my good fortune. . . . This morning in my studio I was able to compose in sheer ecstasy; thus, I found the guts for my Christ, which had been saying nothing to me. . . . One must get truly *beyond oneself* in order to be all that one is capable of."

Improvization (a compulsive discharge) would guarantee authenticity. The stroke or mark should invent itself in the very moment that it is made. In this way, not only does the body communicate directly, without the mediation of scholarly or cultural experience, but the brush immediately synthesizes the basic lines of the object. "In painting," wrote Delacroix, "execution should always be like improvization and herein lies the main difference between [painting and] what actors do. The performance given by the painter will be beautiful only if he is prepared to let go a bit, to find by seeking."

If *alla prima* techniques had always entailed a reduction of control, it was this very factor that Delacroix began to formulate into theory: good painting is impossible without releasing those impulses that spring from elsewhere than in rational thought and craftsmanship. And Delacroix would make every effort to bring about conditions favorable to this surge of creative energy. He was not a man for chaos, frenzy, and directionless flow. Analyzing Titian, Delacroix took care not to confuse the Venetian master's "breadth of facture" with "the monstrous abuse of touch . . . the slack manner of painters [representative] of the decadence of art." He wrote in regard to Berlioz: "That noise is tiresome; it's heroic sludge." And twice in his journal the painter copied this statement by Mozart: "Violent passions

should never be expressed to the point of provoking disgust. Even in horrible situations, music should never hurt the ears, nor cease to be music." For Delacroix, it was important not to give in to an artistic *laisser-faire*, but rather to fix upon a paradoxical task—that is, prepare the unpredictable, organize chance, and program the spontaneous. The artist should master the impulsive components of his action, but for the purpose of bringing them to play in his game. "In painting," writes Meyer Schapiro, "the random or accidental is the beginning of an order. It is that which the artist wishes to build up into an order, but a kind of order that in the end retains the aspect of the original disorder as a manifestation of freedom."[5] These remarks, which were made to explain the work of Pollock and American "action painting," also help clarify the recurring movement characteristic of Delacroix's pictorial practice: "The first lines made by a skilled master to indicate his thought contain the germ of everything salient that the picture will offer. . . . The first idea, the quick notation, which somehow is the egg or embryo of an idea, is usually far from being complete. It contains all, if you will, but one must disengage this all, which is nothing more than the reconciliation of each part." What Delacroix counted on was his finding "that penetrating, quick impression, the rough sketch of that ideal impression which the artist is supposed to have glimpsed or grasped in the first moment of inspiration. With great artists, this sketch is not a dream, a confused cloud; it is something more than a gathering of barely comprehensible lines. Only great artists begin from a fixed point, and it is to this pure expression that it is so difficult to return in the execution of the work, however rapid or prolonged."

The ambition of the painter was thus to return, to transform while conserving, and to bring all his power to bear upon that initial movement through which the idea leaped forth. The realization of the picture would be an anamnesis, an advance toward a point situated behind, according to a regressive process that resembles the workings of a dream. That "point of departure"—that "fixed point"—is also the destination.

248. Jean-Baptiste Greuze (1725–1805). *Lamentation over the Dead Christ.* c. 1768.
Pencil, pen and brush, sepia wash, 14¼′ × 9¾″. Collection Lord Clark.

## On sheets washed with bistre, the untouched areas represent relief and light

249. Henry Fuseli (1741–1825). *Enyo, Goddess of War,
and the Personification of Fear Awaken a Sleeping Warrior.* 1790–95.
Charcoal, pen and brown ink, gray wash on paper, 2′2½″ × 1′8¾″.
Kunsthaus, Zurich.

In the art of Greuze as in that of Fuseli, it is the drawings, with their peculiar intimacy, that reveal the master at his most audacious. Large, flat monochrome areas, all broadly brushed, and an abstract use of reserves as illuminated zones disclose how these artists saw the content of the painting surface as primarily a matter of masses, balances, and contrasts even before it became a convocation of the Biblical or mythological, edifying or convulsive figures who constitute the work's ostensible theme.

From Rembrandt, Fuseli took the principle of flat, generalized passages applied with a sharp, thin brush that has not necessarily followed the contour of an actual form. In his *Enyo* (Fig. 249) the gray, somewhat somber flows, proportioned in relation to the lighter shapes of the reserve, are articulated by a fine network of pencil lines (above), while the foreground is enhanced with a dense concentration of linear notations, made with the incisiveness of etching.

In *Eve at the Forbidden Tree* (Fig. 250) the line closely adheres to the curves of the body, but then it also extends and expands into the wide, thick mark used for the arms. Here one is reminded of the late ink drawings of Matisse, made in 1950–52. For the rest (the tree, the rather singular serpent), Fuseli used a series of rapid, vehement, discontinuous notations structured here and there with strokes of heavier ink.

Greuze, meanwhile, in his great *Lamentation* (Fig. 248), may have gone still further toward abandoning morphological conventions. The curtain of bistre stain suspends its diagonal flow across the sheet only to allow—in approximate patches—the highlights of hair and arms to shine through. In this work shadow is, more than anything else, surface. Aggressively anti-illusionistic, the strokes do nothing to conceal the technique employed to create the drawing: leaving the paper support untouched as a means of representing relief and light. Here, as well as in other drawings by Greuze, a sense of tragedy arises from more than the harshness of the theme. It is already implied in the handling of the washes, which suggest a rent veil, shredded linen, or even ravaged flesh. The wretchedness of the actual figures barely emerges from the inky texture, as if the traumatic shock produced by the scene prevented the image from assuming coherence—as if coherent thought itself had become inadequate.

250. Henry Fuseli. *Eve at the Forbidden Tree* (Milton, *Paradise Lost* IX, 780ff). 1794–96.
Pencil, brush, brown ink, brown wash on paper, 1′8″ × 1′1½″. Kunsthaus, Zurich.

103

251. James Jefferys
(1751–84).
*The Blinding
of Polyphemus.*
*c. 1779.*
*Pencil, ink*
and wash on paper,
1′10″×1′2½″.
Private collection.

# The extravagant and paroxysmal "mannerism" of Jefferys

252. James Jefferys. *Prisoners*. c. 1779. Pen and ink over gray wash, 1½' × 22". Ashmolean Museum, Oxford.

253. James Jefferys. *Four Figures and a Spider*. c. 1779. Pencil, pen and wash on paper, 9 × 11½".
Fogg Art Museum (bequest of Richard L. Feigen), Harvard University, Cambridge.

In reaction against Winckelmann, the theoretician of Neoclassicism who wanted to see in antique art nothing but ideal serenity, an international group formed around Fuseli in Rome during the 1770s. For the Anglo-Swiss artist, as for Sergel, Runciman, Abildgaard, and Romney, Greco-Roman themes were simply vehicles for their fascination with erotic, violent, or macabre situations. They took their inspiration directly from the Michelangelo of the Sistine Ceiling and from the 16th-century Mannerism of Parmigianino, Rosso Fiorentino, Pontormo, Bandinelli, and Goltzius. Thus, it is a Mannerist *stupore* that reigns over the scenes drawn in Rome, during June and July 1779, by a young Englishman named James Jefferys. Selected from an album executed in a matter of days, the artist working as if in a trance or a state of suspended consciousness, the drawings are part of a series of "hallucinations" and "nightmares," all populated by figures given over to dramatic gestures and extravagant postures.

Jefferys, whose premature death came at age thirty-two, claimed license for the imagination and the right to subjective distortion. "I may be excused for putting bones and joints out of their place," he wrote on a sheet dating from 1774–75, "as painting in this sense is no longer Imitative but *Creative*." In his *Polyphemus* (Fig. 251), the expressive athletes, with their long fluid legs, loop garland-fashion along the full length of a bowed stake aimed at the sleeping giant's pineal eye. Meanwhile, tension and terror grip the shackled, gesticulating prisoners in the Oxford drawing reproduced in Fig. 252, just as they do the woman in Fig. 253, who cringes before a spider. (The female bodies drawn by Jefferys are, like those of Pontormo, approximations transposed from male anatomy.)

The artist clearly had a remarkable way of filling his picture surface—by disposing across it a chaplet of light areas representing figures, with the arrangement seized as an integrated whole—but in the drawing at left the rather singular emplacement of the images is the result of later cropping.

In Jefferys, two methods alternate or combine to produce the shadows and the shallow space: parallel hatching, either vertical or horizontal, and irregular washes that by contrast make the bodies stand out in all their whiteness, which is that of the paper itself.

Until recent years, these drawings were, *faute de mieux*, attributed to a hypothetical "Master of the Giants." It was Nancy L. Pressly who, in 1977 proposed Jefferys as their actual author.

## Stretched over a great width,
## the "reserve" becomes ever-more brilliant

254. Henry Fuseli (1741–1825). *The Apostate.* 1772. Pen and brown ink, gray wash on paper, 1′3″×2′1¼″.
British Museum (courtesy of the Trustees), London.

255. Jean-Baptiste Greuze (1725–1805). *The Death of a Cruel Father Abandoned by His Children.* 1769.
Brush, wash of India ink and brown ink, pencil on white paper, 1′6½″×2′1¼″. Musée Greuze, Tournus.

256. Henry Fuseli. *Thetis Mourning the Body of Achilles.* 1780. Brown and red-brown wash and pencil on paper, 16½×22″. Art Institute of Chicago.

The high-voltage flash of a white form crackling across the full width of the sheet gives the drawings of Fuseli and Greuze the intensity demanded by their subjects. The *Apostate* (Fig. 254) features a scene the artist would have witnessed at Rome's Santo Spirito Hospital: a dying man refusing the sacrament of Extreme Unction and attempting to escape the clutches of the attendant priests.

The scene of horror depicted by Greuze (Fig. 255) involves a father who dies in an alcoholic convulsion, as his terror-stricken wife flees and his small son watches from the doorway. Neither here nor in the Fuseli drawing can the violent theme alone account for the power of the work. Whether it derives

from the linear handling that subsumes all the figures into the same dynamic movement, or from the texture of the paper reserve that fuses everything into one white patch, the unifying effect stands in wrenching contradiction to the actions portrayed. The continuity of line and of the paper's own whiteness reunites characters who, at any price, want to separate.

Gestural and muscular excess lies at the very heart of the aesthetic developed by Fuseli. Goethe considered him ''an inspired mannerist who parodies himself.'' The tense, exasperated world he painted is one with which the artist identified completely while he was creating it: ''Consider it as the unalterable law of Nature,'' he wrote in

his *Aphorisms,* ''that all your power upon others depends on your own emotions. Shakespeare wept, trembled, laughed first at what now sways the public feature; and where he did not, he is stale, outrageous or disgusting.'' This could be compared with an observation made by de Quincey in his *Confessions of an English Opium-Eater:* ''We hear it reported of Dryden, and of Fuseli in modern times, that they thought proper to eat raw meat for the sake of obtaining splendid dreams.''

If the violence in Greuze lacks epic grandeur, it is none the less frightening. This was certainly felt by the artist's contemporaries, who encouraged him to return to the sugary scenarios that had made his reputation. After seeing the

work just discussed, Féron wrote: ''What a subject! . . . This theme shocks me. I feel angry that a Frenchman could have imagined it.'' For *Thetis Mourning the Body of Achilles* (Fig. 256) Fuseli went to Homer: ''We saw him fallen like a great oak, immense, his limbs flung out on all sides.'' Once again it is the reserve— now discontinuous, however—that links the actors: the dead hero, his mother standing vigil near the rocks, and the enigmatic little figure who, armed with a sort of oar, flies into the depths of a fraught landscape (a landscape, moreover, that anticipates the more gestural drawings of Fuseli's exact contemporary, the English painter George Romney [Figs. 257–260]).

257. George Romney (1734–1802).
*A Foregathering of Witches.* c. 1792.
Watercolor and black ink, 15×22½".
Fitzwilliam Museum, Cambridge.

258. George Romney.
*A Foregathering of Witches.* c. 1792.
Watercolor and black ink, 15¼×20½".
Fitzwilliam Museum, Cambridge.

If George Romney made his reputation as a portraitist and a rival of Reynolds, he also achieved a remarkable, though still little known, corpus of some five thousand drawings that stand in marked contrast to the generally conventional character of his painting. On these broad sheets, where the artist relentlessly explored his innermost impulses without any thought of publication, Romney filled and structured the surface with imperious flourishes of ink or watercolor, making no attempt to conceal the energy of his working hand. Figures and objects take form sometimes in black on a white ground and sometimes in reverse, with paper-white reserved within the somber surround of ink. The drawings as a whole reveal the artist's objective to have been not the delineation of forms upon a ground, but rather the activation of the surface through a quantitative balance of mutually stimulating blacks and whites.

The four compositions seen on these pages apparently had their source in the opening scene of *Macbeth*, which, after calling for "Thunder and lightning," has three witches enter and speak the first lines: "Fair is foul, and foul is fair/ Hover through the fog, and filthy air." From this Romney created a sort of moving picture, with each sheet a frame and the frames succeeding one another as the equivalents of an inspiration that accelerated and renewed itself from sheet to sheet. The surface seems to have been covered ever-more rapidly and with a progressively broader stroke.

We can almost see the haste with which the artist turned the pages of his sketchbook, creating effects that border on those achieved by Kandinsky in 1909–10, when he gradually and systematically effaced the figural elements of his painting.

The four Romney drawings date from the period when the artist, as an ardent supporter of the republican cause, suffered the consternation of seeing the French Revolution turn into the Terror: "The accounts today from France are dreadful: all the priests that were confined are murdered, perhaps the city of Paris is at this time in flames. I am so agitated with the tremendous situation of that poor country, I am not able to do anything."

259. George Romney. *A Foregathering of Witches.* c. 1792.
Watercolor and black ink, 15¾×21¾". Fitzwilliam Museum, Cambridge.

260. George Romney. *A Foregathering of Witches*. c. 1792. Watercolor and black ink, 15¾×21½". Fitzwilliam Museum, Cambridge.

Tension builds and accelerates from page to page
in the album of a virtuoso master

261. William Blake (1757–1827). *The Circle of the Lustful: Paolo and Francesca*. 1824. Watercolor, 14½ × 20½″. Birmingham Museums and Art Gallery.

to 5

## A volute of amorous bodies sweeps across, up, and out of the pictorial field

From the series of more than one hundred watercolor illustrations that William Blake executed for Dante's *Divine Comedy*, the composition devoted to the Paolo and Francesca episode stands out by virtue of its visionary and spatial amplitude. It was no doubt this page that Kenneth Clark had in mind when he wrote in 1956: "Sometimes it was as if the old Celtic spiral had been wound up tight and was ready to impel his figures through space." Here the spiral becomes the amplification or dilation of a line that has been fattened until it could contain and hold in suspension bodies that, despite the torturing discomfort of their postures, continue to obey, almost without deformation, both the canons of beauty inherited from Michelangelo and the most precise kind of linear definition. "A spirit and a Vision," wrote Blake, "are not, as the modern philosophy supposes, a cloudy vapour, or a nothing: they are organized and minutely articulated beyond all that the mortal and perishing nature can produce."

The supremacy—indeed imperialism—of Blake's tendency toward linearity finds its ultimate fruition in the perpetual movement of the whirlwind that fills and traverses the entire surface, before finally disappearing into the upper left corner of the sheet. "Nature," Blake insisted, "has no outline, but Imagination has." He called for forms or lines that make receptacles for the intellect.

For Blake, as for Mondrian in the 20th century and his fellow practitioners of geometric art, linearity stood for long-held attitudes of moral rectitude: "Leave out this line," Blake explained, "and you leave out life itself; all is chaos again, and the line of the Almighty must be drawn out upon it

before man or beast can exist." But this insistence upon the importance of line should not obscure Blake's remarkable work in color. Anthony Blunt, in his *Art of William Blake* (1959), analyzed all the Dante illustrations and concluded: "He began by laying in the main design in the broad washes which are traditional in the medium . . . but then he works over the whole surface in a series of small touches, almost as if he was painting in tempera, frequently going over the same area many times. . . . but the miracle is that Blake manages to avoid the messiness which normally comes with working over the same part several times in water-colour. The different touches are superimposed, so that the upper ones do not disturb the freshness of the lower layers. The artist must have taken the greatest care not to add one touch until the lower layers had completely dried, and he probably used his paint as dry as possible." Thus, it was the time necessary for the pigment to dry that set the pace for the elaboration of this work. Blake accepted the physical properties of the medium he chose and subjected his creative impulse to their requirements. The scene reproduced here, taken from Canto V of the *Inferno*, concerns the moment when Dante, having just heard Francesca tell her story, falls into a faint, while the two lovers rejoin the endless round in which those who have committed sins of the flesh are caught up. Represented in the illuminated medallion over Virgil's head is the encounter that earned Paolo and Francesca their eternal damnation:

*. . . . While thus one spirit spoke,*
*The other wail'd so sorely, that heart-*
*   struck*
*I, through compassion fainting, seem'd*
*   not far*
*From death, and like a corpse fell to the*
*   ground.*

111

## The arching line of a circle becomes expressive through its relationship to the rectangular shape of the canvas

Moved by the Gaelic poems of Ossian (see also p. 187), the Danish painter Abildgaard decided to illustrate an episode from the Macpherson saga, choosing the one in which the mother of the hero Culmin learns from his apparition that her son has died in battle (Fig. 263). While the barking dogs express their own sense of an unearthly presence, the powerful arc of the mourning woman imposes its rhythm upon the entire picture, where it is amplified in the nude body of the warrior, then echoed on a minor scale in the shield and crescent moon. Responding to one another, these curves bring together on the surface and unify not only the two figures but also two different spaces: that of the living and that of the dead, one frontal and the other projected into perspective depth where it fades away. Only the dogs interrupt the play of curving lines, which simply makes the animals seem all the more incongruous.

Abildgaard was the first artist on the Continent to take up Ossianic themes (he actually owned four different editions of Macpherson's poem) and to join, "in perfect accord, Neoclassical art and the Romantic consciousness."[6] Actually, Culmin had its immediate source in the 1781 version of the *Nightmare* by Fuseli. This Anglo-Swiss artist, during his 1770s sojourn in Rome, had exercised a profound influence upon Abildgaard, whom he saw virtually every day, thereby forming with a mutual friend, the Swedish sculptor Sergel, the core of a group that met for discussion and extremely productive work (see pp. 102–109).

It was Fuseli (Fig. 262) who called attention to Michelangelo's drawing at a time—the late 18th century—when the creator of the *Last Judgment* was beginning to replace Raphael in the pantheon of artists worshiped by the English (such as Reynolds and Blake). The striking authority of the arching figures seen on these two pages has its ancestry in the Delphic Sibyl and the *ignudi* of the Sistine Ceiling.

262. Henry Fuseli (1741–1825). *Cupid and Psyche*. c. 1812. Oil on canvas, 3'5¾"×2'5¼".
Yale Center for British Art (Paul Mellon Collection), New Haven.

263. Nicolai Abraham Abildgaard (1743–1809). *Ossian: The Ghost of Culmin Appearing to His Mother*. c. 1794. Oil on canvas, 2′½″×2′6¾″. National Museum, Stockholm.

264. Pierre-Paul Prud'hon (1758–1823). *The Empress Josephine*. 1805.
Oil on canvas, 8′×5′10½″. Louvre.

## Melancholy or sensuality conveyed by softly inflected arms

Languid and sinuous, the women of Reynolds and Prud'hon escape the Neoclassical rigor that David glorified in France and that subsequently found its confirmation in England. Now Reynolds challenged the endless stream of "lifeless," "insipid" derivations from the antique and stated his perference for the melting contours and soft transitions of Correggio, the art of Titian, Rubens, and Watteau, and "the magical splendour" of Rembrandt's light (Fig. 265). He whom Blake called "Sir Sloshua Reynolds" was an eclectic and a connoisseur. And, according to François Benoît in his monograph on the artist, Reynolds carried his approach "to the point of detaching particles of paint [from the Old Master works in his collection] so as to discover in this substance the secret of their beauty."

But in his passion for textural experimentation Reynolds managed to spoil many of his canvases. He shared the view of William Gandy, a friend and confrere, who said that "a picture ought to have a richness in its texture, as if the colours had been composed of cream or cheese, and the reverse of a hard and husky or dry manner."

After long study of Titian and his pupils in Venice, Reynolds observed that "their general practice appeared to be, to allow not above a quarter of the picture for the light, including in this portion both the principal and secondary lights; and another quarter to be kept as dark as possible; and the remaining half kept in mezzotint, or half shadow." And it was just such economy that he applied to the picture in the Hermitage (one of several versions) in which some have wanted to see the legendary beauty of Lady Hamilton (Fig. 265). Reynolds painted it in the aftermath of a 1781 sojourn in the Low Countries, where he stood wonderstruck before the art of Rubens, while also adopting something of van Dyck's brushwork and coloring.

One of the charms of the work reproduced on the opposite page arises from the game of hide-and-seek played throughout, as in the face that peeks at us while trying to conceal itself, the garment that falls away and is being untied, the shading that melts the fleshy roundness of the arms.

In the art of Prud'hon (Fig. 264) as in that of Reynolds, the figure stands out and reflects the light. Pensive, dressed in a white gown and a dark red stole, which harmonizes with the crepuscular tones of the garden at Malmaison, the Empress has adopted the head and arms posture so often seen in contemporary sculptures (Canova's *Amor and Psyche, Hebe, Pauline Borghese*). The tender melancholy thus expressed ran counter to the spirit of the "severe school." As a result, it can hardly surprise that the picture elicited an expression of feigned indulgence from David: "That one has his proper place, as the Boucher or Watteau of our time. Let him do what he wants; it can have no bad effect, given the state of painting today. He is wrong, but it is not permitted to everyone to be wrong as he is. His talent is real. What I cannot forgive him . . . is his continuing to do the same head, the same arms, the same hands. All his figures have the same expression . . . always the same grimace. This is not how we should visualize nature, we who too are disciples and lovers of antiquity!"

265. Joshua Reynolds (1723–92). "*Snake in the Grass*." 1784–88.
Oil on canvas, 4′2″×3′3¾″. Hermitage Museum, Leningrad.

267. Pierre-Paul Prud'hon. *Crime Pursued by Justice and Vengeance.* After 1808. Oil on canvas, 5'4½" × 6'6". Musée Hôtel Sandelin, Saint-Omer.

# Crime trapped by a mirror reflection of curves

Prud'hon's most famous work was painted not for the serene confines of a museum but for the criminal court in Paris' Palais de Justice. One should imagine it placed above a string of judges, lawyers, and miscreants. Prud'hon explained his conception in an official letter written in the hope of obtaining a commission for the proposed painting: "Veiled by night, in a wild and remote place, greedy Crime slits the throat of his victim, seizes the gold, and looks back to make sure that no life remains to compromise his gain. Foolish man! He does not see that Nemesis, that terrible agent of Justice, following like a vulture bearing down upon its prey, will overtake and deliver him to her inflexible companion."

The version reproduced in Fig. 267 is not the one in the Louvre, ruined by the artist's use of bitumen, but that at Saint-Omer, which is largely from the artist's own hand, even if the transfer and placement of the figures were done by his pupils, Constance Mayer and Carrier. Prud'hon left the canvas unfinished at his death.

A distinctive feature of the work is the ease and freedom of its composition, in which a single curve, constituting one ample movement, unites the two celestial deities from the wing of Vengeance to the feet of Justice. Responding to this is the nearly comparable, but inverse, curve of the victim's body, which glows with a Correggesque luminosity. Together, these mirror-image shapes form a sort of visual trap from which we know that the criminal, with his brutish face and Caracalla look (see Fig. 149), will not escape. As Helen Weston has noted, Prud'hon's allegory takes its power from a double contraction—of time and of space. The murderer, his victim, and the avenging deities, for instance, all crowd into a limited area. They could almost touch one another. Thus, time too is contracted, since the crime, the flight, and the approaching punishment all appear in the same image.

The unfinished state of the picture permits a better understanding of how Prud'hon worked. Covering the entire canvas is a cream-colored ground, several fragments of which are still visible: the foot of Justice and the forward edge of Vengeance's tunic. But the bodies too have been built up from that reserve, which the artist discreetly altered so as to shade and model the forms into roundness. The great appeal of Prud'hon lies in the indissoluble relationship between his elegiac tenderness and the melting quality of his manner. (Delacroix declared him to be "the only painter of that period whose execution was equal to his conception.") He did not paint sentimental figures; rather, sentiment resided in his very touch, in the softness of his color, or in his way of stroking canvas or paper.

The study for the head of Vengeance (Fig. 266) is remarkable for its extreme economy, in which the whole support has been delicately modulated by a veil of light-toned bistre. It is the reserve—the actual exposure of the tinted paper—that serves to indicate hair, eye, ear, and neck. The sparkling highlights come from a few accents made with white chalk, while touches of charcoal, caressed into a blur, endow the image with life and movement.

266. Pierre-Paul Prud'hon (1758–1823). *Head of Vengeance.* c. 1804.
Charcoal and white chalk with stumpwork on blue paper, 20×15¾". Art Institute of Chicago.

268. Pierre-Paul Prud'hon
(1758–1823).
*Head of the Virgin*. c. 1810.
Charcoal heightened
with white chalk and
stumpwork on paper, 9½×6¾".
Musée des Beaux-Arts, Dijon.

By accentuating the procedures of Correggio, his Renaissance model, Prud'hon created certain drawings that offer the possibility of a dual reading. A *close-focus* examination of the *Head of the Virgin* (Fig. 268, enlarged by one-sixth) permits us to appreciate the roughness of the chalk and, even more, of the charcoal, both applied with angular, stiff strokes that are broken up and ''fissured'' by the pronounced grain of the paper. Here, in the tradition of Watteau's three-color studies, is a further increase in the conflict between, on the one hand, the representational function of a line, the requirement that it describe recognizable forms, and, on the other, its own reality *per se,* as a mark, sooty or gleaming, an autonomous stroke of the hand.

A *distant* reading, however, is required in order for the hatchings to fuse in the viewer's eye. Before they can become legible as a face, the overlays of parallel lines—dense for the cheekbones, open for the neck—must blend into one another through the process of optical mixture. And this can occur—allowing abstract marks to transform themselves into a continuous nap of gray-beige medium—only when the drawing is viewed from a certain distance.

If possible, the ''academy'' in the Lille Museum (Fig. 269) carries the effects of double reading still further. Viewed up close, the highlights, which seem to have been applied at great speed, look like scarification. They do not take their proper place or dissolve in the eye until held off at more than arm's length. Prud'hon would appear to have adopted the techniques of engraving, while enlarging them to an extreme degree.

The potential for experiencing a drawing or a painting as both a fabric and a figural scene became one of the period's great aspirations. Gainsborough, according to Reynolds, claimed credit for it: ''That Gainsborough himself considered this peculiarity in his manner and the power it possesses of exciting surprise, as a beauty in his work, I think may be inferred from the eager desire which we know he always expressed, that his pictures, at the Exhibition, should be seen near, as well as at distance.''

269. Pierre-Paul Prud'hon. *Academy (Male Nude).* c. 1788. Sketch, black pencil with white chalk on paper, 1'11½" × 1'5¼". Musée des Beaux-Arts, Lille.

# With its network of vigorous hatching, drawing affirms the activity of the artist's hand

## By means of all-over, generalized scumbling, the painter takes account of the physical surface

By covering vast surfaces with a methodical application of scumbled pigment, David at the end of the 18th century offered a conception of the picture plane totally different from that of Poussin, a painter with whom, however, David was often compared, by himself as well as by others. "After 1780," Louis Hautecoeur tells us in his biography of the artist, "all the while that he subjected his groups to a rigorous framework of geometric or harmonic lines, [David] simplified his technique bit by bit, limiting impasto to highlights, filling in the backgrounds

272. Jacques Louis David. *Portrait of Monsieur de Joubert.* 1786. Oil on canvas, 4′2″×3′1¾″. Musée Fabre, Montpellier.

271. Eugène Delacroix (1798–1863).
*Academy (Female Nude): Mademoiselle Rose.* 1817–24.
Oil on canvas, 2′8″×2′1½″. Louvre.

270. Jacques Louis David (1748–1825).
*Portrait of Madame Trudaine.* c. 1790–91.
Oil on canvas, 4′3¼″×3′2½″.
Louvre.

with scumbled medium, and using thin strokes for the rest of the picture. He deliberately denied himself the sensuousness of *belle matière.*"

What resulted was lean painting, and a lean painting that became highly functional as soon as David wanted to activate the surface through an accumulation of small strokes fluctuating between light and dark, a mottling whose differences in paint thickness would then counter the effect originally sought by providing shadows and by blurring the impressive "murality" of the plane. Whether this "scumbling" is very apparent (as in the works thought, possibly in error, to be incomplete; see Fig. 273) or simply

allowed to show through the transparency of an upper film of paint, "endowing David's *matière* with a secret vibration,"[7] the technique serves to reinforce the planarity of the canvas by a system of simultaneous contrasts that cause the ground to seem more present and resistant. Here was the logical predispositon of an artist who in color never ceased to advocate the separation of hues and optical mixture (in the eye of the spectator) more than chemical mixture (on the palette). David, wrote Delécluze, taught "that it was necessary to apply [colors] one next to the other while trying to blend them, not with the brush, but by juxtaposing them rather precisely, so that they follow one another without offense to the eye, and by expressing the differences among tones and the gradations of light." This refusal to blend strokes and colors anticipated the concerns of Cézanne and Seurat almost a century later.

Some five years apart, the portraits of Mme Trudaine (Fig. 270) and M. de Joubert (Fig. 272) disclose the same sort

of scumbling technique. This can be seen in the backgrounds, but also in the clothing, where it has been both concealed and enhanced with long, dark strokes. In the faces the handling can hardly be detected, owing to successive applications and a greater density of pigment. (For the range in David's brushwork, note the pressure on the coat button around which the form of M. de Joubert has been organized and the loose, Fragonard-like arrangement of curly hair enveloping the head of Mme Trudaine.) This filling in of the picture with scumbled medium implies that the painter, from the outset of his work and even before delineating the figure, took account of the physical dimensions of his canvas by covering it from edge to edge. The effect of the overall play and repetition of small strokes was to block out the isotropic surface as a plane or a kind of screen.

The young Delacroix essayed David's method (Fig. 271) before discovering in Michelangelo and Rubens a more compulsive as well as a more cursive conception of painterly gesture.

## Against a wall of painterly brushwork, the languorous death of an antique ephebe

On July 11, 1794, David was asked to arrange a patriotic ceremony in tribute to a pair of young martyrs of the Revolution. Interrupted by Thermidor (the fall of Robespierre, which ended the Reign of Terror), the event did not take place. Of the scenario plotted out by Robespierre, only the picture reproduced here has survived, and it was left in what would appear to be an incomplete state. (But ''incompleteness'' loses meaning in regard to David, who instinctively knew when to suspend work once the canvas had attained its maximum effectiveness, and who signed at least one portrait created with the same system of *frottis*, or ''scumbling.'')

The success of *Bara* derives from the contrast between an ample surface covered edge to edge with a generalized, monochrome hatchwork of loose brushstrokes and the pathetic curve of an adolescent male body fallen to the ground. On the left, a burst of light announces the advance of a flag. As for color, it can be found only in the tiny object—a cockade—clutched by the dead boy. Like David's homage to Marat (Fig. 156), *Bara* offers not action but rather its effect, not the murder but the victim's mortal remains. The work seems to illustrate a principle enunciated by Winckelmann, the German theoretician of Neoclassicism: ''The more the attitude of the body is calm, the more apt it is to show the true character of the soul'' (1755). All commentators have emphasized the ambiguous nature of the young drummer. Friedlander mentions ''his somewhat feminine hips bent sharply out,'' and goes on to say that the subject ''might be a Narcissus seeking his own image in the pond. . . . This is no more than a nude youth, beautiful, if somewhat hermaphroditic.'' Starobinski describes ''an antique ephebe, almost an Endymion or an Antinous.'' Here we touch upon the homosexual side of Neoclassicism, in which ostensibly virile themes coexist—often in the work of the same painter—with ''decadent'' imagery. In David's studio, where professional modeling was abolished, the students themselves posed. According to one of them, Delécluze, ''those among the young men whose age or general perfection of form made them suitable as models had their names inscribed upon a list and took turns posing entirely nude.'' It is known, moreover, that Bayard, a Davidian pupil, served as the model for Bara.

273. Jacques Louis David (1748–1825). *The Death of Bara*. c. 1794. Oil on canvas, 3'10½"×5'1". Musée Calvet, Avignon.

# The arabesque line of indolent bodies articulates the canvas with a slow, undulating rhythm from edge to edge

274. Anne Louis Girodet (1767–1824). *The Sleep of Endymion*. 1791. Oil on canvas, 6'5½"×8'6¼". Louvre.

"I endeavor to free myself as much as possible from [David's] approach, and to this end I spare neither pain, nor study, nor model, nor plaster. If I end up badly . . . it will be my fault." The obsessive willfulness of this break with the teaching of Jacques-Louis David was translated by Girodet into his *Endymion* (Fig. 274). Note, for instance:
• the Mannerist elongation of the academic canon of proportions;
• the tendency of the body to assume the form of an arabesque, which traverses and lends its rhythm to the entire surface;
• the smooth, porcelain-like quality of the flesh, the disappearance of muscles, nerves, morphological angularities of the flesh, and concrete accidents of skin in the unctuousness of the pigment;
• the volumes that no longer reflect light selectively (as in the Caravaggesque tradition revived by

David) but seem, rather, to become the source of the light that courses over the body's contours.

*Endymion* became something of a manifesto and achieved great success at the height of the Terror when shown in the 1793 Salon. It was generally perceived to be a departure from the "Roman" style of David, thus a harbinger of the post-Revolutionary period. Girodet's correspondence reveals something of the picture's genesis in Rome, when the artist was twenty-four years old: "I am doing a sleeping Endymion. Amor spreads apart the branches of the trees near which [Endymion] lies in a way that makes him reflect the moonlight beaming through the aperture, while the rest of the body remains in shadow. I don't think it a bad idea; as for the effect, it is purely ideal and as a result very difficult to realize. The desire to do something new that does not seem labored may

have caused me to take on more than I can handle; but I want to avoid plagiarism." Several years later he would become more specific: "The invention came to me from a bas-relief in the Villa Borghese. . . . I thought I should not in any way represent the face of Diana. It struck me as improper to paint, in the very moment of her one amorous thought, a goddess renowned for her chastity. The idea of a beam appeared to me more delicate and more poetic, in addition to the fact that it was new at the time."

In his *Iris and Morpheus* of 1811 (Fig. 275), Guérin borrowed and even exaggerated the languid pose formulated by Girodet for his *Endymion*. The pale shaft of light, which in Girodet's picture passes through the very precisely rendered vegetation, has here been replaced by a stream of acidulous colors and, as Rosenblum has noted, gives effect to a "voluptuous, nocturnal

fantasy that locates [the subjects] less in a public domain of shared myth than in a private realm of the spectator's own erotic dreams."[8]

The abandonment of both David's moralizing content and his realist preoccupations produced a kind of aesthetic kitsch. Henceforth, images would draw their power from a strangeness cultivated in direct reaction against the great master's own principles.

275. Pierre Narcisse Guérin (1774–1833). *Iris and Morpheus*. 1811. Oil on canvas, 8'2¾"×5' 10". Hermitage Museum, Leningrad.

# The gestures of heroic love link together in one continuous curve

For the picture in Fig. 276, Broc went to Ovid and found the theme of Apollo supporting the mortally wounded body of his young friend Hyacinth, killed by a discus (see bottom foreground) rebounding from a throw made by the god himself. Once he knew the youth could not be revived, Apollo would transform him into a flower and every year sing his praise on the lyre. According to Delécluze, Broc was "a Gascon who did not lack aptitude, but in whom certain singularities of character had produced a puerile vanity." Benoît tells us that Broc was also the foremost painter in the group known as the "Thinkers," "Meditators," or *Barbus* ("Bearded Ones"). Although nurtured in David's own studio, the Barbu faction responded to the *Sabines* by calling its creator (David) "Vanloo, Pompadour, Rococo" and by accusing him of being frozen in the canons of Italian art, or even classical art of the Greco-Roman tradition. The rebels advocated a return to the purest, most archaic kind of primitive spirit, as this could be found in Homer, Ossian, and, above all, the Bible. "Right away," wrote Delécluze, "the simplest compositon on an Etruscan vase was ranked above masterpieces recently brought from Italy" by Napoleon's armies.

Even if the Broc picture only partially reflects what Delécluze's eyewitness account tells us about the principles held by this sect (flatness, abstract purity of line, suppressed shading), the work nonetheless remains astonishingly precocious not only in form but in content as well. "The erotic intensity of Broc's painting is typical of the more complex explorations of sexual feeling that emerge in the late 18th century," writes Robert Rosenblum.[9] The same author goes on to say that "the

277. Claude Marie Dubufe (1790–1864). *Apollo and Cyparissus.* 1821. Oil on canvas, 6'2" × 7'5¾". Musée Calvet, Avignon.

crystalline effect of Broc's lighting, whereby contours are suddenly illuminated in contrast to the rest of the body, which is largely shadowed, is yet another formal device employed by younger Davidians. . . . The strong silhouettes that emerge from this curious luminary effect emphasize the planar disposition of figures in a manner that corresponds to the growing taste around 1800 for Greek vases and Italian primitive painting." But it was left to Ingres (that year's winner of the Prix de Rome) to make the most of Barbu ideas.

Twenty years later, Dubufe, another Davidian student, selected a similar theme—Apollo consoling Cyparissus after the latter has accidently killed his pet deer (Fig. 277)—and with it produced a "great machine" in which figures of enamel-like perfection stand out against a 17th-century landscape, as if caught at the center of converging spotlights.

The Neoclassical movement as a whole attached great importance not only to the young male body but also to the ideal perfection of its form. Wincklemann, in his *Thoughts on the Imitation of Greek Works in Painting and Sculpture* (1755), objected to what he called "little smart wrinkles." In the art of the Greeks, "the skin never, as on modern bodies, appears in plaits distinct from the flesh." But even while sublimating reality in smoothness, the author of *The History of Ancient Art* (1764) dreamed of antique palaestrae: "The young Spartans were bound to appear every tenth day naked before the Ephori, who, when they perceived any inclined to fatness, ordered them a scantier diet. . . . The Gymnasies, where, sheltered by public modesty, the youths exercised themselves naked, were the schools of art. . . . The fairest youths danced undressed on the theatre."

276. Jean Broc (1771–1850). *Death of Hyacinth.* 1801 Oil on canvas, 5'9" × 3'11¼". Musée des Beaux-Arts, Poitiers.

The jewelry of classical antiquity—
cameos and intaglio-carved
gemstones—provided a source of
inspiration for David's students who,
like Girodet and Gérard, wanted to
reshape and move beyond the
monumental style of their master. In
Girodet's atelier, Jean Adhémar writes,
"much was made of Greek and Roman
coins, for their beauty as well as for
their documentary value." But the
bodies painted by Girodet—round and
full, free of wrinkles and every other
kind of irregularity—also recall,
Friedlander has noted, the Mannerist art
of a Parmigianino or a Bronzino, and
even more—when it comes to a work
like Girodet's *Danaë* (Fig. 280)—the
sensual goddesses of Primaticcio at
Fontainebleau.

*Danaë* was in fact a bit of revenge
taken by the artist upon Mlle Lange, an
actress who had expressed her
dissatisfaction with a first portrait by
addressing Girodet thus: "Please, sir,
be so kind as to withdraw from
exhibition the portrait that, it is said,
brings no glory to your reputation and
compromises my reputation for
beauty." After taking the picture down,
Girodet cut it up and sent the pieces
wrapped in a table napkin to the actress.
He then replaced the portrait at the
Salon with the version opposite, which
the artist produced in two weeks of day-
and-night effort. The new picture
constitutes an allegory in which every
detail makes a scabrous allusion to the
light morals and rapacity of Mlle Lange,
beginning with the turkey in whose
features contemporaries saw a striking
resemblance to the subject's husband
(see the ring on the bird's foot). Another
devastating reference can be found at
the actress' feet, where the script of
Plautus' *Assinaria* refers to a play about
a courtesan who bestowed her favors
simultaneously upon both a father and
his son. If this settlement of accounts
made Girodet seem notoriously
malicious, the scandal also cost the
victim her career in the theatre. Mlle
Lange went into exile in Italy, where
she languished and died, as would the
heroine in Edgar Allen Poe's *The Oval
Portrait*.

The anecdote behind Girodet's
vindictive portrait points up a system of
composition that bears some analogy to
the "emblematic" one that reigned in
European art throughout the 16th and
17th centuries. Just as "emblemata,"
"devices," or *imprese* stood for
Falsehood, Vice, or Justice by the
appositeness of their attributes (scales,
etc.), Girodet constructed his picture not
by simulating an actual space in which
he adhered closely to his model, or even
a space of his own invention, but rather
by accumulating and *assembling*
symbols (gold, the faunlike mask under
the bed, the peacock plumes being stuck
into the turkey's tail, etc.), which he
then organized in a way designed to
seem representationally plausible.

Begun in 1796, Gérard's *Cupid and
Psyche* (Fig. 278) has been compared by
Friedlander to figurines made in biscuit.
The marmoreal polish of the bodies also

recalls the sculpture of Canova—
especially his Graces and Venuses, even
though Gérard based the head of Psyche
upon an actual model. Generally
regarded as the painter's masterpiece,
the picture impresses less by the purity
of its contours (some would say its
preciousness and affectation) than by
the contrast between a "sculptural"
group, trapped in an artificial pose, and
the springlike atmosphere of the quite
"natural" landscape. But for all its
success at the 1797 Salon, *Cupid and
Psyche* found no buyer, which
somewhat cooled Gérard's ambitions.

For the sake of comparison, we have
also reproduced here one of the famous
*Greek Maidens* (Fig. 279) by Vien,
David's master, who worked thirty
years earlier than Girodet and Gérard.
The older artist took his lead from the
wall paintings uncovered at Pompeii.
What this produced was a prim
voluptuousness, lascivious chastity, and
erotic ingenuousness, placing Vien's art
at the very crossroads of Neoclassicism
and the Rococo. The style is a
composite one, like that of David's
disciples later on.

278. François Gérard (1770–1837). *Cupid and Psyche*. 1797.
Oil on canvas, 6'1¼" × 4'4". Louvre.

279. Joseph Marie Vien (1716–1809). *A Greek Maiden at Her Bath*. 1767.
Oil on canvas, 2'10¼" × 2'6". Museo de Arte, Ponce.

280. Anne Louis Girodet (1767–1824).
*Mademoiselle Lange as Danaë*. 1799.
Oil on canvas, 2′1½″ × 1′9¼″.
Minneapolis Institute of Arts.

A cluster of human beings grasp a tree branch that gives way allowing the desperate victims to sink into the flood. Already dead from drowning is a woman—almost an Endymion—floating in the lower left corner of Girodet's *Deluge* (Fig. 282). Constructed upon a diagonal, the picture takes its meaning from the play of tensions that gather at the bottom, in the savage pull on the hair of the mother (whose face remains strangely calm), and extend all the way to the breaking branch, passing through the theme around which the entire composition has been organized: the linked arms of man and wife. Even in his earliest studies—like that in the Cailleux collection (Fig.

281), where all the actors are present but not in the same order—it can be seen that Girodet intended that this straight, taut line should provide the structural motif of his picture.

"An improbable scene, forced poses, slick, glassy paint, dull colors, and leaden shadows," wrote art historian François Benoît in 1897 concerning this immense canvas (more than 14 feet high), and Robert Rosenblum has spoken of "the hysterical acrobatics of the Michelangelesque nudes." It is as if Girodet had excerpted a detail from a Deluge painted by the Carracci or by Poussin, then enlarged and pushed the fragment until it became a convulsive melodrama. Such a work permitted the

*bizarre* to make a spectacular entrance into French painting. Here it springs from the contrast between the precariousness of the situation depicted and the extreme finish of the handling, as in the cleanness and clarity of the contours, the precision of the anatomies and their draperies. "Bizarre" was also the word used by David in commenting on his pupil's work: "If the door is opened to such a subject, there is no reason to stop what already has made such a good start. Farewell to the dignity of art and the *beau idéal*, the only two goals toward which history painting should strive. . . . This genre borders on a kind of absurdity normally sought in melodrama. . . . such contorted figures look like monstrosities."

Girodet himself would reflect these sentiments in a phrase recorded by Coupin: "I prefer the bizarre to flatness." The creator of *Endymion* (Fig. 274) was fascinated by extreme situations, which he called "the edge of the abyss." "He was interested," Levitine notes, "in this eerie spirit of the night [as the artist characterized it] which comes out in sleep, sleep-walking, and disease." For Levitine, what appealed to Girodet—especially in his *Deluge*—was the confounding of two genres that until then had remained completely separate: the *study of character*, which derived from comic literature, and the *study of passions*, which had its source in tragedy. The artist grafted the comic mode (the exaggeration of character and detail) onto the tragic mode cultivated by the Davidians. Girodet's *Deluge* thus becomes a sad burlesque, a hybrid like those the period was then fabricating for the theatre, thereby assuring the triumph of melodrama and *opéra comique*.

## The *terribilità* of Michelangelo transformed into the bizarre

282. Anne Louis Girodet (1767–1824).
*Scene of a Deluge.* 1806.
Oil on canvas, 14'1¾" × 11'9¾".
Louvre.

281. Anne Louis Girodet.
*Study for Scene of a Deluge.* c. 1806.
Oil on canvas, 12¼ × 8¾".
Collection Cailleux, Paris.

# Whether stylized or rendered naturalistically, the female body retains its melodic line

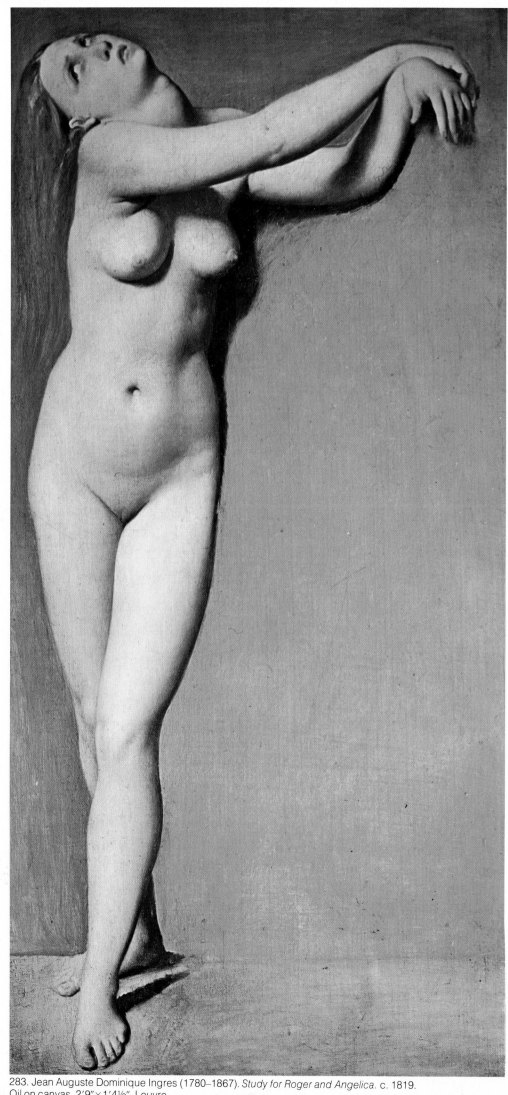

283. Jean Auguste Dominique Ingres (1780–1867). *Study for Roger and Angelica*. c. 1819. Oil on canvas, 2′9″ × 1′4½″. Louvre.

These two studies represented successive ideas pursued by Ingres for his *Roger and Angelica* (1819) now in the Louvre, a painting whose theme the artist took from Ariosto. The oil sketch made from life (Fig. 284) displays the most explicit realism, with the hand of the model joined behind her back. In Fig. 283, meanwhile, is a more stylized and dramatic essay, which came very close to the final version, where the victim's hands have been placed in front and raised to shoulder height.

In Delacroix's journal for March 22, 1855, we find the following entry: ''M. Jeanmot, who was just here this morning, mentioned the fine sketches about which Ingres says: 'One finishes only on what is finished.' '' Ingres in fact proceeded always from certitude to certitude, with the result that even his freest sketches reveal the same kind of execution as that found in the final works. Each study took him closer to his ultimate objective: figures formed and masterfully disposed across the surface in a way conducive to the continuous unfolding of an arabesque line. In the Louvre study at left (Fig. 283), the contour line, if followed along its full circuit of the figure, seems like a *tone held and prolonged* to the full extent possible in its melodic development, conforming one by one to the various shapes of the female body, and completing its course only when interrupted by the painting surface. The figure looks like a capital letter in a historiated text. This is because the human body attracted Ingres only to the degree that it gave rise to the sensuality of an abstract curve. The artist had a horror of anatomy as such, calling it a ''dreadful science that I cannot think of without disgust.'' For him, the body was not a mechanism articulated by muscles and tendons, but rather a play of proportions subject to correction for the sake of rhythmic form. ''The painter should attach little importance to anatomical musculature, but a great deal to those osteological parts that, in particular, make for attenuations and the relationship among attenuations.''

Such a harmonious conception of the body presupposes the suppression of individual detail—the accidents of flesh and skin: ''To arrive at beautiful form, one must not proceed by square or angular modeling; one must model for roundness, without noting interior details.''

284. Jean Auguste Dominique Ingres. *Study for Roger and Angelica*. c. 1818. Oil on canvas, 1′6″ × 1′2½″. Fogg Art Museum (bequest of Grenville L. Winthrop)., Harvard University, Cambridge.

285. Théodore Chassériau (1819–56).
*Venus Fresh from the Sea.* 1838.
Oil on canvas, 2'1½" × 1'9¾". Louvre.

286. Théodore Chassériau. *Apollo and Daphne.* 1844.
Oil on canvas, 20¾ × 13¾". Louvre.

"Born in Santo Domingo in 1819," writes Henri Focillon, in *Painting in the 19th Century,* "he would seem to retain in his art certain Creole reveries, nostalgia for a distant people, for soft, wild women and lost treasures." The art of Chassériau, more than any other of its time, never ceased to nourish the exotic and erotic fantasies of writers. Théophile Gautier, who followed Chassériau step by step throughout his career, extolled the *Venus* reproduced above, "still moist from the kisses of the sea," a work executed when the artist was a youth of twenty. Six years later Gautier would praise "the strange grace, the Greco-Indian quality of *Apollo and Daphne*" (Fig. 286), and make this avowal in the funeral oration he delivered at the tragically early date of 1857: "Other artists have been purer, more complete, and explicit, but none has troubled us as much as Théodore Chassériau."

The "trouble" created by Chassériau is mentioned by Focillon in his

description of *Esther* (Fig. 287): "*Esther* has the charm of a Persian miniature interleaved with the pages of an old Bible. It is truly a hidden treasure, the incomparable daughter steeped for many moons in perfumes and palm oil for the purpose of pleasing the king of kings. . . . She belongs to a very old religion, honoring the sensual within the secret heart of mysteries, doing so by lamplight and to the sound of tambourines."

But the exotic themes of Chassériau become expressive only by virtue of his sensitive use of the arabesque drawing learned from close looking at the art of Ingres, his *Odalisques, Venuses,* and *Angelicas* (Fig. 283), whose canon of proportions the younger master attenuated still further, while also endowing the flesh tones of his subjects with a creamier, more Venetian quality. Here was the art of serpentine curves the secret of which Chassériau would lose once he fell under the power of Delacroix.

Beginning in 1845–46, with a journey to North Africa, Chassériau allowed his somewhat contrived opulence, the rather facile seductiveness of his Oriental bathers, and an almost literal repetition of Delacroix's themes to become dominant in his art, thereby inducing a stylistic collapse. No longer employed as the governing principle of the entire picture, the arabesque was now limited simply to the contouring of objects. This severed the relationship between the rectangular shape of the canvas and the circulation of lines. It made Baudelaire apprehensive: "The position he wants to create for himself between Ingres, whose pupil he was, and Delacroix, whom he tries to plunder, produces something equivocal for everyone and something of an embarrassment for him. That M. Chassériau should find his advantage in Delacroix is easy to understand; but that he should be so obvious about it—despite his talent and precocious experience—there is the problem."

287. Théodore Chassériau.
*Esther.* 1842.
Oil on canvas, 17¾ × 13¾". Louvre.

# Symmetry—an image of mourning . . .

Friedrich found one of his most effective themes in the relationship he saw between symmetry and death. Scorning the idea of composition, the artist transformed most of his works, with their horizontal layout, into acts of defiance against the whole process of counterbalancing plastic elements and the compositional *cuisine* this entails. Symmetry—the division of the field into two interchangeable zones—offers the most "primitive" solution to the problem of composition, which in Friedrich can be seen as an elementary form of the artist's aesthetic rebellion. But the finicky care with which the German master pursued this approach—insisting that the iron fence in *Entrance to the Cemetery* (Fig. 288) display an equal number of bars on either side and that both the crown of thorns above and the stretcher below appear right on the median—evokes a sense of transcendant order, an *axis mundi,* a Law capable of organizing things and controlling the destiny of human beings.

Something similar occurs when Friedrich, by means of formal rhyming, draws a comparison between a "regular" stand of pines and the thicket of spires sprouting from the top of a Gothic cathedral (Fig. 290). But symmetry remains inexpressive without the presence of certain deviant details that, by contrast, serve to make the rigor seem all the more striking. In the watercolor by the Swiss artist Wocher (Fig. 289), painted at the very end of the

18th century, identical forms correspond from left to right, with the exception of the widower and his children, three anomalous silhouettes which neither can nor want to enter the static world that prevails all about them. As for Friedrich's yawning portal (Fig. 288), against which a mourning couple press so close they are hardly discernible from the pier, it opens onto a chaos of tombstones—some erect, some tilted—all of which, other than the central menhir, tend to dissolve into the mist-shrouded folds of earth.

Friedrich's professed ambition was to produce a Christian art divested of all the Biblical imagery that had become attached to it since the Renaissance. The artist painted no Christs on the Cross, only crucifixes. "God is everywhere," he said, "in the smallest grain of sand. I also wanted to show him in the reeds." Still, despite everything Friedrich said, his painting reflects the uncertainties suffered by the Christian conscience in the aftermath of the Enlightenment. "No one believes anymore!" exclaimed Chateaubriand in 1797. The nostalgia and elegiac climate of Friedrich's pictures have subsequently elicited some singular reactions, like that of the writer O. H. Von Loeben in 1817: "This sensation of becoming lost in the infinity where the art plunges us is always anticipated by a wish to die and by an interior death, even when the wish passes so quickly that we hardly realize it was there."

289. Marquad Wocher (1760–1830). *Epitaph for Chris Chona Staehelin.* 1799. Pen and watercolor on paper, 22¾×17¼". Kunstmuseum, Basel.

288. Caspar David Friedrich (1744–1840). *Entrance to the Cemetery.* 1825. Oil on canvas, 4'8¼"×3'7¼". Staatliche Kunstsammlungen, Gemäldegalerie, Dresden.

290. Caspar David Friedrich. *Cross and Cathedral in the Mountains.* c. 1812. Oil on canvas, 17¼×14¼". Kunstmuseum, Düsseldorf.

# . . . and of Christian hope

291. Carl Gustav Carus (1789–1869). *Allegory on the Death of Goethe.* 1832. Oil on canvas, 15¾ × 22″. Frankfurter Goethe Museum, Frankfurt am Main.

292. Carl Gustav Carus. *Monument to the Memory of Goethe.* 1832. Oil on canvas, 2′4″ × 1′8½″. Kunsthalle, Hamburg.

With all its linear simplicity, William Blake's watercolor in Fig. 293 is actually a complex work that embodies and condenses several different meanings, doing so through the device of symmetry. John Murdoch tells us that the artist hoped his angels might convey a sense of two other latent images, the ogival vault of Gothic architecture and a pair of hands clasped in prayer: ''Such allusions and associations were certainly invited by the artist who regarded the Bible as a field for the free play of imagination.''

But Blake went even further and in this one work integrated two episodes from the Old and New Testaments. The margin bears an explicit reference to a passage in Exodus (25:18) where God describes in detail the contents of the Ark of the Covenant: ''And thou shalt make two cherubim of gold, of beaten work shalt thou make them, in the two ends of the mercy seat. . . . Even of the mercy seat shall ye make the cherubim on the two ends thereof. And the cherubim shall stretch forth their wings on high, covering the mercy seat with their wings. . . .'' Blake then associates this description with a passage in John 20:11 describing Mary at the tomb of Christ: ''But Mary stood without at the sepulchre weeping: and as she wept, she stooped down, and looked into the sepulchre, And seeth two angels in white sitting, the one at the head, and the other at the feet, where the body of Jesus had lain.''

By conflating these two scenes into a single image, Blake proceeded to make an interpretation. Thus, the symmetry he effected in graphic terms has its counterpart in time and history by virtue of the identification the artist made between the body of Christ and the ritual instrument through which Yahweh wanted to speak to Moses. Here Jesus becomes the mediator between God and humanity, the propitiatory agent par excellence. Meyer Schapiro, in *Words and Pictures,* has shown how the illustrators of the earliest printed Bibles excelled in this type of concordance. Slipping images from one context into another, they played upon factual coincidences, as in collage, to effect interpretations that the texts themselves could not support.

In the homages paid by Carus to his friend Goethe (Figs. 291, 292), symmetry plays an explicitly allegorical role. The Romantic and classical components of the Frankfurt picture (Fig. 291), with its lyre at the center standing erect above an agitated sea, signify two antagonistic tendencies that the poet tried to reconcile at the end of his life, most notably in his reworking of the third act of *Faust.* A round-headed format reinforces the static character of works in which the natural elements—clouds, rocks, trees, waterfalls—are, by contrast, distributed quite freely.

A disciple of the philosopher Schelling and a pupil of Friedrich, Carus was distinctive in his dual commitment to art and science. (He was a psychiatric doctor as well as an anatomist and a naturalist.) In his *Letters on Landscape Painting,* written between 1815 and 1824 and published in 1831, he clarified the Romantic position—principally that of Friedrich—by indicating that it was not a matter of avoiding or transcending material nature but rather of scanning it, even to the point of minute scrutiny, for the purpose of achieving art, the end and crowning glory of all knowledge. Taking the example of Goethe's poem on clouds, Carus wrote: ''[Goethe] made a point of observing, evaluating, and classifying cloud formations until he had acquired a knowledge of them based not only upon simple visual observation but also upon the penetrating insights that only scientific research can yield. Once he had done all that, the vision of his intelligence brought together all the various aspects of phenomena—and raised them to the level of art. Thus viewed, art appears as the highest form of science. By clearly perceiving the secrets of science and clothing them in beauty, art actually becomes mystical or even, says Goethe, orphic.''

293. William Blake (1757–1827). *Angels Hovering over the Body of Christ in the Sepulcher.* Pen, ink, watercolor on white vellum, 16½ × 12¼″. Victoria and Albert Museum, London.

# A single graphic motif—the ogive arch—assures the formal and thematic coherence of painting

294. Karl Blechen (1798–1840). *Gothic Ruin with Resting Pilgrim.* 1826. Oil on canvas, 4'2¾"×3'1¾". Staatliche Kunstsammlungen, Gemäldegalerie, Dresden.

295. Joseph Mallord William Turner (1775–1851). *Transept of Tintern Abbey, Monmouthshire.* c. 1794. Watercolor and pencil, 13¾×10¼". Ashmolean Museum, Oxford.

Gothic architecture, which underwent a vigorous revival of interest at the turn of the 19th century, drew two strikingly different yet fascinated reactions from painters and illustrators.

On the one hand, they saw it as mysterious, cryptic, and romantic, what Montaigne had already termed "the somber vastness of our Gothic cathedrals." For the writer Joseph von Görres, whom Mme de Staël quotes, "the dark arcades of the church cast their shadows over those who lie buried there. One could believe oneself in the midst of a forest whose branches and leaves have been petrified by death, so that they can no longer sway or flutter when the centuries sweep like night winds through the long tunnel under their vaults."

On the other hand, the Gothic structure attracted "as much by its lightness as by its flutelike attenuation,"

in the view of a critic writing at the turn of the century. And Benoît cites this contemporary comment: "Gothic buildings, by the wonder of their construction, the thinness of their piers, and the daring of their vaults, command admiration and provide models for art." The young Goethe himself, in his famous 1772 pamphlet glorifying Strasbourg Cathedral, which he believed to be an expression of Germanic genius, felt not only "a sensation of totality, of grandeur," but also the organic, structural unity of an edifice in which "everything converges in the whole."

It is this structural conception that the painters seen here transposed into their own practice. Whether it concerns the soaring lines of an extant building (Tintern Abbey [Fig. 295], for instance, which lent its name to the celebrated lyric poem by Wordsworth) or an

imaginary architecture (as in the oils of Blechen and Oehme [Figs. 294, 296]), Gothic construction, *in the very heart of the image,* provided the framework for a generalized system of plastic echoes and rhymes. On the greatest possible diversity of scale, it permitted the repetition of a linear module and a graphic scheme (the ogive or pointed arch) that the artist could redouble and multiply, thereby assuring the overall morphological unity of his work. If Oehme and Blechen borrowed the Gothic theme from Caspar David Friedrich, their master and inspiration, they also extended its formal possibilities until these sufficed for structuring the whole of the picture surface. Something comparable, but in a different context, can be found in the cyclopian, repetitive vaults from which Piranesi drew the magic of his *Prisons.* Meanwhile, it should also be noted that

if the three works reproduced here evince a unity of linear scheme (the ogive), they also share the strong value opposition between a dark foreground and an illuminated midground. In Fig. 296 Oehme emphasized the contrast by confronting the brilliance radiating from the altar all the way to the highest point of the church's tall lancet windows and the chill tonality of the gray early-morning atmosphere.

Oehme and Blechen painted their pictures at a moment when the reconstruction of Cologne Cathedral was being prepared. With the already extant fragments (the choir and one tower) as their point of departure, the architects undertook to develop the building as a whole, deducing the proportions and the tectonic coherence of the façade from a strict observance of principles already present within the stones.

296. Ernst Ferdinand Oehme (1797-1855). *Cathedral in Winter.* 1821. Oil on canvas, 4'2"×3'¼". Staatliche Kunstsammlungen, Gemäldegalerie, Dresden.

## A magical and hypnotic precision

297. Caspar David Friedrich. *Grove of Trees under the Snow.* 1828.
Oil on canvas, 12¼ × 9¾″. Staatliche Kunstsammlungen, Gemäldegalerie, Dresden.

298. Caspar David Friedrich (1774–1840). *Dolmen in the Snow.* c. 1807. Oil on canvas, 2′ × 2′7½″.
Staatliche Kunstsammlungen, Gemäldegalerie, Dresden.

Friedrich's almost excessive concern for acuity stands in marked contrast to his vague atmosphere and vaporous mists (Fig. 370). Whatever the motif—the contour of a plant, a Gothic rib, a ship's mast—the artist painted it with keen and precise strokes. But in sharp focus as in soft, he sought an "inhabited" nature, a nature saturated with presence and powered by "a primitive cosmic force" (Schelling).

It was through his methodical application of highlights that Friedrich succeeded in endowing trees and branches, even ground-hugging bushes, with a quality of hyperrealist precision. This precision, which is not that of the human eye, produces a quasi-hypnotic effect. It comes from the stark juxtaposition of white snow and dark wood, which replaces the fluid relationship that seems normally to prevail between the illuminated and shaded parts of a limb. If Friedrich all but eliminated shading, as in a world struck by zenithal light, it was because he wanted to harden tonal contrasts and suppress intermediate values.

According to William Vaughan,[10] the pietistic tradition of Northern Germany was particularly open to the pantheism that gripped pre-Romantic Europe at the end of the 18th century. Theobul Kosegarten, a Pomeranian pastor and poet especially close to Friedrich, emphasized a direct communication between God and nature, asserting that it was in Nature—"the Bible of Christ"—that the message of divine salvation could be read. But an allusion to still older associations can also be found in Friedrich's trees, for the oak symbolized courage in Germanic legend. It corresponded more or less to the *Colossos* of archaic Greece, where this term, in the words of Jean-Pierre Vernant, "does not designate effigies of gigantic dimensions [but rather] something erect and upright"—column-statues and menhir-statues—whose function was to receive and "double" for the deceased, to become his "shade," his "spirit." The island of Rügen, Friedrich's ancestral home, lent itself to such evocative encounters (Fig. 288), since it contained numerous menhirs. Visiting Northern Germany in 1819, Friedrich's disciple, the painter-savant Carus, noted the persistence of an ancient custom, whereby every male, upon arrival at maturity, was required to plant an oak tree. This legendary subculture was not unrelated to the plastic choices made by Friedrich. Indeed, it accounts for the strong silhouetting of his images, as well as for their erectness and isolation.

299.
Caspar David Friedrich.
*Oak Tree in the Snow*.
1829.
Oil on canvas, 2'4" × 1'7".
Nationalgalerie,
Staatliche Museen
Preussischer Kulturbesitz,
Berlin.

143

With a fanlike movement, the picture opens
to embrace the dimensions of the sky itself

300. Hubert Robert (1733–1808). *Decentering of the Pont de Neuilly*. 1772. Oil on canvas, 2'2"×4'4¼". Musée Carnavalet, Paris.

301. Francisco Goya (1746–1828). *The Meadow of San Isidro*. 1788. Oil on canvas, 1'5¼"×3'1".
Museo del Prado, Madrid.

By raising the ground line at the lateral extremities of his frontal plane, Goya produced an effect of expansiveness in our perception of the landscape in the *Meadow of San Isidro* (Fig. 301). As we look at the picture, we seem to experience a broadening of our vision, a dilation of the pupils. ''The composition unfolds like a fan,'' writes Jeannine Baticle, which accounts for the sense of personal involvement that gradually takes hold of the viewer, as if by approaching the picture we might widen our field of vision and discover the potential immensity otherwise hidden from view. A comparison of this disposition of elements with that of many battle pictures, where the entire field can be assimilated in a single glance, reveals that in Goya's canvas it is the ''hidden'' that increases the sense of spatial amplitude, and that in blocking one part of his panorama, the artist stimulated the spectator's implicit urge to enter that very part. A clever composition, it integrates our own desire to participate in the activity of a scene that draws us forward.

Goya's *Meadow of San Isidro* was done as a sketch for a tapestry meant to adorn the Pardo Palace. The final work—never executed—was to measure 11 by 24 feet. At that scale, the foreground figures would have been lifesize relative to their distance from the viewer, making the illusionistic mechanism even more effective and the spectator's motor impulse still more urgent.

One cannot but be struck by the airiness of the picture (which is twice as wide as it is high) and the ease with which the artist disposed the crowd, the Manzanares River, the city, and the sky in depth. The success here flowed from the strong accent that Goya placed on the foreground, through the size of the figures as much as through the light tonalities of their clothing. The lacework of white strokes extending almost the full width of the frontal plane echoes the various chalky or silvered whites found on the opposite bank. By virtue of their correspondence, these light areas enclose the dim mass of humanity that promenades within a

narrow band measuring no more than one-fifth of the total height. As Eugenio d'Ors wrote in his *Life of Goya* (1928): ''The *Meadow of San Isidro* is a white picture, a painting of silver, an ashen or unpolished silver. The transparency of the high-key colors seems to disclose a ground of white lead, the way touches of watercolor come alive and open up on the whiteness of the bristol or paper support.''

Goya's ''fan'' effect had a precedent, albeit in a less pronounced form, in Hubert Robert's *Decentering of the Pont de Neuilly* (Fig. 300). Here, the artist captured the moment when the collapsing structural forms hit the water, sending up splashes that fountain into the air where they expand into the billowing vastness of the clouds. With the greatest adroitness, he played with light and shadow as a means of animating the field sown with figures all across the foreground (among them Louis XV, Mme du Barry, and the royal ministers). Diderot, who never had much appreciation of Robert, could not bear his ''facility,'' allusive manner,

and *non finito*. From *Salon* to *Salon* the critic scolded the painter as if he were a child (''Develop the habit of finishing, Monsieur Robert!''). In 1775, writing not about the sketch seen here, but about the final version (now lost), Diderot had this to say: ''Ah! Monsieur Robert, how poor, badly colored, and ineffectual is *Decentering of the Pont de Neuilly!* The weakly drawn figures! . . . Robert, after such a long time spent on sketches, can't you do a finished picture?''

302. Joseph Mallord William Turner (1775–1851). *Petworth Park: Tillington Church in the Distance.* 1830–31.
Oil on canvas, 2′3¾″ × 4′6¾″. Tate Gallery, London.

In classical landscape painting, the foreground becomes subject, more or less overtly, to the affirmation of a horizontal that echoes that of the horizon itself. The position of the viewer—his "viewing point"—is assured by this stable fact, which in turn echoes the geometry of the frame, as well as the stability of the ground where the spectator stands.

J. M. W. Turner took a different approach—but one neither more nor less arbitrary—in *Petworth Park* (Fig. 302). The convexity of the foreground plane emphasizes the panoramic character of the format, with the result that the view seems to expand, causing the spectator

to breathe more deeply in the presence of the space depicted. The landscape becomes an extended ellipse, an oculus, while the cloud banks fall into a line that in mirror image reflects the contour of the park below. According to John Gage, Turner was interested, mainly around 1810–12, in optical devices, the *camera lucida* of Wollaston (1807) in particular.

(Beginning with Canaletto in the 18th century, painters rapidly increased their experimentation with mechanical devices, thereby anticipating photography while also questioning the closed nature of traditional composition. Abandoning classical perspective, they

## Through convex or concave spaces, the painter renders landscape into personal experience

303. Caspar David Friedrich (1774–1840). *The Large Enclosure Near Dresden.* c. 1830–32. Oil on canvas, 2'4¾" × 3'4¼". Staatliche Kunstsammlungen, Gemäldegalerie, Dresden.

occasionally found themselves reviving the investigations of curved spaces made by Fouquet and Dürer.)

The rule which holds that to disturb the horizontal is to produce instability and unsettle the viewer was exploited by Friedrich in Fig. 303 so as to reinforce *Weltegefühl*, the cosmic feeling with which this painter drenched his works. The "Large Enclosure," a vast marshy zone on the right bank of the Elbe, is shown at twilight, with the sun's final rays reflected in the watery flats as a back-lighted boat gradually disappears in the gathering darkness. Here the concavity of the lines, which is the very opposite of the inflection found in

Turner's painting, transforms the landscape into an enlarged projection of the artist's own interior space. The system resembles that explicated by the philospher Schelling in 1807: "It is here, in the absolute oneness of the Spirit *within us* and of Nature *outside us,* that a solution should be found to the problem of the possibility of a nature beyond ourselves. . . . It is not, as we understand it, that nature by some random chance coincides with the laws of our own inner being (through the intermediary of a third principle), but that, of necessity and from the outset, she *herself* expresses the laws of our spirit, and not only that she expresses

them but that she also *gives effect* to them, that she is and can be called Nature only to the degree that she does both one and the other."

Landscape becomes a private experience, a kind of ascesis. "I should be entirely on my own," Friedrich explained to a young Russian poet who hoped to travel with the painter. "And I know that if I am alone, it is in order to perceive nature completely. Nothing should come between her and me. So as to become what I am, I must give myself entirely to my environment. I must melt into the clouds and rocks. Were my best friend to be at my side, it would destroy me. . . . I once spent a

whole week in the Uttewalder Grund, among the rocks and pines—and throughout this time I did not encounter a single living soul. I realize that I could not recommend such an approach to anyone else. Even for me, it was a bit much. One ends by falling into melancholy. . . ." Melancholic, expectant, suspended on the brink of what may be an impossible fusion, "Friedrich," so wrote the French sculptor David d'Angers, who visited the German master at Dresden in 1834, "[was] the sole landscape painter who until then had the power to move every part of my soul, the one who created a new genre: the tragedy of landscape."

## Storms provide the occasion for
## a peremptory affirmation of the gesturing hand

Whereas a mid-18th-century painter like Joseph Vernet would have organized his storms from "the exterior," as in scenography, by a disposition of conventional signs—zigzag lightning, a heeling ship, tumultuous waves—the modern artist realized a tenebrous sky by striving to get inside the image, to produce form and stroke, sign and gesture at one and the same time. If this corporeal proximity—this physical identification—remains relative in the art of Valenciennes, trained as he was in the classical tradition (Fig. 305), it bursts forth in Georges Michel (Fig. 306) for whom a tempest is a material precipitate, a whirlwind or cataract of pigment that can also congeal into almost incongruous forms—such as those tonglike shapes that together constitute both a rainbow shooting out from a muddy sky and the foreground extension of a river.

Michel was a marginal artist, an anarchic autodidact who was rediscovered by the Barbizon School. Montmartre served as his Alps and the Saint-Denis Plain as his Roman Campagna. A great connoisseur of Dutch painting, he earned his living for a while around 1800 fabricating "Ruisdaels" and "Hobbemas," which the dealer Le Brun appears to have sold as originals. But Michel's own style, like that of Constable, moved away from these influences, for the relation between his touch and the referent (the object painted) is even looser than in Cuyp or Van Goyen. The Frenchman's impetuous manner and his thick, flat impasto, which anticipated Courbet's Doubs landscapes, tend to identify pictorial material with telluric matter, clay with pigment.

304. John Constable (1776–1837). *Stonehenge.* c. 1836. Watercolor, 15¼×23¼". Victoria and Albert Museum, London.

305. Pierre Henri de Valenciennes (1750–1819). *Storm over a Lake.* c. 1784. Oil on paper on cardboard, 15¾×20½". Louvre.

306. Georges Michel (1763–1843). *Storm over the Seine Valley.* c. 1835. Oil on paper mounted on canvas, 1'8″×2'3½″. Musée des Beaux-Arts, Lyon.

Constable so manipulated the image in his watercolor of the megaliths at Stonehenge (Fig. 304) that this work stands apart from the main current of the artist's production. The painting matured over a long period (some sixteen years from the first sketches to the final version). And if the viewing angle and the disposition of the stones were fixed from the start, the sky assumed its character only at the end. Then, when he addressed himself to the sky, the painter worked rapidly, literally wiping the rainbow onto the paper (possibly with a sponge) and scratching in the clouds with a wide, stiff brush (most obviously in the darker areas). In order to bring out the brilliance of the whites, bits of paper were stripped away in the foreground as well as in the stones. Constable placed considerable importance on his skies. ''That landscape painter,'' he wrote in 1821, ''who does not make his skies a very material part of his composition, neglects to avail himself of one of his greatest aids. Sir Joshua Reynolds, speaking of the landscapes of Titian, of Salvador, and of Claude, says: 'Even their *skies* seem to sympathise with their subjects.' I have often been advised to consider my sky as '*a white sheet thrown behind the objects.*' Certainly, if the sky is obtrusive, as mine are, it is bad; but if it is evaded, as mine are not, it is worse; it must and always shall with me make an effectual part of the composition. It will be difficult to name a class of landscape in which the sky is not the keynote, the standard of scale, and the chief organ of sentiment.''

307. George Stubbs (1724–1806).
*Horse Attacked by a Lion.* c. 1765.
Oil on canvas, 2'2"×3'2¼".
National Gallery of Victoria
(bequest of Mr. Felton, 1949),
Melbourne.

308. George Stubbs.
*Horse Attacked by a Lion.*
c. 1760–65.
Oil on canvas, 8' × 10'10¾".
Yale Center for British Art
(Paul Mellon Collection),
New Haven.

# The horse, an ideogram of energy

Early in the 1760s, Great Britain's George Stubbs took inspiration from an antique group he saw in Rome—possibly also from an actual scene witnessed during a Moroccan sojourn—and, using a few synthetic, profile features (bent right leg, neck stretched backward and swollen, wild mane), assembled the emblematic image of a horse under attack—an image (Figs. 307–309) that would fertilize the Romantic imagination and come to full flower a half-century later (Figs. 310, 311). (The Louvre owns a copy of Stubbs' desperate horse, made in reverse, that is attributed to Géricault. See also the works of Ward, Barye, etc.) This was the period when Edmund Burke had just published his essay entitled *A Philosophical Inquiry into the Origin of Our Ideas of the Sublime and Beautiful* (1756), in which the author stated: "Whatever is fitted in any sort to excite the ideas of pain and danger, that is to say, whatever is in any sort terrible, or is conversant about terrible objects,

or operates in a manner analogous to terror, is a source of the sublime." Then, turning to the Bible (Job), Burke cited the example of the horse: "The horse in the light of an useful beast, fit for the plough, the road, the draft; in every social useful light, the horse has nothing sublime; but, is it thus that we are affected by him, 'whose neck is clothed with thunder, the glory of whose nostrils is terrible, who swalloweth the ground with fierceness and rage, neither believeth that it is the sound of the trumpet?' In this description [from Job 39], the useful character of the horse entirely disappears, and the terrible and sublime blaze out together."

A review of the dates on which Stubbs executed the many variants of his horse picture discloses a progressive expansion of the landscape surrounding the central theme, as if the image of energy and terror, initially concentrated in the animal group, were gradually diffused throughout the whole of nature. Compare the versions reproduced here.

309. George Stubbs. *Horse Attacked by a Lion*. 1762. Oil on canvas, 3'1½"×4'1¼".
Yale University Art Gallery (gift of the Yale University Art Gallery Associates), New Haven.

310. Eugène Delacroix (1798–1863). *Horse Frightened by a Storm.* 1824. Watercolor. 9½ × 12½″. Museum of Fine Arts, Budapest.

## A powerful propulsive discharge that, because of its truth, must be granted full sway

Delacroix, who in 1825 spent four months in London with his friend Bonington, took up Stubbs' horse theme (Figs. 307–309) and proceeded to rework it in rather significant ways. Whatever remained of classical geometry in the British prototype—the parallelism between the horizontal horse and the shape of the canvas, between the animal's profile attitude and the painting surface, all of which reflect the tradition of antique reliefs—was rejected by Delacroix (Fig. 311). The better to create the effect of an animal erupting onto the scene, the French master played on the illusion of depth and invested the central image with a violent, rotational movement. The horse's breast is broadly painted and then frontalized by patches of white, the

latter created by the nearly untouched paper. Meanwhile, the ascendant arabesque that traverses the entire sheet (from the tiger's tail to the horse's muzzle) functions mainly as a foil for the rectilinearity of the support. To Delacroix, art was the peremptory advent of a curve (or a play of countercurves). If the line retained something of the energy of the hand that drew it, any accompanying imperfection or loss of detail mattered little, since benefits of a more important kind had been gained. "My picture acquires a torsion, an energetic movement that must absolutely be completed," the artist wrote in 1824 concerning his *Massacre at Chios*. Later, referring to the hunting scenes of Rubens, he said: "I love his grandiloquence, also

311. Eugène Delacroix. *Tiger Attacking a Wild Horse*. c. 1825 28 Watercolor varnished in places, 7×9¾". Cabinet des Dessins, Louvre.

his extravagant and liberated forms. . . . There is as much to learn from his exaggerations and swollen forms as from exact imitations.''

To begin with, Delacroix saw painting as a powerful, propulsive discharge that, because of its essential truth, had to be granted full sway. The artist spoke in 1850 of ''the fury of the brush'' and of ''lucky accidents that are the artist's passion'' and extolled ''the pictorial licenses [to which] every master often owes his most sublime effects: Rembrandt's lack of finish and Rubens' extravagance. Mediocrities would never dare such things: they never exceed themselves.'' And four years later: ''I pity those who work tranquilly and coldly. I am convinced that everything they do can only be cold

and tranquil, and only put the viewer in a worse state of coldness and tranquility.'' This would seem to imply that what must occur between the conception a project and its final state is a laisser-faire freedom, the playing out of an irrational and uncontrollable urge, the work of an incoercible physical drive. The painting is declared as much as it is formulated. It ceases to be the product of preliminary thought subsequently projected upon the painting surface and becomes the adventure of a hand following its own random impulse across the sheet. The work of art invents itself in the process of being made. If Delacroix's *Horse Frightened by a Storm* (Fig. 310) does not lack for morphological analogies with the watercolor above (Fig.

311),provided it is viewed in reverse, the artist did go further here in manifesting a concern that would preoccupy him for thirty years: how to make the work an organic whole in which fore- and background share the same treatment. In this instance he succeeded by means of an overall light and fluid texture whose transparency everywhere discloses the underlying white of the paper.

## Painting derives its impact not from details but from the furious movement that sweeps them up

312. Eugene Delacroix. *Tiger Hunt*. 1854. Oil on canvas, 2′4¾″×3′¼″. Louvre.

313. Eugène Delacroix (1798–1863). *Combat of the Giaour and the Pasha*. 1853. Oil on canvas, 2′5¼″×1′11½″. Musée du Petit Palais, Paris.

A quarter of a century later, a four-month sojourn in Morocco (1832) continued to provide Delacroix with his favorite subjects. In 1854, when commissioned by the state to paint a picture on a theme of his own choice, the artist decided on a lion hunt (the sketch for which is reproduced in Fig. 428), certain that it would express both his admiration for Rubens and his taste for the Orient. And at the same time that this continuity would evince the unforgettable experience of North Africa, it would also assure him a repertoire of forms and colors that could be treated according to his own fantasy, without his having to be overly concerned about realism. The exotic was, above all else, a device for gaining narrative freedom.

In the paintings seen here, Delacroix laid out upon a blocked, irregular ground a kind of chromatic vortex, an oval and rather flat mass of color that looks as if it might have been generated by an expanding, girational movement. The strokes, ''plunged deep like sword thrusts'' (Théophile Silvestre), reinforce the lightning swiftness of the action. Each one assumes ''the direction of the form itself,'' as Thoré noted in 1847, ''and contributes toward a sense of relief. As the modeling turns, the artist's brush turns in the same direction, and the impasto, which follows the direction of the light, never goes against the illumination radiating throughout the picture.'' ''The objective,'' Silvestre continues, ''is not only achieved but also traversed by the violence of the artist's hand.''

Renewing a tradition that, by way of Rubens, went back to Leonardo da Vinci's *Battle of Anghiari,* Delacroix sought to seize the most intense moment of a crisis. He painted the precise instant when the sharp edge of a blade is about to slice into the flesh of an animal or a warrior. In the words of Baudelaire: ''He expresses power not by the thickness of the muscles, but by the tension of the nerves.''

The picture ceases to be an accumulation of forms and becomes an organism. Its impact does not derive from details and their treatment but from the furious movement that sweeps them up, distorting the imagery as required in order to subordinate each part to the effect of the whole. ''Delacroix,'' Silvestre wrote in 1855, ''gives his figures movements and pathetic gestures that, carried away by forces of energy beyond the material limits of nature, conspire by their very disorder to produce an illusion in the mind of the viewer and draw him irresistibly into the world of dreams.'' As for the artist, a journal entry made as early as 1822 gives this evidence of his feeling: ''In painting, a mysterious bridge is erected between the soul of the figures and that of the spectator.''

The period had a great interest in the circulation of fluids and in the energy thrown off by bodies. ''We project outside ourselves a wealth of power,'' asserted Balzac, who believed that ''we influence by means of that living power, which seeks to impose itself on the beings and things that surround us.'' For Delacroix, the picture was a place through which energy would pass and accumulate before moving on to irradiate the viewer. Matisse too was to believe in the therapeutic virtues of art.

314. Eugène Delacroix. *Arab on Horseback Attacked by a Lion*. 1849. Oil on canvas, 18×14½″. Art Institute of Chicago.

# Unity guaranteed by the repetitive automatism of the painter's energetic wrist

315. Eugène Delacroix (1798–1863). *Lion Devouring a Horse.* c. 1840. Watercolor, 7¾ × 10¼″.
Cabinet des Dessins, Louvre.

Delacroix used stabbing, repetitive gestures to fix his wild felines' bristling manes from end to end. The automatism of the wrist—not, the artist insisted, the hand or the fingers—guaranteed the unity of the lion's head reproduced opposite (scaled larger than the original), whatever the medium used: graphite or watercolor. In Fig. 316 the comma-like strokes begin at the muzzle and expand centrifugally, as if combed over the sheet. Delacroix then enclosed the head in a wide halo of brown, applying it later just as he did the gray highlights. It was his gesture, with its power to weigh upon pencil or brush and thus modulate the thickness of strokes, that truly interested Delacroix. Thus, the concern in the work seen here was less the drawing of a lion than the evolution of the animal through the action of the hand.

In *Lion Devouring a Horse* (Fig. 315), the disheveled mane looks like the raveled ends of the dark, "braided" hatchings formed all over the creature's coat. The graphite marks preceded those from the brush, which were not superimposed but made to play their role side by side. A chaplet of white reserve runs the full length of the beast's left front paw and leg, while additional reserves form the claws on the left paw and the horse's extended tongue.

The contemporaries of Delacroix all noted his fine-tuned nature, often comparing him to a hypersensitive seismograph. "Endowed with an impressionable, nervous, intuitive, and melancholic constitution, a nature open to passions and sorrows alike, he suffers every quiver and quake that human beings can experience," wrote Théophile Thoré in 1837. According to Théophile Silvestre, "the atmosphere in his studio is so hot that grass snakes would be happy living there. This ardent, yet cold-blooded man is always coiled up like the python in the zoo. . . . The sensations that course through his delicate nerves—faster than electricity on telegraph wires—send him reeling twenty times a day" (1855).

316. Eugène Delacroix. *Head of a Lion Roaring.* c. 1843. Watercolor, 7 × 7½". Cabinet des Dessins, Louvre.

## Delacroix strove to preserve the impulse of primary sketches . . .

''Delacroix,'' wrote Baudelaire in his long obituary of 1863, ''was passionately in love with passion and coldly determined to seek out the means to express passion in the most visible manner.'' The whole elaborate preparation of *Sardanapalus* (see also Figs. 319–322) involved nothing more than a determined effort to retain, right through to the finished work, the incandescence of an inspiration clearly nourished by personal obsessions and to transmute ''into musical and arabesque terms'' (as the artist expressed it) all that his erotic reverie had aroused within him. (Philippe Jullian, in his biography of Delacroix, speaks, in his own way, of ''an assembly of women twisting and prostrating themselves under the sword as if in rapture''.) The artist began with various pencil sketches—almost formless things rendered in a ''naïve'' style—designed to establish certain features that haunted him (the hand of Sardanapalus, the woman seen from behind). Rather quickly, however, he advanced to a general study made in ink and then in oil, working impulsively, even brutally, and using a stroke much more violent and broken than any seen in the large picture reproduced in Fig. 320. Here was the decisive moment of the entire process, and it established once and for all the painting's diagonal disposition, its rhythm, and the cursive movement of the drawing. What remained was the clarification of certain details or figures so as to make them more legible in the ultimate version measuring more than 16 feet wide. This stage then brought forth the large pastel studies reproduced in Figs. 317 and 318, studies that the artist would incorporate virtually unaltered into the Salon painting.

Delacroix's work consisted mainly of ''organizing'' his compulsions and of ''proceeding fast enough and with sufficient sureness to allow nothing of the intensity of the action or idea to evaporate,'' according to Baudelaire. The artist extended this thrift into the whole of his life, causing him to become suspicious not only in love but even in the ordinary exchanges of daily existence. ''He feared conversation as if it were debauchery,'' continued Baudelaire, ''a dissipation in which he risked losing his power.'' This also accounts for the maniacal concern that the artist had for the pristine cleanness of his implements. ''That was very understandable insofar as every precaution had to be taken in order to assure agile and decisive execution.''

317. Eugène Delacroix (1798–1863). *Study for the Death of Sardanapalus.* 1827–28. Pastel, red chalk, white chalk on brown paper, 15¾ × 10¾". Cabinet des Dessins, Louvre.

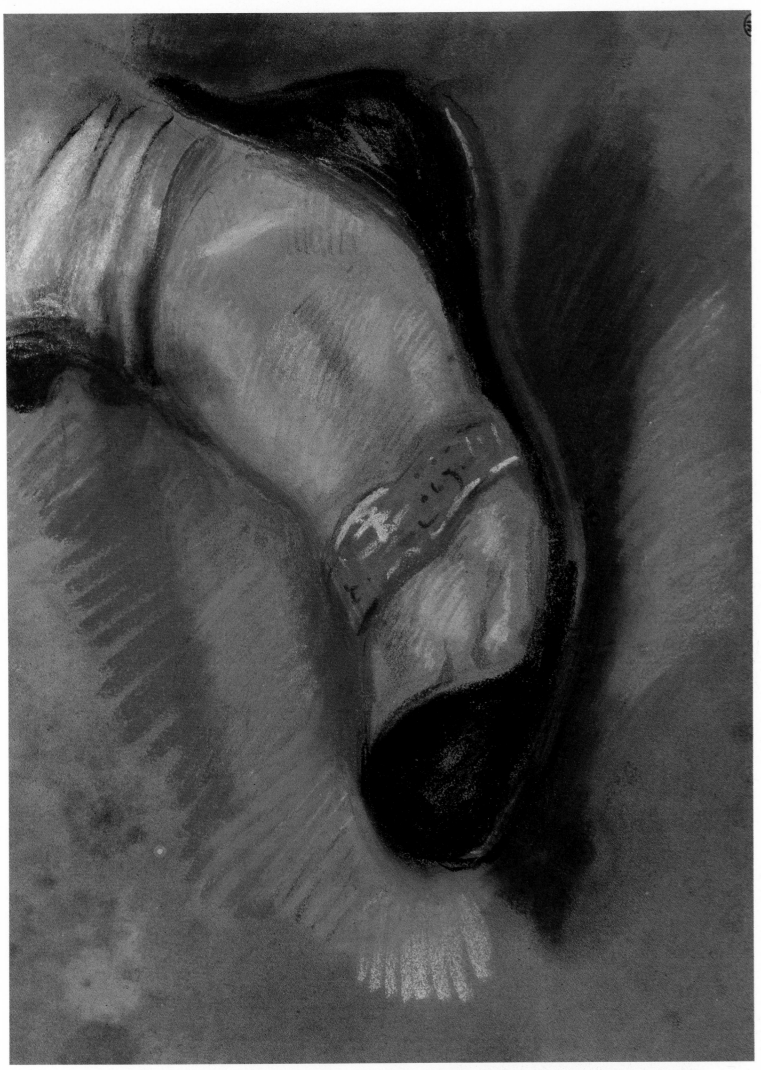

318. Eugène Delacroix. *Study for the Death of Sardanapalus*. 1827–28. Pastel, conté crayon, red and white chalk on brown paper, 11¾×9″.
Cabinet des Dessins, Louvre.

159

### . . . and the feverish élan of drawing right through to the finished work

319. Eugène Delacroix (1798–1863). *Studies for the Death of Sardanapalus*. 1827–28. Pastel over pencil and chalk (red and white), 7¾×17¼″. Cabinet des Dessins, Louvre.

320. Eugène Delacroix. *Sketch for the Death of Sardanapalus*. 1827–28. Oil on canvas, 2′8″×3′3¼″. Louvre.

321. Eugène Delacroix. *Death of Sardanapalus*. 1828. Oil on canvas, 12′11½″×16′3″. Louvre.

Delacroix simply unleashed his exploding impulses whenever he needed, for example, to solve a problem of linkage between two disparate components, as in the lower left corner of the despot's couch and the foreground area strewn with tangled jewelry (Fig. 322). Such a study actually reveals how the artist "trusted" his hand to invent an arrangement capable of blending heterogeneous elements into the same movement.

We know that *The Death of Sardanapalus* (Fig. 321) had its source in Lord Byron's 1821 play about the fall of the last king of the second Assyrian dynasty, which came as he lay in his besieged palace at the end of the 9th century B.C. "Lounging upon a splendid bed, at the top of an immense pyre," Delacroix wrote in the catalogue to the Salon of 1828, "Sardanapalus orders the eunuch and guards to slaughter his women and pages, even the horses and dogs belonging to his favorite. None of the objects that had served his pleasures was to survive him. . . ." As it has very often been observed, Delacroix's massacre was a pastiche of his own making, and the play, like the antique sources themselves, contained no collective sacrifice, no woman hanged in the background, and no ceremonial bed. Byron, in fact, had simply mentioned a favorite's suicide, an event that occurred offstage. The Marquis de Sade, it would seem, had taken over from Byron in the artist's imagination, as if to illustrate this remark made by Sainte-Beuve in 1843: "I venture to state without fear of being contradicted that Byron and Sade . . . have been the principal sources of inspiration for our moderns, the one official and visible, the other clandestine, but not too clandestine."

J.J. Spector, in his book entitled *The Death of Sardanapalus* (1974), remarked that the flames mentioned in the text are scarcely evident, their place assumed by the spiraling bodies of the concubines. As for the artist's

322. Eugène Delacroix. *Study for the Death of Sardanapalus.* 1827–28. Pen, watercolor and pencil, 10¼ × 12½".
Cabinet des Dessins, Louvre.

contemporaries, they were generally taken aback and even scandalized by the painting's organization. ''He wanted to create disorder and forgot that disorder itself has a logic,'' wrote Jal in 1827. And indeed Delacroix had attempted to reconcile a diversity of styles:

● On the one hand, he cropped the scene in a highly modern way, allowing the frame to interrupt and thereby suspend the narrative. (In Fig. 321 see the man on the right cut in half and on the left the head and breast of a horse, a horse that recalls the manner of Gros);

● On the other hand, he devised a scenic space of little depth whose ground plane is tilted forward like a theatre stage and divided between a foreground aligned parallel to the painting surface, in keeping with Neoclassical principles, and a receding perspective, like that in Baroque paintings, crowned by the half-erect bust of a monarch, ''swathed in muslin, and posed like a woman'' (Baudelaire), his fingers and toes adorned with rings.

323. Richard Dadd (1817–86). *Sketch of an Idea for Crazy Jane*. 1855.
Watercolor, 14¼ × 10¼". Bethlem Royal Hospital and the Maudsley Hospital, Beckenham.

# A linear web, or trap, of grasses "manages" the surface and assures its planar continuity

For his *Crazy Jane* (Fig. 323) Richard Dadd (see p. 88) borrowed a character from a popular English ballad about a young girl who went mad when abandoned by a lover. But the picture's effect of unreality may depend upon a single detail: the thin filament of shadow that seems to double all the various stems and stalks brandished by the heroine. It makes the botanical vestiges look pasted down, upon a sky painted like cardboard and pressed flat against the figure's silhouette. (The same sort of treatment appears in the skirt, here however without violating the conventions of realism.) Raised up like a net or curtain, the linear, floating web of branches, ribbons, ivy, and peacock feather assures the continuity of a pictorial surface on which colors and masses progressively lighten toward the top of the image. Patricia Allderidge has observed in her catalogue that the dark band across the bottom of the skirt serves as an extension of the tree-lined horizon, as if to consolidate the figure and provide a better anchor for it. We are told that the model for Jane was a male, a fellow inmate of the artist at Bethlem Hospital.

In Dadd's *Bacchanale* (Fig. 324), the startling accumulation of faces in a twice-reduced space (in width as well as in depth) would recall the crowded scenes painted by Hieronymus Bosch (*Christ Carrying the Cross*) or Dürer (*Christ Among the Doctors*) were it not for the fact that the smallest plastic component here is not the human image but rather the abstract curve. The almond eyelids, the irises, pupils, and brows, the lips, the cup and its content, even the large grasses projected across the entire surface, share in the general principle of curvature and flexion, thereby reinforcing the picture's feminine, nostalgic theme.

324. Richard Dadd. *Bacchanalian Scene*. 1862.
Oil on wood, 14¼ × 9½". Private collection.

The twisting thrust
of tree limbs
projects
the freedom of drawing
into every corner
of the planar space

325. Jean-François Millet (1814–75). *The Carrefour de l'Épine, Fontainebleau Forest.* 1866–67. Pastel, 1′7″×2′½″.
Musée des Beaux-Arts (Donation Granville), Dijon.

326. Achille Etna Michallon (1796–1822). *Oak and Reeds.* c. 1820. Drawing, three pencils on paper, 14½×19¾″.
Cabinet des Dessins, Louvre.

327. Pierre Henri de Valenciennes (1750–1819). *Large Tree*. c. 1874. Oil on paper, 13¾×18½". Louvre.

In Valenciennes' oil study reproduced above (Fig. 327), the tree limbs trail off into thin brown filaments drawn with a light touch and the edge of a drying brush, as if to explore, occupy, and survey the picture surface.

The liberated calligraphy in the handling of the foliage, consisting of simple strokes applied, or dabbed on, with the tip of a brush, succeeds in creating a screen between the spectator and a distant landscape (Italy's Lake Nemi). The formula is one that the Impressionists would revive almost a century later. As worked out here, the theme permits a loosening of the natural link or contiguity between branches and leaves. In the *Large Tree,* therefore, the linear component (the boughs) has not been invariably articulated on the mass of color held in suspension (the leaves).

Moreover, Valenciennes also anticipated Impressionism by punctuating his trunks with light-toned, lozenge-shaped, form-defining accents whose effect is to break up the appearance of woody compactness.

(The same sort of coiling, convoluted movement can be found in another iconographical genre, that of the fantastic. The hydras, dragons, and other sea serpents which populated Western painting from the time of Uccello and Carpaccio had a plentiful resurgence at the end of the 18th century in the art of Mortimer, West, Fuseli, Blake, etc.)

Pupil of Valenciennes and friend as well as teacher of Corot, Michallon became, despite his premature death, an all-important trail-blazer in the formulation of modern landscape

painting as Valenciennes taught it at the École des Beaux-Arts (see p. 197). Even if Michallon's manner recalls that of the Dutch, the drawing in the Louvre (Fig. 326), its trunk glinting and even broken up with reddish lights, conforms to the main line of recommendations made by Valenciennes: "Do not fail to do studies of beautiful trees, either isolated or in a mass. Apply yourself to all the details of bark, moss, roots, branch system, even the ivy twining about it. . . ."

In Millet's painting of a dead birch (Fig. 325) the solitary limb standing erect and parallel to the picture plane resembles a fracture, like that of a cracked window. Consummate science and highly diversified execution animate every inch of the surface. The treatment of the trunk, for instance, is so precise

that, along with its haunting profile, the vaguely anthropomorphic form all but assures a sympathetic identification on the part of the viewer. It is in this textural sophistication, in the infinite variety of the individual touches, that we must see the most likely source of the divisionism practiced by the Italians Segantini, Previati, Pellizza, etc.

# Pigment troweled onto the canvas in large, flat strokes

329. Thomas Couture (1815–79). *The Grand Duchess Stephanie of Baden, study for the Baptism of the Prince Imperial.* c. 1856–62. Oil on canvas, 2'1½" × 2'8". Musée National du Palais, Compiègne.

328. Jean-Baptiste Carpeaux (1827–75).
*Madame Carpeaux en déshabillé.*
c. 1873.
Oil on canvas, 12¼ × 8".
Musée du Petit Palais,
Paris.

The development of the rough sketch at midcentury was the doing of artists who sought to reveal and express the "painterliness" of painting. This can be seen not only in the art but also in the teaching of Couture, and in the pictorial work created by Carpeaux as a sideline to his sculpture. What such artists wanted to do was emphasize that aspect of the painting process which refers to nothing but the handling and not to any program of commemoration, education, or description.

The bravura of Carpeaux (Fig. 328), in his intense, vigorously worked sketches and his powerfully built-up impastoes, resembles nothing so much as the transposition of the gesture of a sculptor pressing his bits of clay against the yet-unformed mass present upon the prop. As for Couture (Fig. 329), he advocated long brushes conducive to a generous application of pigment.

Opposed to colors mixed on the palette, he counseled his pupils to construct in successive layers, while making the most of the paint's transparency: "Ask the suppliers for what they call *couleurs broyées serrées* ["fine-ground colors"]; still better results can be had from their superimposition."

The sketch reproduced above is the product of a rapid sequence of operations: the application of gray underpainting partially covering a black ground; the distribution of white accents to model the dress; the disposition of a fine web of tiny bistre veins to define the folds; and finally the application over the whole of a new series of fat, white touches, all rough and grainy, which heighten and extend the train toward the left in a chaplet of masterly flourishes signifying nothing but the freedom and bravura of the artist's hand.

Couture was fascinated by his own studies but had little understanding of how in the final work to preserve the "fire" of the first stroke. He left a great number of unfinished canvases, even those begun under official commission, and his *Baptism of the Prince Imperial,* ordered by Napoleon III, would never see the light of day. Thus, it is mainly rough sketches that account for the present revival of interest in Couture. Albert Boime has demonstrated how Manet, who other than Puvis de Chavannes was Couture's most famous pupil, continued to show the influence of his teacher even after master and pupil had broken with one another. The study reproduced in Fig. 329 is a "curiosity," since it bears, upside down, a male "academy" that tradition, owing to an inscription on the back of the canvas, attributes to the young Manet.

330. Jean-Baptiste Carpeaux (1827–75). *Berezowski's Attempt upon the Life of the Emperor.* c. 1867. Oil on canvas, 4'3¼"×6'4¾". Louvre.

331. Jean-Baptiste Carpeaux. *Ball at the Tuileries.* 1867. Oil on canvas, 2′1½″ × 1′9¼″. Louvre.

## From the *prestezza* of Carpeaux, an art that reaches halfway from El Greco to the gestural painting of modernist abstraction

Brilliantly virtuoso, the slashing, lightning-speed style of Carpeaux and the sheer authority of his touch give this artist a singular position, halfway between El Greco and Magnasco and the gestural painters of the 20th century. But we should also note that, for all its velocity, the brush remains subordinated to the object it denotes (dress or horse) and refers directly to that object. The process simply involves reduction rather than equivalence. Respecting both identity and structure, a stroke of white in the *Ball at the Tuileries* (Fig. 331) suffices to indicate trousers, while a gather of orange streaks can be read as an evening gown. The doublet worn by Alexander III, with the Empress Eugénie on his arm, has been rendered as a red patch fringed about with white accents. In *Berezowski's Attempt upon the Life of the Emperor* (Fig. 330)—its subject an event that Carpeaux witnessed on June 6, 1876, near the cascade in the Bois de Boulogne (when Napoleon III was

saved by a rearing horse)—each light-toned dab, as in Guardi, stands for a face or an arm. Also from the year 1867 is Manet's *View of the Universal Exhibition,* where the system of touches is of a different order. A few arbitrary Xs of red on a green ground signify by simple allusion a planting of flowers. Here we see not reduction but transposition, a calculated liberation of the stroke, which no longer stands for an object but merely provides the raw elements of a suggestion, an atmosphere. If Carpeaux makes contact with the modernist sensibility, it is through his nervous intensity, the *prestezza* of his brushwork, more than in his figural mode, which remains traditional.

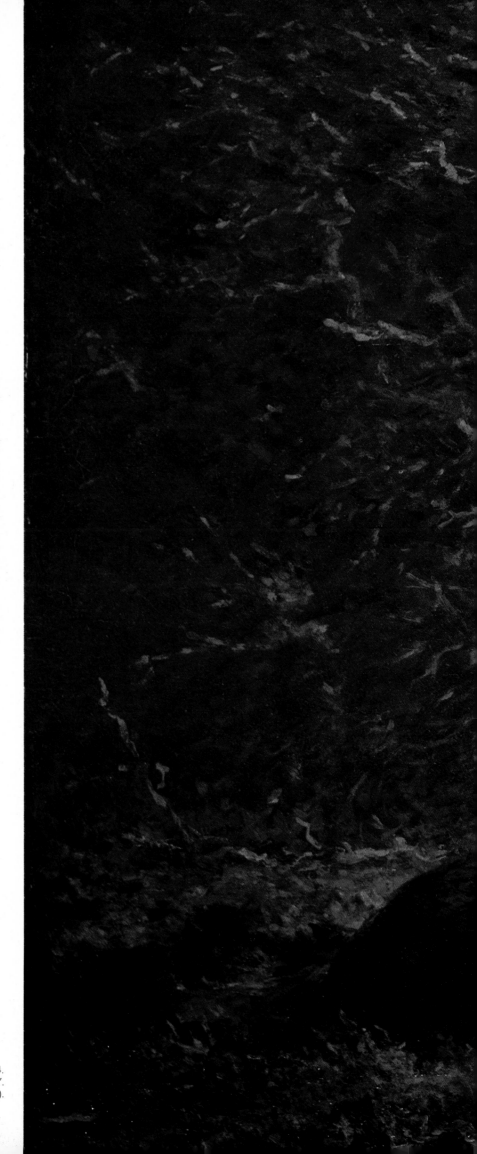

## Trapped in a fretwork of fiery tongues exploding from edge to edge

In what appears to be a genre scene, Millet adopted an hallucinatory mode to describe a memory that, in the last weeks of his life, had suddenly come to him from his youth in Normandy. ''When I was a child,'' he explained to a visitor, ''there were great flights of wild pigeons that perched in the trees by night. We would go there with torches, and the birds, blinded by the light, could be clubbed to death in the hundreds.'' ''And you have not seen that again since you were a child?'' ''No, but everything comes back to me when I work.''[11]

Whether pressed against a luminous, backlighting zone or all but absorbed into the ground where they crawl, the actors seem virtually trapped by the enveloping fretwork of fiery tongues. (The effect resembles the woven, radiating mass of a bird's nest, a mesh of hair—or indeed a net.) From edge to edge the picture surface has been activated by accents of high-key color—broken lines, scrapings, serpentine trails of thick medium, flourishes—all of whose turns and breaks reflect the painter's impulsive, jerky gestures and evoke something like an organic implosion, a commotion, or violence that has been suspended and even frozen.

''As the mood of the painting works its effect on us,'' writes Herbert, ''we instinctively realize that in the apocalyptic nature of this light and in the violence of the action, the artist is describing a horrifying event, for which the only appropriate term is murder.''

332. Jean-François Millet (1814–75). *The Birdnesters.* 1874. Oil on canvas, 2′5½″×3′¼″. Philadelphia Museum of Art (the William L. Elkins Collection).

# CHAPTER III

# The Blurring of Form

333. D. Mondo (1730–1806).
*Saint Vincent Ferrer.* c. 1800.

334. F. Goya (1746–1828).
*Witch and Wizard.* 1820–22.

335. H. Daumier (1808–79).
*Waiting at the Station.* 1858.

The Neapolitan painter Mondo, like Goya and Daumier, painted with a thick, heavy medium. Heads seem modeled in the cushion of pigment. Instead of faces depicted upon a support, there is a crust of paint in which faces are implied.

336. T. Gainsborough (1727–88).
*Study for the Portrait of Lady Clarges.* c. 1778.

Reynolds (1788): "I have often imagined that this unfinished manner contributed even to that striking resemblance for which [Gainsborough's] portraits are so remarkable. . . . in this undermined manner there is the general effect; . . . the imagination supplies the rest."

In his *Philosophy of the Enlightenment* Ernst Cassirer has demonstrated how the art of 17th-century classicism derived its coherence from the logico-mathematical model developed by Descartes (1596–1650). There was, Cassirer found, a "perfect accord between the scientific and the artistic ideals of the age, since aesthetic theory had no other ambition than to follow the path already broken by mathematics and physics." Reducing matter to extension and the body to finite space, the Cartesian model implied a rigorous, univocal, and intangible definition of the depicted object.

Meanwhile, parallel to this normative mode, another current emerged toward the end of the 17th century, an aesthetic that would receive its philosophical formulation a century later in Germany. "It might be said," writes Cassirer, "that alongside the aesthetic ideal of rigor and exactitude there is another, diametrically opposed ideal—that of inexactitude. . . . The aesthetic faculty . . . is not the prisoner of the 'clear and distinct.' Not only does it allow a certain margin of indeterminacy, it also demands and creates such a margin, since the aesthetic imagination takes fire and develops only in the presence of something that is not yet fully defined or thought out. . . . The accent falls less on proximity than on distance with regard to the object. . . . Nevertheless, an aesthetic idea [derives its value and its charm] from the multiplicity of relations it condenses within itself, and this charm is hardly diminished by the fact that we can never visually possess this multiplicity, or resolve it analytically into its constituent parts."

These few observations help us perceive the aesthetic links that join painters as different as Gainsborough and Goya, Turner and Delacroix. Inexactitude, indetermination, a sense of distance from objects, formal and figural polysemy, the infinity of meaning—these are some of the characteristics of a kind of painting that Paul Valéry has classified as generalized or *formless form*: "Objects, colors, masses, contours, volumes . . . whose only property is to take up space. . . . To say that these things are formless is not to claim that they have no forms, but that their forms do not allow us to replace them with something clearly delineated and identifiable. . . . And, in effect, generalized or formless forms leave behind only an impression of potentiality. . . ."

Amorphousness resists denomination. Fleeting and fluctuating, the inchoate shape cannot be reduced to a name. According to Germaine de Staël, the arts *pre-exist* verbal language: "They are above thought. Their language is that of color, or form, or sound. If we could depict the impressions to which our soul is susceptible prior to the acquisition of verbal language, then we would better understand the effects of painting and music."

This implies a clear distinction between the object depicted (the subject, theme, or motif) and the pictorial (formal, plastic) elements of line, material, color, etc. The separation of subject and form might occur first as the relative autonomy of the painter's stroke vis-à-vis the exigencies of representation. Here, we have only to consider the "blurriness" of the portraits painted by Gainsborough or Goya (Figs. 333–336). But it also entailed the increasing independence of the painter's medium—his pigments—which tended to break free of the motif, to become simply patches of color and create texture—

to "speak" for themselves. Eventually, the idea took root that pleasure results from the artist's dual care for, or oscillation between, two competing demands: fictive three-dimensionality and the ostensible presence of pictorial elements. Thus, it became impossible for the viewer to submit to the picture's illusion without his being continually aware of the empirical means by which the illusion was produced.

This explains the Romantics' eagerness to retain in the final work the qualities of the sketch, the study, the preparatory drawing. The painter, in his disposition of mass, would refuse to specify, preferring to leave genus and species indistinct. And the less defined the theme, the more articulate the material. Herein may lie the difference between this approach and that of Leonardo da Vinci in his *non finito.* With Leonardo, "the difficult birth of the work, [the artist's] flight before its completion, his indifference to its ultimate emergence," as Freud put it, expressed an individual situation, a symptomatic state more than an intellectual choice. Characteristic of his time, the great Florentine viewed the sketch as merely transitional, a work leading to something more final and finished. For him, vagueness and imprecision were important only insofar as they led to the pictorial realization of the object (the closed sign).

An important distinction, introduced by Goethe, between *allegory* and *symbol* sheds light upon the two opposing approaches to figuration: "Allegory transforms appearance into a concept, the concept into an image, in such a way that the concept remains wholly within the image, allowing itself to be grasped and possessed integrally, and can thus be stated verbally. The symbol transforms appearance into an idea, the idea into an image, but in such a way that the idea in the image remains forever active and beyond attainment." In his commentary on this passage, Tsvetan Todorov remarks that, for Goethe, "the meaning of an allegory is finite, that of a symbol infinite, inexhaustible; moreover, in allegory meaning is complete, final, and thus in some sense dead; whereas in the symbol it is active and alive. Here again, the difference between symbol and allegory is defined primarily by the task it imposes on the mind of the spectator."

As soon as the work becomes inexhaustible (indeterminate, polysemic), so does the commentary made upon it. This brings us into the age of interpretation. For example, the antirationalist Romantic theoretician Wackenroder wrote that "the pleasure afforded by great works of art never ceases; it lasts forever. We always believe that we can penetrate such works even more deeply; yet they always exceed our grasp, and we cannot conceive of a point at which our soul will have depleted them." And if no amount of looking can penetrate to the bottom of such a work, then every consideration of it will be different. No longer is the picture a self-contained object, an ever-present, all-evident entity that speaks its truth once and for all, but rather a set of *relations* between the painting and the probing consciousness that scrutinizes it. This means a 90-degree rotation, wherein the spectator emerges as the essential conduit of all aesthetic speculation. *Empiricism* triumphs. For Hume, Cassirer notes, "a supposedly correct value judgment does not pretend to deal with the thing itself, but only with the *relations* between objects and ourselves, subjects who per-

337–340. A. Cozens (1717–86). Four plates from
*A New Method of Assisting the Invention
in Drawing Original Compositions of Landscapes.* 1785.

The teaching method devised by Alexander Cozens
involved a figurative interpretation of random blots or
stains produced accidentally upon the paper support.
Cozens insisted that the artist could obtain several
different drawings from the same blot.

ceive, sense, and judge. This relation may, in each particular case, be 'true' without always being strictly the same, since the nature and thus the truth of a relation never depends on only one of the two terms it unites, but on the way in which they are reciprocally self-defining." Hume wrote that "all sentiment is right, . . . Beauty is no quality in things themselves: it exists in the mind which contemplates them, and in each mind perceives a different beauty."

Aesthetics merges with psychology, and a painting, from its inception, seems to contain, like a mold, the presence of the viewer as *coproducer.* For Hogarth, in the mid-18th century, this incorporation of the spectator required nothing more than the stimulation of his eye. It was simply a matter of mobilizing the sensory-motor apparatus by an abstract system of linear or chromatic contrasts based on irregularity, surprise, a change in the direction of curves, and the optical fusion of colors. The depicted scene would matter less than the "wanton kind of chace" in which the eye is engaged.

Later formulations would allow the spectator to be addressed in a less automatic, more imaginative way. Alexander Cozens, for example, provided a kind of theoretical guide and illustrated demonstration in a *New Method of Assisting the Invention in Drawing Original Compositions of Landscapes* (1785). Here the English artist-writer set out to systematize one of the intuitions experienced by Leonardo, who advised painters to "look upon a wall covered with dirt, or the odd appearance of some streaked stones," certain that they would discover there "several things like landscapes, battles, clouds, uncommon attitudes, humorous faces, draperies, etc. Out of this confused mass of objects, the mind will be furnished with an abundance of designs and subjects perfectly new." The stains that Cozens worked with were not taken from walls, but freely produced, with pen and ink, on sheets of paper. Through a series of interventions he made them yield up figurative compositions (Figs. 337–340). "The blot is not a drawing, but an assemblage of accidental shapes, from which a drawing may be made. It is a hint, or crude resemblance of the whole effect of a picture, except the keeping and colouring; that is to say, it gives an idea of the masses of light and shade, as well as the forms, contained in a finished composition."

The *tachiste*—the artist who works with blots, stains, or patches—does not refer either to an existing site or to a model painting. He himself produces the textural *magma* from which his figures will emerge. Instead of the ancient studio technique—prescribed from Alberti in the 15th century through Ingres and Couture in the 19th century—of squinting before an object in order to apprehend its large, overall masses, the painter could now commence with an a priori inscription, on a sheet of paper, of a chaplet or sequence of ink blots. Generated by the chance movements of the hand, they constitute a "natural" and not an iconic ground. Cozens' method is *inductive* rather than *projective*, which means that his landscapes emanated from material givens (and thus constraints) instead of springing forth, fully formed, from the painter's brow. (For more on this distinction, see Chapter II, pp. 97–101.) The artist was keenly aware of the difference between what he called *sketching* ("transfer ideas from the mind to the paper") and *blotting* ("make varied spots and

shapes with ink on paper, producing accidental forms without lines, from which ideas are presented to the mind. . . . To sketch, is to delineate ideas; blotting suggests them."

In actual practice, the distinction that Cozens made between chance (the arbitrary) and predetermination (the motivated) was not as rigorous as this formulation would suggest. To view the stains on the page as purely aleatory would be to assume that the moving hand represented "nature itself" at work, thus a hand free in its operations of all cultural influence. But the artist himself admitted that this was not the case: "All the shapes are rude and unmeaning, as they are formed with the swiftest hand. But at the same time there appears a general disposition of these masses, producing one comprehensive form, which may be conceived and properly intended before the blot is begun." And as Gombrich observes, however freely formed these ink-spotted sheets may appear, their general morphology embodies the classical landscape conventions defined by Claude in the 17th century. The hand may believe itself to be wandering at random; in reality, it reproduces cultural schemata that the artist has interiorized. The sky, for instance, is always carefully placed. Moreover, Cozens suggested that his method be applied to history painting since "it is the speediest and the surest means of fixing a rude whole of the most transient and complicated image of any subject in the painter's mind."

The respective contributions of the arbitrary and the motivated remain variable and thus fluctuate. However, it is not their complex relationship that interests us in this chapter, but rather the method's propaedeutic function within the general context of an age that modified the way in which works of art would be read. Cozens' method assumed the status of a precedent or model, insofar as it furnished material proof in support of the new interpretive mechanisms demanded by the paintings of Turner, Goya, or Delacroix. What Cozens demonstrated was the role the viewer would play in the scene represented. In realizing on the paper support the passage from the *blot* to the precise delineation of a landscape, the interpreter is not so much painting the scene as rehearsing the process of elaboration that will eventually be required of the spectator. To elaborate is not to decipher. It is not a matter of deriving a solution that the artist has foreseen from the start. The work contains no meaning already in place. Each agglomeration of marks, Cozens insisted, calls for an unlimited number of readings (and readers). The mark is not merely polysemic, it is *open*[1]—that is, both formally predetermined (the array of manipulated blots) and indeterminate, by virtue of the numerous, or even innumerable, solutions that the modified marks suggest to the spectator or spectators.

Moreover, as Jean-Claude Lébensztejn has remarked, Cozens' *Method* also proposed, in principle, the equivalence of inked and "reserved" zones. Indeed, the author defined the "true blot" as "an assemblage of dark shapes or masses made with ink upon a piece of paper, and likewise of light ones produced by the paper being left blank." White equals black and neither has any meaning except through the presence of the other. Thus, the interpretive function assumes ever-greater importance as the virgin, untouched areas acquire the character of images and themselves, in their structural relation to

341. J. B. Greuze (1725–1805).
*Study for the Punished Son.*

Applied rapidly, ink joins with the "reserve" to form a light-dark pattern that transcends the delineation of figures.

342. J. H. Mortiner (1740–79).
*The Captive.* 1781.

343. F. Goya (1746–1828).
*General Folly,*
from *Los Disparates.* c. 1815–24.

"Reserves" form a network of bright, interdependent touches challenging the coherence of the figuration.

their opposite (the inked zones), come to represent large segments of the landscape.

What Cozens made visually explicit—what he demonstrated—by his *Method*, theoreticians like Roger de Piles had, from the beginning of the 18th century, perceived as important. "As there are styles of thought," wrote de Piles, "so there are also styles of execution . . . the firm style and the polished style. . . . The firm style animates the work and makes us forgive its flaws; and the polished style finishes and clarifies everything in detail, leaving nothing to the viewer's imagination, which, however, takes delight in discovering and concluding what it attributes to the painter, even though this derives from the viewer's own imagination."

By midcentury, still other theoreticians had adopted a similar position, but usually only in regard to sketches and drawings, as if license could be allowed in these supposedly intermediary genres simply as a means of assuring the linear integrity and finish of the final painting. Thus Caylus wrote: "The difference that I see between a beautiful drawing and a beautiful painting is that, in the latter, we can read, in direct proportion to his powers, everything that a great artist has wanted to represent, whereas, in the former the viewer himself finishes the object that is offered to us."[2] Diderot was of the same opinion: "In a painting I see something pronounced; in a sketch how many things have I imagined that were barely uttered!" Even Burke supported this position, declaring that he had often received greater pleasure from a simple sketch of some vaguely defined subject than from the most finished canvas. This was because he found his imagination flattered by the promise of more than was actually there.

Such conceptions and such tolerance could only encourage working methods that lent themselves to ambiguities of meaning and deliberate vagueness of expression. Hubert Robert began each work by tracing out a perspective matrix with all the proper convergence upon a vanishing point. But in the final work, he would sometimes subvert the gridlike regularity by introducing displacements calculated to blur its stereometry. This leaves the viewer to deal with the distortions—either by correcting them or by admitting to the spatial instability they produce. Another significant factor was the *counterproof*, which produced in reverse image a second, somewhat paler version of a drawing once a sheet of paper had been pressed against the original. Jean Cailleux has alerted us to Robert's frequent use of the technique. The artist liked to return to his "first thought," now weakened by the transfer process, and complete—while also blurring—it with a line deliberately placed off the original mark, applied with a brush or grease crayon. The counterproof presupposes a technical intervention whose effects are not entirely predictable. Thus, the aleatory, or chance, effects of the hand join those of the painting process. In this way, the grain of the original paper, flattened by the press, does not coincide with that of the now-modified, receptive surface, and traces of graphite are either crushed together or fragmented. Moreover, the artist has introduced a temporal dimension into his process. The final product is the result of several chronologically distinct interventions, each of which represents a "correction" of its predecessor. *Pentimento* (a term, signifying the traces or "ghosts" of earlier drawing, whose usage dates to 1798) is the basis of such works, just as creative difference is the goal. Robert did not go back over the counterproof in order to restore the original, nor did he seek to produce a definitive or "improved" version. It was the variation, the paraphrase, the critical reprise that interested and delighted him. His conception was sequential and procedural, with the accent falling on displacement and difference. (We are reminded of the astonishing manipulations wrought by Hercules Seghers, the 17th-century Dutch engraver who inspired Rembrandt and an artist whose etchings, forgotten for two hundred years, were not rediscovered until 1829, as if contemporary practice had finally made them legible again.)

Any consideration of incompleteness and variation should also include the procedures utilized by Greuze (Fig. 341), himself a master of the counterproof, or by Saint-Aubin, a virtuoso of the incomplete (Figs. 493, 494), or even by Cochin *fils*, who multiplied the states of his engravings in order to stimulate the interest of connoisseurs of the rare. Finally, we should examine the mezzotint process of engraving that the French call *au berceau*, for the fine-toothed wheel that is rocked back and forth over the plate to create, as Jean Adhémar writes, "a facsimile of a drawing executed on grained paper." Here, a significant reversal occurs, since the print, which for so long had been dedicated to the "imitation" of painting, would now mimic the hazardous course of crayon over the texture of a minutely pebbled surface.

The near-universal taste for drawing, which began in the 1750s and embraced classical drawing as well as, increasingly, contemporary drawing, marks above all else the triumph of what henceforth would be regarded as an independent genre. "Drawings," writes Jean Adhémar, "were made to be sold, self-sufficient drawings, drawings that were no longer sketches for paintings, but works of art possessing intrinsic aesthetic value." Such sheets fascinated collectors because they were expressions of the artist's primary inspiration, his "fire" (see also Chapter II, pp. 97–101), but also because they were works "to be completed" (by the viewer).

A survey of 19th-century literature reveals how vision itself was gradually transformed through the observer's confrontation with the new objects presented by modern life. The crowd, for example, became the *masses*, as Balzac in 1833 contemplated "that human tapestry woven, between two and three in the morning, by the male and female habitués of the distillers." He then added: "Tapestry is the word. The rags and faces harmonize so well with each other that you can never tell where the rags end and the flesh begins, where a bonnet is, where the nose belongs, etc."

The masses become mass in literature, just as they do in Goya's *corridas* and sabbaths (Fig. 343) or in Turner's banquets (Fig. 381) and apocalypses (Fig. 389), where a few random commas, distributed across (or ploughed into) the thickness of the pigment, suffice to denote faces and bodies. Here the touch has nothing to do with the inimitable swiftness of Fragonard (Fig. 240), the synthetic punctuations of Guardi (Figs. 183, 184), or the nervous accents of Magnasco (Fig. 239). All such artists, however great their graphic agility, invariably attempted to relate each object to a stroke and each stroke to an object. Goya, however, no longer respected this identification of signs with things (a small dab for each head,

344. T. Gainsborough (1727–88). *Wooded Landscape with Cow Standing Beside a Pool.* c. 1778.

With his technique of applying tone on tone, of working within a narrow range of values, and of juxtaposing strokes of closely related hues, Gainsborough produced optical instability, most notably in his foliage. The blending has ceased to be atmospheric and become retinal.

345. H. Daumier (1908–79). *Don Quixote.* c. 1868.

The head of the hero has been reduced to a patch of ocher, utterly devoid of delineation—like the silhouette of Sancho Panzo in the distance.

346. C. Guys (1802–92). *Two Women and a Man.*

Guys made the dissociation of contour and color the principal means of his aesthetic of instantaneity.

a zigzag for the folds of drapery). His crowds are splashes of medium, with his figures extruded therefrom.

Vagueness becomes a virtue. "If your imagination is poor, and in fog you see nothing but gray," wrote Friedrich, "then this aversion is understandable. All the same, a landscape enveloped in mist seems vaster, more sublime, and it animates the imagination while also heightening suspense—like a veiled woman. The eye and the imagination are generally more intrigued by vaporous distances than by a nearby object available to the eye."

Delacroix, who in his youth discovered the spirit of German Romanticism through Germaine de Staël's *De l'Allemagne*, placed vagueness and incompletion at the heart of his aesthetic. He admired his friend Chopin's compositions for their "floating, indefinite contour, which constitutes the charm of his ideas . . . this cloudy, blurred indecision which, while destroying the rigid framework of form, drapes it in long coils of what seem like sheets of mist." One evening in September 1854, Delacroix entered a church in Dieppe, where he encountered "the most grandiose of spectacles, that of a darkened church illuminated by a half-dozen smoky candles placed here and there. I challenge the opponents of vagueness to create a comparable sensation with precise, well-defined lines." Ambiguity and vagueness are consubstantial with painting, which is "even vaguer than poetry, despite [painting's] static form. One of its greatest charms."

Théophile Silvestre devised an ingenious metaphor to demonstrate the precarious status of contour in Delacroix's aesthetic: "Imagine a bas-relief placed horizontally and half-submerged in water. The portion that remains above water, visible to the eye, is certainly not a network of contours and clear lines, but a salient ensemble. Given this situation, who can define the importance proper to line without this being purely hypothetical?" Delacroix compared painting to a ruin: "The sketch for a painting, for a monument, for a ruin as well should have all the more impact upon the soul because of what the soul adds to it in the course of gaining an impression of the object." It is only one step from the ruin to total effacement. A composition is truly perceived only after the work has been removed from sight: "In the absence of the painting that has aroused certain emotions [in the soul], it must be reconstructed from memory; then the unity of the work will dominate, provided such a quality was actually there."

Thus, we see Romantic art oscillate between *vagueness* and *transposition*, between the blurring of the object and the compensatory displacement of signs and their effects. "It is not the thing that must be made," writes Delacroix, "only the semblance of the thing." Whether it concerns the immersion of an object in misty, atmospheric haze, or the substitution of graphic or chromatic equivalents for the iconic denotation of objects, certain generalized zones of color and texture come forward and invite interpretation, reverie, and free association. Looking at Gainsborough's paintings, Reynolds was struck first by "those odd scratches and marks," "this chaos, this uncouth and shapeless appearance," that "lightness of hand," but then conceded "that in this undermined manner there is the general effect; enough to remind the spectator of the original; the imagination supplies the rest." It was precisely this fluctuation of meaning and effect, of denotation and

general reverie that Gainsborough wanted to systematize when he "expressed, that his pictures, at the Exhibition, should be seen near, as well as at a distance."

The primacy of the painting's *painterliness* (its material constituents: texture, surface, color) has also been acknowledged by John Robert Cozens (Alexander's son), whose works are so delicate that photographic reproduction can never do them justice (Figs. 207, 208). In his minutely sensed, lyrically elegiac Italian landscapes, this artist gave effect to volume by means of tiny monochromatic patches, loosely spaced and frontalized in a way that anticipated Corot or Cézanne. These patches, whose function is to mediate between two contradictory realities—the flatness of the support and the fictive depth of the scene (which gives each patch a tendency to oscillate, even to shimmer, despite the pigment's matness)—are generally disposed in chaplets or chains of the same color, all joined to other series of patches similar in shape but deeper or higher in tonality. Their discrete, repetitive character evinces the autonomy of touch vis-à-vis the depicted object. The absence of modeling and the abundance of reserve areas contribute to an ambiguity of spatial recession, and it is up to the viewer—as it would be a century later with Cézanne—to locate and order what, within a mass of foliage or on the side of a hill, is near or far.

Turner, who studied and copied J. R. Cozens' demonstrations during his apprenticeship in the "academy" of Dr. Monro (beginning in 1795), produced an art that summarizes the whole set of issues broached in this chapter. Haziness, vagueness, ambiguity, the blurring of elements and materials are magnified into a general vision of the world, brought about in an oeuvre that is said to link up with Claude Lorrain on one side and on the other with the American painter Mark Rothko. Clouds, smoke, sea, snow—so liquid and aerial were the material and thematic components of Turner's pictures that for Constable the works appeared to have been painted with "tinted steam." In Turner scientific observations on the behavior of light are inextricably bound up with an archaic, regressive vision. His conception of light, borrowed, according to Gowing, from the second book of Newton's *Optics*, assumed the interpenetration of all luminous particles: "Darkness or total shade," the painter wrote, "cannot take place while any angle of light reflected or refracted can reach an opposite plane. . . . We must consider every part as receiving and emitting rays to every surrounding surface." It is this continuum that Turner wanted to paint, while here and there allowing forms and beings to emerge—after the fact. *Light and Color* (Fig. 389), for example, was conceived by the artist "as encapsulated within a bubble, on whose spherical surface can be seen prismatic refractions of colour." For Turner, light—often dense and thick—was the medium, almost the pretext, for a reversal of procedure, wherein substance or material came first and forms or figures later, as effects or extrusions of primary matter. Thus, process itself yielded a metaphor of the genesis and effacement of beings and things in the material world. The relation is not between an object and a sign, but between an overall theme and an overall painting.

Here was an art devoted to nothingness, to undifferentiated matter, to submersion within primordial

347. H. Daumier. *Pierre Bailliot*. 1833–35.

348. H. Daumier. *Auguste Ganneron*. 1833–35.

The face has become an excrescence of clay, a geological terrain with all its folds, cavities, and depressions.

349. A. Préault (1809–79). *Slaughter*. 1834.

By means of crowding and collision, Préault destroyed the order and harmony of the classical relief. The protest against violence takes place through an indictment of compositional rhetoric. In his spatial contraction, scalar distortions, and irregular edges, Préault anticipated the reliefs carved by Gauguin.

substance. In the twilight of a Europe that had drawn its spiritual cohesiveness from a whole baggage of religious beliefs, Turner's melancholy renewed contact with the ancient Greek world's first image of Hell: the "primordial flux" from which the world's variety had emerged. "Hesiod imagined," write Détienne and Vernant, "that the clear distinctions between earth, water, sea, fire in the sky, and misty shadows gradually disappeared into the subterranean world, where opposite elements were reunited in their common root."

A heightened, almost giddy sense of nothingness characterizes the era. From Beckford to Hoffmann, from Nodier to Nerval, European literature is largely a series of desolate or distraught declamations on the situation of a human subject awash in and fragmented by forces over which he has no control: fleeting time, failed memory, vague depression, optical vertigo, phantasms, confused sensations, drugs, madness. Piranesi became the eponymous exponent of this vertigo. His *Prisons* were interpreted sometimes as dream spaces or scenes of madness where an alienated individual could become lost (de Quincey, Gautier), sometimes as the giantism that menaces an urbanized, mechanized police state, or again as the circumconvolutions of the brain, the mystery of cells and thought. Now, we value them for, most of all, the number of formal devices they disclose: broken scale, accelerated and warped perspective, steep, plunging views, repetition edge to edge of a single motif (the arch, the stone rampart), enlarged details of materials, assemblages, found objects (fragments of reliefs [Fig. 469], pedestals, shafts, instruments) which destabilize and decentralize the subject-viewer and deprive him of the certitudes of Euclidean space.

Despite the differences of period and style, Turner had the same interest as Piranesi in a subject unmoored—as if suspended over an abyss—by the suppression of customary spatial references. This can be seen in those paintings and watercolors (the "chromatic veils") in which the English master provides absolutely no clue to the structure of depth. "No visible object," Leonardo insists, "can be properly perceived by the human eye except in contrast to the ground against which its contours are delineated and drawn." The modern critic Clement Greenberg believes that "value contrast, the opposition of the lightness and darkness of colors, has been Western pictorial art's chief means, far more important than perspective, to that convincing illusion of three-dimensionality which distinguishes it most from other traditions of pictorial art." And Greenberg adds: "Turner, really, was the one who made the first significant break with the conventions of light and dark"—thus opening, by the suppression of contrast, the possibilities that would produce, via Monet's *Water Lilies*, the great American painting of the 1950s—the art of Pollock, Still, and Newman.

Vertigo even had its own philosopher in the Englishman Edmund Burke, whose *Philosophical Enquiry into the Origins of Our Ideas of the Sublime and Beautiful* appeared in 1757. Burke found that the sublime could be experienced only by captivating the soul before the mind had been able to work its will. Haziness, vagueness, obscurity constituted the principal vehicles of the sublime: "I think there are reasons in nature, why the obscure idea, when properly conveyed, should be more affecting than the clear. It is our ignorance of things that causes our admiration, and chiefly excites our passions. . . . The mind is hurried out of itself, by a crowd of great and confused images; which affect because they are crowded and confused."

According to Burke, the failure of painting lay precisely in its having sacrificed too much to the circumscription of material things: "Let it be considered that hardly anything can strike the mind with its greatness, which does not make some sort of approach towards infinity; which nothing can do whilst we are able to perceive its bounds; but to see an object distinctly, and to perceive its bounds, is one and the same thing . . . but then it is in my power to raise a stronger *emotion* by the description than I could do by the best painting."

Insensitivity to vagueness, a tight, miserly hold on objects—these were what would render painting impotent. Throughout the late 18th century and the entire 19th century, artists would appear to have embraced such values only to discredit the view espoused by Burke. But by emphasizing allusion at the expense of illusion, by favoring all the formal and material aspects of painting (color, texture, gesture, the shape of the canvas) that permitted escape from the conventional demands of figuration, modern painters achieved an art that even Burke would have found utterly beyond his comprehension.

350. Jean-Baptiste Perroneau (1715–83.) *Portrait of Abraham van Robais*. 1769. Pastel. 2'4¾" × 1'11½".
Cabinet des Dessins, Louvre.

The ovoid of the human head dissolves
under a rain of flat, liquid touches

351. Jean-Baptiste Perronneau. *Portrait of a Magistrate.* 1768. Oil on canvas, 2′1½″×2′.
Collection Cailleux, Paris.

Perronneau did portraits that, by comparison with those of his more successful rival Quentin de La Tour, appear to be unfinished. In them the artist displayed ''less technical virtuosity than Latour's, perhaps quite deliberately,'' notes Michael Levey. We cannot make too much of the fact that Perronneau rendered his faces, in pastel as well as in oil, with flat, vibrant touches more juxtaposed than blended. The strokes remain insistently strokes and cannot be forgotten as such. So utterly is this true that the neck and chin become zones that do not ''turn''—that is, do not assume the quality of rounded volumes. The process was almost ''Cézannian,'' but in fact it perpetuated, as Jean Cailleux has observed, the manner of the 17th-century Dutch master Aert de Gelder, whose art the Frenchman could have encountered during the frequent sojourns he made in The Netherlands before dying there in 1783. As these small planes of color— these green, gray, and ocher facets— break up the ovoid of the head, yet abruptly come together and model the cheeks, they announce a technique that does not serve—as is generally the case with La Tour—to give the form density, to reinforce its concrete nature, or to establish a psychological presence. Instead, it produces a dislocation or confusion of features, an uncertainty about the individual character of a subject whose personal unity is affirmed only by the undeniable sharpness of the gaze.

352. Hubert Robert (1733–1803). *The Royal Family at Their Final Mass*. c. 1792.
Oil on canvas, 1'2½" × 1'6". Private collection.

## Figures seem to partake of the fictive space that surrounds them

So great is the space taken up by the tapestries in the paintings reproduced here—by the Frenchman Robert and the Spaniard Paret, the one working in the royal apartments of the Tuileries and the other in those of Madrid—that the hangings have a distinctly pictorial effect, causing the actual scenes to seem extended into fictive space and making it easy to confuse the figures in the foreground with those on the walls. In the Robert picture (Fig. 352), the ambiguity arises from the perspectival scaling, which is generally consistent from the "real" figures to the "fictive" ones. That is, the diminution required

by distance operates more or less as if the total space—actual and illusory—were unified and continuous.

Moreover, a sequence of red spots associates the two scenes at the same time that it punctuates the borders of the tapestries and the decorative figures above the cornice. And the figures, relative to their individual positions in depth, have all been rendered with the same rather light touch as well as with the same kind of shallow modeling. On the other hand, the two spaces begin their recession from two different points, that of the tapestries being higher than that of the real scene. To

353. Luis Paret y Alcazar (1746–99). *Charles III at Table*. c. 1770.
Oil on wood, 1′7¾″×2′1¼″. Museo del Prado, Madrid.

this is added a certain vagueness in regard to the views represented in the wall hangings. Are they all part of the same scene, or are they different in time and place? Seeing them as a continuous panorama helps to reinforce the sense of illusionistic depth, with this viewed through a large segmented bay window. However, Robert has made no attempt to burden us with a *trompe l'oeil* exercise. As in many of his pictures, the aim here was to hold the painting ''in a state of tension'' by creating a spatial ambiguity capable of making us conscious of the mechanisms of illusion employed by the artist.

The Paret picture (Fig. 353) presents an equally manifest confusion between two spaces, especially in the left half. The various bays, with their mirrors and openings, contribute to the mixture of planes, while the whole is surmounted, if not extended, by a ceiling decoration that happens to be the most volumetric and insistent element of the entire ensemble. But what fixes our interest is the carpet, a bravura piece that fills the foreground (and should be compared to Goya's *Philippines Board* in Fig. 355), while its three emphatically straight edges anchor the composition solidly to the rectilinear shape of the canvas.

354. Jean Auguste Dominique Ingres (1780–1867). *The Interior of the Sistine Chapel.* 1814. Oil on canvas, 2′5¼″×3′¼″. National Gallery of Art (Samuel H. Kress Collection), Washington, D.C.

## Artists paint the distance that separates us from the great and the powerful

Two pictures with a common theme: an illustrious personage represented at the center of a canvas. And two painters with the same purpose: to paint not so much the figure but the void that separates us from him. Such are the factors that relate a pair of paintings executed within a few months of one another. But in every other respect they are opposites, which simply enables us to read them better. In the painting by Ingres (Fig. 354) the artist's neat, immaculate touch is everywhere evident, not only in the sovereign pontif but also in the fifty-four prelates, dignitaries, and Swiss guards that surround him (some of whose images

are portraits). Clearly distinguishable are such details as the gold Christ on the Cross in the rear ground, the papal arms on the dias, the decoration of the pilasters at the left, and the 15th-century frescoes on the upper longitudinal wall. Only the fragment of Michelangelo's *Last Judgment* (right background) remains in fairly deep shadow, as if the system devised by Ingres had just collided with that of his illustrious predecessor. Taking as his motto, "A thing well drawn is a thing always well painted," the French master affirmed that "smoke itself should be expressed in line." Meanwhile, he found his own way of renewing contact with the

355. Francisco Goya (1746–1828). *The Philippines Board.* c. 1815. Oil on canvas, 10'4¾"×14'. Museo Goya, Castres.

tradition of intarsia, the marquetry work of the Florentine Renaissance whose inlaid wood assemblages of precisely contoured and regularly shaped monochrome planes produce an effect of depth.

Goya, on the other hand, chose to approach his scene (Fig. 355) head-on rather than from the oblique angle chosen by Ingres. It is not so much a void that he painted as a gap, which seems all the greater by virtue of the painting's monumental scale (more than 14 feet wide). Indeed, no photograph could reproduce the overwhelming impact that the picture has on viewers in its actual presence. The shareholders in

the Philippines Company—a slack and slipshod lot, their ears, noses, and cheeks constituted of nothing but red dabs—have been shunted to left and right, there isolated and penned up like cattle, as if to exclude them from the receding perspective grid formed by the carpet, whose straight edges have their point of departure in the picture's lower corners. The carpet, in fact, is the star of the painting, its muted luminosity—like that of Bonnard—the consequence of discontinuous strokes overlaid with other equally broken strokes of a different color. The same process was used for the large vertical lines defining walls, windows, and paneling, all of

which have been rendered in a deliberately uncertain, irregular hand, to the point where some strokes have gone dry for want of pigment. Here we have a composition endowed, like Ingres', with every characteristic of a geometric box, but a geometry that is subverted by the handling whose voluntary indecisiveness deprives the spatial system of its certitude. As for the surfaces, all very frontal, their differentiated vibration was also obtained by means of a knowing use of random brushwork. The textural and luminary differences of a lighter tone of gray loosely applied over a first, darker layer of the same color have yielded an

effect of great iridescent beauty. The real source of this shimmer is the underpainting, which has its triumph in the rectangular forms that box in Ferdinand VII from above and from below. There the color glows and radiates with an incomparable warmth that anticipated the large chromatic veils of the 20th-century American colorist Mark Rothko.

356. Benjamin West (1738–1820). *Apotheosis of Nelson.* 1807. Oil on canvas, 2′11½″×2′5½″.
National Maritime Museum, London.

## Crowding supplants the harmony of composition

At the same time that the hero gained access to the paradise of warriors, the painter gained access to the freedom of incorporeal spaces. The theme of celestial apotheosis made it possible to escape the guideposts of the physical and empirical world, as well as the smooth, even contouring and linear gridwork demanded by Neoclassical doctrine.

Simultaneously, immortality underwent a change of nature. The Valhalla of the military ceased to be the Heaven of Christian imagery. Instead, we are invited to step right *in* at eye level, not to witness from *below*.

Girodet, in his picture (Fig. 357), shows the Napoleonic heroes—

Dugommier, Hoche, Marceau, etc.—arriving in Odin's paradise and there joining the shades of Ossian and his warriors. Here we see not only a number of dogs but also a foreground chorus of nymphs, whose supple necks look forward to the Ingresque distortions of *Thetis* (Fig. 167).

"The painter would give the impression, not without reason, of having racked his brains to no purpose," wrote Delécluze, who thereby confirmed the very mixed success the picture had at the 1802 Salon. What caused the greatest shock were the ectoplasmic figures, those luminescent phantoms who appear to have been generated by the gaseous

medium on which they are borne. No one seemed ready to acknowledge a conception already realized by Raphael, who in his *Foligno Madonna* painted gray angels with the same texture as the clouds where they float. Girodet, as was his wont, provided a very precise explanation in his correspondence: "It was essential . . . to identify [the shades] with the fog in which these figures swim and move and *which itself forms their substance*. They had to seem porous, penetrable. . . ." As for the spooky glow beaming through the clouds and radiating from the figures like haloes, the artist had this to say: "The lights that illuminate the scene are a meteoritic glimmer that has neither the hue of sunrays, nor that of the moon, nor that of terrestrial fires, unless it could be understood as modified by the intervention of variously but softly colored lenses. In no way did nature furnish such an effect, or if it provided me with the model, one should again grant that it has been applied in a wholly new way. Thus, it is a sort of creation."

This creation was not understood. Diderot's daughter, Mme de Vendeul, for example, discusses both the work's vaporous atmosphere and its principle of construction, which instead of David's compositional order offered a crush of figures: "Pervading the whole is a magic, a soapy mousse which may be as skilled as it is clever but which I cannot find attractive. . . . To me it does not allow enough space for so many people and objects." As for David himself, he was dismayed: "Ah, that picture! Girodet, is he mad? . . . Either he is crazy or I no longer know anything about the art of painting. Those are figures of crystal that he has done. . . . What a pity! With his beautiful talent, he will never create anything but follies. . . ."

For his *Apotheosis of Nelson* (Fig. 356), the Anglo-American painter Benjamin West borrowed the Deposition and Ascension themes traditional to Christian iconography. But it is Neptune, aided by Victory, who presents Britannia with the celebrated Admiral laid out on a cloud. Filling the canvas is a disorderly allegory in which angels, lions, horses, and family members appear side by side. A disparity of scale simply reinforces the indeterminant character of a deliberately non-Euclidian space.

357. Anne Louis Girodet (1767–1824). *Apotheosis of French Heroes Who Died for the Fatherland during the War of Liberation.* 1802.
Oil on canvas, 6'3½"×6'½". Musée du Château, Rueil-Malmaison.

# The floating spaces of dreams
## transform painting into an irrational montage

359. François Gérard (1770–1837). *Ossian.* After 1801. Oil on canvas, 5'10¾"×6'6". Musée du Château, Rueil-Malmaison.

The Gaelic poems of Ossian, transcribed and largely invented by the Scots poet Macpherson in 1760–70, would not have their full impact in France until the turn of the 19th century under the influence of Napoleon. The First Consul, who was a great reader of the "Northern Homer," commissioned Girodet and Gérard to execute a pair of *ossianesque* pictures for Malmaison. "Escaped from my brushes in less than forty days" (according to a contemporary newspaper), Gérard's original is now lost. However, variations made by the master himself can be found at Hamburg and Malmaison (Fig. 359). "Over a thin, transparent sketch," writes Daniel Ternois, "which allows the support to show through, Gérard painted the figures of his picture in a masterful way, using a heavy impasto that throws a ghostly radiance onto the dead heroes evoked by the Caledonian bard."

With an engraving after the Gérard canvas as his point of departure, Ingres would make his own interpretation of the theme some twelve years later (Fig. 358). Whereas Girodet had presented an allegory endowed with spatio-temporal unity (Fig. 357), Gérard and Ingres painted a phantasm. What we see are the inner workings of a mind lost in a dream, and the image would be impossible without the dreamer represented within it. No longer are we in the presence of a "vision," an "apparition," a prophetic dream of divine origin, as in the art of Giotto or Zurbarán. Here, as Werner Hofmann has noted, it is Ossian who *evokes, conjures,* and produces the surrounding translucent forms. But since Gérard retained spatial coherence (a circle of shades united around the bard who chants their praise), Ingres went further and permitted the dream to disrupt the

scenic order. Superimpositions, transparencies, irresolutions, scalar discrepancies—all contribute toward making an irrational montage, an oneiric *condensation*. The dream world decomposes and recomposes in accordance with rules utterly alien to the canons of classical subject matter.

Ingres added to the complexities by allowing the distinctive qualities of the two scenes—that of the dreamer with his two dogs and that of the dreamed— to seep from one into the other. Thus, the nocturnal blue of the sky overflows onto the phantoms. And these, far from being monochrome, tend toward blue, beige, and green. The light source (the moon) illuminates dream and dreamer

alike. Another interpenetration is the cloud that appears from the right and then floats in front of Ossian. The dream itself consists of a paradoxical substance that seems both marmoreal and transparent. As for the relation of the two lances, it remains ambiguous, since the distant one (the shadow of a ghost) exists without our knowing the source of the light creating the effect.

The *Dream of Ossian,* originally commissioned as a ceiling decoration for Napoleon's bedroom at the Quirinale Palace in Rome, was repeatedly reworked and transformed by the artist and his assistants, with each intervention adding to the singularity of the earlier trials.

358. Jean Auguste Dominique Ingres (1780–1867). *The Dream of Ossian.* 1813. Oil on canvas, 11'5"×9'1¼". Musée Ingres, Montauban.

# In the ambiguities of medium, a sabbath of monsters

360. Francisco Goya (1746–1828). *The Devil's Lamp.* 1797–98.
Oil on canvas, 16½ × 11¾″. National Gallery (courtesy of the Trustees), London.

361. Francisco Goya. *Saint Francis of Borja Attending a Dying Man.* 1788.
Oil on canvas, 15 × 11″. Collection Marquesa de Santa Cruz, Madrid.

"As if by a sort of condensation or spontaneous activation of the principle of darkness,"[3] Goya's penumbra becomes populated with phantasmagorical figures who seem fabricated from the murky element in which they circulate. But it is in a normal-looking space that the chimerical beings (incubi and succubi) come forth, sometimes pale and transparent like retinal after-images and sometimes formed of a rich pigmentary substance that imparts to them the same materiality as that claimed by the living (Fig. 362).

Circumventing the Neoclassicism that dominated late 18th-century Europe, this fusion of rational and hallucinatory space recalls, on the one hand, the Temptations of Saint Anthony painted in the 15th and 16th centuries and, on the other, the Romantic and Faustian imagery of Delacroix and Louis Boulanger. Thus, it was as a Romantic that Théophile Gautier appreciated Goya in his *Voyage en Espagne* (1843): "No one knows better than he how to make the overheated atmosphere of a stormy night roll with huge black clouds filled with vampires, ghouls, demons, or how to silhouette a cavalcade of witches against a sinister horizon." Baudelaire too, looking at *Los Caprichos,* engravings that belong to the same period as these paintings, saw "horrors of nature and human physiognomies wierdly animalized for the occasion." "Goya's great merit," the poet explained, "lies in giving monstrosity the ring of truth. His monsters are born whole and sound. No one pushed further than he in the direction of the likely absurd. All those contortions, those bestial forces, those diabolical grimaces are permeated with *humanity.* . . . The cutting edge or seam line between the real and the fantastic is impossible to discern with certainty." To what degree did the deafness that struck the painter in 1793, following a grave illness, cause the visual hallucinations whose strange fruit was the art reproduced here? No doubt the isolation suffered by the deaf painter helped set him on the oneiric, nocturnal path laid out by artists he had been able to study either in Italy or through engravings: Salvator Rosa, Alessandro Magnasco and his Inquisition scenes, Giambattista Tiepolo (*Capricci* and *Scherzi de Fantasie*), Piranese (*Grotteschi* and *Carceri*). Still, the sketch for *Saint Francis of Borja* (Fig. 361) preceded Goya's 1793 crisis by five years, and here, for the first time, appeared nightmare figures of a sort that for three decades would proliferate in the artist's work, all the way to the walls of *La Quinta del Sordo* ("The House of the Deaf Man," see p. 285). Startling even in all this fantastic imagery is the blood spurting from the Crucifix. But the fantastic takes a more textural form in the ocher underpainting, whose ambiguous presence surfaces in numerous places (curtain, background wall, dying body), causing us to sense everywhere the dark, lurking menace of diabolical concretions.

*The Devil's Lamp* (Fig. 360), with its single touch of red provided by the light, and the *Conjuration* (Fig. 362) form part of a series of six pictures executed for the study of the Duchess of Osuna in her Alemada residence. Sorcery was fashionable in aristocratic circles at the end of the 18th century. Indeed night reigned everywhere in Europe, not only in the diabolism of Goya's Spain, but also in England's "gothik," a taste launched by Horace Walpole in his novel, *The Castle of Otranto* (1764), as well as in the morbid, twilight mood of Edward Young's *Night Thoughts* (1747), translated by a friend of Goya's, and Thomas Gray's *Elegy Written in a Country Churchyard* (1781).

362. Francisco Goya. *Conjuration.* 1797–98. Oil on canvas, 17¾ × 12½″.
Museo de la Academia Royal de Bellas Artes de San Fernando, Madrid.

The light falling from a window or transom upon Rembrandt's philosophers now illuminates Goya's scenes of rapine and murder. In a series of small pictures belonging to the Romana collection, shadow constitutes the texture of crime, the fabric from which the hangman's gestures are knotted, the realm of pure horror, without rule or recourse. The diffuse brightness, which clothes naked bodies or dies at their feet in a thick flow, is a vital substance from which they will soon be cut off (Fig. 363), The gaping orifice of a mouth howling with shock—agony, ecstasy—finds a vast echo in the welling luminosity of the upper zone (Fig. 364). In Goya's art the representation of sexual violence rose to new heights. And the violence committed there is cold, calculated, and driven, an activity in which the victims are objects—human instruments. The artist shows us not only scenes of sadistic aggression but also, probably, the pleasure he drew from them. It would be a mistake to seek the source of this art exclusively in the bloody events of the Napoleonic war in Spain, which Goya witnessed. The canvases reproduced on these two pages, for instance, were executed before the French invasion (Gudiol dates them to 1794–95). And several scenes of savagery and cannibalism—paintings and drawings alike—are generally thought to belong to the years around 1800. Goya proved to be the incomparable observer of an atrocious war, but if he could *see* the horror for what it became, it was because he allowed the sadistic drives within himself to come out, which in turn made him a secret conspirator with that atrocity. The work of art evolved as the product of an effort to objectify and symbolize.

Speaking of early 19th-century medicine, Michel Foucault, in his *Birth of the Clinic*, evokes "the moment when evil, the unnatural, and death—in brief, the whole dark underside of death—come to light, [the moment] when the limits of the visible and the invisible assume new contours. The abyss underneath evil, which was evil itself, has just surged up into the light of language—the light which no doubt was the very one that illuminated *Les Cents Vingt Journées, Juliette* [Sade] and *The Disasters* [Goya]." It was this surfacing of the dark zones of the unconscious, of the perverse and phantasmagorical netherworld that Goya translated into the symbolic statement of the works he painted.

363. Francisco Goya (1746–1828). *Bandits Stripping a Woman Naked*. 1808–10. Oil on canvas, 16½ × 12½". Collection Marques de La Romana, Madrid.

# Light dims, unleashing dark forces

364. Francisco Goya. *Bandit Stabbing a Woman*. 1808–10. Oil on canvas, 15¾ × 12½". Collection Marques de La Romana, Madrid.

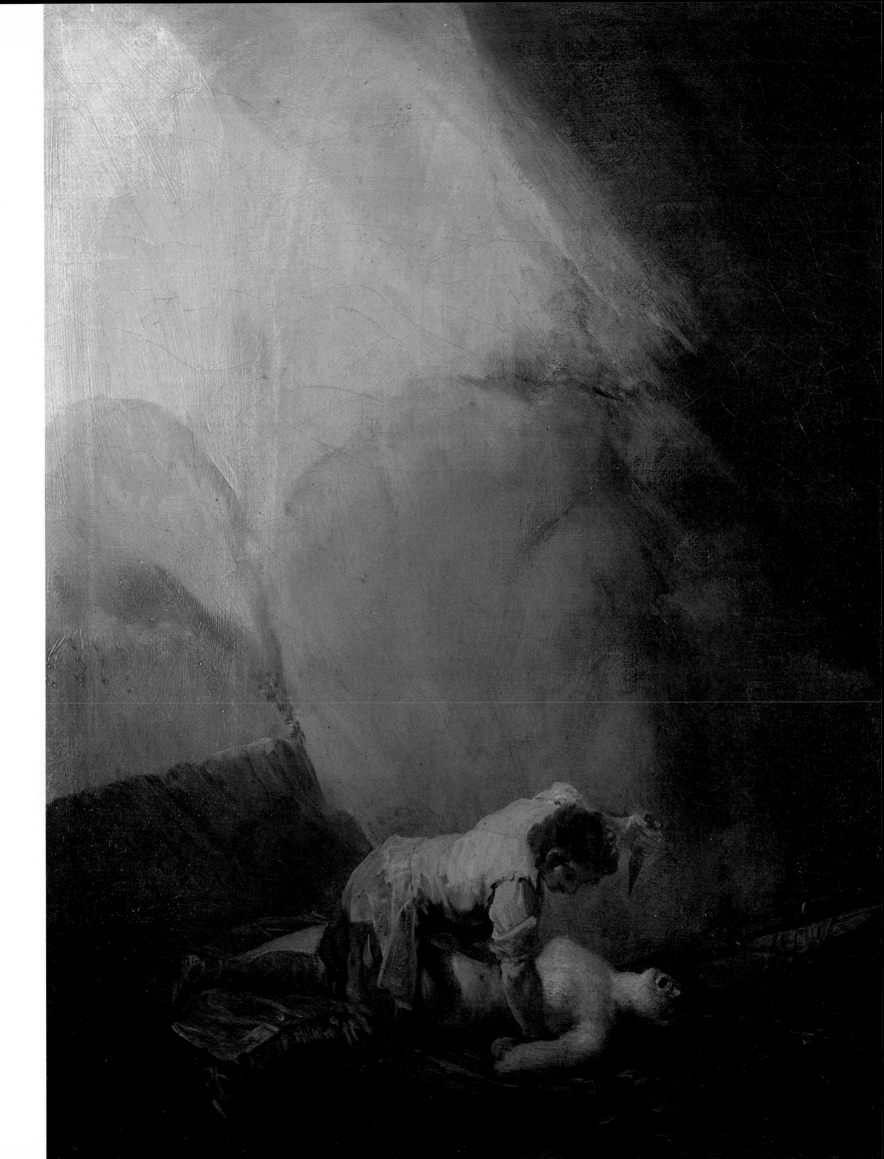

## Through macabre, fantastic themes,
## a singular liberation of artistic powers

365. Ary Scheffer (1795–1858). *Lenore, or "The Dead Go Fast."* c. 1830.
Oil on canvas, 1'11¼"×2'6". Musée des Beaux-Arts, Lille.

A violent theme from literature inspired a pair of pictures that stand out as singular exceptions in the overall production of two supposedly conventional painters. Horace Vernet, the grandson of both Joseph Vernet and Moreau the Younger, as well as the son of Carle Vernet and a nephew of the architect Chalgrin, was famous by age twenty-five for his "brilliant, facile, fecund, and eminently patriotic brush" (in the words of an 1822 account). He concerned himself mostly with subjects related to military life and colonial conquest. "No pompon was foreign to him," wrote Edmond About in 1855, "and he knew his trooper down to the very buttons on his gaiters. With the visor of a shako he would reconstruct a soldier for you, just the way Cuvier would take an ossicle and from it reconstruct a megatherium." Baudelaire, in his 1846 *Salon*, devoted one of his most famous and violent

diatribes to Vernet: "M. Horace Vernet is a military man who paints. . . . I hate that man because his pictures are decidedly not painting, but rather agile and frequent masturbation. . . ."

The author of *Les Fleurs du mal* was hardly more generous toward Ary Scheffer, whom he classed in the same *Salon* among the *singes du sentiments* ("apes of feeling"). Idolized by middle-of-the-roaders and constantly held up to Delacroix as an example of moderation and a "Raphaelesque" brush (Thiers), Scheffer in 1846 would receive forty-five thousand francs for two pictures based upon Goethe's *Faust*, the very year that Delacroix could get no more than a thousand for his *Marguerite in Church*. The unexpected appearance in such careers of canvases as unusual as those reproduced here may have resulted from the conjunction of a new technique with the influence of literature. The fantastic,

macabre subjects of German poetry were feeding the imaginations of the Romantic generation: Delacroix or Louis Boulanger. As can be seen above and opposite, the *Ballade* of Bürger (1747–97), which had been popularized by Mme de Staël in *De l'Allemagne* (1813) and translated by Gérard de Nerval in 1830, tells in the manner of a Schubertian *lied* the story of the vigil made by a young woman whose fiancé had gone to war, then the latter's return concealed by armor and his riding with her through the night, all the while repeating that they would soon reach their destination, since "the dead go fast." Its visor up, the armor disclosed only a skeleton. The picture's nocturnal, morbid content would appear to have been influenced by the recent advent of lithography. "The Romantics were above all 'colorists,' " notes Marcel Brion, "and found in the richness, pliancy, and velvety softness of

lithography an expressive means almost as efficacious as polychromy." Scheffer (Fig. 365) treated the anecdote in a rapid style, *alla prima* ("a fiery sketch tossed off in a moment of reverie and forgotten in a corner of the studio where Scheffer accidentally rediscovered it," according to Philippe Burty). Through the unevenness of its scumbling, the red-ocher surface discloses silhouettes that are barely sketched in (below left and behind the horse). Vernet, by contrast (Fig. 366), cultivated a smooth facture, but one that is also enlivened by a series of luminous points (see the dazzling death mask) as well as by red touches (the eyes of the owl, the horse's nose, the statue, etc.) that enhance the work's infernal atmosphere. Both canvases evince the recurring effect that a new printmaking process had on painting, for the figures seem to have been emitted by the surface itself, the products of a rich ambiguity of tone.

366. Horace Vernet (1789–1863). *The Ballad of Lenore, or "The Dead Go Fast."* 1839.
Oil on canvas, 2'×1'9¾". Musée des Beaux-Arts, Nantes.

# The canvas activated by
# effervescent constellations of color and energy

367. François André Vincent (1746–1816). *Battle of the Pyramids*. c. 1803.
Oil on canvas, 3'11¼"×5'10¾". Private collection.

For the *Battle of Nazareth* (Fig. 368), his first picture on such a subject, Gros arranged a chain of nodes and nebuli separated by voids, all enveloped by the smoke of combat and illuminated by a zenithal sun. The impression is one of endless movement, in which red and white patches constantly impell the eye from one group to another. Effervescent chromatic constellations, the scenes partake of the general flux at the same time that they retain their anecdotal identity. "One sees the mass before the details. Still, one soon comes to them," wrote Ernest Chesneau. More than van der Meulen and the battle painters of the 17th century, Gros' canvas recalls the girational dynamism of Rubens' *Kermesse* (Louvre), with its empty expanses and its distribution of colors— the Rubens that Gros called *sublimissime* and who more than David was his true master. (In 1793, while staying in Genoa, Gros returned each day to a chapel where he could see the

368. Antoine Jean Gros (1771–1835). *The Battle of Nazareth*. 1801. Oil on canvas, 4'5¼"×6'4¾".
Musée des Beaux-Arts, Nantes.

369. François Louis Joseph Watteau (1758–1823). *Battle of the Pyramids*. 1799. Oil on canvas, 13¼″ × 3′11¼″. Musée des Beaux-Arts, Valenciennes.

Antwerp master's *Saint Ignatius Healing the Possessed*.) Also related to Rubens is the extreme freshness of the French artist's greens, especially in the distance with its sprinkling of light-toned spots representing the fleeing, burnous-clad warriors. The subject of the *Battle of Nazareth* was submitted to a competition announced for 1801, its purpose being to celebrate the victory of Napoleon's General Junot, who two years earlier had led several hundred men against six thousand Arabs and Turks. Gros received the prize, but for the final version of his picture, which was to measure 49 feet wide, he managed only to sketch it in, since

Bonaparte, legend tells us, took umbrage at the importance given to Junot. We can estimate the scale planned for the picture from the painter's *Pesthouse at Jaffa* (Fig. 423) and *Battle of Aboukir* (Fig. 507), both of which are known to have been executed on the canvas cut for *Nazareth*. What remains of that work is the Nantes Museum's ''sublime study'' (Delacroix), about which Focillon said: ''The vanquished of Nazareth, henceforth, is David; the new blazing conquest is color.''

In François Watteau's *Battle of the Pyramids* (Fig. 369) we also have an apportioned distribution of clusters over

a vast surface, which seems all the more vast by virtue of the painter's unabashedly plunging perspective. There the individual elements tend to blend into a mass that would be indistinct were it not for the vermicular rhythms of the horses' rumps, upturned stomachs, and necks. In all this frenzied motility, each of the tumults resembles a miniature version of a battle scene by Giulio Romano or Pietro da Cortona, or one of Rubens' hunting episodes.

Vincent, in his superb study for the *Battle of the Pyramids* (Fig. 367), chose to make the frankest possible opposition between the regular formation of the French forces, all positioned to fire, and

the gesticulating, centrifugal chaos of their adversaries. Here the tangle of proliferating lines would appear to have been produced by a scrawling hand working around the white oval of a horse's haunches. The dramatic (and Manichaean) dichotomy of two tactics and two cultures produced a collage-like effect. Most of all, however, it signaled the eruption in French painting of a system of construction based upon the linear expansion of an erratic gesture—such as that developed from what Gros and then Delacroix would call an ''egg''—the better to invest the surface, as if by a process of metastasis, with tone, substance, and weight.

## Sheets of fog obscure the landscape, frontalizing and flattening the image

The spectator could be subject to a compounded sense of insecurity when confronted with the fogs painted by Valenciennes (Figs. 371, 372) or Friedrich (Fig. 370), for while the atmospheric confusion muffles contours, frustrates focus, and obscures spatial guides, the absence of foreground serves equally well to produce an effect of instability. As early as 1808 the writer Ramdohr complained that Friedrich's *Teschen Altar* made the viewer feel suspended "in air," floating over an abyss. No longer was his position fixed by perspective lines whose point of departure was the observer.

370. Caspar David Friedrich (1774–1840). *Morning Mist in the Mountains*. 1808. Oil on canvas, 2'4"×3'5". Staatliche Museen, Schloss Heidecksburg, Rudolstadt.

In classical landscape painting, on the other hand, everything had been subordinated to the existence of an active viewer who controlled the spatial organization and was its agent. However grand or heroic the themes—vast mountains upon distant horizons—the perspectival organization would

371. Pierre Henri de Valenciennes (1750–1819). *The Rocca di Papa in Fog.* c. 1782–84. Oil on paper mounted on cardboard, 6×11″. Louvre.

372. Pierre Henri de Valenciennes. *The Rocca di Papa under Clouds.* c. 1782–84. Oil on paper mounted on cardboard, 5½×11¾″. Louvre.

simply affirm all the more emphatically the reality of the spectator in front of whom and for whom nature's constituent elements ("ideal" and "composed") were arranged.

Thus, the difference does not reside in the choice of theme—mountains and clouds—but rather in the viewer's position, centered or shifting. Classical landscape painting, notes Fritz Novotny, postulates the organizing presence of an individual person, thereby implying the art's essentially humanist nature. But the organizing individual loses his footing before the fragmentary, unstructured, dedramatized, arhythmical views—views devoid of emphases—offered by Friedrich and Valenciennes. They reduce the viewer to the status of supernumerary, a passive, contemplative, even precarious bystander. Nature deploys itself without reference to him.

Still, the selection of formless motifs—clouds and mists—was most certainly not fortuitous (nor were the clear analogies with the Chinese conception of landscape painting). Indeed, the subjects painted made it possible to maintain verisimilitude while also dismantling the kind of spatial structure that had dominated European painting since the Renaissance.

The paradox presented by Valenciennes derives from the fact that as an academician, a professor, and the author of a treatise on perspective, this master spent a lifetime defending, indeed insisting upon, the primacy of history painting and the *grand style* inspired by Homer and Virgil. But while in Rome, he made several dozen studies designed, like the works reproduced above, to capture the transient moment and the fragmentary perception. Known to his pupils, Valenciennes' Roman studies have, with all justice, been viewed as one of the wellsprings of modern landscape painting.

197

373. Caspar David Friedrich (1774–1840). *The Watzmann.* c. 1824–25. Oil on canvas, 4¼″×5′7″. Nationalgalerie, Staatliche Museen Preussischer Kulturbesitz, Berlin.

## Through a delicate disturbance of atmospheric perspective,

The pictures reproduced here do not possess the "visionary" simplicity that Friedrich and his contemporaries wanted to see in them. The German master constantly insisted that his works were simply dictated to him by an interior, uncontrollable impulse. For Friedrich as for the idealist philosopher Schelling (1775–1854), art transcended intellectual prescription. The artist was merely a medium. He "introduces into his work," wrote Schelling, "beyond what clearly enters his conscious will, as if he instinctively obeyed a certain element of eternity that is not accessible, in the fullness of its

revelation, to any finite intelligence." This was more or less what Friedrich declared in 1821 during a conversation with the Russian poet Zhukosvsky: "Sometimes I try to think, and nothing comes to me. But I can drift off and suddenly it is as if someone were shaking me. Gripped all over, I open my eyes, and what my spirit sought looms up before me like an apparition. I immediately take up my pencil and draw, for the main task has been accomplished." Some years later the following statement would be found among various other fragments from the artist's hand: "Close your physical eye,

so as to see your picture first with the spiritual eye. Then, bring to light *what you have seen in your darkness,* so that it may in turn act upon others, from the exterior toward the interior."

But how much credence should we grant to positions taken up in a polemical context for the purpose of combatting the realist and naturalist wave then beginning to establish itself in Germany? The very care with which Friedrich prepared his pictures—all preceded by pencil and chalk drawings and then worked up in watercolor—and the extended period required for their execution, sometimes staggered over

several months, or even years, exclude the possibility of instantaneous illumination and thus a work "revealed" in one sudden stroke. The distortions in Friedrich's art were never violent or overt. This was his ruse. If he appropriated the phenomena of nature (sunsets, haloes, fogs), it was done gently. At the most he wanted to suggest a diffuse, indefinite presence, a discreet strangeness—a climate, not a message. His sworn objective was to "naturalize" the divine, to infuse it without disturbing the appearance or coherence of things. Viewers should be conveyed into reverie, melancholy, and

198

374. Caspar David Friedrich. *Winter Landscape with Church*. 1811. Oil on canvas, 13×17¾″. Museum für Kunst und Kulturgeschichte der Stadt, Dortmund.

## Friedrich induces a sense of great mystery

prayer by a twist so delicate that they understand what has happened only after close consideration. It was, however, the clever, almost tricky aspect of his art that captivated certain young painters beginning around 1820. Adrien Ludwig Richter, for instance, refused to be convinced by Friedrich's "nature," confusedly perceiving the Dresden master's skill at bearing it away from empirical evidence: "He engages us in abstract thought, using the forms of nature in a purely allegorical manner, like signs and hieroglyphs meant to have a precise meaning" (1824). The technical sophistication sensed by

Richter consists in three procedures that, individually or together, contributed to Friedrich's "magic":
● the elimination of the foreground plane and the floating of a viewer deprived of, thus unanchored by, a central vantage point (see pp. 196–197);
● the assemblage of natural but incompatible elements solely for the purpose of including a sense of an extra-natural presence (see p. 303);
● finally, the dissociation of *linear* perspective and *atmospheric* perspective, which produces visual malaise and, once again, suggests a law other than that governing empirical

experience. All this can be seen in the paintings reproduced here. Linear perspective, since the time of Leonardo, has been understood as "the diminution sustained by the size of bodies" relative to their withdrawal from us, and atmospheric perspective as their progressive alteration under the effect of distance, meaning that the more distant the object, the more indistinct it appears. In Friedrich, the traditional conjunction of these two perspective systems is often disturbed. "Resolution"—to borrow a term from photography—works counter to the spatial scale. Friedrich painted "very

tight" or "very loose," or yet "tight/loose/tight." Mount Watzmann (Fig. 373), which the artist never saw (but took his model from the watercolor of a student), has been rendered with extreme precision, even in the shaded areas, while the terrain within a few feet of the spectator seems more dissolved than resolved. In *Winter Landscape* (Fig. 374), however, the foreground, with its crutches, pines, crucifix, and the sick man leaning against a rock, stands forth in surreal clarity, while the neo-Gothic structure in the background has all but disappeared in an extreme condensation of mist.

375. Joseph Mallord William Turner (1775–1851). *Sunrise, a Castle on a Bay: "Solitude."* c. 1840.
Oil on canvas, 2'11½"×3'11¼". Tate Gallery, London.

376. Joseph Mallord William Turner. *Palestrina: Composition.* 1828.
Oil on canvas, 4'7"×8'2". Tate Gallery, London.

For Turner, Claude Lorrain constituted the model the artist had to assimilate and then surpass. (He was also the most popular painter in 18th-century England.) In 1811, while teaching at the Royal Academy, Turner spoke of a "golden orient," an "amber coloured ether," and an "aerial color."

The pictures reproduced on these two pages disclose the steps in a veritable dissolution of form, as if by phagocytosis. Here we can see how the bucolic landscapes of Claude have been relentlessly analyzed, all the way through to the English master's canvas of 1840 (Fig. 375)—an "elevated pastoral" or "ideal landscape" in which the trees seem like a gauzy tissue, gossamer, spectral, and fibrous.

But Turner also went to certain of Claude's canvases (even more than to those of Ruisdael) for his freedom in cropping or framing the image, a freedom that allowed a spread of foliage or a grove to be suddenly interrupted by the picture's edge. This is what makes the scene look "like a fragment of the visible world cut out at random," with the result that "the image appears to be a stranger in its own frame" (to use the description that Heinrich Wölfflin, the formalist theoretician, gave of what he called "open form").

In 1819, the famous portraitist Thomas Lawrence wrote to the painter-diarist Farington as follows: "Turner should come to Rome . . . the subtle harmony of this atmosphere, that wraps everything in its own milky sweetness . . . can only be rendered, according to my belief, by the beauty of his tones."

# Turner's art erodes objects until they have the consistency of a spiderweb

377. Joseph Mallord William Turner. *Arricia: Sunset.* c. 1828. Oil on canvas, 1'11½"×2'7½". Tate Gallery, London.

378. Joseph Mallord William Turner. *Coast Scene near Naples.* c. 1828. Oil on cardboard, 15¾×23½". Tate Gallery, London.

379. Joseph Mallord William Turner. *Music Party, Petworth*. c. 1830. Oil on canvas, 4′×2′11½″. Tate Gallery, London.

## Flooded by radiance, a patrician salon assumes the appearance of an aquarium

A comparison of *Interior at Petworth* (Fig. 380) with *The Slave Ship* (Fig. 430) reveals that whatever the subject—a tragedy or the intimacy of a patrician residence—Turner allowed the picture to be dominated by an amorphous medium wherein beings and things struggle to emerge and assume individual identity. "In Turner," writes Lawrence Going, "light is not only glorious and sacred, it is voracious, carnivorous, unsparing. It devours impartially, without distinction, the whole living world." This subordination of every trace of life to a general principle—paint and light—was soon recognized by the artist's contemporaries. In 1816, Hazlitt was protesting against pictures that seemed "too much abstractions of aerial perspective and representations not properly of the objects of nature as of the medium through which they were seen." This analysis is astute, even though negative in attitude, and it applies equally to another scene painted at Petworth (Fig. 379). "Strawberry Rembrandt" is a phrase sometimes used to characterize such hotly colored scenes. Here too Hazlitt was prescient, suggesting that Turner's colors are "not local colours but a combination of gaudy hues intended to become a striking point of attraction on the walls of the exhibition." Baudelaire would say the same thing about Delacroix, but for the purpose of validating his art (see p. 236).

380. Joseph Mallord William Turner (1775–1851). *Interior at Petworth.* c. 1837. Oil on canvas, 2′11″×3′11¼″. Tate Gallery, London.

381. Joseph Mallord William Turner (1775–1851). *George IV at the Provost's Banquet in the Parliament House, Edinburgh.* 1822. Oil and watercolor on wood, 2'¾"×2'9½". Tate Gallery, London.

Banquets, commemorative or tragic, offered painters an occasion for projecting endless perspectives in which the durability of the human figure would be challenged by the mistiness of distance. At the same time that bodies partake of a vague continuum, which is nothing more than color and medium, there seems to occur, as Henri Lemaître observed in regard to Turner's landscapes, "a sort of assimilation of nature by dream." In these dramatized, swiftly receding perspectives, it is either the atmospheric component that carries

them off (dissolving contours and lines) or the linear component. This can be seen in Robert's rendition of the banquet prepared for seven hundred guests in the Louvre's Grande Galerie to celebrate the victories won by Bonaparte's forces in Italy (Fig. 383). If the figures retain a certain amount of definition in the picture by Delacroix (Fig. 382), who was grappling with the essentials of an historical subject from Walter Scott, the human image elsewhere (Fig. 381) ceases to be much more than a small silhouette or a rather free stroke of pink

pigment—even when the face is royal.

Turner was famous for his extraordinary powers of technical invention. In the banquet scene just referred to, the surface in the upper zone has been barely touched. A few trails of maroon paint and a stippling of white suffice to indicate a coffered ceiling and the chandeliers hung from it. Two fat stains of violet "juice" stand for a pair of background loges. Most of the identifying features of the frockcoats and chairs were obtained by scratching into the red ground, then highlighting

here and there with a bit of white piping. Quite simply, the huge banquet hall and its press of humanity have been realized by a combination of dense color flooding the foreground, a background left largely virgin, and a few accents.

Such parsimony should not be equated with aesthetic avarice. Turner did not economize on color but only on signs. That he was capable of the most minute description is borne out by his topographical work (Fig. 295). Since the end of the 18th century, English watercolor had taught painters to notate

## Racing perspectives give banquet scenes new, dreamlike dimensions

382. Eugène Delacroix (1798–1863). *Murder of the Bishop of Liège.* 1829. Oil on canvas, 2′11¾″×3′9¾″. Louvre.

allusively and to suggest lightly. In the art of John Robert Cozens, for instance (Fig. 208), the stroke does not always reconstitute the structural truth of an object but only a fairly free equivalence, to such an extent that Cozens' style sometimes seems to anticipate Corot and Cézanne. If Turner, who practiced both techniques at the same time, applied to watercolor the methods he acquired in oil, he also did the reverse, transposing into his major canvases the thrift and economy of watercolor painting.

383. Hubert Robert (1733–1808). *Banquet Given in Honor of Bonaparte in the Louvre's Grande Galerie.* c. 1797. Oil on canvas, 14½×16½″. Musée des Arts Décoratifs, Paris.

# Surging forth from an amorphous "mattress" of medium: the machine

According to Novalis, art is an organic reality that is produced *in* nature *in the same way* that nature produces, but a reality that is nevertheless an autonomous system, with its own logic and conventions independent of any presupposed referent. Nothing demonstrates this principle better than the reversal that Turner effected between thickness and thinness. While large volumes of high density—buildings, figures, trees—are generally rendered in a medium of slight consistency, as if they had been pulverized by a vibrating flux capable of eroding away their definition (Figs. 375–378), the immaterial components of nature—light most of all—are stroked on with a palette knife in fat, structuring deposits. *Rain, Steam, and Speed* (Fig. 384) exemplifies the latter technique, especially in the clouds of the upper right corner, the locomotive's lantern, and the three plumes emitted by the smokestack. Here the painter has transmuted countless impalpable, unstable, ethereal, diaphanous data into an opaque, crustlike texture, the medium so thickly applied that the relief formed by its contours on the flat painting surface casts shadows when struck by a raking light. We should also note the emphasis placed on the radiance emanating from under the arch in the foreground, where the pigment simulating light is not only much heavier than that for the stone structure itself but has even been incised with fingernails or a brush handle.

The imperious thrust of the perspectival axis finds itself intercepted and blunted at midground by an amorphous, cottony "mattress" (cf. Fig. 381). Such a generalized cushion of color leaves viewers to free-associate as they wish, to find within themselves a latent sense of the image offered by Turner's painting, to see in the high-key strokes to the right of the boat, for example, a group of bathers, nymphs—or just bits of pigment.

This picture is the masterpiece of a type that art had been moving toward since the end of the 18th century, a work in which sublime themes are translated into the language of modern techniques. Turner painted the fusion of industrial vapor with those traditional constituents of atmosphere—rain and fog—the fusion brought about by a new factor: speed. (Indeed, the artist may have conceived the idea for his picture while leaning out the window of a train as it traveled over this very site.)

384. Joseph Mallord William Turner (1775–1851). *Rain, Steam, and Speed: The Great Western Railway.* 1844. Oil on canvas, 2'11¾"×4'. National Gallery (courtesy of the Trustees), London.

# Out of a sweeping, tumultuous storm of color and gesture, the picture is born

385. Joseph Mallord William Turner (1775–1851). *Rockets and Blue Lights (Close at Hand) to Warn Steamboats of Shoal Water.* 1840. Oil on canvas, 3′1¼″×4′. Sterling and Francine Clark Art Institute, Williamstown.

In Fig. 386 an explosion of *matière* ("medium") develops into a spiraling movement that is made all the more pronounced by the visible trails left by a furrowing brush. The picture seems born of the rapid rhythms struck by an arm sweeping across the canvas. With gesture counting for more than image, the emotional experience of a storm is expressed through corporeal mobility. The catalogue of the 1842 exhibition insisted that "the author was in this storm on the night the *Ariel* left Harwich." Certain stylistic analogies with other works, notably the Williamstown picture painted just two years earlier (Fig. 385), would suggest a slow maturing of an audacious plastic conception, rather than an actual participation in the storm. (The artist was then sixty-seven years old.) This seems all the more likely given the fact that a similar anecdote accompanied *Rain, Steam, and Speed* (Fig. 384). But the literal truth matters less than the obvious determination on the part of the artist to place himself not *in front* but at the *very heart*—at the epicenter—of his material. It all came about as if Turner had been interested not so much in the *mist* that envelops things as in the original *mix* from which things emerged only later, less the atmospheric fog than a primordial lack of differentiation among species, genera, and textures. The artist would seem to have sought a regression to the old pre-Socratic cosmogonies, in which earth, water, fire, and air were understood to have been mingled in "the netherworld," in Tartarus, whose dark immensity resembled the sea. Not *Poros*, the buoyed, domesticated sea, but "*Pontos*, with its thousand routes [that] resemble an endlessly effaced highway, a road that is never laid out, a path that is closed as soon as it is opened. In this chaotic expanse, where each crossing takes the form of a voyage over an unknown and forever unrecognizable region, motion reigns without end."[4]

386. Joseph Mallord William Turner. *Snow Storm—Steamboat off a Harbor's Mouth Making Signals in Shallow Water, and Going by the Lead. (the Author Was in this Storm on the Night the Ariel Left Harwich).* 1842. Oil on canvas, 2'11¾"×4'. Tate Gallery, London.

387. Joseph Mallord William Turner (1775–1851). *The Angel Standing in the Sun.* 1846. Oil on canvas, 2'11¾"×4'. Tate Gallery, London.

## Images materialize from a magma of painterly substance

388. Joseph Mallord William Turner. *Undine Giving the Ring to Massaniello, Fisherman of Naples.* 1846. Oil on canvas, 2'4¼"×2'6¼". Tate Gallery, London.

Several of Turner's last works, executed when the seventy-year-old artist was ill and melancholic, seem possessed of a slow girational movement. They make one think of an imploding nebula or the gradual extinction of a lantern. For the exhibition of the *Angel Standing in the Sun* (Fig. 387), representing the Archangel Michael announcing the Last Judgment, Turner added a pair of quotations to the catalogue. One came from the Revelation (14: 17, 18): "And I saw an angel standing in the sun; and he cried with a loud voice saying to all the fowls that fly in the midst of heaven, come gather yourselves together unto the supper of the great God; that ye may eat of the flesh of kings, and the flesh of captains and the flesh of mighty men, and the flesh of horses, and of them that sit on them, both free and bound, both small and great." The other was borrowed from *Voyage to Columbus,* a poem by Turner's friend Samuel Rogers: "The morning march that flashes to the sun; / The feast of vultures

when the day is done." Into his painterly stew the English master threw Biblical fragments, then seasoned the mixture with barely formed beings— Adam and Eve, Cain, a skeleton, Samson and Dalilah, Judith and Holophernes (above)—or kneaded into it a fatty pigment studded with thronging figures (opposite). Images from time immemorial surge up from the general stir of the painterly substance. Almost a half-century earlier, the painter Farington had already observed: "Turner has no settled process but drives the colours abt. [sic] till He has expressed the Idea in his mind." It was this inductive process that here found its ultimate realization. The subjects were not prepared in advance by any kind of mental drawing; rather, they emerged from the texture and took shape from a humus-like ground, their identity fixed only by a rare accent of color.

It was with some ostentation that Turner made a habit of going to the

Royal Academy during the three days reserved for "varnishing" and there finishing pictures that he had delivered in an almost formless state (Fig. 117). No doubt he wanted to demonstrate and thus emphasize a practice that for him seemed the very foundation of his art.

*Undine* (Fig. 388) derived from the same method, albeit under a more anecdotal guise. This Neapolitan fantasy shows a fisherman netting a marine goddess who can attain immortality only by stealing the soul of a mortal through marriage to him. Here she offers the man a ring. The picture draws the viewer in mainly by what seems to be a compositional vortex. Replacing the articulation, coherence, and equilibrium of parts is a kind of luminous zone glowing from within the central nucleus. Meanwhile, Vesuvius burns in the left background. (Gerald Finley, in the November 1979 *Burlington,* has published a detailed study of *Undine* and *Angel Standing in the Sun.*)

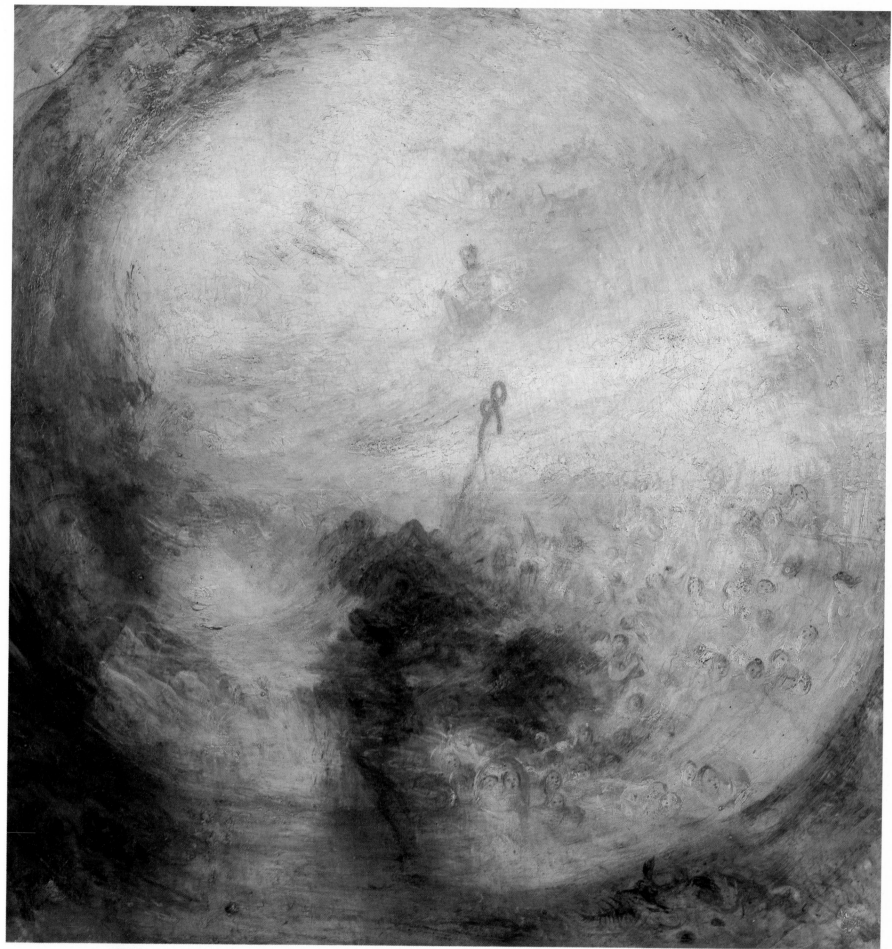

389. Joseph Mallord William Turner. *Light and Color (Goethe's Theory)—The Morning after the Deluge—Moses Writing the Book of Genesis.* 1843. Oil on canvas, 2'6¾" × 2'6¾". Tate Gallery, London.

# CHAPTER IV

# The Exploration of Color

390. P. J. de Loutherbourg (1740–1812).
*A Coal Mine at Night.* 1801.

391. J. M. W. Turner (1775–1851). *The Burning of the Houses of Parliament.* 1834.

392. P. J. Volaire (1729–1802).
*Eruption of Mount Vesuvius.* c. 1780.

393. J. Wright of Derby (1723–97).
*Eruption of Vesuvius.* 1774–75.

The cataclysms of nature, urban catastrophes, the nocturnal fires of industry—all provided the artist with an occasion to display sublime spectacles capable of exalting the soul. As the architect Boullée wrote: "A volcano vomiting flames and death is an image of horrible beauty!" But fires, eruptions, and tall furnaces were also a pretext for spreading a great quantity of vivid color over the canvas without regard for the traditional balance of light and dark.

At the very outset of his authoritative *Grammaire des arts du dessin* (1867), Charles Blanc hazards a metaphor that says much about what had always been viewed as the "evil" character of color: "Drawing is art's masculinity; color, its feminity. . . . It is essential that drawing retain its dominance over color. Otherwise, painting will fall into ruin; it will be lost through color just as humanity was lost through Eve." Color is feminine, therefore fickle, transient, uncontrollable, and suspect, whereas form is "precise, contained, palpable, and constant." And this curious Manichaeism even took on a political tone, with color likened to an "overture," or indeed an "adventure." "[Color] was associated with freedom and line with tyranny," notes Francis Haskell in *Rediscoveries of Art* (1976). Whatever their politics, colorists found themselves branded as "heretics," even as "disturbed" and "crazed."

Assumed to be irrational, color figured hardly at all in teaching, and when it did, the lessons usually took the form of academic recipes. Since the 17th century, students had begun by endlessly and patiently copying line engravings known as "drawing models." The method had a profound impact, conditioning young artists to adopt a linear manner even when working from a live model or before a landscape motif. "This elementary drawing instruction encouraged stylistic tendencies that would affect painting techniques as well," Albert Boime tells us in *The Academy and Painting* (1971). Marigny, Directeur des Bâtiment under Louis XV, made certain that students at the French Academy in Rome devoted themselves not simply to drawing but to "history" drawing. In a letter to Natoire, then head of the Academy, Marigny wrote: "Insist that pupils have the pencil in hand more often than the brush."

For Winckelmann, who was then formulating the theory of what would become Neoclassicism, "color contributes to beauty . . . whose essence [however] consists not in color but in shape." The same sentiments were to be heard even from Fuseli, an apostate Neoclassicist: "When it is the object of the arts . . . to make sense the minister of mind . . . . *Design* [drawing], in its most extensive as in its strictest sense, is their basis; when they stoop to be the mere playthings, or debase themselves to be the debauchers of the senses, they make colour their insidious foundation."

The same was true of David, who for twenty-five years reigned over both a prolific studio and the whole of French painting. This artistic tsar viewed color as merely "a related element, a complement of drawing, an aspect of objects, a supplement to value; it does not of itself afford pleasure." As long as painting remained subordinate to the expression of established paradigms, of presupposed meaning (indeed, to the illustration of a moral lesson, as in David), as long as form was to be the product of a prior commitment and to appear upon the canvas only as the sign of an external world of preexistent givens, color continued to be treated as *supplementary.* Color could reinforce meaning, but not produce it. In the words of Rousseau: "Beautiful, nicely shaded colors are pleasing to the eye, but this is purely a pleasure of the senses. It is the drawing, the imitation that gives these colors life and soul. . . . The lines in a touching picture touch us even in a print. Remove these lines from the picture, and the color no longer does anything."

It should also be mentioned that before the gradual spread of museums in the 19th century, most paintings were hung in inaccessible private collections. Thus, painters and art lovers had to depend upon engravings or written descriptions (such as those in Diderot's *Salons*) for their knowledge of older or even contemporary art. "The effects of both these indirect forms of communications in guiding general taste can hardly be overestimated," writes Francis Haskell. They produced a taste for drawing and the crisply delineated image, a taste that, when applied to the past, made linear styles—those of 15th-century Flemish and Florentine "primitives"—seem preferable to the painterly, vaporous manner of the Venetians or Correggio. (There was considerable circulation of prints among painters. In the 19th century Constable, despite his modest means, owned some five thousand.)

Thirty years after Rousseau, Kant adopted a similar position in his *Critique of Judgment* (1790). Here, colors are merely "charming." "Certainly," the 18th-century philosopher declared, "they can make the object seem sensuously alive, but not beautiful and worthy of being contemplated. Indeed, they are more often than not restricted by the requirements of beautiful form, and it is only beautiful form that lends them dignity even where the charm is tolerated." A bit further along in his argument Kant undertook to classify the fine arts into three main categories: the verbal arts, the figural arts, and the arts that play upon the senses. This means, as J. C. Lébensztejn has noted, that Kant separated painting from color, for while his system included painting (along with architecture and sculpture) among the figural arts, it relegated color to the third category, in company with music.

Carried to its ultimate conclusion, this logic would totally exclude color from painting. But to isolate color as a constituent element of the picture, to distinguish its effects and consider the specific rules and controlling principles that give it life (contrast, shading, optical mixture, etc.) was to grant that the pictorial components do interact upon one another. Moreover, it was to question the unity of a project or a practice that, since the Renaissance, had been based exclusively on the idea of imitation or the subordination of painting to denotation.

A century after Diderot, such critics as Blanc and Silvestre still felt obliged to justify their interest in Delacroix on the basis of realist considerations. For them, color would have its place wherever it alone could render certain aspects of the world. "When it comes to painting sensations produced by inorganic matter and the feelings that well up from our innermost selves, color becomes the means par excellence," admitted Charles Blanc. Silvestre put it this way: "Only color gives us a sense of reality, movement, the location of figures in relation to one another, and the air they breathe."

Going further, however, and tolerating color as a mode of expression without strictly subordinating it to depicted objects would, in the view of Blanc, reverse the order of things and lead to objects chosen solely for the purpose of producing coloristic effects. "In *The Massacre at Chios* [Fig. 394]," wrote Blanc, "a particular *sabretache* was placed in that corner

394. E. Delacroix (1798–1863).
*Sketch for the Massacre at Chios.* 1823–24.

Distributed over the canvas in flat, planar zones, the reds
serve to activate the whole scene. A second network of
silvery white performs the same function.

395. E. Delacroix. *Page from
the Moroccan Sketchbook.* 1832.

During his travels, Delacroix noted and elaborated the
effects of color.

396. J. B. Corot (1796–1875). *The Dream.* 1870.

During the night of September 9–10, 1870, Corot dreamed
that the Prussians took Paris by surprise and burned it. He
then made this sketch, depicting the fire in horizontal trails
of red. The capital would in fact be put to the torch several
months later by the French Commune.

because [Delacroix] needed an orange accent
there." What the painter risked was making not only
his choice of theme but soon even his whole composition subject to purely sensory imperatives. Finally, "the physical impression" would supplant
denotation. The tendency was fatal, since "it is well
known that the dominance of color over design
would result in the usurpation of the absolute by the
relative, of permanent form by transient appearance, and the empire of the spirit by the physical
impression."

Now this attack upon the absolute, upon the
spirit, upon the "dignity" of painting was precisely
what Baudelaire applauded in 1855 when he wrote
in a famous statement: "Viewed at a distance too
great to permit analysis or even an understanding of
the subject, a picture by Delacroix has already produced upon the mind a rich, happy, or melancholy
impression. . . . It seems that this color . . . thinks
by itself, independently of the objects it clothes."

This emancipation can be grasped, however, only
by taking into consideration the work of scientists
who, beginning with Newton in 1704, set out precisely to investigate color as a specific, measurable
phenomenon endowed with its own laws. Their
study of the decomposition of light, the chemistry of
pigment, and the physiology of vision would eventually have its effect in painters' studios. Once the
primary colors were understood as measurable, it
became possible to organize them into a system. No
longer were they, as Kant wrote, "pure sensations,
but already the formal element determining the unity within a variety of sensations." Once there is
measure, there is form, and the form/color opposition loses its pertinence.

Le Blon, in his *Traité du coloris* of 1756, stated
the existence of the primary colors: red, yellow, and
blue. At the end of the century Schiffermüller in Vienna and Harris in London scientifically proved the
complementary nature of the three primaries and
the three secondaries. He also suggested their possible relevance to painting. At the same time, the
investigation of after-images and the presence of
color in shadows provided evidence that, as John
Cage has phrased it, "the eye 'demanded' a complementary juxtaposition of colours, and induced it au-
tomatically when one colour was looked at for some
time." Around 1800 most painters were in command
of the principle of complementarity among hues.
Thus, despite the weight of academic dogma and the
canonical commitment to imitation, color was now
perceived as having its own economy.

Delacroix, during an 1832 journey, saw Morocco
and Spain primarily in terms of color patches. His
journal is filled with such notations as these: "A Jew-
ess stands out vividly: red cap, white drapery, black
dress"; "Men illuminated along the edge of one side.
Shadows on white objects full of blue reflections.
The red of saddles and turbans, almost black." In the
drawing reproduced here (Fig. 394) color forms a
patch as much as it does a sign. And if, over the
years, Delacroix paid so much attention to the radiance within nature (the color of shadows, the play of
complementaries) he did so less for the purpose of
"faithfully" reconstituting the landscape than for discovering formulas that could be applied to the color
combinations in his works, whatever the theme. Delacroix looked at nature the same way he looked at
pictures.

For Goethe, color had its beauty; hence, there
was no need for it to represent anything. It responds
to a biological, instinctual, indeed a therapeutic necessity. "In general," he wrote, "human beings experience great happiness at the sight of color. The
eye needs light. . . . Therapeutic effects have been
attributed to colored gemstones—perhaps because
of this deep feeling of ineffable well-being." The
*Theory of Colors* (1810), to which Goethe devoted a
great many years, records innumerable experiments
with prisms, convex lenses, irisations, etc., in which
color is produced for its own sake and praised for its
"charm," "intensity," "power," "finesse," etc. It was
in this context that Goethe devoted an entire page
to ways of blowing bubbles and to their chromatic
effects: "The most ordinary kind are soap bubbles,
whose beauty is the most striking. But they can also
be formed with wine, beer, pure spirits, and, especially, chocolate when whipped into a mousse."

Here was color enjoyed for itself, scrutinized,
analyzed in the gleam of a soapy film—but also on
the basis of a vision in which objects and forms would
hereafter be treated as secondary or supplementary.
"Extraordinary though it may seem," Goethe declared, "we insist that the eye does not distinguish
form—rather, it is light, shadow, and color that
come together and permit our vision to distinguish
one object from another. With these three elements—light, shadow, and color—we construct the
visible world and at the same time make painting
possible." Goethe therefore concentrated all his effort on the task of liberating color from the denota-
tive function to which it had been subordinated and
of reversing the academic tradition that had made
drawing the vehicle of beauty and meaning. Color
has the capacity, he wrote, "to contribute to the
highest aesthetic aims." Thus, in the same para-
graph, he added: "We should not be surprised by
the effects [that color], in its most basic and general
manifestations, has on the eye, to which it is the
servant par excellence—and, through the eye, on
the sensibility, even without there being any reason
for the substance or the form of an object on the surface where we see it."

But once a color has been unburdened of its debt
to objects and presented as an abstraction, meaning,
which abhors a vacuum, returns by another route,
that of associative symbol. Goethe saw hue as the
vehicle of atmosphere and mood. He divided the
spectrum into two zones: *Plus*, which contains the
*warm* colors—yellow, orange, red lead, and vermi-
lion (all of which "make us inclined toward anima-
tion, vivacity, and effort"); and *Minus*, designating
the *cool* hues—blue, blue-red, and red-blue (which
evoke suffering, fatigue, anxiety). In regard to yellow, for example, Goethe stated that "in its purest
state, it conveys the very nature of light and possesses the character of serene enjoyment and sweet
stimulation." Red "gives the impression of gravity
and dignity as well as benevolence and grace." As
for red-yellow, "it is not surprising that vigorous,
healthy, hearty people find this particular color
agreeable." In contrast to Newton, who considered
light refracted through a prism as nothing more than
a simple phenomenon of particle physics, Goethe
attempted to reintroduce a system of meaning. To
each he attributed a personality, a role in a psycho-
physiological continuum, and an anthropological coherence that—albeit pure fiction—tended to re-

397. T. Rowlandson (1756–1827). *A French Dentist Showing a Specimen of His Artificial Teeth.* 1811.

The violent effect of such enlarged details and chromatic aggressiveness anticipated Ensor and 20th-century Expressionism.

398. W. Blake. Detail of Fig. 399.

399. W. Blake (1757–1827). *Newton.*

A Michelangelesque figure is set against a madreporic material in which color has run free of all constraint.

400. J. E. Millais (1829–96). *The Blind Girl.* 1856.

The Preraphaelites reinforced their hyperrealist precision with flat, vibrant color.

store stimuli, sensations, and emotions to a universal vision of man. "What, in brief, Goethe rejected in Newton's theory," observes Gaston Bachelard, "is its failure to see anything but the *superficial* aspects of color. For Goethe, color is not merely a play of light, it is an *action* within the depths of our being, an action that awakens essential, sensitive values. 'Colors,' said Goethe, 'are the actions of light, actions and sorrows.' "

Forty years later, Goethe's color symbolism was to be echoed by Delacroix ("Everyone knows that yellow, orange, and red generate and represent ideas of joy, richness, glory, and love"). And still later Kandinsky would incorporate the system just as it was in his *Concerning the Spiritual in Art* (1912), one of the first manifestoes of pure abstraction. Goethe's own source would have to be sought in the emblematic codes of heraldry and religion. But Robert Klein has found another precedent in the mystical ideas of the Mannerist master Lomazzo, an early 17th-century Milanese painter and theoretician who classified the emotional properties of color in relation to astrology. Goethe's thinking partakes of a long irrationalist and alchemical tradition that flourished even in the writings of that great man of the Renaissance: Alberti. In a pre-Socratic manner, he declared: "There is the color of Fire, so to speak, that we call red; there is that of the Heavens, which is called celestial or blue; the color of Water, which is green; the color of Earth, an ashen color." This ties the hues to the four Elements, creating a relationship that Bachelard would call "the imagination of matter."

Hegel, in his *Aesthetics* of 1835, subscribed in part to Goethe's analysis. He too spoke of the "magic of colors" and granted them primacy over drawing, which "forms only the external framework of painting. . . . It is therefore color or coloration that constitutes the element par excellence of painting . . . its utmost vitality." But the symbolic conception so dear to Goethe was discreetly relegated to history: "One could also search for symbolic import in the way the painters of former times employed primary colors, especially when it came to blue and red. . . . The Blessed Virgin, who when shown enthroned as Queen of Heaven, wears a red mantle, in contrast to the blue mantle that she wears in her role as Mother." In reality, Hegel saw color as free of all prescription: "Already drawing is less reducible to general laws than linear perspective, but color escapes altogether. The meaning of colors should be a quality that is individual to each artist, a particular mode of vision and conception of existing tones and shades, as well as an essential aspect of the artist's imagination and powers of invention."

The main difference, however, lies elsewhere. Hegel could not accept the principle of color's expressive autonomy as formulated by Goethe. To whatever extent color may be primordial, it is because color "makes objects seem endowed with life and spirit." For the Berlin philosopher, the best demonstration or supreme proof of color, "its ideal side, so to speak," is rose or pink, "the tone of human flesh that, in a remarkable way, combines all colors, without any of them becoming dominant." Joy being both the best of all themes and the paradigm of all painting, the challenge is to paint flesh while also making the picture become flesh (come to life), with all the transparency and luminosity, all the subtle,

unctuous, melting qualities that oil encourages. If Hegel had no difficulty visualizing a nonobjective painting, he also made a point of warning that such a development would precipitate the end of painting as a specific practice. He even suggested that color contains a destructive principle: "That magic produced by colors manifests itself mainly where the substantiality and spirituality of the object have disappeared in order to take refuge in, during the process of animating, the conception and utilization of colors. One could say, in general, that the magic consists in treating all colors so as to produce a nonobjective play upon appearances." Once "content" has been diminished and neutralized, "painting, through the opposition and harmony of colors, through their contrast or reciprocal reinforcement, begins to approximate music, just as sculpture, in the process of evolving into bas-relief, begins to approximate painting."

This takes us back to the schema devised by Kant: the more color, at the heart of the pictorial organism, takes precedence over denotation, the more painting resolves itself into music. The approaches taken by Goethe and Hegel intersect without overlapping. For the one, color is autonomous, independent of all referent, but loaded with a constant symbolic charge; for the other, color remains obligated to denotation, but independent of all symbolic systems. Nineteenth-century painting would oscillate between these two positions until finally overcoming them dialectically, thanks to the conception of *differential* color, a conception that emphasizes color as a combinative in which each hue becomes expressive only by virtue of the hues that are adjacent to it.

But what is immediately striking, even before this notion can be examined, is the degree to which color, from Diderot to Baudelaire, had assumed importance, in both theory and practice, as an expressive force and a major element of painting. That "hyperbole of color" which the critic Jal deplored in the work of Delacroix exhibited at the 1828 Salon became this master's most significant quality in the opinion of Baudelaire. "For those people," wrote the poet, "color does not dream, does not think, does not speak." It was Fauvism that Baudelaire anticipated when he exclaimed: "I would have fields dyed red and trees painted blue." As in his reply to Alphonse Karr's criticism of the "pink" horse in Delacroix's *Justice of Trajan*, Baudelaire complained that "it was as if pinkish horses did not exist and as if, moreover, the painter had no right to make one."

The case of Ingres is significant, since he feigned contempt for color ("A thing well drawn is always sufficiently well painted") all the while that he proved himself a remarkable colorist in a number of works whose audacity astonishes even today (Figs. 401–405). "M. Ingres," wrote Silvestre, "has nothing in common with us. He is a Chinese painter wandering through the 19th century in the ruins of Athens. . . . The violence of the tones, reacting against the correctness of his lines, makes the figures advance or withdraw counter to the will of the painter who staged the scene. . . . The various planes have been indicated and the figures disposed according to their linear scale, but in vain. That false coloring manages to upset everything, transforming voids into solids, destroying distance, suppressing atmosphere, crowding, suffocation, crushing, and flatten-

215

401. J. D. Ingres (1780–1867). *Portrait* of J. B. *Desbédan*. 1810.

402. J. D. Ingres, *Wounded Amazon*. c. 1806–12.

403. J. D. Ingres. *The Duke of Alba at Saint Gudule's in Brussels*. 1815.

Although accused of being an indifferent colorist, Ingres actually engaged in extremely bold experiments with color: the coloring *à l'antique* in Fig. 402; the tone-on-tone effect in Fig. 401; the warm, sumptuous reds of Fig. 403.

ing all the figures one against the other like a deck of cards."

But what Silvestre considered a weakness would soon be regarded as a decisive innovation to which Matisse and Picasso would pay ample tribute. Ingres' strategy (as his drawings of Roman architecture suggest) consisted in unsettling the perspectival arrangement common since the Renaissance in order, by means of color, to affirm the frontality of the picture. "Create perspective with colors," wrote Leonardo, "in relation to the size of objects; that is, colors lose some of their nature to the degree that bodies, at different distances, undergo a diminution of their natural quantity." Ingres proceeded to work in opposition to this system. Whenever he had to deal with depth (and many of his pictures show that he avoided this altogether [Figs. 165–170, 416, 417]), the master disallowed as much as possible the reduced intensity demanded by atmospheric perspective (Fig. 404).

However, it was only Ingres's student Amaury-Duval who would sense what makes the coherence of such an approach, showing how much color, in a picture like *Roger and Angelica* (Fig. 283), reinforces the very factor that the arabesque line has already affirmed: the presence of the flat painting surface. In his memoirs (1878), Amaury-Duval judiciously recalls "those Japanese paintings that a young, new school claims to have discovered, M. Ingres admired them sixty years ago. The proof of this is in the portrait of Mme Rivière and in the Pourtalès *Grande Odalisque*, about which the critics said: 'This work resembles the colored drawings that sometimes decorate arabic or Indian manuscripts.'"

Meanwhile, in the same period, the advent of color was also being confirmed on the other side of the artistic scene, by Turner in his semiabstract watercolors (Figs. 440, 441) as well as in his oils (Figs. 430, 431), where the immateriality of light is expressed by means of thick crusts of pigment laid on with a palette knife (Fig. 406). Here was a new technique, "a combination of gaudy hues intended," as Hazlitt phrased it in 1816, "to become a striking point of attraction on the walls of the exhibition," whose freedom of facture convinced contemporary critics that the painting had been executed willy-nilly with whatever tool happened to be lying about. The image of Turner "sweeping" a canvas with a broom (Fig. 117) corresponds to the apt description that Théophile Gautier has given us of Goya's method: "He collected color in buckets, applied it with sponges, brooms, dusters, and anything else that fell into his hands; he troweled and masoned his tones like mortar, and made his expressive touches with great strokes of the thumb. Aided by these expedient and peremptory procedures, he could cover some 30 feet of wall in one or two days. . . . Using a spoon as his brush, he executed the *Third of May, 1808*, in which we see the French shooting down the Spaniards. It is a work of incredible verve and fury. . . ."

At the same time that they caricature, such anecdotes acknowledge and even render commonplace a new conception of how to paint. Thus, as indicated earlier, the 19th century is notable for its general awareness of the *differential* and *structural* character of color. For Baudelaire, isolated hues did not exist, and color was "the harmony of two tones. The

warm tone and the cool tone, in whose opposition all things reside, cannot be defined in an absolute way; their existence is purely relative." And Charles Blanc: "Without even touching a color, one can fortify, sustain, thicken, and neutralize it virtually by working on adjacent colors."

This relativity of hues—hues that in themselves have no reality since they are literally produced or effected by other hues (which also depend upon other hues, and on and on)—discloses the existence of *significant color*—an autonomous chain of chromatic reactions, which functions alone and "manages" the surface without any longer being obligated to the figurative component of the picture. The notion of *local color* loses its pertinence since it now becomes impossible to pretend that color has either identity or permanence. As soon as Delacroix began thinking of color as an independent "martingale," as a play of reflexes and interactions, an ineluctable distance came to be established between process and "subject." This subject, as the trip to Morocco indicates, would itself soon constitute nothing more than the occasion for chromatic combinations. Another example appears in a journal entry made by Delacroix in 1849: "Returned via Ourville. Coming from Cany, a beautiful view: cobalt tones appearing in the verdant masses of the background in contrast to the vigorous and occasionally golden tones of the foreground." Here, color has "devoured" objective detail and nullified the concrete existence of form. Nature is abolished in the opposition of blue and green. As Fritz Novotny has observed: "The painting of Delacroix contains the first hints of that painterly structure which dominated the art of the latter part of the 19th century, the first presage of the subjection of the illustrative element to the play of chromatic forms."[1]

Painters also discovered that color obeys certain laws, which themselves are linked to the psychology of vision, and that these laws somehow function without regard to the individual artist and his intentions. Contemporary science confirmed this sense of dependency or nonmastery on the part of painters grappling with the uncontrollable effects of hues. In 1839 Chevreul published his work on "the law of the simultaneous contrast of colors." There we read: "To place a color on a canvas is not merely to give that color to everything the brush has touched, it is also to color the surrounding area with its complementary. Thus, a red circle is surrounded by a halo of light green, which will progressively weaken as it extends outward." One does not simply produce the interaction; it is already there, imposing itself from without on the artist's design. Thus, the painter acknowledged a resistance that he began to be able to name, to objectify in a rule. In this respect, color is comparable to language, since one can "speak" a language only by respecting its system.

Delacroix made every effort to measure these constraints methodically, to adapt himself to them, to turn them to his own advantage, and to apply them on every scale, from a small bit of canvas to the wall-size composition. "Rather than simplify local colors by generalizing them," wrote Silvestre, who had watched Delacroix paint, "he multiplied the tones to infinity and opposed them one to the other in order to give each a double intensity. . . . If green dominates a figure on its shaded side, red will dominate on the illuminated side. If the light-struck

404. J. D. Ingres. *Odalisque with Slave*. 1842.

405. J. D. Ingres. *Sleeping Woman, Nude*.

In closely related themes. Ingres developed two radically opposite conceptions of color, exemplified by the white, linear brilliance of the odalisque in Fig. 404 and the deep, warm tones of the nude in Fig. 405, whose radiance seems produced by light refracting off the surrounding decor.

406. J. M. W. Turner (1775–1851). *The Fighting Temeraire* (detail). 1839.

The effect of an immaterial sky is created by a crust of paint so thick it stands out in relief.

407. F. Goya (1746–1851). *The Executions of the 3rd of May, 1808* (detail). 1814.

The martyred body stains the canvas. Since the 15th century, blood (as in the Crucifixion, the Crown of Thorns, and Veronica's Veil) had given license for a free handling of both color and texture, where a sly complicity with medium can be detected.

part of the figure is yellow, the part in shadow is violet. If it is blue, orange is placed in opposition, etc., throughout the painting."

Perceived from a certain distance, depending upon the size of the strokes or zones of paint, colors tend to melt together and blend. This is *optical*, as opposed to *chemical*, mixing. Delacroix became a passed master of the technique, which, he said, gives "painting an accent that colors mixed on the palette cannot." Here again, the aim was to exploit the constraints of vision as fully as possible. Enlarged to architectural scale, the process culminated in the half-nude figure in the central cupola at the Luxembourg Palace, where, despite the height and darkness of the site, Delacroix managed to effect what Charles Blanc called "the most delicate, transparent, and appealing hue." By what miracle did he do this? "By the boldness with which Delacroix brutally slashed the figure's nude torso with hatchings of strong green, which, partially neutralized by its complement, rose, forms with that rose, while being absorbed by it, a tone whose blend and freshness can be sensed only from a distance."

Obviously, these methods did not originate with the painter of *Sardanapalus* (Figs. 317–322), and the artist himself had observed them in Veronese and Rubens. In the mid-18th century, Hogarth considered it common knowledge, "that had the colours there [in the paintings of Rubens] been so bright and separate, been all smooth'd and absolutely blended together, they would have produced a dirty grey instead of flesh-colour." Even David, the head of the Neoclassical school and often regarded as a master of smooth painting, insisted on being credited with the broken quality of his brushwork: "If you examine my pictures carefully . . . you will see that they are not worked over any more than necessary. If they seem much worked over, it is because the value of the colors and the vigor of the brushwork are calculated in relation to planes and combined according to the distance from which the spectator should view the picture. In painting this is what constitutes finish. As Doyen used to say . . . finish does not finish."

But if optical mixing was not an altogether novel painting technique, the 19th century did initiate the process of systematizing and theorizing its effects, to the point where the age finally understood color as a relatively autonomous element in the economy of the picture. This evolution corresponded, meanwhile, to a certain "surfacing" of color, a process whose realization passed through the "divisionism" of Seurat and Signac to culminate in the art of Robert Delaunay and Paul Klee. It was in a restrospective, indeed nostalgic, vein that Goethe wrote in 1810: "Artists formerly practiced a method that consisted in painting on a light ground. This ground was constituted of chalk affixed in a thick layer on canvas or wood and polished. Then one would make a drawing, after which the image was covered in a wash of blackish or brownish color. . . . As one colored, the image below the light wash continued to act. For example, one painted a garment in a transparent color, through which the white would show, giving life to that color. At the same time, the part already given over to shadow attenuated the color without its being altered or dirtied."

Here was the old charm of transparency, of layer upon layer, of glazing. It would require the whole intelligence of Matisse, at the beginning of the 20th century, to structure a work upon the tension between the two tendencies: the old one, which favored transparency and glazing; and the new one, which validated the effects of surface and optical mixing.

Caught in a lava flow
of filament-like strokes,
figures seem absorbed into
the earth-colored ground
upon which they are painted

408. Jacques Gamelin (1738–1803). *Cavalry Charge*. 1786.
Pen, wash, gouache, watercolor, pastel, 11½ × 16½". Collection Galerie Joseph Hahn, Paris.

Jacques Gamelin, who made his career mainly in the Midi (Toulouse, Montpellier, and Narbonne) after a ten-year sojourn in Rome (1765–74), developed the technical aspects of his art as if medium itself could yield a kind of handling capable of embodying his particular conception of the figure and its effacement. He painted on slate, on copper, ''on marble by a process of penetration and firing,'' all the while that he also did paintings on canvas for large ceiling decorations and even miniatures.

In the works seen on these pages, where several processes have been combined, the physical consistency of figures and horses seems threatened, owing to the images' bare emergence from an ocher ground spread over the entire surface (which radicalizes an effect found in the 17th-century works of a Benjamin Cuyp or a Philips Wouwerman), or to their entrapment in the debacle of colors and long, filament-like strokes. The deposits of pigment resemble a lava flow, impelled as if by its weight to become lost in texture (canvas or earth), the substance doing less to constitute figures than to disintegrate them.

What happens here with respect to color—the relation of bodies to a material that absorbs them—the artist repeated elsewhere in engraving. His *New Collection of Osteology and Myology Drawn from Nature,* meant for artists and scientists, is a monument of black pre-Romanticism (Fig. 27)—''the most incredible collection of funeral scenes ever assembled since the *danses macabres* of the 15th century'' (François Pupil).

409. Jacques Gamelin. *Cavalry Charge*. 1786. Pen, wash, gouache, watercolor, pastel, 11½ × 16½". Collection Galerie Joseph Hahn, Paris.

# Fires and other catastrophes call for pure color

411. Hubert Robert (1733–1808). *The Burning of Rome.* 1787. Oil on canvas, 2′8″×2′2½″. Hermitage Museum, Leningrad.

412. Hubert Robert. *Burning of the Opéra in the Palais-Royal, Viewed from a Crossing in the Louvre.* 1781. Oil on canvas, 12½×9½″. Musée de L'Opéra, Paris.

As an excuse for allowing every kind of red to explode over the canvas—billowing masses, incandescent clouds—the theme of fire assumed a new amplitude at the end of the 18th century, mainly in the art of Hubert Robert, who confessed to being "fascinated by flames and their forms."

In the 16th and 17th centuries, Sodom, Troy, Hell, and Neronic Rome had given rise to a rich play of chromatics, notably in the Low Countries. Robert brought the subject up to date by making himself the chronicler of great urban dramas, which he observed firsthand from his apartment over a crossing in the Louvre (Fig. 412). "There is no spectacle we so eagerly pursue, as that of some uncommon and grievous calamity," wrote Burke in his treatise on the sublime and beautiful, "so that whether the misfortune is before our eyes, or whether they are turned back to it in history, it always touches with delight." In Robert, the scene is mediated and observed by one or several groups of spectators, placed in the distance, and framed by an intervening structure that holds the subject at its position in depth (Figs. 410, 411), as if to illustrate another statement by Burke: ". . . terror is a passion which always produces delight when it does not press too closely." This was the aesthetics of catastrophe, and Stendhal paid tribute to it in 1812 during Napoleon's withdrawal from Moscow, four years after Robert's death: "We left the city illuminated by the most beautiful fire ever seen, an immense pyramid that, like the prayers of the faithful, had its base on earth and its summit in the heavens. The moon appeared above that atmosphere of flame and smoke. An impressive spectacle, but to enjoy it one would have had to be either alone or among spirited people."

410. Hubert Robert. *Burning of Paris' Hôtel-Dieu in the Middle of the Night.* c. 1773. Oil on canvas, 4′9″×3′7″. Collection Cailleux, Paris.

## A vision of Hell demands
## the deployment of a thousand shades of red

From a somewhat marginal family in northern England came one brother who developed into a sort of street philosopher, another who led the life of a firebrand, before ending up in a mental hospital, and, finally John Martin (''mad Martin''), one of the most popular painters of his generation and the sworn enemy of all academic institutions (which found his canvases contrived and vulgar). And the esteem this artist enjoyed was accorded not only by the masses susceptible to vast ''machines'' but also by certain Continental writers who, beginning in 1830, considered Martin to be his country's greatest artist, the master of vertiginous effects and fabulous invention. His influence can be felt even in the 20th-century cinema. Indeed, D. W. Griffith seems to have incurred a debt to Martin for the Babylonian section of *Intolerance* (1916), the American filmmaker's masterpiece.

Martin specialized in the gigantic. His pictures usually portray immense geological or historical convulsions, such as the fall of Nineveh, the destruction of Sodom, or the Last Judgment. Overwhelmed by universal chaos, his populations founder in the collapse of empires or in the yawning chasm of doomsday. The artist was a true master of rushing perspectives and loved to exploit the contrast between minuscule silhouettes—solitary or literally countless figures—and immeasurable spaces strewn with colossal composites of architecture. The inspiration for all this came from Piranesi, that virtuoso of broken scale, and Turner, whose epic nature and sense of Alpine grandeur (Fig. 525) Martin appropriated. Spectacularly descriptive

pictures like that reproduced here, coincided with certain contemporary scientific conceptions, which presented the history of the terrestrial globe as a series of violent disruptions, geological and climatic disintegrations, and cataclysmic changes. This was particularly the position of the paleontologist Cuvier, who saw in Martin's disasters a pictorial expansion upon his own theories. The French savant even visited London in order to congratulate the artist on the scientific conformity of his visions.

With Milton's *Paradise Lost* as its point of departure, the canvas reproduced in Fig. 413 constitutes a lurid fantasy on the theme of Hell. Far in the distance on the left, whole files of the damned can be seen in an orderly procession behind banners, edging their way along a sea of molten lava, all the while that in the right foreground several of Lucifer's minions argue and meditate in the manner of Arcadian shepherds. Martin may have discovered his model in the spectacle of modern metallurgy, with its foundries and streams of white-hot iron. The connection can be found as early as 1851 in Théophile Gautier's reverie *à la Martin* in which the author evoked, like a true Romantic or an Expressionist *avant la lettre,* the industrial world in all its giantism and inhumanity: ''Under the city of the living spreads the city of the dead, the dark city of immobile inhabitants. Wide air shafts, gaping like the jaws of Hell, lead to the area of crypts and syringes. In the vomitory cities labor funereal races, tribes of gravediggers, slaves of death; those who fuse natrum and bitumen in crucibles. . . .''

413. John Martin (1789–1854).
*The Fallen Angels Entering Pandemonium.* c. 1841.
Oil on canvas, 2'½"×2'6". Tate Gallery, London.

## Pigment structures the canvas in large, monochromatic zones

By building up a wall of yellow behind the portrait subject (a celebrated actress) and making the color both rich and intense, laid on in large unequal patches—the facture becoming the picture's most pregnant and energetic theme—Goya, in Fig. 414, violated principles formulated and followed throughout the 18th century, preeminently by Rousseau and Kant, who held that color, the generator of pure sensation, was merely an *extrinsic* element of pictorial art. "In painting, in sculpture, and indeed in all the plastic arts, in architecture, in the art of gardening as well as in the fine arts, the essential factor is drawing," wrote Kant in his *Critique of Judgment* (1790). "That which, for reasons of taste, makes it the fundamental condition is not that which produces an agreeable sensation, but uniquely that which pleases for its form. The colors that illuminate drawing are not the attraction; they can enliven the object for the sake of sensation, but not make it worthy of being looked at and beautiful."

All of Goya's art rejects this position. Not only is it the massive eruption of color that unifies his painting, assuring the work's impact and coherence, but it even establishes itself as indissolubly bound to the other constituent elements of a picture. In a passage like that of the yellow settee, we cannot possibly think of the color without simultaneously thinking of the direction of the strokes and the grain of the pigment. The further Goya went in his art— particularly in the works created for himself at La Quinta del Sordo (Fig. 505)—the more he made color a substantial reality in which chromatic

radiance is always conceived as a consistency. What color loses of the concrete, in terms of representation, it regains in material weight, in terms of texture.

A vigorous and flamboyant painting, John Singleton Copley's *Lord Heathfield* (Fig. 415) anticipates, in its cropping as well as in its liberated color, the most daring of the large portraits by Toulouse-Lautrec. The canvas above is a sketch worked up in the presence of the model preparatory to a vast battle picture: *The Siege of Gibraltar*. The universal power of red to produce shock and optical excitement has been guaranteed by the suitably "uniform" tone spread over much of the ocher ground.

415. John Singleton Copley (1738–1815). *Lord Heathfield.* 1787. Oil on canvas, 2′2½″ × 1′10¾″. National Portrait Gallery, London.

414. Francisco Goya (1746–1828). *Antonia Zarate.* 1810. Oil on canvas, 3′4½″ × 2′8¼″. Collection Sir Alfred Beit, Blessington.

# Isolated against a dark ground, color becomes mass

416. Jean Auguste Dominique Ingres (1780–1867). *The Iliad* (after *The Apotheosis of Homer*). c. 1850. Oil on canvas, 13¼ × 20¾″. Private collection.

The 20th century has very largely rejected the old, hackneyed antithesis of Ingres the draftsman and Delacroix the colorist, which was a modern extension of the dichotomies that have never ceased to become systems in the aesthetic discourses of the West, pitting Raphael against Titian, Poussin against Rubens, etc. ''Both [Ingres and Delacroix] expressed themselves in *arabesque* and *color*,'' Matisse wrote in 1945. ''. . . They forged the same links in the chain. Only nuances prevent their being confused with one another.'' And to indicate the importance of Ingres, who was one of his sources of inspiration, just as he was for Picasso, Matisse went on: ''The first, he would use pure colors and limit them without denaturing them. . . .''

If, at age seventy, the painter of the solemn and chilly *Apotheosis of Homer*

(1827, Louvre) felt the need to extract from that immense composition the personifications of the *Iliad* and the *Odyssey* so as to make them into two separate paintings, it was probably because he wanted to afford himself the experience (and the pleasure) of color for its own sake, while also giving the lie to the tiresome anagram that had been made of his name: *En-gris* (''In gray'').

Like such 16th-century German masters as Dürer, Cranach, and Baldung Grien, Ingres posed his figures against a black, smooth, dense ground (unlike the *Apotheosis of Homer,* where the images appear before a stone pedestal). This dark field lends all its warmth to the drapery's hue, green or red. By means of the figures' skewed postures as well as by their reduced shading and modeling, Ingres succeeded in

contracting depth (he loved to denounce ''the dumb show called *trompe l'oeil*''), the better to offer, at first glance, a frontalized field—a high note—of pure color.

Still, color here is not merely a matter of extreme opposition among three hues: flesh, drapery, and background. Far from strictly monochrome, the draperies are shared by two or three juxtaposed values of the same hue. Thus, in the *Odyssey* (Fig. 417), the green-yellow used as a base color has been heightened by a darker green. Through subtle manipulations, the artist introduced here and there, in the flesh as well as in the fabric, a few gray tones that seem to echo the black ground.

Viewed from a lowered angle, the monumental figures of the *Iliad* and the *Odyssey* have been painted in the finest layers of pigment, utterly without impasto. At the time Ingres insisted upon a facture as thin ''as the skin of an onion.'' ''Apply medium evenly throughout,'' he said. ''I do not see in nature either pronounced touches or highlighted colors.'' Jules Laurens, in his *Légende des ateliers,* shows Ingres ''taking three strokes of the palette knife to scrape down a student's pointlessly impastoed canvas: 'What remains will be enough!' '' He also described the master ''planted before a house painter on the Rue Vavin who was painting a grocer's shop front: 'Well now! *cher Maître,* what are you doing here?' asked a passing colleague from the Institute. By way of response, Ingres pointed to the workman: 'Look,' he said, 'and admire. He takes and puts on *only what is necessary!*' ''

417. Jean Auguste Dominique Ingres. *The Odyssey* (after *The Apotheosis of Homer*). c. 1850. Oil on canvas mounted on wood, 2′ × 2′9¾″. Musée des Beaux-Arts, Lyon.

# Glitter from the calculated disorder of color touches

418. Francisco Goya (1746–1828). *Ferdinand VII*. 1814. Oil on canvas, 6'11½"×4'9½". Museo del Prado, Madrid.

A screen of yellow touches glitters on the red ground of the King's mantle. Crushed, scraped touches, fat, square ones standing out in relief, sometimes sectioned by the point of a brush handle—the freedom learned from Velázquez here bursts out in chromatic incontinence (Fig. 418). It was not so much the smooth, obstinate face of Ferdinand VII (painted from old studies made in 1808 and as inexpressive as the heavy white hose encasing the figure's calves) that appears to be the real subject of this picture, as the surging, streaming color (see Fig. 419). The artist had only to load the mantle border with the necessary *quantity* of reds, yellows, and blacks in order for the desired effect to occur. The point was not to paint an object but to provide a chromatic equivalence of it. If the dabs of color—left unmixed—seem strewn over the surface one by one, where they accumulate like superimposed and mingled stitches, close looking confirms that any supposed disorder in the brushwork is in fact the product of great calculation. See how the rain of pigment was suspended to allow the red ground to come through, in exact proportion to the other colors. To push the enlargement to an arbitrary degree—to take a detail from the detail—would produce what might pass for a picture by Jackson Pollock, the American Abstract Expressionist of the 1950s whose "dripped" surfaces, viewed at the same scale, would probably seem not so far removed from Goya's colorism in this simple fragment from a large canvas.

Goya did not believe in the pictorial reality of line. "Lines, lines," he said, "and never forms! But where do they find lines in nature? I see only illuminated bodies and bodies that are not illuminated, planes that advance and planes that recede, reliefs and hollows. My eye never sees features or details. I do not count the hairs in the beard of the man who passes by, nor do the buttonholes of his clothing prove any more arresting for my eye. My brush should not see any better than I do. As opposed to nature, those simple masters go from the detail to the whole, and their details are almost always fictive or false."

419. Francisco Goya. *Ferdinand VII* (detail of Fig. 418).

## The picture is nebulousness that densifies bit by bit

420. Antoine Jean Gros. *Napoleon Decorating the Artists* (detail of Fig. 421).

421. Antoine Jean Gros (1771–1835). *Napoleon Decorating the Artists* (sketched in). 1808. Oil on canvas, 11'5¾"×21'. Musée National du Château, Versailles.

Gros' giant sketch reproduced in Figs. 421 and 420 shows Napoleon giving the Legion of Honor cross to David, surrounded by painters at the 1808 Salon. Here the hues have been applied in large fluid zones and unified by their veil-like thinness and transparency. These sheets of partially superimposed color possess a texture that varies by their size as well as by the constantly shifting gesture of the brushwork, with each new change of direction releasing a different kind of illumination. The colored shadows were obtained by means of a more continuous tissue of tone. If Gros borrowed from his master David the technique of *frottis*—that loose, brushy kind of "scumbling" seen in *Marat* (Fig. 156) and *Madame Trudaine* (Fig. 270)—he also altered its function. The author of *Bara* (Fig. 273) had shown the most minute concern for the contours of his figures before transferring them one after the other to a surface already prepared with a vibrant layer of regular strokes. With Gros, however, the figures proceed directly from the color, through a gradual densification of the tints, emerging upon the surface like so many nebulae whose materialization occurs bit by bit. Gros thought of his canvas as the sum of his interventions, or as a collection of fields or "gauzes" that he would progressively accent by the addition of flat, light colors (the white belt worn by the small boy, the pale parts of the mother's dress). The entire canvas should "come up" at the same time. "Bring out every part simultaneously," he said to his pupils, "so that if the task is interrupted, there will be homogeneity throughout, whatever the state of advancement."

Such characteristics can also be found in Gros' study for the *Pesthouse at Jaffa* (Fig. 422), a huge floating, rather shapeless cloud populated by convulsive specters, a realm in which the abstract structure of the hospital room seems drowned in a thick texture striated by strokes from a disorderly brush. Even the figure of Bonaparte, carrying one of the *pestiférés*, disengages itself with difficulty from the surrounding central group. But all this confusion has dissipated in the final, carefully crafted version (Fig. 423), where the scene is now dominated by a play of arcades reflecting, as Friedlander noted, a surprising interest, for a fanatic disciple of David, in the period's Gothic Revival. The picture, Delacroix tells us, had an immense success: "Great numbers of workers, men of the people, banging at the doors or climbing onto one another's shoulders, appeared at the windows, six-franc pieces in their hands, and begged Gros to let them in."

The work was intended to efface the bad impression produced by the French

422. Antoine Jean Gros. *Sketch for Napoleon in the Pesthouse at Jaffa*. 1804. Oil on canvas, 2′4¾″×3′¼″. New Orleans Museum of Art.

423. Antoine Jean Gros. *Napoleon in the Pesthouse at Jaffa*. 1804. Oil on canvas, 17′5½″×23′7½″. Louvre.

army's massacre of Jaffa's civilian population, and by the summary execution of four thousand Turks who had surrendered on the promise that their lives would be spared—who, however, were dispatched first with bullets but then, for reasons of economy, by the sword. Bonaparte wanted to reverse the emotional charge contained in the name "Jaffa." The painting achieved its purpose to perfection, offering the image of a thaumaturge, or miracle worker, calmly touching the sores of the afflicted, like Saint Louis at an earlier time caressing the scrofula of the plague-stricken.

The transfiguration of the ordinary into the epic was the generative force behind Gericault's *Chasseur* (Fig. 425), painted when the artist was twenty-one (at the time of Napoleon's invasion of Russia) and inspired by an ordinary spectacle on the public highway: "The initial idea for his *Chasseur* came to [Gericault] one day when he was going to the festival at Saint-Cloud. Along the route he saw one of those big delivery wagons that the artisans of Paris rent at a fixed rate and transform on such occasions into omnibuses, this one drawn by a gray horse of no beauty but full of fire and magnificent in color. Little accustomed to harness, the high-spirited animal reared in the midst of dust under a brilliant sun, eyes bloodshot, mouth foaming, and mane caught up by the wind. The artist had found his picture. The sun was the one at Austerlitz. The dust became the smoke of battle, and the horse, a battle charger intoxicated and crazed by the smell of gunpowder, the clash of arms, and the thunder of cannon" (Charles Clément, 1868). This was the kind of heroic transmutation that constituted the very soul of Géricault's creative genius. Later the artist would explain that every morning during his work on the *Chasseur* he had himself brought "a hackney horse sometimes streaming with water and covered in mud. 'It had nothing,' he added, 'of the activeness that I needed, but I looked at it and this took me back to the [Saint-Cloud] horse.' "

Géricault, however, could formalize this stop-action excerpt from everyday life only by pressing it into the mold of established painting. Thus, the first version of *Chasseur* (Fig. 424) has strong affinities with David's *Napoleon at Saint-Bernard* and with the figure of Murat in Gros' *Battle of Eylau* (Fig. 510), executed four years earlier. But from study to study Géricault progressively effected a radical reversal of the composition. The curvilinear conception of the "first thought" (Fig. 424) was then traversed (Fig. 426) by a diagonal of a much more violent nature, the beast's leg in the lower left foreground stretched out like an expanded coil, assuring the image its dynamic thrust. Meanwhile, that flat, gaudy blob serving as the general form of the cavalry officer and his mount radiates and expands, touching the edges of the sheet with hooves, tail, and shako plume.

Directly descended from Rubens and Gros, color has been disposed in a play of thick, vigorously applied accents, like so many cores of energy: slabs of red for the cape, the plume, and the jacket cuff, but also an edging of the same intense hue around the trousers, the horse's foreleg, etc. These effects provide strong contrast with the zones of vivid yellow and with the heavy deposits of pigment punctuating the rump and the panther skin. "Where does this come from?" exclaimed David standing in front of the final picture at the 1812 Salon (Fig. 425). "I do not recognize that touch."

424. Théodore Géricault (1791–1824). *Study for the Charging Chasseur*. 1812. Oil on canvas, 20×15¾". Private collection, Paris.

## Applied in slabs and accents, pure hues invest the picture with new energy

425. Théodore Géricault. *The Charging Chasseur*. 1812. Oil on canvas, 9'7"×6'4¾". Louvre.

426. Théodore Géricault. *Study for the Charging Chasseur*. 1812. Oil on paper mounted on canvas, 17×13¾". Musée des Beaux-Arts, Rouen.

# Whether slow or turbulent, the stroke or patch of color precedes figuration

427. Théodore Géricault (1791–1824). *Cavalryman Striking the Enemy.* c. 1820. Pen, watercolor, and gouache, 11×15". Musée des Beaux-Arts, Lille.

By its concentration of colored energy, the large sketch (Fig. 428) that Delacroix made for his *Lion Hunt* represents a triumph of that "breadth," that "high-strung" quality, that "verve" and "fire" which the artist sought to project into his "most beautiful inflammations." Baudelaire characterized the final version as "a veritable explosion of colors. . . . Never did more beautiful or intense colors penetrate to the soul by way of the eyes."

But "the virulent and frenetic patchiness of this sketch, its exuberances of color raised to maximum intensity, with its dominant reds and yellows 'electrified' by dark blues and browns,"[2] also constituted a triumph of

method (another application of which can be seen in Fig. 429). According to the late-19th-century painter-theoretician Signac, Delacroix took every care to "superexcite" his colors by using color on color as a means of shading and colors separated by only short intervals on the chromatic scale: "He made a point of not spreading a uniform color over his canvas. He caused a hue to vibrate by superimposing on it strokes of a very close hue. For example, a red would be studded with touches either of the same red but in a lighter or darker value or of another red, a somewhat warmer one—with more orange in it—or a chillier, more violet one."

This modulation through the

juxtaposition of closely related color tonalities struck Delacroix's contemporaries: "Where even the color of Rubens glows like a tranquil lake, that of Delacroix glitters like a river pelted by a rainshower," wrote Théophile Silvestre, who often watched the painter work. And, we have this from Charles Blanc, writing in his *Grammaire des arts du dessin* (1867): "He made his surfaces throb with hue on hue. . . . Instead of applying his color flatly, he dabbed it on top of the same, but more saturate, hue, which would show through slightly everywhere and evenly enough to produce, from a distance, the impression of unity, while also giving an unusual depth to the hue thus

428. Eugène Delacroix (1798–1863). *Lion Hunt*. 1854. Oil on canvas, 2′9¾″×3′9¼″. Private collection.

modulated—thus vibrating—upon itself. . . .''

But after submitting momentarily to the charm of Delacroix's chromatic effervescence, the same author, who was an academician and the founder of the *Gazette des beaux-arts,* recognized the threat all this posed to the principles taught by the École des Beaux-Arts, an institution wholly dedicated to the primacy of drawing and ideal form: ''The passionate colorist . . . invents his form through color. . . . For him everything is subordinate to the brilliance of hue. Not only does drawing give way to it and should give way, but composition is governed, hindered, and brutalized by color. In order to introduce here a violet that will super-

excite a certain yellow drapery, one must arrange a space for that hue, invent an accessory which may be unnecessary.''

Color has its own laws. It disturbs the harmony afforded by drawing. And Delacroix (''the chaos man,'' as the painter Couture called him) was at the genesis of those ''deformations'' that modern art would sanction. ''I should be little surprised,'' wrote van Gogh, ''if soon the Impressionists find fault with my way of working, which has been more fertilized by the ideas of Delacroix than by theirs. Because instead of seeking to render exactly what I have before my eyes, I use color more arbitrarily in order to express myself powerfully.''

Contrary to Delacroix (or Rubens), Géricault for the most part never attempted to realize an immediate, organic whole in the first study or sketch that he did for a painting. He followed the procedure established by David, working up a succession of ideas and finally transferring them to the canvas. The watercolor in Fig. 427 appears to be a copy made from memory of a fragment of George Jones' *Waterloo,* which the French artist had seen in London. It may be that Géricault used the little exercise as the central motif in one of his last works: the Wallace Collection's *Charge of the Cuirassiers.* On paper partially covered with gouache and watercolor (in which silhouettes are discernible here and there), we can see

how figures emerge out of the reserve, take their form from the broad flat areas (which look forward to Rodin's washes) and, by virtue of the modeling and the disposition of highlights, progressively detach themselves from the surface.

## Thick and fatty, color "thinks" by itself

Preparing for his large encaustic *Pietà* at Saint-Denis-du Saint-Sacrament (Fig. 429), commissioned by the Préfecture de la Seine in 1840 and executed in 1844, Delacroix worked up a superb sketch in which he pushed to the limit his conception of color as a radiant, autonomous force. For the general disposition of the picture's contents, the artist borrowed rather freely from the so-called *Écouen Pietà,* painted in France during the 16th century by the Italian master Rosso Fiorentino and installed in the Louvre under Napoleon. But the chromatic material—fat, heavy, and stirred about like pigments on a messy palette—typifies the 19th century. Both in his journal and in remarks to Baudelaire Delacroix reveals his commitment to a three-fold principle:

● Color functions at the level of the subconscious, where it becomes a "much more mysterious and perhaps more powerful [force]; it acts, so to speak, without our knowledge.

● Color generates specific effects that are not lined to the objects represented. "Delacroix's color is often plaintive," observed Baudelaire, who in 1850, guided by the painter himself, articulated his celebrated formulation of abstraction: ". . . Viewed at a distance too great to permit analysis or even an understanding of the subject, a picture by Delacroix has already produced upon the mind a rich, happy, or melancholy impression. It could be said that the painting, like sorcerers or mesmerizers, projects its thought from a distance. . . . It seems that this color . . . thinks by itself, independent of the objects it clothes."

● Finally, color favors the frontal unity of the surface: "In almost all paintings that are not coloristic," wrote Baudelaire, "one can always see voids, that is, great holes produced by tones that are not, so to speak, on the same level."

In the 20th century, many artists would struggle to eliminate those "holes"—meaning all sense of value contrast—and to invent an *isotropic* painting, a painting equally "resistant" at every point of the planar space. For this reason a great appreciation developed for the interrelationships that Delacroix had achieved among hues. These functioned as a system, for, as Théophile Gautier noted in 1855, "his color does not impress by the great vivacity of its reds, greens, or blues, but by the range of nuances that validate one another. His rich tonalities are not beautiful in themselves; their brilliance results from their juxtapositions and contrasts. Muffle a certain shrill-seeming stroke, and harmony would be destroyed. It is as if you removed the keystone from a vault." Here is a conception that should be familiar from its legacy in the art subsequently produced by the Neo-Impressionists, van Gogh, the Fauves, etc. But Delacroix gave it additional nourishment, according to his contemporary Théophile Thoré, from pantheistic and cosmological associations, convinced that the structural interdependence of colors reflects the notion of a "great natural harmony," a universal system in which all forces are interrelated. This may have been what Delacroix meant when he wrote: "My palette freshly arranged and brilliant with the contrast of colors suffices to fire my enthusiasm."

429. Eugène Delacroix (1798–1863). *Pietà*. 1843. Oil on canvas, 11½ × 16½". Louvre.

430. Joseph Mallord William Turner (1775–1851). *Slavers Throwing Overboard the Dead and Dying—Typhoon Coming On.* 1840. Oil on canvas, 2'11¾"×4'. Museum of Fine Arts (estate of Henry Lillie Pierce), Boston.

According to Hugh Honour, *The Slave Ship* (Fig. 430) was a product of the antislavery campaign that began to rage in Great Britain around 1840. The African trade had just been written up in a book containing, notably, "a spine-chilling account of the slave ship *Zony* in 1783, when the captain had a large cargo of slaves thrown overboard during an epidemic, so that insurance, payable for those lost 'at sea' but not from disease, could be claimed."[3]

Turner's picture stupefied the public when it was exhibited in 1840. Thackeray mused about the work in an article: "Is the picture sublime or ridiculous? Indeed I don't know which." But he went on to describe the "flakes of white laid on with a trowel; bladders of vermillion madly spirited here and there . . . gasping dolphins redder than the reddest herrings; horrid

spreading polypi, like huge, slimy, poached eggs, in which hapless niggers plunge and disappear."

But the canvas has elicited other, closer interpretations. Lawrence Gowing, for instance, tells us that the youthful Turner had planned to paint a picture illustrating a phrase from the Apocalypse: "And water turn'd to blood." "It could not be painted then," writes Gowing, "it was to be one of the basic themes of his life."[4] Blood is the vehicle that gives its unity and color to *The Slave Ship*. The fiery red blazing on the horizon constitutes a lyrical expansion of a substance suggestive of blood, pus, and vomit, something resembling the disaster of a slashed and broken body enlarged to global dimensions. The most singular touch of all may be the woman's leg extended above the waves in the foreground, its

shackle still attached, while all about swim a school of white, flirtatious fish.

*Ulysses Deriding Polyphemus* (Fig. 431) is, by comparison, a relatively resolved picture in which the ships' rigging, the decoration on the sides of the vessels, and the figures of the nymphs at the waterline have been minutely described. Ulysses, standing on the top deck, defies the blinded giant cowering just beyond the mountain ridge. The work is one in which the norms of 19th-century mythological painting have been observed. But with its fanlike disposition radiating from two patches of crusted white, the color could not but stir contemporary viewers. "The sunrise throwing its rays upon the golden vessel dyes the waves a dazzling yellow," we read in the French magazine *L'Artiste* (1836). The general character of the sky was obviously

obtained by scraping a palette knife across the canvas, an action that crushed the substantial heaps of pigment as the instrument moved. Thus, the color seems less deposited than dragged. The solar rays having been invested with the greatest thickness, the paint becomes progressively thinner toward the left. And so, here again, we find the paradox mentioned on page 206: the more diffuse and impalpable the effect, the harsher and heavier the handling.

# Gold, blood, and light—color takes fire

431. Joseph Mallord William Turner. *Ulysses Deriding Polyphemus—Homer's Odyssey*. 1829.
Oil on canvas, 4'2¾"×6'6¾". National Gallery (courtesy of the Trustees), London.

# The scene empties, making way for the abstraction of clouds

432. Alexandre François Desportes (1661–1743). *Cloud Study at Sunset.* c. 1700?
Oil on paper, 11×13″. Manufacture Nationale, Sèvres.

The scene empties, as if by the shift of one's gaze, while concrete objects move to the margins, giving way to variegated, mutating masses of clouds (see also Figs. 489–492). Desportes, the *animalier* who painted abundant decorations for princely houses, left a studio crammed with some six hundred studies—watercolors and drawings still largely unknown—that with real justice are regarded as inspired anticipations of *plein-airisme*. His oils on paper (Fig. 432) were executed before the motif. According to his son, Desportes "carried his brushes and loaded palette into the fields, [the materials packed] in a tin box. He had a cane with a long pointed steel tip to hold it firmly in the ground, and the steel head that opened contained a small frame of the same metal, to which he attached the portfolio and paper. He would not go into the country, visiting friends, without taking this light luggage, which never bothered him and which he never failed to use."

What this practice established a century before Constable was the freedom of a chromatic and compositional approach stripped in one stroke of all academic bias. A genre was being created, albeit for documentary reasons (furnishing models to the Manufactures Royales), that would remain unchanged right up to Impressionism.

Valenciennes (Fig. 435), at the end of the century, reinvented the same method (see also Figs. 305, 327, 371, 372), multiplying his views of the Roman Campagna where he sought particularly to capture the metamorphoses of light and the changing play of clouds. "Every study made from nature," he wrote in *Réflexions et conseils* published in 1796, "should be made rigorously within an interval of two hours at the most. And if it is a rising or setting sun effect, no more than a half-hour should be allowed. . . . It is good to paint the same view at different times of day in

433. Eugène Delacroix (1798–1863). *Sky Study.* c. 1849. Pastel on gray paper, 7×9½″. Cabinet des Dessins, Louvre.

434. Eugène Delacroix. *Sky Study*. c. 1850. Watercolor, 10¾ × 15¾". Cabinet des Dessins, Louvre.

order to observe the differences produced on forms by light. The changes are so sensitive and so astonishing that one can hardly recognize the same objects.''

If in Desportes the *plein-air* study still served an essentially practical purpose, in Valenciennes the connection between such experiments and the artist's Salon work has already become much looser. And this proved all the more true with Delacroix, whose brittle, broken strokes in Fig. 433—executed, it would seem, from a window at Champrosay—have no corollary in the master's oils. And the discrepancy becomes all the more marked in the curious cloud (Fig. 434) where the fullness of the white form developed from a progressive expansion of the blues on the virgin paper (which was then darkened with traces of gray).

Brilliant contrast, overlapping forms, and an arabesque traversing the page suffice to justify a work that is less a ''rendering'' than a ''handling.''

435. Pierre Henri de Valenciennes (1750–1819). *Sky Study Made from the Quirinale*. 1782–84. Paper on cardboard, 10¼ × 15". Louvre.

241

which should increase his awareness through visual classification."

The source of Constable's recurring preoccupation with the rainbow (see Fig. 304) can be found in the last, large landscapes of Rubens. In both instances, the rainbow was important for its *plastic* value, which permits the picture surface to be traversed, occupied, and articulated by a regular curve, a firm geometry, a color offering a vigorous contrast to that of the sky (the ground)—even if it means achieving this, as Turner did in Fig. 437, by playing upon the whiteness of the paper.

The rainbow is a frontal form, parallel to the picture plane and generally symmetrical (when represented whole)—thus a form that recapitulates and reinforces the two-dimensional character of the painting. For a modernist eye educated by Delaunay and Malevich, this peremptory intervention by color in the chromatic and compositional economy of the work has a meaning quite different from any understood by Constable. Now we can perceive in the rainbow image a minimalist reduction of the painting to one feature that alone sums up the entire landscape, since the form contains virtually the whole of the spectrum. A watercolor like that in Fig. 438 (reproduced one-third larger than the original) could be seen as a sort of "zero degree" of figuration, realized in a single multicolored line.

But it can also be viewed with the eyes of Cézanne, who wrote in 1904: "Light does not exist for the painter" (meaning that Cézanne recognized only color). From his perspective, the rainbow becomes an instance in which color-light is transformed into color-pigment (into medium and texture) by the painter, and the work remains simply that: the revelation of this passage or change, this "substantiation." The modernist reading may be anachronistic, but it also shows why, without it, this type of sketch was hardly even taken seriously before the 20th century.

436. John Constable (1776–1837). *Landscape and Double Rainbow.* 1812. Oil on paper, 13×15″. Victoria and Albert Museum, London.

# The rainbow, like an incision cut into the canvas

"The modern vice today is bravura, the need to go beyond truth," wrote Constable at the early date of 1802, and the theme of sincerity, of authenticity—in which the Englishman prefigured the Impressionists—would be a leitmotiv of his existence. It was in this spirit that Constable explored those meteorological phenomena: clouds and rainbows (Figs. 436, 438). Later, his library was found to contain a copy of Thomas Forster's *Atmospheric Phaenomena* (2nd ed., 1815), duly annotated by the artist. Moreover, he had copied the cloud studies in Alexander Cozens' *New Method* (1785), studies prepared by the 18th-century author as learning aids for his students. E. H. Gombrich, in *Art and Illusion,* has been instrumental in showing that the vaunted naturalism of Constable had its limits and that his supposedly immediate rapport with nature was filtered through a variety of cultural experiences. What Constable found in Cozens, writes Gombrich, was "a series of possibilities, of schemata,

437. Joseph Mallord William Turner (1775–1851).
*Landscape with a Rainbow.* c. 1820. Watercolor, 8¾×11″.
Collection Sir Edmund Bacon, Bart.

438. John Constable. *Sky Study with a Rainbow.* 1827. Watercolor, 9×7″.
Yale Center for British Art (Paul Mellon Collection), New Haven.

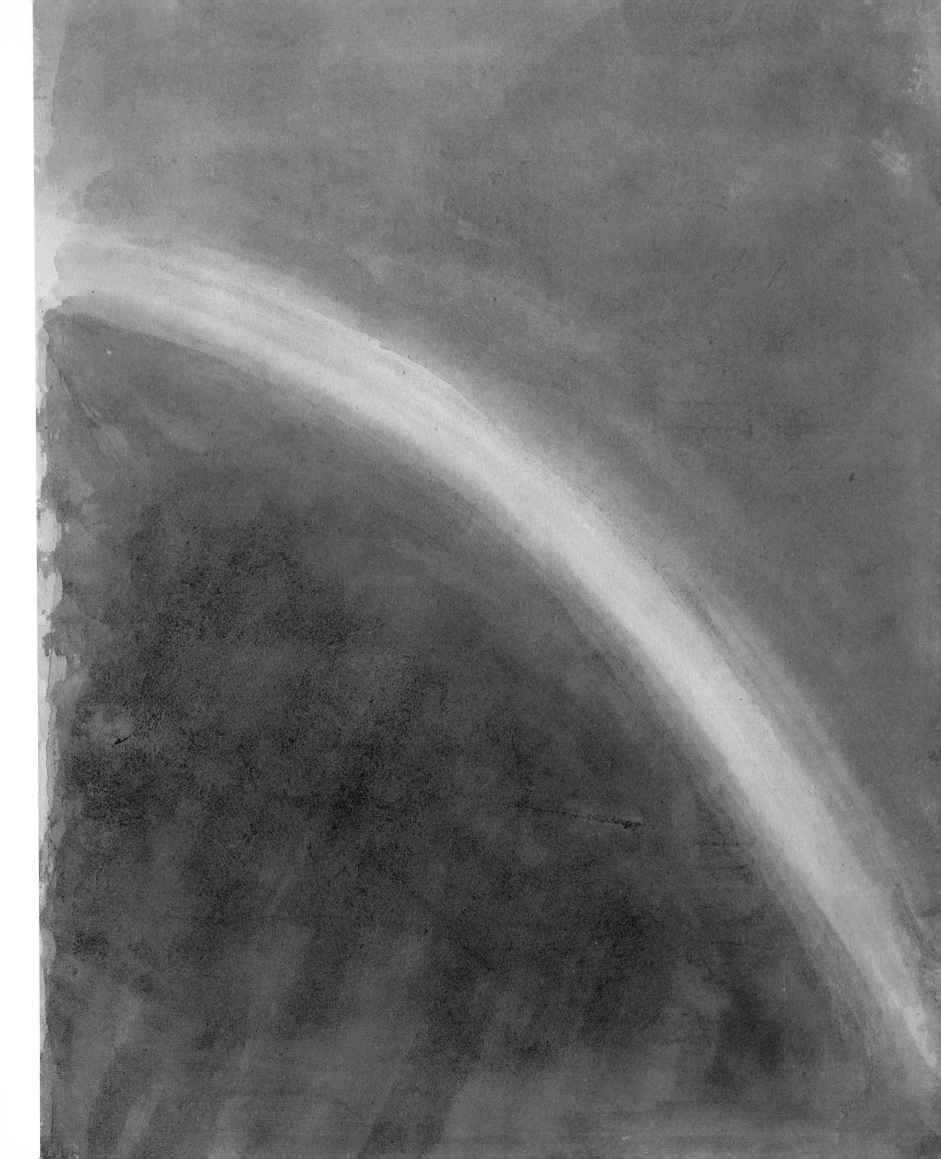

Among the 19,049 drawings and watercolors that Turner left to the British nation, certain sheets—now called ''colour-beginnings''—offer nothing more than wide areas divided into two or three parallel, horizontal zones painted edge to edge. As Lawrence Gowing has emphasized, the ''beginnings'' preceded the formation of objects that subsequently occurred in the course of gestural and color interventions—dripping, marbling, tearing, etc.—made while the paper remained damp. Thus, figuration serves only to interpret the disposition of colors to which it is subordinate.

The watercolor in Fig. 439 dates to 1799, when Turner was twenty-four years old. It comes from a series commissioned by William Beckford, the author of *Vathek* and a famous eccentric who wanted a visual record of the country house, a ''gothic abbey,'' that he was then having built at Fonthill (Fig. 77). Turner took up a position at considerable remove from his motif, which resulted in the large frontal zone occupying two-thirds of the sheet. More important, the sheet was immediately filled in its totality. In other words, the reality of the surface intervened in the art as an active force: It conditioned the proportions of the image and thus determined its plastic character.

This cannot be said of *Ehrenbreistein* (Fig. 441), which shows the fortress near Koblenz. At first, one sees only an area of pink, an acid color that in the artist's time was itself an amazing motif. Then the small dark strokes begin to appear, pen strokes that denote a bridge drawn in perspective. Next comes forth the road up to the citadel, obtained by scratching into the pigment. Finally, the church, the boat, etc., assume form. The suggestive power of that diaphanous medium is all but endless. For Turner, the surface was simply a means. He could add to it (by strokes of the pen) and infiltrate it with color (by soaking), but he could also produce highlights or figures by stripping away particles of paper. For this procedure the artist cultivated his famous ''eagle claw,'' a sharply filed thumbnail. Early on Turner developed the habit of working with his fingers, and most of the watercolors he produced bear the imprint of his thumb. He even thinned color with his saliva—and had handles put on the underside of his drawing board so that at any moment he could plunge it into water and thus soften the forms on the attached sheet. Here, therefore, was a master who integrated the accidental and the imponderable into the artistic process. Turner, in fact, wished and hoped for the unforeseeable reaction of his medium. As Gowing has very well put it: ''He never lost an accident.''

## Fluid, generalized zones, the world before the advent of objects

## In Blake's symbolic system, color is message

443. William Blake (1757–1827). *Ancient of Days*. 1794–1827. Watercolor, black ink, and gold paint on etched matrix, 9×6¾". Whitworth Art Gallery, Manchester.

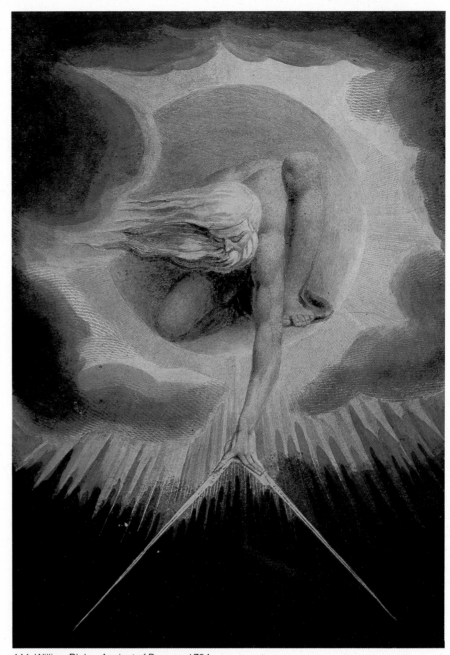

444. William Blake. *Ancient of Days*. c. 1794. Engraving touched with pen and watercolor, 9×6¾". British Museum (courtesy of the Trustees), London.

For Blake, the choice of color had nothing to do with aesthetic intentions or even with figural and mimetic needs. Indeed, the artist railed against the descriptive conception of painting represented by a Titian or a Veronese, which he associated with powder and patches:

*Venetian, all thy Colouring is no more Than Boulster'd Plaster on a Crooked Whore.*

And he said as much for Rubens: "To my Eye Rubens's Colouring is most Contemptible. His Shadows are of a Filthy Brown somewhat of the colour of Excrement; these are fill'd with tints & messes of yellows & red. His lights are all the Colours of the Rainbow, laid on Indiscriminately & broken one into another."

Blake, by contrast, saw color as a code, as emblematic and symbolic. His color refers to everything but itself. "For example," wrote Henri Lemaître, "the relations between yellow and red constitute in Blake a sort of magical process through which humanity gains access to the spiritual universe. . . ."

The same attitude obtains in regard to the *medium* of color. Blake rejected oil because he detested its rich substance

and ambiguous thickness, as well as its abundant content of mineral elements: earthen Sienna, zinc white, etc. It was watercolor—in all its lightness and translucency—that the English master found appropriate to his mystical flights.

*Glad Day* (Fig. 442, slightly enlarged) illustrates the transcendent quality that Blake attributed to color, expressed even in the way it radiates from the triumphant form of the Adam-like figure. The work, as Anthony Blunt has observed, seems in its freshness to be completely spontaneous. Actually, however, it derived from the famous diagram proposed by the Roman architect Vitruvius—a man proportioned to fit perfectly within a superimposed circle and square—and realized in its most spectacular form by Leonardo da Vinci. (As his model, Blake would have used a woodcut made after Leonardo by Scamozzi.) But Blunt also draws attention to another source: a pair of engravings representing a bronze faun, published in 1767–71 in a collection devoted to the excavations at Herculaneum. The double origin of *Glad Day* reveals how Blake appropriated—often unconsciously—all sorts of noble or trivial imagery, which he proceeded to condense and

reconstitute by a process of transmutation in which color was the determining factor. The work seen here began in 1780 as a black-and-white engraving. It was then redone in 1795 as a color engraving, which the artist finished in watercolor. Of particular interest are the lower left area, where the ground has been realized in a free proliferation of hues, all dominated by a spotting of red, and the dark zone on the right, with its thin rays scratched into the cushion of paint.

According to Blake himself, the *Ancient of Days* (Figs. 443, 444) originated in a "vision" that, he said, hovered overhead at the top of the stairs. So often did Blake have such illuminations that in a 1797 petition, the epithet "visionary artist" appeared after

his name, as if the highly individual works he created partook of an established pictorial genre. But the *Ancient of Days,* no less than *Glad Day,* was the product of the various sources, which Anthony Blunt has surveyed: medieval manuscripts and engravings after Mannerist pictures. Blake made his print as the frontispiece to one of his "prophetic books"— *Europe*—executed in 1794. On his deathbed the artist was still at work coloring one of the extant versions, each of which is distinguishable by its color. In the *Ancient of Days* he visualized the creator of the world as a divine geometer who is the antithesis of the painter-poet. For Blake the compass symbolized reason's claim of dominance over the tangible world.

442. William Blake. *Glad Day*. 1780–95. Color print touched with pen and watercolor, 10¾×7¾". British Museum (courtesy of the Trustees), London.

# Germinating and saturated with light, the mystical vegetation of Palmer

445. Samuel Palmer (1805–81). *Pear Tree in a Walled Garden*. c. 1829. Watercolor and gouache, 8¾×11″.
Collection Eugene Victor Thaw, New York.

A half-century before van Gogh, the Englishman Samuel Palmer (see also Figs. 521, 522), painted vibrant, ecstatic watercolors in which the forms—trees, flowers—resemble so many energy cells charged with radiant vitality. They are visionary works, articulated by proliferating curves (clouds, moon, chestnut trees, hills, sheep), pregnant with diffuse power and insistent with germination, through which their creator, a disciple of William Blake, wanted the viewer to sense, as if by condensation, the omnipresence of divine grace.

To achieve his purpose, Palmer devoted himself to a veritable regimen of spiritual conditioning. According to Kenneth Clark, the painter ''became a visionary by an act of the will.'' Living in retirement at Shoreham, a village in Kent, periodically joined by other painters, and sheltered from the industrial society that he abominated, Palmer established during those several years a quasi-hypnotic relationship with the exterior world. Clark speaks of ''visual experiences made more intense by the unconscious element of self-identification.'' The artist arrived at this state through prolonged contemplation, by reading Christian poets and the great mystics (Jacob Böhme, Milton, Swedenborg, Blake), and through a close study of 16th-century art (Dürer, Lucas van Leyden). Thus, he did not address landscape as a present fact, but instead filtered it through a kind of clairvoyance, a mystical consummation, a sensory exacerbation, an emotional densification. It was this hypersensitivity that caused him to raise his color key to a level then completely unknown. ''Sometimes,'' Palmer wrote in 1825, ''landscape is seen as a vision, and then seems as fine as art; but this is seldom, and bits of nature are generally much improved by being received into the soul, when she thinks on such supernatural works as Mr. Linnell's picture by Lucas van Leyden.''

A lingering memory from childhood, retold by the artist at the end of his life, sheds light on the character of Palmer's imagination: ''When less than four years old, as I was standing with [my governess], watching the shadows on the wall from the branches of an elm behind which the moon had risen, she transferred and fixed the fleeting image in my memory by repeating the couplet:

*Vain man, the vision of a moment made,*
*Dream of a dream and shadow of a shade.*[5]

I never forgot these shadows, and am often trying to paint them.''

446. Samuel Palmer. *In a Shoreham Garden*. c. 1829. Watercolor and gouache, 11½×8¾″.
Victoria and Albert Museum, London.

447. William Holman Hunt (1827–1910). *The Dead Sea from Siloam*. c. 1854–55. Watercolor, 9¾ × 13¾".
Birmingham Museums and Art Gallery.

## Violet, sulfurous, and bleached, the manic exoticism of Holman Hunt

Holman Hunt, even more than his fellow members of the Pre-Raphaelite Brotherhood, was a fanatic about "real" documentation. To regenerate painting, he assigned it a moral and spiritual function and served this by paying the most scrupulous attention to the tiniest aspects of nature. So great was his concern for the authentic Biblical setting of *The Scapegoat* (Fig. 448) that the artist planted his portable easel on the very soil of Palestine, at the site of ancient Sodom on the shore of the Dead Sea, in one of the most arid and uncomfortable regions on earth. Working from morning till night under the protection of a parasol, accompanied by a bodyguard, and himself armed to the teeth against marauders, Hunt

448. William Holman Hunt. *The Scapegoat*. 1855. Oil on canvas, 2'9¾" × 4'5½". Lady Lever Gallery, Port Sunlight.

brought off the violet-toned landscape in which everything has been rendered ''after nature''—even the animal, which was painted a bit later in Jerusalem.

Leviticus provided the theme. In accordance with the prescriptions of Yahweh, a goat charged with all the sins of Israel was to be led each year into the desert and left there to die. Here Hunt saw a symbol of Christ, the burdened and abandoned Redeemer. (When exhibited in 1855, the picture had only a qualified success, largely because the comparison it drew seemed a bit strained.)

*The Scapegoat* is the product of two contradictory orientations, one toward an extreme realism and the other toward a no less extreme form of symbolism.

The painter has given us every hair on the animal—a creature of sad, accusing eye—and then asked us to see in all this an image of Christ. A didactic parable has been grafted onto the work of a naturalist. (Some critics were unkind enough to suggest that the canvas should hang in the Museum of Natural History.) But the real contradiction lies elsewhere, for the power and ''pop'' charm of *The Scapegoat* derive principally from the fact that in it the hard and the sharp interlock with the soft, the pallid, and the perished. The animal's hooves sink into a viscous, gummy substance afloat with cadaverous remains, animal skeletons, and spongy tree limbs. Decay affects the entire landscape, an immense basin

where matter and organisms return to an undifferentiated state under a bleaching sun. The violet cast of the landscape, with every seam and fold of its sulfurous crests picked out by the dual illumination of sun and moon, contributes to the sense of nature stricken with inertia, reverting through a process of dessication to a primordial condition of mineral chaos.

The ''heroic'' decision made by Hunt to risk his life for the sake of painting ''on location'' can be explained by his need to find a ''speaking,'' eloquent site that could express the barren horror of the world before the Redemption and thus permit the artist to adhere to his naturalistic principles. He did not paint the landscape violet because he saw it

that way (because he was concerned about fidelity to the model); rather, it was because the landscape was violet that he chose to paint it (in order to reinforce his religious message).

Executed in the same region, the study reproduced in Fig. 447, with its daringly cropped, tree-filled foreground and its Dead Sea in the distance, reveals the ''atmosphere'' that the English master sought to capture in his large picture (provided, as we assume, the watercolor was meant to serve in some way as a ''trial proof'' for *The Scapegoat*). This splendidly ample, lunar panorama, all encrusted with white rocks, betrays only one sign of life: the shepherd's fire in the left midground.

# CHAPTER V

# Construction by Assemblage

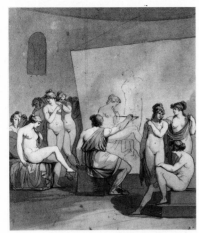

449. A. Kauffmann (1741–1807). *Zeuxis Painting the Most Beautiful Women of Crotona.*

450. H. Robert (1733–1808). *Statues in the Capitoline Museum.*

451. H. Fuseli (1741–1825). *The Artist in Despair over the Grandeur of Antique Fragments.* 1778–80.

452. G. D. Tiepolo (1726–96). *Studies of Sphinxes, Heads, and Fish.* 1750–53.

Three types of assemblage: In Fig. 449 Angelica Kauffmann depicted the myth of the painter Zeuxis who chose features from several beauties to obtain the ideal model. This was montage, but on the level of anecdote. In Figs. 450 and 451 Robert and Fuseli combined objects with different scales in the same unified space. Tiepolo (Fig. 452) juxtaposed disparate objects in a disjunctive space.

While it may be true that all of painting derives from various methods of assemblage—technical, representational, compositional—it was not until the end of the 18th century and the beginning of the 19th that artists undertook to make a candid disclosure of these procedures. Pictures began to reveal their construction; indeed, construction became a manifest theme. Simultaneously, fracture lines developed, threatening the unity of the image. "To those who wander in last," wrote Michel Foucault in *The Archaeology of Knowledge*, "must we point out that a *tableau* [meaning "scene" as well as "picture"] . . . is formally a 'set within a series?' "

The notion of montage, already alluded to in Chapter II (pp. 97–101), had long been central to the classical tradition inherited from the Renaissance. "Claude Lorrain," wrote Reynolds, "was convinced, that taking nature as he found it seldom produced beauty. His pictures are a composition of the various draughts which he had previously made from various beautiful scenes and prospects." Reynolds, in his *Discourses*, also insisted upon the validity of an idea that had been accepted since the 16th century, namely, that the artist should study the masterpieces and incorporate their most worthy and admirable details in his own work. It was this dual appropriation of fragments from, on the one hand, nature and, on the other, the art of the past that Turner, in 1811, demanded for a genre then thought to be directly dependent upon the motif: modern landscape painting.

The Zeuxis myth, revived by a number of artists around the turn of the 19th century, makes an effective illustration of this need for montage (Fig. 449). Commissioned to create an image of Helen of Troy for the Temple of Juno at Crotona, the illustrious Greek painter trusted neither his own genius nor the charms of a single model. Thus, Alberti tells us, Zeuxis "chose from the city's youth the five most beautiful maidens, so that he might combine in his painting whatever features of feminine beauty were most exquisite in each of them." The procedure, once carried forward to the tragic and morbid side of the 19th century, has certain points in common with the approach taken by Géricault, whose preparation for the *Raft of the Medusa* (Fig. 218) included seeking out and painting the heads of the dead and moribund in the hospitals of Paris (Fig. 514). The difference lies less in method than in the personal involvement of the modern painter in studies that proved to be as much ends unto themselves as intermediate steps. The final work therefore assumes the character of an impossible contraction of all the emotional states captured in Figs. 517 and 518. The kind of difficulty that Géricault generally experienced in his attempts to conclude a work (see Delacroix's view reported on p. 97) suggests that the picture may have come to seem inadequate in its capacity to contain the multiplicity of expression that the artist found surging up within himself, at a moment of great personal and historical tension (see p. 82).

Such artistic conduct went against Renaissance and Neoclassical tradition (that is, against Guérin, Géricault's own master [Fig. 153]), as well as against the traditions of academic precept and the idealism espoused by Winckelmann. All these systems required that the painter control and contain, that, in brief, he *compose*, in the twofold sense given the word by Littré: "To form a whole with different parts; to harmonize, to arrange by making concessions." As Albert Boime explains in *The Academy and French Painting in the Nineteenth Century*, the studios preparing students for the Prix de Rome in the 19th century encouraged their charges to think of the image as a conjunction of separately prepared details. Part by part, the pupils learned to draw eyes, nose, lips, and then the three together (full face or profile). Afterwards came the chin and ears, and finally the head, taken as a whole. The process continued with the foot, the leg, etc. Right away, at its very origin in the 17th century, this additive conception of academic drawing received its most perverse form from Le Brun, in his various attempts to combine human features and animal physiognomy. For instance, he drew a lion and a horse with human eyes. Conversely, when the father of French academicism wanted to suggest the relationship between a particular character and a certain animal temperament, "his faces have," according to J. Baltrusaïtis, "the eyebrows and eyes of the corresponding beasts." Some of Le Brun's plates juxtapose "the appearance and movement of the eyes and brows" of a man, a monkey, a camel, a tiger, a lynx, etc., making "a sort of table of species among which one could choose. . . . There is something dramatic in this presentation of living organs, whose natural origin is not immediately evident and that seem to be easily interchangeable." Curiously, added Baltrusaïtis, Le Brun's experiments, which drew upon an ancient store of popular imagery, had no impact on contemporary art. More than a hundred years had to pass, but then, in the late 18th century and the first half of the 19th, the cross-grafting of images initiated by Le Brun exploded into a veritable mode, which culminated in the frenetic and bizarre caricatures of Grandville. From the Academy to Grandville, the same process of assemblage was at work, and merely transposed from convention to aberration, from normalcy to delirium.

Also dependent upon the principle of assemblage was the classicizing idealism advocated by Winckelmann, first published in 1755 and a considerable influence upon European art all the way to and including Ingres. A true Platonist, the German theoretician believed that the Greek artist understood how to isolate within the visible world (especially in human morphology) the essential lines that he bore latent within himself as Ideas already inscribed upon his consciousness. Innate models engraved upon the soul even before birth, these Ideas could be recovered through a process of abstracting and distilling empirical experience. The Greek artist would select, then condense and assemble the quintessential features of nature for the purpose of revealing ideal, "divine" beauty. For reasons peculiar to his condition—climatic, social, political reasons—he mastered, once and for all, the whole technique of synthesis, which made the Greek approach the example that modern artists would be exhorted to follow, totally and exclusively. Classical art became the unsurpassable model for all modernity. It was true "nature," pure and noble, unlike the anecdotal, prosaic nature to which Dutch painters, for instance, subjected themselves in the 17th century.

The identification of nature with Greek art gave rise to a number of claims that are troubling for the 20th-century sensibility. David and Ingres, those

453. H. Robert. *The Razing of the Bastille.*

454. L. Moreau (1740–1806).
*Demolition of the Bastille.*

Simultaneously painting the same event, Moreau produced a light-toned, distant, asymmetrical, fragile image, while Robert took a low vantage point in order to emphasize the mass and volume of the towers. Whereas Moreau toned down the motif (thus the occasion it signified: the explosion of the French Revolution) and showed it in sparkling daylight, Robert dramatized the forms by means of an enlargement that threatens to "explode" the picture.

456. E. F. Burney (1760–1848). *The Eidophusikon of Loutherbourg.* c. 1782.

457. J. M. W. Turner (1775–1851). *Frontispiece to the Liber Studiorum* c. 1811.

Beginning in 1781, the painter Loutherbourg presented a spectacle of movement and sound based upon an assemblage of paintings on canvas and wooden panels manipulated from different axes. The program included visions of storms, avalanches, and Niagara Falls. The image was produced by a constantly changing montage, causing nature to appear like a passing articulation of heterogeneous elements. The scheme indirectly influenced Turner (Fig. 525), whose engraving in Fig. 457 has certain formal analogies with the luminous screen of Loutherbourg's *Eidophusikon.*

great *chefs d'école*, saw no contradiction in requiring their students simultaneously to make a "literal" copy of the exterior world and to do a strict imitation of the ancients. Meanwhile, Winckelmann, who usually is blamed for the bad pastiches that inundated 19th-century salons and museums, in no way recommended the servile copying of antique prototypes. Instead, he urged a synthesis of the Greek synthesis, a montage of montages. As Léon Mis has written, in his summary of the German theoretician's ideas: "What the Greeks did in relation to nature, their model, the moderns would do in relation to the models provided by the masterpieces of Greek antiquity." By taking advantage of the distillation process as already effected under the ideal circumstances provided by antiquity, artists found the means of escaping the ever deceptive, ephemeral, and trivial facticity of everyday reality.

Indeed, David, the chief exponent of French Neoclassicism, departed significantly, in practice, from the Winckelmann position. While periodically reproaching himself for not being sufficiently "Greek" in his painting, he attempted to combine the antique model with the precise handling typical of 15th-century Flanders. In his large sketch for the *Tennis Court Oath*, we can see that David began his figures as academic nudes, which he then developed into detailed portraits of the various political personages actually present at the scene. Here was montage, but by superimposition—that is, two heterogeneous styles overlapping one another in a precarious balance. "In the crispness of the drawing, in the eloquent purity of the gestures, in the beauty of the 'anatomies,' it is the *ideal* that [David] offers us," writes Jean Starobinski, "but the faces, even where a noble transport crowds out every other passion, reflect the *characteristics* of the individual being, the irregularities of a living nature that mimetic fidelity prevents from being reduced to an ideal 'type.'" Yet, this singular manner of reconciling the irreconcilable enriched French art with some of its greatest masterpieces (Figs. 151, 152). At the other extremity of the artistic spectrum, a Friedrich (Figs. 526, 527) or a Runge (Fig. 520) never challenged the nature of montage. Whatever their views on Winckelmann's idealism, they did not question the idea of assemblage, but rather the need for referring to ancient Greece. The same is true of Delacroix, from whom we have a famous dictum: "Nature is a dictionary." This meant lifting details and fragments from the factual world, not for the purpose of stringing them together on the canvas like a sentence, but rather of mixing them together in an organic whole that would erase their distinctive traits. "Even though every detail may be perfect, let us say inimitable," wrote the artist, "the combination of these details rarely presents an effect equal to that which results, in the work of a great artist, from the overall sense of wholeness and composition." Born of montage, the painting emerges from an effacement of the montage—which, it so happens, cannot be distinguished except when the creative process has been arrested. As Théophile Silvestre so aptly put it in the language of the period: "For [Delacroix], every composition is a combination of external elements that he has seen and recalled with his own passionate feelings."

Art history, too often divided into narrow specializations, has difficulty accounting for the effect pro-

duced by an interweaving that causes seemingly antithetical practices not only to coexist but even to influence and overlap, interfere and compete with one another. The 18th century was especially conducive to such interpenetration. Painting, scenography, architecture, interior decoration, and garden design were in constant contact, often because it was the same men who excelled in several or all of them. Moreover, the genesis of form was itself a montage, since the mutations that such schemes as perspective and fragmentation underwent in one field—even when interdependent in their evolution—could just as well be transposed to another area. "At the beginning of the 18th century," writes Marianne Roland-Michel and Daniel Rabreau, "a new generation of Venetian and Piedmontese scenographers required that even stage flats create the illusion of a new mobility. The introduction of double and triple vanishing points, frequently located off-stage, created a fragmentary space, suitable to the succession—continuous or discontinuous, according to the situation—of locales required by the dramatic action." Baroque scenographers—mainly the Bibienas—introduced *la scena per angola*, or diagonal décor, that continued beyond the spectator's range of vision. They invented a dilated, complex, uncontrollable space that anticipated Burke's reflections on the infinite and sublime: "There are scarce any things which can become the objects of our senses, that are really and in their own nature infinite. But the eye not being able to perceive the bounds of many things, they seem to be infinite, and they produce the same effects as if they were really so." In order to produce this *"effect of the infinite"* in a limited space, two conditions, wrote Blake, must prevail: *"Succession;* which is requisite that the parts may be continued so long and in such a direction as by their frequent impulses on the senses to impress the imagination with an idea of their progress beyond their actual limits"; and *"Uniformity;* because, if the figures of the parts should be changed, the imagination at every change finds a check; you are presented at every alteration with the termination of one idea and the beginning of another."

These reflections, which read like a commentary on Bibiena scenography, are also very much in keeping with many of Piranesi's engravings, which were contemporary with Burke's writings. Piranesi was certainly a disciple, if not a student, of the Bibienas, whose sense of vertiginous perspective he drew upon and adapted to his two themes: ruins and prisons (Figs. 233, 234). This visionary art would influence numerous painters such as Hubert Robert (Figs. 181, 182, 487, 488), who in turn affected the evolution of architecture and garden design (actually creating several of the most famous ones). Panini, also a pupil of the Bibienas, invented the genre called *caprice* (or *capriccio*), pictures in which architectural monuments "excerpted" from various sites are juxtaposed in a plausible décor or environment (Fig. 481). In addition to Robert (Figs. 479, 480), another Panini student, Servandoni, took up the genre and singlehandedly illustrated the extreme permeability of the various artistic practices. Architect, creator of the portals at Saint-Sulpice, titular and triumphant scene designer to the Opéra (where Boucher would succeed him in 1742), scenographer at the Salle des Machines, and elected to the Academy in 1731 for his ruins pictures (Fig. 483), Servan-

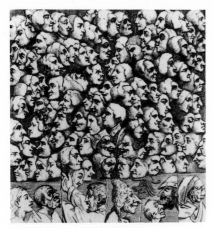

458. W. Hogarth (1697–1764). *Characters and Caricatures.* 1743.

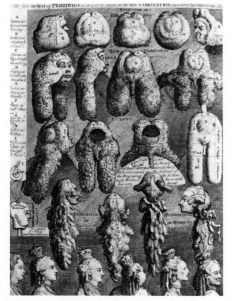

459. W. Hogarth. *The Five Orders of Periwigs.* 1761.

Hogarth filled his surface with identical elements arranged side by side. A tabular conception, it excludes all compositional hierarchy.

460. C. N. Ledoux (1736–1806). *Elevation, Hosten Houses.* 1795.

According to Gallet, Ledoux "created an indefinitely extendable ensemble and conceived the notion of serial architecture whose application came in the great complexes of the 20th century."

461. C. N. Ledoux. *Perspective View of the Entrance to the Hôtel Thélusson.* c. 1780.

Ledoux's triumphal arch framed a distant view of a great mansion, the scheme influenced by Piranesi and Robert (Figs. 190, 411, 412).

doni applied his perspective combinations and dramatic assemblages in whatever arena he worked.

Thus, we see how the general circulation of plastic schemes transgresses the scholarly categories of art history. Here we give only a few examples, since no linear genealogy could do justice to a movement so diffuse, abundant, and multidirectional. In landscape architecture, for instance, designers began by referring to the *paysage composé* of Claude Lorrain, Salvatore Rosa, Poussin, and Gaspard Dughet. In 1739 Alexander Pope, a true authority on the subject, declared that the art of the garden derived from that of landscape painting and should be compared to a picture on the wall. Even the three colors of atmospheric perspective were applied to actual parks: brown for the near ground, green for the middle ground, and blue for distances. The "eye-catcher," a sham ruin situated upon the horizon, would function like a pictorial accent and momentarily hold the stroller's attention. In France, around 1780, Le Rouge isolated the rocks in Vernet's painting and copied them with the idea of proposing the motif as amusing bits of garden décor. Carmontelle, the creator of Paris' Parc Monceau, devised the following program: "Let us change the arrangement of gardens the way we shift scenery at the Opéra; let us have in reality what the most skilled painters would be able to offer as decoration, at all times and everywhere."

Soon, however, landscape itself began to have its effect on painting. By the middle of the century it was being said that while a painting could offer only one view, the garden provided hundreds. In 1794 Humphry Repton, then England's greatest landscape architect, wrote that whereas the painter had to work from a fixed vantage point, the gardener could change his view of the landscape merely by walking through it. This perpetual displacement of the stroller revealed, by way of contrast, the particular and arbitrary fixity of a painting's observer. The consequence of this would be neither immediate nor literal; in painting, the two-dimensional representation of multiple points of view became programmatic only much later, with the advent of Cubism in the early 20th century.

Still, as soon as centralized, monocular perspective came to be perceived, consciously or not, as a convention, painters immediately began to challenge both its pertinence and its permanence, whether by exaggerating or disturbing its lines (Figs. 381, 383), by blurring its order with afocal effects (Figs. 370, 379, 380, 384–389); or by reducing its volume through tabular arrangements (Figs. 532, 533), as in the juxtaposition of objects that tend to reproduce in two dimensions the polynuclear system of the garden—which was not based upon the compositional balance of plastic elements (since these were always shifting), but rather upon a rectilinear structure with multiple focuses all linked together by the stroller's progress.

A scriptural metaphor used by the landscape architect Capability Brown sheds light upon the way the period had of distributing elements through a dispersion of radiating points, rather than by means of a closed system: "There, I place a comma, and here, where a more marked change is needed, I use stronger punctuation." These punctuation marks could be vegetal (groves, copses, etc.), but also monumental, with memorials to every culture on earth

assembled in one place. The gardens of William Kent (Stowe), Chambers (Kew), or Cormontelle (Parc Monceau) all contain a number of *fabriques* or *follies*: Roman temples, porticoes, or Gothic ruins, all sham constructions and arranged according to a model derived from the Chinese. "The Chinese," writes J. Baltrusaïtis, "do not divide the terrain geometrically but by scenes, each of which has its own vantage point marked by an object, a bench, or a building." This multiple-focus aesthetic, where each *topos* functions as an inducement to reverie, accords with the philosophical attitudes of Joseph Addison, who would have a lasting influence upon the whole of 18th-century England. Anticipating by two hundred years the psychological mechanisms described by Proust, Joseph Addison asserted in an issue of *The Spectator* (1712) that an object or circumstance could awaken an infinity of ideas until then lying dormant in the imagination. Stimulated by an odor or a color, the mind would suddenly conjure the meadows and gardens—with all their rich imagery—where such sensory experiences had first been encountered.

An "associationist" movement, which got under way at this time, viewed perception as the vehicle of mnemonic linkages. A simple detail could draw forth a whole chain of old sensations. The view itself was less important than the play of associations that it released. The gardener Humphry Repton revived the notion at the end of the century when he praised the pleasure afforded by the "accidents" of landscape—a bench, a tree, a turn in the path—that remind one of old events. Landscape became a trap for feelings, an emotional arrangement. It seemed nothing so much as a tactical disposition of sensuous objects and radiating nuclei, whose placement depended less on plastic *données* than on psychological considerations. Empathy counted for more than composition. Painting, which was closely allied to this landscape development (especially in the work of such artists as J. R. Cozens, Gainsborough, Girtin, Cotman, and Constable), gained a "depth" that no longer had anything to do with perspectival illusion. The artist now permitted himself to offer nothing but allusion, litotes, and fragments of his own experience. As a corollary, the spectator was invited to exploit the least mark to whatever extent he found it echoed in his own memory. The picture became a condensation or treasury of sensations, each of which constituted the point of departure for a whole chain of meaning. What the work might lose in clarity (see Chapter III, pp. 173–177), it would gain in complexity. It was no longer the depository of ideas, but rather the bearer of a web of diffuse emotions.

The London museum-home of the architect John Soane (1753–1837) can be seen as both a transposition into three dimensions and a culmination of the system of emotional montage. Not only is it a montage of *spaces* (three houses integrated by means of courtyards, corridors, and labyrinthine cellars) but also a montage of *objects* (works of every size and style displayed side by side: Egyptian sarcophagi, bracketed vestiges of ancient architecture, busts, columns, furniture, pictures hung and superimposed by means of movable walls, with most of the paintings—whether by Hogarth or Clérisseau—depicting accumulations of figures or ruins). Instead of stylistic or chronological coherence, the arrangement reflects the affective relationship that Soane

462. J. J. Lequeu (1757–1825). *Young Man Pouting.*

463. J. J. Lequeu. *The Big Yawn.*

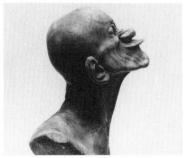

464. F. X. Messerschmidt (1736–83). *Self-Portrait Grimacing.*

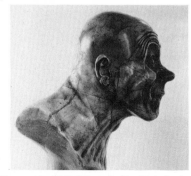

465. F. X. Messerschmidt. *Self-Portrait with a Bird's Beak.*

A grimace is like the enlargement of an enlargement, heightening the image to the level of pain.

had with his collection. The ensemble invites each visitor to take a different direction, his progress accelerated by a multitude of mirrors (convex or lamellated, hidden in door frames, ceilings, and library stanchions) and by the great number of openings (windows, interior balconies, perforated partitions). Mirrors and openings serve to expand the various spaces, while also making them dissolve into one another, to compound their ambiguities, and, most of all, to juxtapose them unexpectedly wherever some fragmented object or space outside the room suddenly surges into view by way of a mirrored door or a hole in the wall. Such visual "collages" dramatize what is a purely emotional mode of presentation and accentuates the strangeness of the effect. The violence of the combinations redoubles the disparity of the objects.

Simultaneously broken and blended—that is how we can read both the age's Anglo-Chinese gardens, with their surprises and sudden disclosures, their unexpected sites, and the two-dimensional *Caprices* and *Fantasies* of Tiepolo (Fig. 452), Piranesi (Fig. 469), and Robert (Fig. 450). Here, depicted adjacent to one another within the confines of a sheet or a canvas, are works of art, instruments, and stone fragments, all belonging to different spaces and scales.

But even more than architecture, painting, gardens, and scenography, it was the human subject that in the 18th century came to be viewed and described as split, divided, parceled out in bits and pieces, and totally subordinated to sensations that, from the exterior, seize and disperse him. In 1740 David Hume wrote that while some philosophers might affirm the individual's continual consciousness of his so-called self, he (Hume) found that whenever he had been able to penetrate most intimately within himself, he always encountered some particular perception—some "other"—be this heat or cold, light or darkness, pain or pleasure. The Scottish philosopher maintained that he could never, at any moment, grasp his own inner reality without also seizing upon the perception of something else. Indeed, he insisted that he could conceive nothing except in terms of perception.

The fracturing of the subject gave rise to nostalgic thoughts of ancient Greece, imagined as a privileged moment in history when the unity of the human creature found reinforcement through its fusion with nature. "Why was every Greek," wrote Schiller in his "letters" *On the Aesthetic Education of Man*, "the qualified representative of his era, and why does no modern have the right to take such a role? Because the first received his form from nature, which unifies all, whereas the latter has his from knowledge, which dissociates everything." Schiller attributed the fragmentation of contemporary man to the explosion of science (an inexorable development, moreover), to the class system, and to the division of labor. He indicted the modern state ("an ingenious clockwork in which a mechanical life is created by an assemblage of innumerable but inert pieces") and the reduction of the individual to the narrowness of his social and productive function.

Painting too reflected these strains and ruptures—by questioning its own unity. It was in the 18th century that Hogarth's engravings and paintings offered a convulsive, polycentric image of popular or bourgeois morality. Here the scene breaks down into innumerable dramas—incon-

gruous, prosaic, violent, obscene—any one of which is paroxysmal enough to threaten the existence of the overall space. While fires, defenestrations, murders, and collapsing masonry occupy some parts of the image, life—impervious to it all—goes on in other parts. *Bedlam* (1733–35) became the model of such frenetic situations. Here, as anywhere else, but neither more nor less, the alienated individual lives out his delirium without paying any attention to the surrounding world, which, however, he influences and disturbs.

Paroxysm and excessive crowding called for the subdivided image. Replacing the paradigm of the *Last Supper* (Renaissance, static, synchronic) was the *Way of the Cross* ("primitive," dynamic, diachronic). Goya needed six pictures to paint the murder of the bandit El Maragato by a monk, and Géricault structured his *Affaire Lualdès* into six episodes. In a totally different mode, meditative, religious, or pantheistic, Friedrich and Turner painted diptychs; Runge, the Nazarenes, and Palmer, whole series.

Delacroix, meanwhile, pondered the plastic effectiveness of disproportionality: "Part of the effect produced by the statues of Michelangelo is due to certain disproportions or unfinished passages that augment the importance of the completed portions. . . . Should disproportion be a condition of admiration? If, on the one hand, Mozart, Cimarosa, and Racine astonish less as a result of the admirable proportionality of their works, should not Shakespeare, Michelangelo, and Beethoven, on the other hand, owe some of their effect to an opposite cause? For my part, I think so."

To this question Turner also made a positive response. The English artist used two methods at once in order to challenge the compositional economy of classicism. While he tended to efface contrasts (see Chapter III, pp. 173–177), he also broke up the scene with aggressive cropping. Here again, it was Burke who showed the way, in his deliberations upon the *production* of infinity. For Burke, as we have seen, infinity had to be *produced*. Immensity, left as such, "says" nothing. Sheer quantity is not enough. To *create* a sense of bigness, artifice is required. The true artist, wrote Burke, would charm the viewer by means of a creative imposture, since a plane that is large only in terms of its dimensions expresses nothing but a common or retarded imagination. Only the deceptive work has the power to make a grand impression. This would become the program of painters taking the Alps as their theme and source of inspiration: Wolf, J.R. Cozens, Towne, Turner (Figs. 201–204, 206–208). If they chose such a motif, they did so precisely because it was *too* big. Far from wanting to reproduce a mountain or a whole range viewed from afar and in totality, they sought to isolate a fragment that, in occupying the entire canvas, would express the incommensurate character of the ensemble. Confronted with a stone rampart enlarged to fill the surface edge to edge, the spectator has the opportunity to imagine all that extends beyond, right into infinity. From the picture as an assemblage of fragments, we come to the fragment as a picture (Fig. 488).

In the case of Ingres, however, it is the difficulty of combining a great many figures on the same canvas that comes into question. The artist's enchantment with the specific *morceau* and the "studied"

466. N. de Largillière (1656–1746). *Study of Hands.*

467. J. D. Ingres (1780–1867). *Study of Hands and Feet.*

Painters began to feel the particular charm of the disparate. Both Largillière and Ingres (Figs. 533–535) lavished great care on their assemblages of fragments, well beyond the needs of mere documentation.

468. G. D. Tiepolo (1726–96). *The Flight into Egypt.*

Studio drawing allowed the coalescence of incompatible scenes. Here the painter could give his subconscious associations free rein.

469. J. B. Piranesi (1720–1827). *Lapidary Fragments.*

A tiered display of objects has replaced composition. The juxtaposition of broken scenes and inscriptions prefigured the modern process of collage.

detail, which the preparatory exercises evince (Figs. 533–535), proved less and less reconcilable with his concern for the kind of plastic or formal homogeneity that "makes a picture." In this regard, Ingres collided with the same resistant forces that Géricault had encountered. Something in him rejected synthesis (which he managed to achieve only in his single-figure works). And for this very reason, his studies may be more modern—closer to Cubism, for instance—than those of Géricault (Figs. 514, 517, 518). Whereas Géricault painted anatomical fragments in a uniform space, Ingres gave effect to fragments of figures in a shattered space. In the first case, it is the referent that has been dismembered; in the second, it is the picture. Ingres ruptured the mimetic (iconic) link between the structure of the external scene and the internal economy of the canvas.

Works like these, based as they are upon the dispersion of their figural components, bring into the open the fear of chaos that, from Alberti to Diderot, haunted the history of Western art. For the Renaissance man, "[the painter] should, above everything else, endeavor to make all the parts harmonize with one another, and they will do this if in quantity, in function, in type, in color, and in every other respect they harmonize with a single beauty." The argument of *Della pittura* is directed entirely against the menace of disintegration. Whether apparent or concealed, the pictorial devices ("veil," perspective grid) put into place by the Florentines had no other purpose, by Alberti's own admission, than to bolt down what tends to come apart and to hold "the surface together." *Harmony* was a victory over the precariousness of a shifting ground that had to be controlled throughout. Thus, even voids—the areas free of marks—were absorbed into the perspective matrix, which quantified them while also denying their actuality as material and surface (and, at the same time, suspending the opposite effect this material as such could have up on the viewer). Each square inch of the canvas, regardless of whether it bears some sort of denotation, refers, by the very fact of the perspective apparatus, to the concrete, measurable spaces of empirical reality. The system allows nothing to escape its control.

The eternally affirmed and eternally questioned unity, which medievalizing and Mannerist developments attempted here and there to transgress, was in fact violated by a "closet" practice that for centuries had been confined to the studio: the quick sketch, the study, the "initial inspiration" that functions like the painter's unconscious (Figs. 466–468). Here, the juxtaposition of fragments, the overlapping, the duplications refer to no rule or a priori order, submitting neither to the yoke of perspective nor to the authority of the unifying subject himself (the painter). Inscription depended upon two factors: the obsessional perseverence of a theme that is drawn in the mind of the artist at the same time that it appears on the paper; and the residual possibilities of a surface occupied, indeed loaded, with the artist's successive interventions (close-ups, shifted axes, repetitions, etc.). The sheet becomes saturated with incompatible details. Here, *composition* has been replaced by *coalescence*, and harmony by *agglutination*. This is what occurred in the condensations of Tiepolo (Fig. 468) or Ingres (Fig. 467), or in a study by Girodet (Fig. 512) where incoherent odds and ends of a battle scene float about. All set down upon the same sheet, such details remain irreducible to a closed, self-contained totality.

Drawings like these (as well as Ingres' studies for *Saint Symphorian*) suggest that the picture may be nothing more than a suspended instant of an ongoing process of dispersal, a moment of order in a permanent, continuous activity of construction and deconstruction—in brief, "a feeble unity," as Foucault put it. And painting, which for centuries had incessantly concerned itself with the same gestures, the same bodies, the same postures, would now assume the character of a charnel house, trafficking in scattered members, samples, grafts, *membra disjecta*, and deriving in the history of art (according to the nature of the fragment) from decalcomania and collage. Once presupposed, unitary, denoted composition had been blunted, once coalescence had replaced it, pictorial production as a whole would range freely throughout a vast field of visual thought: ideas and activity of dreams, mnemonic imagery, phantasms, rebuses, memory arts, cartography, geometry, cinema, photography, etc.—not to mention what visual language offers in the way of diagrams, equations, or symbols. These are all unstable formations with ambiguous boundaries and self-dissolving specificities, formations that communicate among themselves with the same movements of attraction that Freud attributes to dream fragments: "distorted," broken up, and reunited like floating mirrors."

# Chimeras and hybrids: the return of monsters

470. William Blake (1757–1827). *The Beast of Revelation*. 1799–1810. Watercolor, 15¼ × 13¾".
National Gallery of Art (Rosenwald Collection), Washington, D.C.

plenitude of monsters and hybrids. In Blake, who drew his inspiration from medieval illuminations, Asian art (of Persia, Egypt, and India), and collections of engraved emblems, the subject tends to orient itself entirely toward the frontal plane. Such a tabular conception favored the equal validation of all the diverse details and accessories of an image whose primary purpose was to deliver a message or provide a vivid interpretation of a text, whether by Dante, Milton, or Blake himself, or yet taken from the Bible. In shifting the text, the artist commented upon and interrogated it as if in turn to realize, dialectically, a new text. *The Beast of Revelation* (Fig. 470), one of the fifty watercolors on Biblical themes commissioned from Blake in 1799, is not a literal illustration of Revelation 13, which commences: "And saw a beast rise up out of the sea, having seven heads and ten horns." Not to be found here, for instance, are the sword of fire and the cudgel, nor is the dragon mentioned as having several heads. Text and image appear less to overlap than to extend one another. Such a formulation, in which exegesis is always implied, cannot but flout the demands of "natural" space so as to reconstitute itself as a montage of symbols. "No man since," wrote Blake, "ever supposes that copying from Nature is the Art of Painting; if Art is no more than this, it is no better than any other Manual Labor; anybody may do it and the fool often will do it best as it is a work of no Mind."

With Mortimer, on the other hand, the art of the hybrid is restored to classical three-dimensional space (even if, as in Fig. 471, the perspective has been partially obstructed by a curtain of smoke). Indeed, the very horror of the image arises from the relative conformity of the monsters to "ordinary" beings.

Mortimer was a turbulent, scattered person, a lover of rare, disquieting, macabre subjects, and a great admirer of Salvator Rosa, from whom he borrowed themes (notably the Italian master's *banditti*), and of the 17th-century Roman engraver Pietro Testa, whose minute manner he adopted. Dead at age thirty-nine, Mortimer prefigured the Romantic artist, tormented and bohemian. In the Oxford drawing seen here, the figures' twisting movement owes much to *Saul and the Witch of Endor* by Rosa (Louvre), a picture well known from an engraving. Sharp, dry, and tense, the artist's drawing contrasts with his handling of color. Thus, in the background, the lines and washes do not coincide. Mortimer had such a reputation for the virtuosity and speed of his draftsmanship that a contemporary wrote: "He never goes back over a line."

The tradition of the hybrid—to use a term proposed by André Chastel—goes back to the very origins of pagan antiquity. The author of *Fables, forms, figures* defines it as "form that, with a strong feeling of whimsy and caprice, confounds the image of the species, combining animate and inanimate, vegetable and animal, bestial and human in a state of continuous metamorphosis." But if the hybrid expresses a kind of euphoria, it also, according to the Hellenist Jean-Pierre Vernant, communicates a fascination

for indistinct primordial matter and a nostalgia for "a creative power [that prevailed] before the emergence of a clearly differentiated cosmos." Chastel mentions the *bizzarie* of Leonardo (a winged lizzard, a lyre in the shape of a horse's head) and cites the great success of the mixed, amphibious, grotesque, and fantastic assemblages that were created at the very heart of the Mannerist 16th century. England in the second half of the 18th century—with Barry, West, Mortimer, and soon with Blake and Flaxman—produced its own

471. John Hamilton Mortimer (1740–79). *Monsters*. c. 1778.
Pen and watercolor, 16½ × 11". Ashmolean Museum, Oxford.

Painted by two contemporaries equally imbued with antique and Baroque Rome, the pictures reproduced here disclose the same conscious use of the frame as an expressive factor of prime importance. But the solutions the two artists devised proved to be quite opposite. Commenced in 1774, *Philoctetes* (Fig. 472) by the Danish painter Abildgaard shows the wounded and suffering hero compressed, even crushed between the two horizontals of the framing edge, the lower one of which serves as a platform for the figure's left knee and foot. The friezelike disposition of the body gains plastic value only in counterpoint with the rigid shape of the enclosing rectangle. The uncomfortable posture imposed upon Philoctetes corresponds to the unhappy position of Sophocles' hero, who was bitten by a snake and then abandoned on the Isle of Lemnos by companions unable to bear their friend's purulent wound. If the artist's

academic treatment of the subject owes much to Michelangelo, it was from the frescoes of the Carracci in Rome's Palazzo Farnese—with their numerous figures embedded in the *trompe l'oeil* ceiling—that Abildgaard borrowed his conception of the frame.

The same influences fell upon the Irishman James Barry, one of the fathers of Neoclassicism and a fierce champion of both history painting and the antique who, after a visit to Herculaneum, proclaimed: "The moderns, with all their vapouring, have invented nothing, have improved nothing, not even in the most trifling articles of convenient household utensils. . . . Is there anything new in the world?" [1]

It was, however, by exaggerating and enlarging what he found in the Carracci that Barry presented his pair of deities in one of the 18th century's most daring compositions. But where Abildgaard crammed his surface full without violating the integrity of the figure,

Barry began by scaling his hero and heroine to twice the normal human size. He then circumscribed them within a "movie screen" format that projects the viewer right into the image, into the intimacy of the two Olympian lovers.

The philosopher Edmund Burke, who was the friend and patron of Barry (financing the latter's trip to Rome), may have encouraged, through his reflections on the sublime, the vast, and the infinite, a work that rises well above its creator's other productions.

472. Nicolai Abildgaard (1743–1809). *Philoctetes*. 1774–75. Oil on canvas, 4′½″×5′8″. Staten Museum for Kunst, Copenhagen.

473. James Barry (1741–1806). *Jupiter and Juno on Mount Ida.* c. 1782–99. Oil on canvas, 3′3¾″×4′2″.
City Art Galleries, Sheffield.

The frame crops into
or contains the image

475–478. Jean-Baptiste Greuze. *The Punished Son* (details of Fig. 474).

## The "scenario" fragments composition into a series of intense, theatrical scenes

474. Jean-Baptiste Greuze (1725–1805). *The Punished Son.* 1778. Oil on canvas, 4'3¼"×5'4¼". Louvre.

In the didactic dramas of Greuze—as in the satires of Hogarth—the emotional excess with which the characters have been endowed demands a narrative or sequential reading of a composition that breaks up into as many fragments as there are figures. The eye is made to isolate each image like a cinematic close-up. The intensity and individuality of the mimicry and the theatricality of the gestures have a fracturing effect. No longer does everything converge upon a central personality, as, for example, in a Renaissance Last Supper, nor is there any relative conformity among the individuals represented, as there would be in a battle painting or in a Dutch drinking scene (where a "collective" type dominates). Instead, Greuze has made his actors compete with one another (even the dog plays his special role). This insistence upon individual performance (Figs. 475–478) recalls the kind of tabular presentation traditional in frieze compositions, where each protagonist is clearly visible. While weakening the picture's synchronic unity, the internal subdivision of the story leads to its multiplication. As in Hogarth, unity is no longer the picture but paired pictures—that is, the series and the sequence. Greuze's *Punished Son* (Fig. 474) echoes another work by the same artist: *The Father's Curse*.

If the *tableaux-montages* created by Greuze seem related on the one hand to literary recitation and on the other to cinema, it is owing to the veritable scenarios that he has given us. His description of *The Mother-in-Law* (a canvas now lost) reads so much like a succession of moments carefully staggered in time that inevitably the modern mind visualizes it through the movements of an imaginary camera. This takes us to the very antipodes of Rubens or Delacroix, who understood the picture as an organic whole conceived and apprehended in one stroke. "I presume it to be dinner time," wrote Greuze, "when the unfortunate young woman will take her place at a table along with the others. Now the mother-in-law takes a piece of bread from the table and, holding [her daughter-in-law] by the apron, strikes her across the face [with the bread]. I have tried to paint in this moment the kind of spontaneous hatred that comes from true aversion. The young woman tries to avoid [the blow] and seems to say: 'Why do you strike me? I have done you no harm.' Her expression is one of modesty and fear. Her grandmother is at the other end of the table. Flushed with the most vivid pain, she raises her eyes and her trembling hands to Heaven and seems to say: 'Ah, my child, what has become of you? What sorrow, what bitterness!' The mother-in-law's own daughter, hardly sensitive to her sister's plight, laughs upon seeing the despair of that respectable woman, and warns the latter by ridiculing the former. The baby, whose heart has not yet been corrupted, holds his grateful arms out to his sister, who minds him. . . ."

# An assemblage of monuments in one fictive space yields an imaginary urbanism

479. Hubert Robert (1753–1808). *Some of the Principal Monuments of Paris.* 1788. Oil on canvas, 3'10"×5'10½". Private collection.

480. Hubert Robert. *Roman Monuments.* 1788. Oil on canvas, 3'1½"×5'3¾". Private collection.

The *Caprices* of Panini and his disciple Hubert Robert comprise arbitrary juxtapositions of famous monuments combined in one fictive space that gives the appearance of an actual city. The older master's *Roman Ruins* (Fig. 481) presents side by side the Temple of Hadrian, the Pantheon, the obelisk in the Piazza del Popolo, the quadripartite Arch of Janus, the Temple of Fortuna, and Trajan's Column. Hubert Robert (Fig. 479) assembled the Louvre's "colonnade" façade, the Porte Saint-Denis arch, the Fountain of the Innocents, and the Sainte-Geneviève church (now Paris' Pantheon). For his *Roman Monuments* (Fig. 480) he followed the same procedure, which had a two-fold objective: to bring together buildings that in reality are dispersed, and to invent a coherent setting, an urban proposition plausible enough to contain them.

The *Caprice* pictures partake of the montage process that can also be seen at work in those Renaissance studies or rooms known as curio cabinets, in the composite sets made for plays and opera, and certainly in that 18th-century phenomenon called the "English garden," with its sham pagodas, mills, temples, rocks, mountains, etc. (Robert, in fact, was often asked for drawings of parks and landscapes devoted to the grandeur of nature.) But the *Caprices* can also be seen as reviving a "hieroglyphic" conception of the picture, especially since such works frequently reassemble the same

481. Gian Paolo Panini (1691–1765). *Roman Ruins*. c. 1740. Oil on canvas, 5'8"×7'3". Walker Art Gallery, Liverpool.

structures in different compositions. As in mathematics, the work becomes a combinative of constant elements. It is like a chessboard whose pieces have been manipulated by the artist to suit his fancy.

The principle underlying classical or "historicized" landscape painting, as formulated by the Carracci at the turn of the 17th century, required that the picture provide a simulacrum of reality in its organization of heteroclite, or disparate, elements lifted from nature and antique architecture alike. In the

works reproduced here, this principle has been pushed beyond all verisimilitude. The assembled images could never have coexisted in the same place. Thus, the caprice gives simultaneously the plausible, the "natural," *and* the clues that expose this "natural" as pure fabrication. It openly declares itself to be an artifice. In one stroke, the picture calls attention to what all previous landscape painting—whether by Bril, by Claude, or by Poussin—had implicitly taken from stage design and from "collage."

# Using ruins as a frame within the frame, the painter candidly declares his system of pictorial illusion

482. Gian Paolo Panini (1691–1765). *An Apostle Preaching in Ancient Ruins.* c. 1725. Oil on canvas, 5′7¼″×8′½″. Louvre.

Along with the ''picturesque genre of ruins,'' established by Panini and his pupil Servandoni, came a kind of configuration that would reappear throughout the 18th century, most notably in Piranesi, Robert, and Guardi. This was architecture treated as an enframing structure that recapitulates the picture's own framing edges. (Ledoux adopted the same conception in his *real* architecture for the portal of Paris' Hôtel Thélusson.)

The scheme employs an archway and flanking columns to draw the eye toward an erect motif—temple or obelisk—located in the middle distance. Thus, the frame within the frame has not been reduced to a simple duplication of the gilded picture frame, even where the resemblance may be evocative. For the modern eye, the fake frame (the ruin depicted in the foreground) seems a

pictorial means of exemplifying or evincing the function of the frame, which is to limit or close the image. The tradition handed down from the 15th century conceived of the picture as an open window (''My first act, when I want to paint a surface,'' wrote Alberti in *Della pittura* (1436), ''is to draw a rectangle of a suitable size, in the guise of an open window through which I might see the subject''), but the 18th-century *ruinistes,* by the displacement they effected, *exposed* what for Alberti had been self-evident. They set forth, *declared,* and inscribed within the picture as its actual subject matter what until then had been the external border, the *non dit* (''never mentioned'') and the *non montré* (''never shown''). They caused us to *see* that to frame is to select, to control the eye and catch the spectator in the trap set by the

perspectival mechanism, to assign us a place in the illusionistic system. (Panini [above] doubled the effect inasmuch as the *tempietto* columns themselves constitute a frame for the statue at their center.)

It is not without significance that Servandoni (''great *machiniste,* great architect, fine painter, sublime decorator,'' according to Diderot) made a brilliant career at the Paris Opéra (1726) before his acceptance into the Royal Academy in 1731 as a ''painter gifted in architecture and perspective.'' Indeed, scenography had a determining effect upon his pictures, even if, as in Fig. 483, the deliberate asymmetry of his ruins compositions departed somewhat from contemporary practices in Parisian stage design. As for Panini (Fig. 482), the genre's true promoter and a tireless inventor of *capricci*

(''fantastic views,'' says J.G. Méjanes, ''made up of elements taken from reality, from antique ruins in particular, and given a literary, philosophical, religious, or merely elegiac character through the addition of a few figures''), the artist formed in Rome, where he was professor of perspective at the French Academy, a whole generation of *décorateurs* and *ruinistes,* among whom Hubert Robert was the most faithful, owning as many as thirty pictures by his master.

483. Jean Jérôme Nicolas Servandoni (1695–1766). *Architecture with the Ruins of an Ionic Temple and an Obelisk.* 1731. Oil on canvas, 8′6″ × 6′4¾″. Musée de l'École Nationale Supérieure des Beaux-Arts, Paris.

The revival of nocturnal, moonlit landscapes around 1740—contemporary with the taste for ruins in painting and garden design—encouraged painters to attempt the kind of multiple-source illumination known from several striking essays made by Elsheimer and Rembrandt in the 17th century.

Dual illumination made it possible to open up in the composition—embed within the unity of the work—a micro-space (a ''bubble'') that in itself constitutes a small-scale picture with its own specific climate. In Vernet (Fig. 486) as in Wright of Derby (Fig. 484), the color of the torch or the wood fire contrasts with the cold clarity of the moon. Here, two antagonistic types of illumination have not been gradually blended, as in other works by the same artists (or yet in Volaire), but rather left separated—and cleverly so—by the surrounding tumulus. (For a comparable effect, see Fig. 296).

The double light source always disturbed those wedded to academic principle, for it threatens the atmospheric coherence of the work, ruptures formal unity, and thus scatters the viewer's attention. ''What is meant by the word *unity*?'' asked Charles Blanc in his *Grammaire des arts du dessin*. ''It signifies that the picture should present neither two light masses of equal density nor two dark masses of equal vigor.''

Joseph Vernet, whose pupils included Alexander Cozens, Richard Wilson,

484. Joseph Wright of Derby (1734–97). *Virgil's Tomb by Moonlight.* 1779. Oil on canvas, 3'3¾"×4'2". Yale Center for British Art (Paul Mellon Collection), New Haven.

# Landscape opens to produce a picture within the picture

485. Hubert Robert (1733–1808). *Grotto*. 1772. Oil on canvas, 12½×17¼". Louvre.

Loutherbourg, Valenciennes, Volaire, and, indirectly through the latter, Wright of Derby, must be considered the principal agent in these experiments with light. Wright, one of 18th-century England's finest painters, was captivated by the spectacle of fireworks and volcanoes. During and after his Italian sojourn (1773–75) he painted some thirty pictures and studies representing Vesuvius in eruption, a theme that Volaire transformed into a specialty after he took up residence in Naples in 1769 (Fig. 392). Wright's painting (Fig. 484) shows Virgil's tomb visited by a 1st-century poet who sits while declaiming his verses. Real or imagined, the tomb was one of the period's recurrent themes, mainly because it could be counted on to induce, as Bernardin de Saint-Pierre wrote, "a voluptuous melancholy."

Robert, in the contemporary picture reproduced in Fig. 485, worked a new variation upon the complex luminary scheme just seen. What he gives us are not competing sources of light but two different reflections of light produced by one external source. Nevertheless, it yields the same spectacular partition of the canvas into two divergent, albeit intersecting, spaces, each of which seems to be organized around its own independent axis.

486. Joseph Vernet (1714–89). *Seaport by Moonlight*. 1773. Oil on canvas, 3'2½"×5'4½". Louvre.

A disciple of Piranesi (whose friend he was in Rome after 1756), Hubert Robert mastered the art of spatial amplification by exaggerating the difference in scale between figures and their setting and by cleverly exploiting the discrepancy. In the picture reproduced below (Fig. 487), he deployed an exquisite garland of young women (dressed *à la Directoire*) against a background of commemorative monuments and perched the accompanying musicians upon the plinth of an obelisk whose shaft would seem to have been broken by a giant hand. The canvas surface is mat, the color having been applied on top of an absorbent ground that produced a ''soaked'' look. The artist painted the work four years after he had barely escaped the guillotine. (Legend has it that another Robert died in the painter's place.)

With *The Pyramid* (Fig. 488) we move from the disprortionate to the incommensurable, from the overscaled object to the limitless object. Here Robert has filled his canvas with a gigantic structure broadly penetrated at the base, populated by minuscule silhouettes, shrouded in expressive shadows and in clouds mixed with smoke rising from what may be a ritual. The work, one of the most spectacular executed by Robert, appears to respond to the philosopher Edmund Burke, who argued that painting could not achieve the sublime, committed as it was to the description and circumscription of objects: ''But let it be considered that hardly anything can strike the mind with its greatness, which does not make some sort of approach towards infinity; which nothing can do whilst we are able to perceive its bounds.''

The colossal form in Robert's *Pyramid* is without boundaries. The artist did not simply paint a large object or even the fragment of such an object; he painted the impossibility of apprehending all with the eye and of controlling all with the intellect. The painting has been related by Monique Mosser to a cenotaph designed in the Egyptian style by the visionary architect Etienne-Louis Boullée.[2] Boullée, at the beginning of the 19th century, proposed building the simplest forms—spheres, pyramids, cones—which he hoped to enlarge to monstrous scales (Fig. 80). What Robert teaches us with his cropping of the image is how to ''read''—how to ''experience''—such an architecture, whose monumentality assumes a new meaning the moment that we supplant our *morphological* conception (which seeks a closed object, a defined, controllable form like a model or a drawing) with a *phenomenal* approach. The latter places the accent upon a subject taking account of his relationship to a volume that exceeds him in every respect, eludes all mastery, and reveals itself only through a fragment, a section of wall, or a texture.

487. Hubert Robert (1733–1808). *Young Women Dancing around a Broken Obelisk*. 1798. Oil on canvas, 3′11¼″×3′3″. Museum of Fine Arts (bequest of Lady Davis), Montreal.

488. Hubert Robert. *The Pyramid*. c. 1760. Oil on wood, 2′×2′4¼″.
Smith College Museum of Art, Northampton, Mass.

The sublime evoked through monuments too colossal
to be apprehended except by fragments

489. Thomas Jones (1742–1803). *House at Naples*. 1782. Oil on paper, 5½×8¾″.  National Museum of Wales, Cardiff.

490. Thomas Jones. *Rooftops at Naples*. 1782. Oil on paper, 6×13¾″. Ashmolean Museum, Oxford.

## Reframing the image subordinates the unity of the site to the intrinsic logic of the picture

Early in the 1780s, the Welshman Thomas Jones—who had been a student of Richard Wilson before going to Italy for seven years—painted a number of Neapolitan views (Figs. 489, 490) in which he disclosed a unique capacity for exploiting the urban motifs laid out before his eyes. The artist's method was to subordinate the unity of the site—the coherence of the referent—to the intrinsic logic of his picture. Jones did not hesitate to reframe and decentralize his composition in order to reveal a play of lines echoing the orthogonal structure of the picture's enclosing edge. The relationships he set forth tend toward the isomorphic, as in a roof whose width responds to the picture's panoramic format (Fig. 490) just as a more vertical wall section responds to a narrower format (Fig. 489). In each instance, we find ourselves confronted with the

fragment of a house that clearly extends beyond the picture's own dimensions. But this "open form" (the manifest prolongation of the motif outside the limits of the work) is compensated for by the rigidity of the verticals and horizontals that reinforce the relation between the image and the rectangular structure of the painting surface. Concentrating on the motif, we have only a fragmentary experience, but if we address ourselves to the play of lines, a sense of internal unity emerges.

The pictures gain in interest by virtue of the fact that both depict the same building at the same hour (witness the shadows). The Cardiff Museum's *House at Naples* (Fig. 489) repeats and enlarges the left section of Oxford's *Rooftops at Naples* (Fig. 490). We can almost see the painter at work, framing, repositioning himself on the roof-terrace

of his Italian lodging (his *lastrica*), and selecting from the façade what interests him for pictorial purposes. One thing remains constant, however, and that is the strictly parallel disposition of the forms vis-à-vis the painting surface.

Jones' rooftop experiments were not in any way involved with preparations for some grand, ultimate composition. Their value lay entirely within themselves, which made their novelty seem all the more striking when the pictures were discovered at a public sale in London in 1954.

Forty years after the Welshman's work in southern Italy, the Danish artist Dahl did paintings of skies in which he further accentuated the frame by limiting the urban scene to a fringe of rooftops or belltowers isolated from their normal context (Figs. 491, 492). Thanks to an "athletically" low angle, which seems almost a demonstration of this principle, a portico rising above the urban sprawl suffices to evoke a complete temple, while a few distant crenelations suggest a castle. Such selectiveness has an analogy in late 18th-century "English" gardens, where the poetic fragment received its fullest expression.

In these little studies, Dahl drew inspiration from the celestial horizons of Friedrich, his master and friend in Dresden, as well as from the research carried out by the meteorologist Luke Howard. The latter's early 19th-century classifications not only caused painters (Constable) and poets (Goethe) to develop an interest in clouds, but it also taught them how to distinguish, name, and paint such phenomena. Dahl, however, tended to escape from the contemplative, mystical climate of Friedrich, as well as from Howard's taxonomic and scientific concerns. The Dane's clouds—particularly in the Berlin study (Fig. 491)—are painterly concretions, solid fields of medium, frontal zones where perspective has not been so much canceled as beaten flat by a vigorous handling that endows both near and far with equal density.

491. Johan Christian Clausen Dahl (1788–1857). *Cloud Study*. c. 1825. Oil on canvas, 8¼×8½″. Nationalgalerie Staatliche Museen, Berlin.

492. Johan Christian Clausen Dahl. *Sunset over Two Belfries in Copenhagen*. c. 1825.
Oil on canvas, 4¼×6″. Kunsthalle, Hamburg.

493. Gabriel de Saint-Aubin (1724–80). *The Salon of 1767.* c. 1767. Watercolor and gouache, 9¾×19″. Private collection.

Gabriel de Saint-Aubin, a prolific draftsman and a contemporary of Greuze and Fragonard, treated Salon exhibitions as if they were landscapes. So great was his skill at rendering these art-crammed interiors—at capturing the essence of each canvas in a few strokes of the pen—that even today the individual works shown on the walls can be identified. Still, one senses that it was not the specific unit or picture that interested him, but rather the closed, confined scene where the works displayed within it agglomerate into a continuous fabric, a multicolored crust of high-key strokes spread the full extent of the walls. In his *Salon of 1767* (Fig. 493), zones of luminous powder float through the room, producing an impressionistic haze that

softens even the geometry of the proliferating frames. The picture has now lost the tectonic firmness that it retained in the 17th-century representations of curio cabinets. Painting has become an environment, an ambience. The painter no longer reproduced pictures; instead, he transformed painting into a world, a "nature," crowned with an allegory of triumph.

In an unfinished view of the 1765 Salon (Fig. 494), where the artist was still in the process of assembling his "motif," we can see that the delineation of the large geometric masses preceded and ordered the placement of the individual works. The lines interlock as a grid in which several of the pictures are linked by the same continuous

straight edge or in a latticework of such edges. (And this particular disposition did not derive exclusively from the type of hanging prevalent in the period's exhibitions; to understand this we have only to consult any of Saint-Aubin's sketchbooks, where the linear matrices evoke drawings made by Mondrian around 1910.) Once again, the unit or individual canvas has been subordinated to a superior, more all-embracing principle.

Saint-Aubin's extraordinary productivity (yielding more than five thousand drawings) was regarded by his contemporaries as neurotic, perverse, or unhealthy. Greuze even spoke of "priapism." Saint-Aubin drew as if afflicted by an itch, and people tired of seeing him drawing "all the time and

everywhere." Finally, he earned a soubriquet: *Monsieur Croquetel* ("Mr. Sketch-all"). Still more dismaying was his reluctance to finish. Unsuited to the solemn programs of Salon painting— mythologies, idealized landscapes—and rejected by the Academy, Saint-Aubin created, as if in spite of himself, a genre out of incompletion. For him drawing was less a professional practice (he made a poor living at it and died in poverty) than a way of life, a mode of being, a fever. But that he belonged to painting is borne out by the many catalogues in whose margins he sketched, with an incomparable gift for synthesis, the pictures sold before his eyes. The catalogue of the Mariette sale alone contains twelve hundred such *croquis*.

From a dense assemblage of pictures,
Saint-Aubin realized a continuous, multicolored fabric
of high-key strokes and fluid atmosphere

494. Gabriel de Saint-Aubin. *The Salon of 1765*. c. 1765.
Black pencil, pen, black ink, gray wash, watercolor, 9½×18".
Cabinet des Dessins, Louvre.

# Saturated with color, shapes, and hyperrealist detail, the museum becomes a delirium of objects

German-born, transplanted to Great Britain in the 1760s, and painter to royal and ducal courts (London, Vienna, Florence, and Parma), Johann Zoffany is best known for his ''conversation pieces,'' paintings in which he assembled, under a hard, uniform light, various types of objects (pictures, sculptures, furniture) and human subjects, all isolated from one another like wax effigies (Fig. 495). Static, stiff, and fixed in the midst of vast collections of art, Zoffany's aristocrats appear to have been deliberated one at a time and finished individually before being transferred to the canvas. (The procedure, however, has an analogy in the work of Goya, Zoffany's contemporary. See Figs. 496, 497.)

The picture reproduced here was commissioned by England's Queen Charlotte (*née* Mecklenburg-Strelitz) who wanted a good pictorial description of the Uffizi. In the 18th century the celebrated Florentine museum provided the triumphal moment of the entire Grand Tour, that journey of cultural initiation made on the Continent by every young Englishman of good family. The beneficiary of advantages accruing from his patroness' rank, Zoffany gathered in one room—the Tribuna, built at the end of the 16th century to house the treasures of the Medici—the foremost masterpieces belonging to the Uffizi. (He even had seven pictures brought from the Pitti Palace.) Among these great monuments he installed groups of *dilettanti* and British notables, some of them displaying the insignia of their status. The oneiric effect obtained in the picture is due mainly to the oddity of the ''collages'' that the artist arranged. In contrast to Saint-Aubin's Salon scenes, where the depicted works lose something of their individual qualities through fusion into an overall climate, every one of the pictures in the Zoffany collection, whether by Carracci or Rubens, Titian or Raphael, has been reconstituted with maximum fidelity, even to the specific touch of each master. But the most impressive aspect of Zoffany's work is the arrangement of its contents, the unexpected combination and juxtaposition of images that differ not only in genre (sculpture, painting, actual people), but also in period (from Egyptian antiquity to the 17th century), and, most especially, in scale. Take, for instance, the passage in the lower right corner

where Titian's foreshortened *Venus of Urbino* has been surrounded by an antique marble of two wrestlers and a clutch of real people. Here the scales of the various forms are *almost* identical, which simply makes the relationships among them all the more unstable and disturbing. It is an environment where heterogeneous images (men, objects, and pictures) are eternally on the verge of spatial compatibility without ever completely attaining it. We should also note the reds that dominate the canvas, not only the color of the wall covering and curtain but also that spotted onto most of the paintings, on the chairs, the carpet, and the clothing worn by the living figures. The pervasiveness and insistence of one hue have a flattening effect and thus confuse our perception of depth. And so does the brilliant, zenithal illumination, which reduces shadows to a minimum and completely eliminates the connective tissue of atmosphere, thereby reinforcing the sense of flat, paper-doll silhouettes, dry contours, and isolation.

The opposition of the rectilinear geometry of the frames above and the jumble of diverse shapes below, the enveloping disposition of the walls, and the contrast between the broken line of the cornice and the encircling head-high dado, with its load of busts—all these disparate phenomena perturb the image of a place dedicated to the serenity of classical genius. The piling-up of masterpieces hovered over by clusters of petrified art lovers produces a kind of cold frenzy, a chaos of forms. At the same time that the 18th-century connoisseur attached ever-greater importance to touch and manner, he also deprived art works of even the last vestiges of the religious significance with which they once seemed pregnant. According to the historian K. Pomian, taste underwent an important change after 1750. Interest shifted ''from the painting to the painter. . . . Aesthetic appreciation ceded primacy to questions of attribution. . . . [Concern centered] not so much on the meaning of the picture as on its material qualities, less on the 'spirit' that had presided over its creation than on the activity of the [artist's] hand.'' As a corollary to this, pictures came to be considered for their speculative or commercial value. The new interest in manner and the rise of the art dealer combined to reduce the physical distance between the work and its admirer.

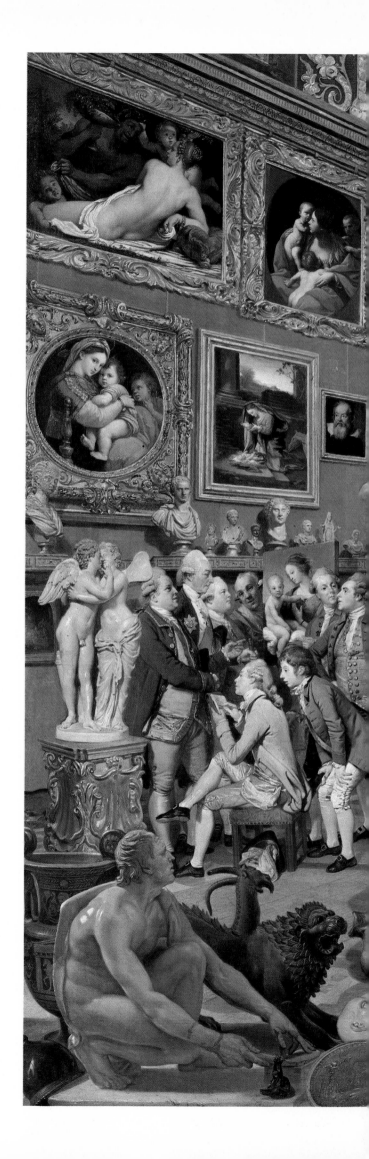

495. Johann Zoffany (1733–1810). *The Tribuna of the Uffizi.* 1772–78. Oil on canvas, 4′½″×5′1″. Royal Collection, London.

496. Francisco Goya (1746–1828). *The Kite*. c. 1777. Oil on canvas, 8′10″×9′4¼″. Museo del Prado, Madrid.

If we took account only of their official purpose, the cartoons executed by the young Goya (aged thirty-one) for Madrid's royal palace (the Pardo) might seem devoid of mystery. Made in the immediate aftermath of the Tiepolos' long success in Spain, the commission was for a series of popular scenes reflecting the contemporary vogue of *majas* and *majos* within the capital's aristocratic circles. Goya delivered six of the cartoons between October 1776 and January 1778.

However, a spirit of disquieting strangeness reigns over these vast compositions. The figures, for instance, seem less to partake of a space than to be heaped up (Fig. 497) or juxtaposed (Fig. 496) like diverse fragments from other works, or excerpts that the artist might have arranged side by side through a process of decalcomania. The picture could be the product not of composition but of a coalescence of pieces—thus, an oneiric association of stiff, phantom-like beings who, with their vacant looks, appear to have no communication with one another. This feeling is reinforced in the *Crockery Vendor* (Fig. 497) by the presence of a third wheel, half-obliterated and ghostly, behind the carriage's own two wheels. Each figure in these paradoxical scenes reflects a documentary concern for truth, in clothing as well as in gesture (see above, for instance, the gleaming knee buckles worn by the *majos*), but everything together produces, under the reassuring guise of a genre episode, a space that breaks up instead of cohering.

Equally remarkable, in regard to the image's decomposition, are the sharp luminary contrasts from one part of the picture to another. In the *Crockery Vendor* this takes the form of an extremely jumbled midground that is backlit by the distant city whose blind tower is almost monochrome. Such nonhierarchical spaces can only scatter the spectator's attention and disconcert the expectations of normal vision.

497. Francisco Goya. *The Crockery Vendor*. 1778. Oil on canvas, 8′6″×7′2½″. Museo del Prado, Madrid.

498. Asmus Jacob Carstens (1754–98). *Ossian: Fingal's Battle with the Spirit of Loda.* c. 1797. Oil on canvas, 2′6¾″×3′3¼″. Statens Museum for Kunst, Copenhagen.

# Ruptured scale gives birth to fantastic beings

Painters used the fantastic as an occasion for admitting figures of different scales into the same scene. Here they were carrying over into classical, geometric space practices derived from archaic, naïve, or medieval modes of figuration. Pictorial coherence and narrative credibility now became dependent upon the viewer's willingness to violate perspectival rules that had been in effect since Alberti in the 15th century. The "classical" conception of pictorial space had always held that size should indicate a figure's location in depth, whereas the newly revived but older systems used size to denote just the opposite: the supernatural character of the spectral beings represented. While the Renaissance tended to impose the same scale on both men and gods, Flaxman (Fig. 127), Ingres (Fig. 167), Turner (Fig. 431), and, above all, Goya (Figs. 504, 505) did the reverse.

Image enlargement had enjoyed a revival of interest in literature ever since Swift and, after him, Voltaire (in his *Micromégas*) had made their well-known use of it for satiric purposes. The texts of these authors lent themselves to illustration, and none other than Goya based a powerful drawing upon *Gulliver's Travels*. But if Swift and

Goya transport us to the realm of the colossal, where the relationship between forms is all but incommensurable, Carstens (Fig. 498) or A. E. Fragonard (Fig. 500) combine mythical or fantastic beings who are no more than two or three times larger than the flesh-and-blood hero. However different the scales, they remain comparable—and thus perhaps all the more troubling.

Alexandre Evariste Fragonard—the son of Jean-Honoré and the author of many successful works done in the *Style troubadour*—painted a knight-commander (Fig. 500) who is exceptional not only in size but also in color and texture.

On the other hand, the Michelangelesque demon painted by Carstens evinces a clarity and a consistency that relate the Dane's figure to his adversary. The picture shows Fingal, the hero of the Ossianic saga, crossing into the sacred aerie of Loda and, surrounded by megaliths, suddenly coming upon the spirit of the place. They engage one another in battle. Struck by Fingal, the spirit cries out as he dissolves into air. Carstens, a pupil of Abildgaard (Fig. 472) and a passionate admirer of Michelangelo, had first tried to reach Rome when he was twenty-nine years old. For lack of

money, he went no farther than Milan and Mantua. In the latter city, he conceived a lifelong admiration for Giulio Romano's Pallazo del Te frescoes devoted to the legendary Fall of the Giants, in which the artist played cunningly upon the contrast between the collapsing architecture and the massiveness of the figures.

In the picture by Mortimer (Fig. 499; see also Fig. 471) queasiness and revulsion result from the dual effect of enlargement and montage, for in the red-stomached monster have been combined the head of a dog and an immense dragon's tail coiling into the background.

500. Alexandre Evariste Fragonard (1780–1850). *Don Juan and the Commendatore's Statue.* c. 1829. Oil on canvas, 1′3″×1′½″. Musée des Beaux-Arts, Strasbourg.

With Blake,
the design of the page
assumes primacy over
proportional relationships

501. William Blake (1757–1827). *Urizen Struggling in the Waters of Materialism.* c. 1794. Color etching finished with pen and watercolor, 6¼ × 4¼". British Museum (courtesy of the Trustees), London.

Isolated within a cloud ring, which accentuates the close-up effect, the giant Antaeus (Fig. 502) delicately deposits Virgil and Dante in the ninth circle of Hell (where Lucifer eternally devours Judas). As much by the violent disparity of the scales as by the precarious balance of the principal character, the image both troubles and stirs us. It is a *vision* rather than a *view*. It also partakes of the awkwardness that remains constant in Blake throughout all his various styles, whether in the angular drawing of the illustrations to Hayley's ballads or in the sinuous contours of the slavery engravings (Fig. 65), which in

their deliberate naïveté have nothing in common, either with one another or with Antaeus' labored contrapposto in the watercolor reproduced opposite. (Here the torso seems to be a stiff, gauche variation upon the *Laocoön,* which Blake had in fact engraved [Fig. 71]).

But if maladroitness is so fundamental and yet so varied in Blake, it is because the artist cultivated the quality. It satisfied an expressive need, proof of which can be found in the perfectly formed academic nudes made by Blake as well as in an impeccably modeled oil copy that he executed of a figure (1776) from Michelangelo's *Last Judgment.* The stiffness compels the eye, tearing us away from the conventions of ideal form. It harks back to archaic, "purer," more "truthful" ages. Jean Starobinski speaks of "massive, disproportionate creatures of wild primitiveness." Blake, he says, was "the annunciator of the end of time, which simultaneously meant a return to the origin of things."

It is in an original, ammoniac matter that Urizen swims (Fig. 501), his body constituted from the very tissue of the colored ground covering the entire sheet (whose upper corners are touched by the god). This print comes from a series that Blake began engraving in 1794. After applying a mixture of glue and pigment to the cut plate, the artist then pressed the proof on by hand, producing a spongy, porous texture. In Blake's personal version of Genesis, Urizen is the incarnation of forces both primitive and demonic, which the artist-poet identifies with the Old Testament Jehovah and with coercive reason. To Urizen, Blake opposed Jesus, the symbol of goodness and liberty. He wanted to superimpose his own enigmatic, swarming pantheon upon traditional Judeo-Christian imagery, whose efficacy would seem exhausted in a revolutionary period.

502. William Blake. *Antaeus Setting Down Dante and Virgil.* 1796. Pen and watercolor, 20⅜ × 14½". National Gallery of Victoria, Melbourne.

HELL Canto 31

## In his giants and cannibals, Goya conjures the phantasms of childhood fears

503. Henry Fuseli (1741–1825). *The Blind Polyphemus, at the Entrance to His Cave, Strokes the Ram under which Odysseus Lies Concealed.* 1803. Oil on canvas, 2′11¾″×2′4″. Private collection, Zurich.

504. Francisco Goya (1746–1828). *A Giant.* 1808–10. Oil on canvas, 3′9¾″×3′5¼″. Museo del Prado, Madrid.

In his famous *Saturn* (Fig. 505) Goya synthesized two themes that never ceased to haunt him: giantism and cannibalism. (They appear in a sanguine sketch dated 1798; meanwhile, the artist devoted several drawings and paintings to scenes of monstrous gluttony.)

*Saturn* is one of fourteen oils that Goya painted directly on the plaster walls of the Quinta del Sordo, his residence on the outskirts of Madrid. He began the series shortly after surviving an illness that almost killed him during the winter of 1819 (when he was sixty-three years old). In the Quinta del Sordo, *Saturn* was positioned facing the main entrance on the ground floor, along with its pendant, *Judith.* The subject came from the most ancient of Greek mythologies. Kronos (called Saturn by the Romans), the son of Uranus whom he castrated with a sickle during the elder god's coupling with Gaea (Earth), has taken his father's

place in the celestial empire. But according to omen, the usurper would be overthrown by one of his own sons. To forestall this, he devoured his male progeny at the moment of their birth, one after the other. Only Zeus, thanks to a maternal ruse, would escape destruction.

On a tenebrous ground, bathed in a lunar light—the product of Caravaggism by way of Ribera—the huge figure has been painted in broad, rapid strokes of thick, mat medium (note especially the legs). Streaks of blood, added only at the end, outline the fingers throughout their length and then turn black while

contouring the victim's form (which could very well be female). The low-angle viewpoint is that of a child addressing an adult, and the whole vision—a vision of horror—seems to express what psychoanalysis would call "castration fears."

During the period of Goya's work on *Saturn,* Goethe felt compelled to voice a warning against the "subjective" and the "morbid," which the German poet had come to associate with "romantic." In a famous phrase, he declared in 1820: "I call classic what is healthy and romantic what is sick." But while denouncing the contemporary fascination with obscurity, Goethe showed just how much all that harkening to the subconscious and all that inner experience entailed a risk—even fingered the mechanism of madness: "There is an empty spot in the brain, a place, that is, where no object makes an impression, just as the eye too contains a blind spot. If man pays attention to this place, he becomes absorbed in it; he falls into mental illness; he imagines things of another world, which in fact are pure nothings and have neither forms nor boundaries, but cause fear like that of night's empty space and pursue more cruelly than specters anyone who does not tear himself from their grasp."

*A Giant* (Fig. 504), painted ten years earlier than *Saturn,* is a less intense work but also based on the improbable interface of two worlds. On one side looms a striding giant, while on the other a crowd flees, the latter realized in a few bits of colored or oily pigment scraped over an earthen expanse. And the giant's face too is nothing but an agglomeration of accents, almost haphazardly applied. This juxtaposition of *disparate* elements (*Los Disparates* is the title given by Goya at the time to a suite of twenty-two engravings that are masterpieces of strangeness and horror) owes its form to a system of construction quite different from that used by Henry Fuseli for his *Blind Polyphemus* (Fig. 503). Whereas Goya presents a brutal confrontation of heterogeneous spaces, Fuseli retains scenic unity, despite the distortions of size effected for the sake of the fable.

505. Francisco Goya. *Saturn.* 1821–23. Oil on plaster transferred to canvas, 4'9" × 2'8¾". Museo del Prado, Madrid.

# Threatening or tragic, a monstrous foreground detail . . .

506. Peter Paul Rubens (1577–1640). *The Fall of the Angels* (detail). Alte Pinakothek, Munich.

In the vast hagiographies that Gros devoted to the Napoleonic campaigns, the traditional function of the repoussoir—assuring, by means of a foreground object or void, the sense of progressive recession into depth—has been replaced by its opposite. Thus, the lower part of the canvas, far from being empty or neutral, is crowded with violent, aggressive images that spill toward the spectator, thereby contradicting the heroic, noble character of the work and asserting themselves as a challenge to it. In *The Battle of Aboukir* (Figs. 507, 508), as in Rubens' *Fall of the Angels* (Fig. 506), a detail—a shrieking mouth right at the picture's bottom edge—decentralizes the composition, its questioning power shattering the coherence of the main argument and confronting us with an almost corporeal threat. The work's triumphal rhetoric is simply swallowed up in this yawning chasm—this cloaca—where the image of death, with its cyclopian eye, freezes us in our tracks.

507. Antoine Jean Gros (1771–1835). *The Battle of Aboukir.* 1806. Oil on canvas, 18'11½"×31'9". Musée National du Château, Versailles.

508. Antoine Jean Gros. *The Battle of Aboukir* (detail of Fig. 507)

In *Napoleon at Eylau* (Fig. 510), just as in *The Battle of Aboukir* (Figs. 507, 508), Gros has given us a form rent by contradictory images, a picture whose main subject is undermined by an overpowering fragment. The eye can scarcely move beyond the foreground, with its heap of thrown-back heads, to take account of Napoleon's blessing hand. The victims pull the picture toward the bottom and begin to ''weigh'' upon the spectators, who, virtually face to face with frozen countenances, are almost forced to look at them.

Five weeks after the bloody encounter with the Russians at Eylau (twenty-five thousand dead), a competition was announced for a painting designed to commemorate the Napoleonic victory. Denon, the director of French museums, dictated the program for the entries: ''The moment is that when His Majesty visiting the battlefield at Eylau in order to distribute aid to the wounded, a young Lithuanian hussar, whose knee had been shot off, rose up and said to the Emperor: 'Caesar, you want me to live. . . . Well, let them cure me and I will serve you as faithfully as I did Alexander!' '' Gros won the competition, in which Meynier also submitted a sketch (Fig. 509), and the similarity of their compositions suggests that Denon had provided a drawing along with his iconographic prescriptions. In his own way Meynier too had success, achieving genuine tragic force with his blood-stained distance and, even more so, with his foreground accumulation of naked bodies (halfway between Signorelli and Géricault). Still, the work is no match for Gros' final 26-foot-wide picture, whose sheer size endows the work with undeniable expressive power. (The impact of the scale can be suggested here only through the artifice of an enlarged detail.) This makes the faces near the lower frame twice normal lifesize. Gros' contemporaries—notably David who had wanted to paint the figures of his *Tennis Court Oath* larger than reality—were well aware of the degree to which the overscaling of the foreground did less to provide a decorative effect than to deny spectators the neutrality of benign or aesthetic contemplation. Such distortion, it was felt, would be certain to challenge attitudes and unsettle complacency. So too would the bayonet covered with frozen blood, as well as the heads and bodies whose upside-down positions render them all the more anonymous, and whose crowding anticipated the charnel houses of modern times. Along with all this come the blued, snow-encrusted faces, the stiff hand cut off by the frame, and under Napoleon's horse a cadaver, ignored and barely visible, while beyond stretches a great plain

510. Antoine Jean Gros (1771–1835). *Napoleon at Eylau.* 1808. Oil on canvas, 17′5¾″×26′3″. Louvre.

strewn with indistinct traces—somber masses, corpses, common pit-graves. The ''counter-argument'' of Gros and Meynier, surreptitious and probably involuntary inversions of the official program, did arouse the suspicions of the police, who complained in a report: ''The artists have collected every kind of mutilation, every aspect of a vast butchery as if they were required

specifically to paint a scene of horror and carnage and make the war seem execrable.'' The art historian Henri Focillon said the same thing: ''Under a black sky, this mass of fallen giants . . . shocked the Salon strategists, accustomed as they were to seeing the warriors of the *Iliad,* as translated by Bitaubé, fall and die with the elegance of dancers.''

. . . shatters
the conventions
of Napoleonic glory

511. Antoine Jean Gros. *Napoleon at Eylau* (detail of Fig. 510).

# The picture emerges in slabs or zones
## of densely agglomerated figures and details

512. Anne Louis Girodet (1767–1824). *Study for the Rebellion of Cairo.* c. 1810.
Colored chalk on tracing paper, 1'9¼"×2'2". Musée des Beaux-Arts, Avallon.

"At the Luxembourg: *Rebellion of Cairo,* full of vigor, grand manner," wrote the young Delacroix in his journal, almost as if to cite the picture as a precursor of Romanticism (Fig. 513). Twelve years after the event, which occurred on October 21, 1798, the reprisal launched to suppress the conspiracy in which General Dupuis died provided Girodet with an occasion to emulate his friend Gros and prepare a spectacle of violence and eroticism, an Egyptian fantasy: "The subject of *The Rebellion of Cairo* offered no particular feature, no important person," observed the contemporary critic Landon, "and the picture has been composed merely of episodes, fruits of the painter's imagination." The presumed vehemence of the encounter (in actual fact, it was done with artillery) permitted Girodet to express his love of arms glistening with blood, severed heads, bronzed bodies, and stunning profiles. (According to his biographer Coupin, the artist surrounded himself "with Mameluks who were, so to speak, in residence with him and whose

beauty he found electrifying." A whole sophisticated savagery was at work here, like that soon to be set forth by Balzac at the end of his *Girl with the Golden Eyes.*

For his *Rebellion of Cairo* Girodet adopted the restricted depth typical of Neoclassical scenes, a fact that elicited comparison with David's *Sabines.* The impetuous flux of a disorderly mass rolls across the canvas from left to right and from bottom to top, the whole articulated by the symmetrically placed figures of the French dragoon and the Arab warrior holding his fallen master. Stendhal found the disposition "extremely energetic" and, in his correspondence, mentioned the pervasive vibration caused by an almost infinite multiplicity of detail: "Imagine a nest of vipers discovered when an antique vase is picked up. Only with difficulty is it possible to follow the same body. To look at it for any time is to become lost in it."

The sketch at Avallon (Fig. 512) reveals Girodet to have had a particular conception of detail. Here, the unit is no

longer an object or a body but rather a pictorial fragment—as if the picture emerged in slabs or patches, or in agglomerations of figures. The decapitated soldier in the foreground, whose helmet hides the headless neck, melds into a specific ensemble or passage, an indissoluble accumulation that includes the crouching form of the turbaned Black, the severed head, and the Arab warrior's leg. And just as the light in *Endymion* (Fig. 274) and the *Apotheosis of French Heroes* (Fig. 357) bit into contours and seemed to radiate from them, the *Rebellion of Cairo* seems to "come forward" by pieces. The *zone* (a fragment of the composition) tends to supplant the *detail* (the study of an isolated object selected from the outside world). Girodet painted in a deliberately artificial environment, for his smooth, precise manner demanded a new kind of illumination. "During the years 1804 and 1805," wrote Delécluze, "he painted at night by the glimmer of lamps prepared for such work, and his four big canvases, *Scene of a Deluge, Atala, Napoleon at*

*Vienna,* and *Rebellion of Cairo,* thus everything he produced up to and including *Pygmalion,* were for the most part created in this way. He began by saying that artificial light was as favorable to painting as daylight, and he finished by pretending that it was better."

513. Anne Louis Girodet. *The Rebellion of Cairo.* 1810. Oil on canvas, 11'8¼" × 16'4¾".
Musée National du Château, Versailles.

514. Théodore Géricault (1791–1824). *Severed Heads*. c. 1818. Oil on canvas, 1'7¾"×2'2½".
National Museum, Stockholm.

In the course of his preparatory research for *The Raft of the Medusa* (Figs. 216–218), Géricault undertook to capture the most daunting aspects of illness and death. The 18th century had certainly not neglected the dissection of cadavers as a means of instructing artists in human anatomy (with such investigations carried out under the supervision of surgeons), but the painters used this science simply to help them in their representations of martyrs or other pious themes, or to assure their grasp of academic principles. If Stubbs around 1750 did numerous dissections of human subjects, as well as horses and other animals, he used them for his

treatises on osteology or mythology and not for pictures. But in some ten "amphitheatre subjects" (eight of which survive) devoted to human remains, Géricault presents us with something quite different: a deliberate confrontation with the intolerable, an attempt to express through painting a fascinated horror of death. "It was [in Beaujon Hospital]," wrote his biographer Clément, "that he studied with avid curiosity every phase of suffering, from the first attacks to the final agony, and all the marks that it left on the human body. There he found models who did not have to feign physical distress or moral anxiety, the

ravages of sickness or the terrors of death. He arranged to have the interns and attendants supply him with cadavers and amputated members." Thus Géricault was able to take home and keep the head of a guillotined thief as well as a pair of legs and an arm (Figs. 517, 518).

*Severed Heads* (Fig. 514) is actually a montage in which the head of a young girl on the left is reputed to be the portrait of a hunchback then generally known as an artist's model. Géricault added the gash on her neck so as to simulate a decapitation. Here, therefore, he betrayed empirical reality for the sake of emphasizing the pathetic.

In Géricault we see the emergence of a secularized, prosaic conception of the funerary image. The human body was achieving a new status in the aftermath of the great Napoleonic slaughter. Death had lost its aura.

In the realism of "still" life,
the artist's age-old study of
human anatomy turns morbid . . .

An abyss (as well as half a century) separate Géricault from the melancholy *écorchés* of Gautier d'Agoty (Fig. 515), whose full-color plates, although made primarily as medical illustrations, occasionally served for instructional purposes in art schools. Here, the tradition of the anatomical subject presented live, a legacy from Charles Estienne or Vesalius (16th century), has been reinforced by the marked individuality of the faces—their expressions as well as their features. These highly imaginative studies were produced in an era (the 18th century) when macroscopic techniques had almost been mastered and when dissection had become a fashion

attracting up to five hundred spectators—society women and actors among them—all gathered around a cadaver. (Thanks to the work of Bichat and his successors, the 19th century was the age of histology, cellular theory, and the anatomy of the nervous system.)

In Gautier d'Agoty, the use of color, often varnished in order to suggest the effect of oil painting, simply accentuates the "surreal" dimension of the image, with its cranium opened to reveal shapes like flowers and shells. In this portrait of a couple, the dialectic of "now you see it, now you don't" opens onto a new abyss, as the surgeon's scalpel discloses nothing so much as still greater mystery.

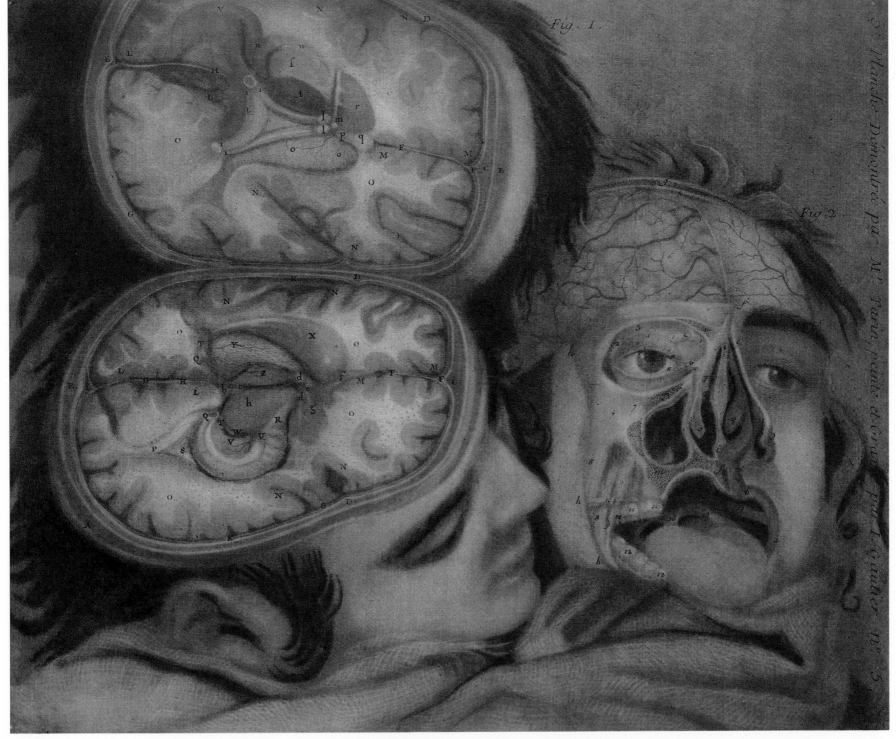

515. Jacques Gautier d'Agoty (1717–85). *Anatomical Illustration.* c. 1748. Mezzotint, 12½×15¼".
Courtesy of the Welcome Trustees, London.

516. Francisco Goya (1746–1828). *Butcher's Counter*. 1808–12. Oil on canvas, 1'5¾"×2'1½". Louvre.

Anthropomorphic allusions simply add to the morbidity of this butcher-shop display painted by Goya (Fig. 516). Charles Sterling, in his book on still-life painting (1951), makes the following observation: "The eye of the sheep, fixed as it may be with the glaucous, faraway look of death, seems a poignant reproach to our cruelty." If, Sterling continues, we find ourselves touched "to the very depths of our sensory organization," it is because these cuts of meat "are appetizing at the same time that they fill [us] with horror, by reason of their fresh blood whose glistening red seems unique—seems to belong solely to blood. In the presence of such simple pictures, with their facile, literal realism, we find ourselves gripped by a malaise, in which cannibalism is as much a component as mortal terror." Here, for Sterling, was "the first expressionist still life."

Géricault reversed the attitudes of Goya, for whereas the Spaniard invested animal meat with human import, the French master brought out everything that is animalistic about the human creature, everything about human flesh that is meatlike (Figs. 517, 518). The violence of Géricault's macabre images (which is the violence of an enlarged, close-up detail) derives from the fact that the cadaver parts are presented with such candor, stripped of all mythic or religious associations. With a leg and two arms, viewed from various angles and artfully rearranged for each picture, the painter produced a terrible synthesis of still (truly "stilled") life and dissection, painting and surgery, museum and medical school.

It seems that for a while Géricault may have wanted to include some evidence of cannibalism in his *Raft of the Medusa* (Fig. 218). But from a process of documentation, the artist advanced to the idea of using his series of "anatomies" as a means of "habituating" or conditioning himself to enter into the whole climate of horror that must have reigned upon the stricken raft.

But there is something repetitive about these studies as well as about other themes favored by Géricault, like that of the foul murder of magistrate Lualdès, which the artist also treated in a series. Dredged from the depths and motivated by a preoccupation with death, such works raise questions concerning the limits of art once their imagery causes the viewer to suspend aesthetic contemplation and thus challenge the old principle originally formulated by Aristotle: "As for those [works] that by means of spectacle arouse not fear but only horror, they have nothing in common with tragedy."

517. Théodore Géricault (1791–1824). *Study of Two Severed Arms and a Leg.* c. 1818.
Oil on canvas, 1'8½"×2'1¼".
Musée des Beaux-Arts, Lyon.

. . . and the
fragmented body
is reduced to
its animal materiality

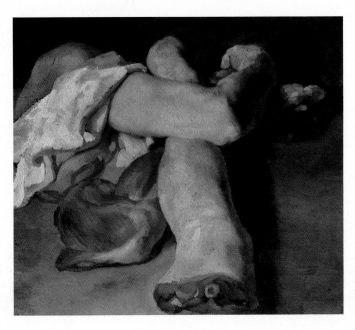

518. Théodore Géricault.
*Study of Severed Arms and Legs.* c. 1818.
Oil on canvas, 14½×18".
Musée des Beaux-Arts, Rouen.

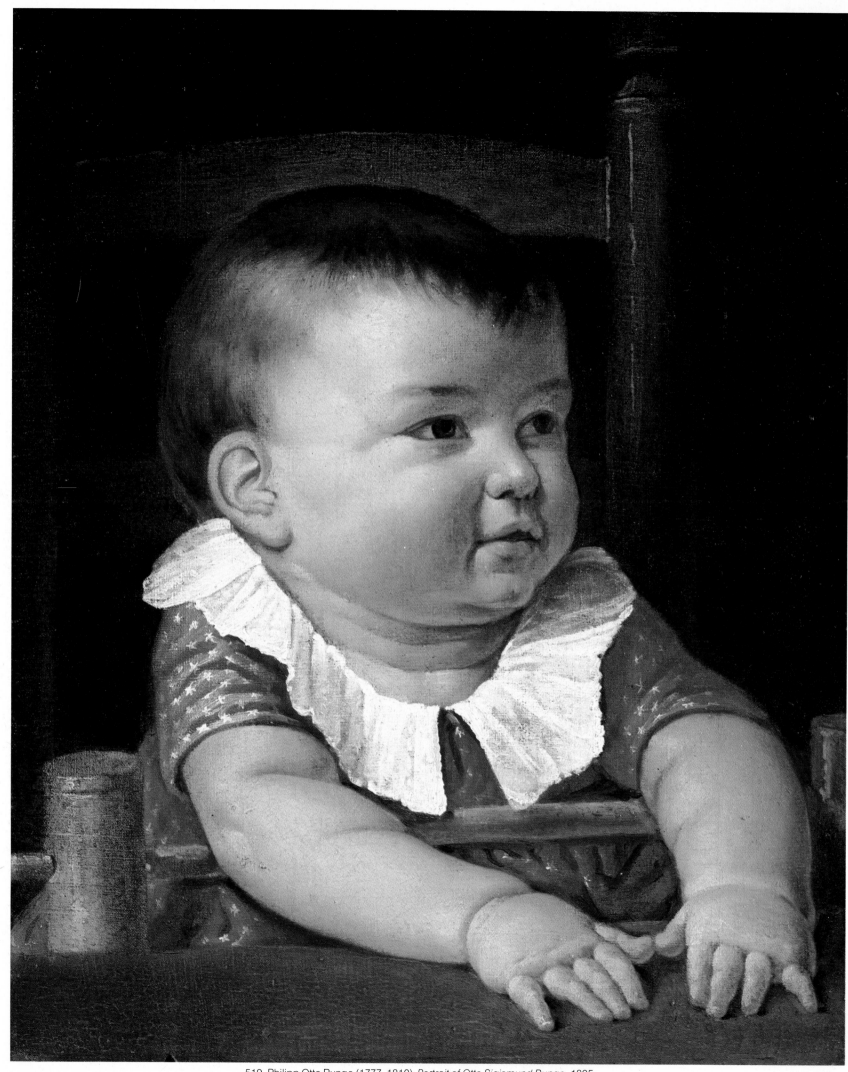

519. Philipp Otto Runge (1777–1810). *Portrait of Otto Sigismund Runge*. 1805.
Oil on canvas, 15¾ × 13¾". Kunsthalle, Hamburg.

# The giant infants of Runge threaten
# to break free of the enclosing frame

520. Philipp Otto Runge. *Portrait of the Artist's Children.* c. 1808–09.
Oil on canvas, 15×19¼". Kunsthalle, Hamburg.

Chubby, almost swollen, and possessed of a voracious, gargantuan vitality, the children painted by Runge all but burst out of their skins just as they threaten to burst out of the picture's enclosing frame. An excess of health here translates as an excess of surface. "The child-plant, the metaphor of innocence that Runge and Novalis share (unknowingly) with William Blake in England" is, according to Werner Hofmann, a concentration of energy, an image potent with the future.

While painting the portrait of his daughter Marie (Fig. 519), two years before his death, Runge used a curious phrase to describe the child: "So solid that even bullets would bounce off her." To give effect to the molecular density of childhood, Runge took a deliberately "naïve" approach, trying for an image of directness and factuality. He obtained it by cropping in as close as possible, by scaling the head larger, and by placing himself at eye level so as to face the subject straight on. (The same procedures, as

Rosenblum has noted, would be adopted and even accentuated by van Gogh in his giant babies, and also by *douanier* Rousseau.)

"We should become children again," wrote Runge, "if we want to attain the highest good." This desire for a return to innocence and primal energy— always a product of the intellect, and one that would motivate Gauguin, Expressionism, and Russian neo-primitivism—contradicts the extreme sophistication of the work that Runge was then pursuing in his *Times of Day*. This cycle of four vast panels, each measuring 26 feet high, was based upon a "symphonic" conception that, once realized, would have combined several different levels of meaning and conflated into the same forms (stars, flowers, newborn babes, etc.) not only the Times of Day but also the Ages of the World, the Four Seasons, and the Stages of Life. Here was programmatic painting, saturated with religiosity, a tabular, allegorical work whose polysemous qualities evoke the

emblematic, Masonic imagery of ancient times.

Runge envisioned a building designed to house the project, a place where music would also have played a role. He hoped to realize "an abstract and pictorial, fantastic and musical work." His premature death suspended the grandiose but obscure scheme, which now survives only in a few drawings, a series of engravings, and a large study for *Morning*. But the artist's linear style and decorative borders would be echoed a century later in Art Nouveau, a style that borrowed Runge's arabesque while rejecting his program.

The artist also wrote *The Sphere of Color*, a theoretical work published in 1810, the same year that Goethe's *Theory of Colors* appeared. Partially influenced by the ideas of Jacob Böhme, the 17th-century German mystic, the Runge treatise has served, according to Eric Michaud, as the model and source for "almost all subsequent color theory: Chevreul, Kandinsky, Klee, and Johannes Itten."

# Tragedy expressed in a face cleansed of all pretense

Painted when the artist was twenty-eight, Palmer's *Self-Portrait* (Fig. 522) presents an intense countenance of hallucinating fixity, a visage whose proximity—one could even say "promiscuity"—reveals nothing so much as the subject's closed and impenetrable character. Here was a new kind of image, a harbinger of the 19th century's existential crisis, already burdened with the anguish that would be voiced by another Christian, Palmer's contemporary, the Dane Kierkegaard. On a paper of omnipresent color, which constitutes the principal material of the face, the hair, the collar, and the background, a series of white touches simultaneously produce both modeling and highlights, their application broad enough to suggest the weight and density of the skin, even its puffiness. Sharp, black strokes form the hair, contour the eyes, and limn the cleft of the mouth.

Palmer did this portrait two years after meeting William Blake, who encouraged the young artist in the mystical and antinaturalistic direction along which he had been trying to discover himself (Figs. 445, 446). But Palmer's moment of transcendence did not extend beyond 1832 or 1833, when he concluded his so-called Shoreham period and established himself in London (thereby losing contact with the source of his best inspiration).

The painting in Fig. 521 belongs precisely to that pivotal interlude. And, in the opinion of Allen Staley, the work is not a portrait of the artist as Christ, but rather a pious image for which Palmer borrowed, *faute de mieux* in the solitude of Shoreham, the general outlines of his own face. At the time he did in fact wear his hair and beard long (Fig. 120), but self-enhancement with a halo would hardly have been consistent with the painter's ardent yet modest faith.

Palmer had the habit of surrounding himself with religious images as a means of sheltering his mind from evil, and this icon may very well have performed such a function. Certainly, the work is striking for the riveting quality of the subject's attitude and gaze as well as for the almost mineral heaviness of its impastoes. One could believe that Palmer, by the end of his Shoreham experience, was approaching a quasi-animistic conception of painting and believed it possible to capture in the work itself the very presence of God.

521. Samuel Palmer (1805–81). *The Artist as Christ.* c. 1833. Oil on wood, 13½×9½". Collection D. C. Preston.

522. Samuel Palmer. *Self-Portrait*. c. 1826. Black chalk, heightened with white on buff paper, 11½×9″. Ashmolean Museum, Oxford.

# The solitary figures confronting
# the enigma of the world

523. Caspar David Friedrich (1774–1840). *Woman in Morning Light*. 1818.
Oil on canvas, 8¾ × 11¾". Museum Folkwang, Essen.

The large figures that Friedrich executed from the back must be counted among this master's most celebrated works. Since the 17th century, European painting had produced many images disposed in this fashion, but whereas Claude, Watteau, Domenico Tiepolo, Géricault, or Ingres had bathed both figure and setting in a generalized illumination, Friedrich isolated the human form against a spread of sky and clouds (Fig. 523) and planted it upon a rocky outcropping (Fig. 524), which simply accentuates the effect of silhouette, almost as in Chinese ink painting. The subject, male or female, serves as a repoussoir. The figure remains outside the world it contemplates, and if Friedrich's avowed purpose was to evince the communion of humankind with divine light (light understood as both material and

metaphoric), the pictorial approach taken by the artist demonstrates just the opposite—for man and woman alike stand outside and look upon a world from which they are excluded. This feeling of *orbitas,* of abandonment and dereliction, can also be found in, for instance, the dual movement of *Hyperion,* published in 1797 and 1798 and reissued in 1822, where the poet Hölderlin sings of hope (''To be at one with all living things, to return through radiant selflessness to the whole of nature—this is thought and joy in their highest form''), at the same time that he groans in misery (''Yes, I have become thoroughly rational in your presence; I have become perfect in my understanding of how to distinguish myself from my environment—and so here I am isolated from the beauty of the world, exiled from the garden where I once flourished, withering away in the noonday sun'').

In the two pictures reproduced here—especially in *The Wanderer* (Fig. 524), which is more conflicted and thus more achieved—Friedrich manifests a strong feeling of ''territory'' (in the ethnological sense of the word). It holds us at the exact distance necessary for us to experience these figures simultaneously as different, removed, ''other'' *and* as projections of ourselves. The viewing angle—which in *The Wanderer* is arbitrary, since it postulates a spectator suspended in space—reinforces the twofold feeling of alienation and intimacy. This is the trap in which the artist catches us: We project ourselves, through empathy, into the figure with its back turned, but only to be excluded, along with the figure, from the radiant field whose spectacle the figure contemplates. Such duality and conflict cannot but evoke the dream mechanisms described by Freud, for whom the presence of the dreamer in his own dream (seeing himself in action) constitutes proof that memory is acted upon and altered by the subconscious, since in reality ''one finds oneself at the center of the situation [where] one pays attention not to oneself but rather to the exterior world.'' Herein may lie a valid analogy for Friedrich's ''oneirism,'' for the shifting back and forth of the self-image between an internalized subject (but not totally ''other'') and an externalized subject (albeit not completely ''me,'' the viewer) that re-presents the viewer's self-image on the canvas.

524. Caspar David Friedrich. *The Wanderer above the Mists*. c. 1818.
Oil on canvas, 3'2½" × 2'5½". Kunsthalle, Hamburg.

Whereas classical landscapists had combined heterogeneous sites—woods, ruins, hills—and made this process the very principle of their art, Turner and Friedrich, each in his own way, embraced forms so radical that they threatened the spatial unity of the canvas.

For his evocation of Hannibal's journey across the Alps (Fig. 525), Turner—who loved to fantasize about the destiny of Carthage and the decline of empires—admitted to having integrated a mountain view with a detail representing a storm he had witnessed near York two years earlier while staying with a patron-friend. Not content to juxtapose two motifs taken from utterly separate sources in empirical reality, the artist clapped together a pair of disparate elements whose scales make them not only disproportionate but even incompatible. Thus, the picture consists of a vastly enlarged view of swirling snow imposed upon an overall, panoramic scene swarming with thousands of tiny figures—and receding to a distant perspective on the warm, sensuous waters of an Italian bay. By thus playing upon differences in scale, Turner broke with compositional tradition, which had endeavored to effect coexistence only among plastic constituents sharing the same approximate degree of enlargement or reduction—among objects, that is, capable of being related to the same external nature. Like a modern collage, Turner's assemblage of heterogeneous forms produces a rather marked spatial commotion. Thus, it is not only Hannibal's army that is swept by cataclysm, but also the whole economy of scenic painting as this had prevailed from the advent of Claude Lorrain and the Dutch masters, Turner's first models, all the way through Joseph Vernet and Loutherbourg (Figs. 456, 457). However, for the next twenty-five years after his *Hannibal,* Turner would rarely return to a system of construction based upon disproportion, in the true sense of the word. (It was John Martin [Fig. 413] who would vulgarize the formula in his huge Biblical and Babylonian machines.) Liberated by his daring experiment, Turner could now concentrate on developing the kind of fluid space that became the foundation of his fame.

The montage effect may be less spectacular in Friedrich (an artist with a fundamental aversion to all showiness), but it was nonetheless based upon what Werner Hofmann terms ''an arbitrary combination of natural phenomena . . . that are mutually exclusive.'' Like most of Friedrich's pictures, *Rainbow* (Fig. 526) is not solely a conflation of several natural sites. Its contradictions, for instance, are meteorological as well, although this may not be apparent at first glance. Since a rainbow, to be visible, requires a light originating behind the observer, the one presented here—all compactness and symmetry—could not have been created by moonbeams. But if the needed illumination derives from the sun—which is suggested in the foreground where the hiker basks in light—the moon, with its placement high up in a nocturnal sky, becomes inexplicable.

The same can be said of *Abbey under Oak Trees* (Fig. 527), the shadowy scene of a monk's burial. The luminous circle hovering over the horizon, and gradually darkening toward the top, permits us to suppose that the sun is in the process of rising (or setting) directly ahead of us, which somewhat reduces the improbability of the bright glow emanating from a tall, traceried Gothic window at the center of the composition. By means of his calculated incoherences, Friedrich causes the prosaic order of things to be questioned—and implies the immanent presence of another Law.

525. Joseph Mallord William Turner (1775–1851). *Snow Storm: Hannibal and His Army Crossing the Alps.* 1812. Oil on canvas, 4'9″×7'9″. Tate Gallery, London.

526. Caspar David Friedrich (1774–1840). *Rainbow*. 1810. Oil on canvas, 1′11¼″×2′9″. Museum Folkwang, Essen.

The legendary
and the mystical
evoked through
a montage of
disparate sites
and climatic conditions

527. Caspar David Friedrich. *Abbey under Oak Trees*. 1809–10. Oil on canvas, 3′7¼″×5′7¼″.
Staatliche Schlösser und Gärten, Berlin.

## In bizarre mixtures of materials and techniques, letters become landscape

528. Victor Hugo (1802–85). *Visiting Card.* c. 1860. Drawing with watercolor, 5½×7½". Maison Victor Hugo, Paris.

529. Victor Hugo. *Visiting Card.* 1856.
Pen and brown ink wash, watercolor, gouache, scumbled with charcoal, printed with lace on white paper, 5×3½".
John Rylands University Library, Manchester.

Like William Blake a half-century earlier, Victor Hugo felt tempted to endow script with materiality, to give body and substance to the alphabetical components of language. The poet produced almost countless drawings, and the three thousand or so examined by Pierre Georgel reveal an incredible freedom of technique, "all sorts of bizarre mixtures" (as Hugo himself phrased it) used either in combination or one at a time—coffee grounds, coal, soot, prints made from ferns or laces (Fig. 529)—and processes as diverse as crumpling, tearing, and scratching. Also to be found in Hugo's graphic works are a certain number of attempts to integrate the "readable" and the "visible," the alphabetic sign and the iconic sign, what comes from gesture and what comes from language. The startling *Marine Terrace* (Fig. 530)— the largest drawing to survive, according to Georgel, from the Jersey period—is the product of a series of mental operations whose effect was to replace the images of Victor Hugo and Juliette Drouet with their patronyms and then to reduce these to their initials,

which were in turn transformed into vegetal and animal motifs (vine and serpent) intimately mingled or "coupled." What results is a meteoric image, simultaneously frightening and triumphant, an image in which the poet's two initials seem literally to cling to the large D (for Drouet).

Hugo also created a set of *cartes de visite* that he sent to friends as a New Year greeting at the outset of 1856 (Fig. 529). Now he used the letters of his name, dispersing them over the surface, but in a less illusionistic manner than in *Marine Terrace,* where the effect of depth is quite insistent. Thanks to the "reserves" (the areas of virgin paper), the letters seem inscribed upon the same plane as that occupied by the architectural motifs: castles, ruins, city halls, etc. The painted, or historiated, letters, long known from medieval Gospel books, would become the object of numerous experiments on the part of 20th-century masters, from the Cubists to Paul Klee, who, in the context of their painting, learned to exploit the inherent ambiguity of letters, which constitute both form and sign.

530. Victor Hugo. *"Marine Terrace."* 1855. Pen and brown ink, brown wash, heightened with gouache and charcoal stumpwork, 1'4¼"×1'1".
Private collection.

MARINE TERRACE

## By the additive process of filling the picture with similar but discreet forms, the painter abolishes composition in favor of assemblage

531. Eugène Delacroix (1798–1863). *Babouches (Turkish Slippers)*. 1832. Oil on canvas, 6¼ × 7¾". Louvre.

Géricault's study of horses (Fig. 532), painted when the artist was twenty-two years old, represents a complete rupture with Neoclassical conceptions as professed by Géricault's master Guérin, whose atelier the younger man still sporadically frequented in 1813. Thus, while the main objective of Géricault may have been to enrich his palette with appropriate exercises while also satisfying his passion for horses, the painter permitted himself something more—a disposition of elements in a series of superimposed bands, each with a different spatial reference. As in a link chain, the arrangement made possible a repetitive, systematic, and even reversible (left to right) juxtaposition of the very similar but discreet forms (horses' rumps) that fill the canvas surface edge to edge. Here the idea of composition (with all the formal balances that presupposes) loses its relevance in favor of a notion of assemblage. It is precisely the similarity of the objects depicted that permits us to transcend the three-level division and

sense it as perfectly correct. Such a reading is also encouraged by the restricted depth of the ensemble, the shallowness reinforced by the play of blacks and browns, which in one place denotes the animals and in another, shadows and background.

The picture, which the artist kept above his bed (as shown by Ary Scheffer's *Death of Géricault*), was bought for 2,850 francs at a posthumous sale ("a considerable sum," notes Philippe Grunchec, "more than the price for *The Wounded Cuirassier*, acquired by the Duc d'Orléans").

Albeit less conclusive, Delacroix's little study (Fig. 531) seems also to evince a pleasure in enumeration. The effect of the Turkish slippers—similar forms disposed radially upon an evenly textured ground—derives as much from their repetition as from their color. Perhaps still more than the artist's *Women of Algiers*, the *babouches* merit the appreciation that Gustave Planche wrote in 1834: "It is painting and nothing more."

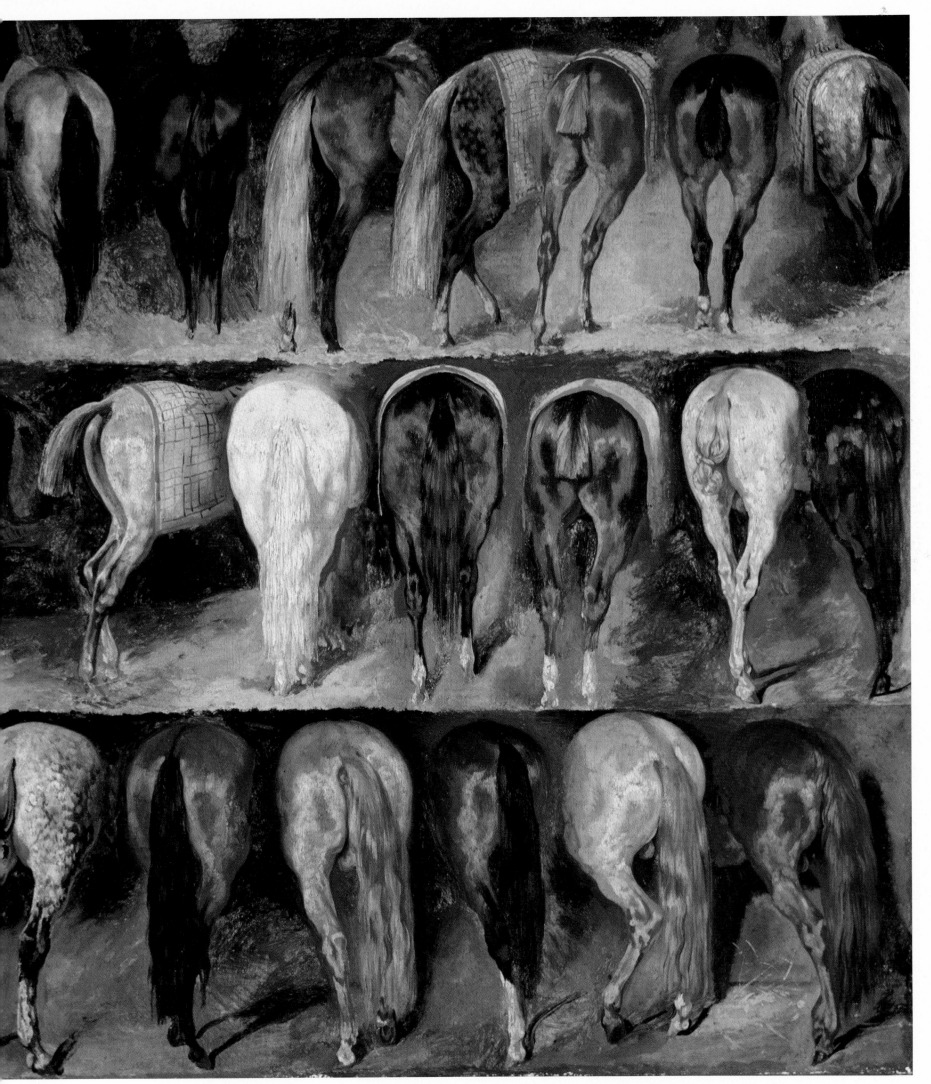

532. Théodore Géricault (1791–1824). *Cruppers.* c. 1813. Oil on canvas, 2′5¼″×2′11¾″. Private collection.

533. Jean Auguste Dominique Ingres (1780–1867).
*Study for the Martyrdom of Saint Symphorian.* c. 1834.
Oil on canvas, 2'½" × 1'7¾". Fogg Art Museum
(bequest of Grenville L. Winthrop), Harvard University, Cambridge.

While striving
for Raphael's unitary coherence,
Ingres gives in to
the tensions of his time
and declares the "final" work
to be only a stage

534. Jean Auguste Dominique Ingres. *Study for the Martyrdom of Saint Symphorian.*
c. 1834. Oil on canvas, 2' × 1'6¾".
Musée Ingres (collection Henri Delaborde), Montauban.

By signing his studies for *Saint Symphorian* and by selling them to collectors, Ingres confirmed that he intended these productions to have a life of their own as independent works of art. Indeed, they disclose a cast of mind much more modern than the creator of the *Turkish Bath* would himself have admitted.

All his life, Ingres dreamed of achieving the sovereign ease of Raphael in the organization of his multifigure pictures. "What is most admirable in [Raphael's] compositions," he said, "is the link that unites all the figures in a group, relates the groups to one another, and causes them to resemble, so to speak, various clusters of grapes harmoniously joined to the main stem." And these well-conceived works of Raphael, all projected upon the surface with such grace, struck Ingres as having "flowed from his intelligence in a single stream." But it was just such mastery of vast ensembles that Ingres could never achieve (witness not only *Saint Symphorian* but also *The Apotheosis of Homer,* despite its scholarly symmetries, and the huge *Golden Age,* left unfinished at the Château de Dampierre), as if something in the

rebellions and tensions of his time prevented the artist from producing the desired harmony. In the general weakness of their disposition, Ingres' large paintings seem like so many provisional solutions devised in the course of a continuing search. (Moreover, Ingres never ceased going back over most of them, just as he never ceased transposing certain figures, such as the *Valpinçon Bather,* from one work to another, all the way to the final *Turkish Bath*). It is this potential mutability, this floating quality of the Ingresque picture that is anticipated and thus expressed in the studies for *Saint Symphorian* (Figs. 533–535). They are like the muddlings of an impossible synthesis, debris from a cataclysm, or an incident that would fall first on one side and then on the other (or drop out altogether) of classic compositional logic. Broken, fractured pictures, juxtaposed fragments and "rejects," an amalgam of anatomical parts. Images that always had to be redone and redistributed. The key to these assemblages may have been provided by Théophile Silvestre when, in his malicious portrait of Ingres, he wrote in 1857: "I see him there, an agitated

figure surrounded by an enchanted circle of engravings, a Popilius circle from which he cannot exit, turning, returning, taking an attitude here, another there, a head, an arm, a hand, a figure, a group; a tomb, a column, a caryatid, a temple; placing a personage, another, yet another; replacing the first, the second, the third, etc., absolutely as if he were maneuvering the king, the queen, the knight, the rook, the bishop on a chessboard." Silvestre reveals

Ingres working on the pictorial table, manipulating his pawns and figures in a match with no clear winner, a process in which the "final" work is only a stage. In such a practice we can perceive everything that was shattering traditional order and the unitary coherence of depicted space. Here was a problem, or a process, that after the turn of the 20th century would give the Cubists the basis of their own concentrated program.

535. Jean Auguste Dominique Ingres. *Study for the Martyrdom of Saint Symphorian.* c. 1834.
Canvas mounted on wood, 2'½" × 1'7¾". Fogg Art Museum (bequest of Grenville L. Hicks), Harvard University, Cambridge.

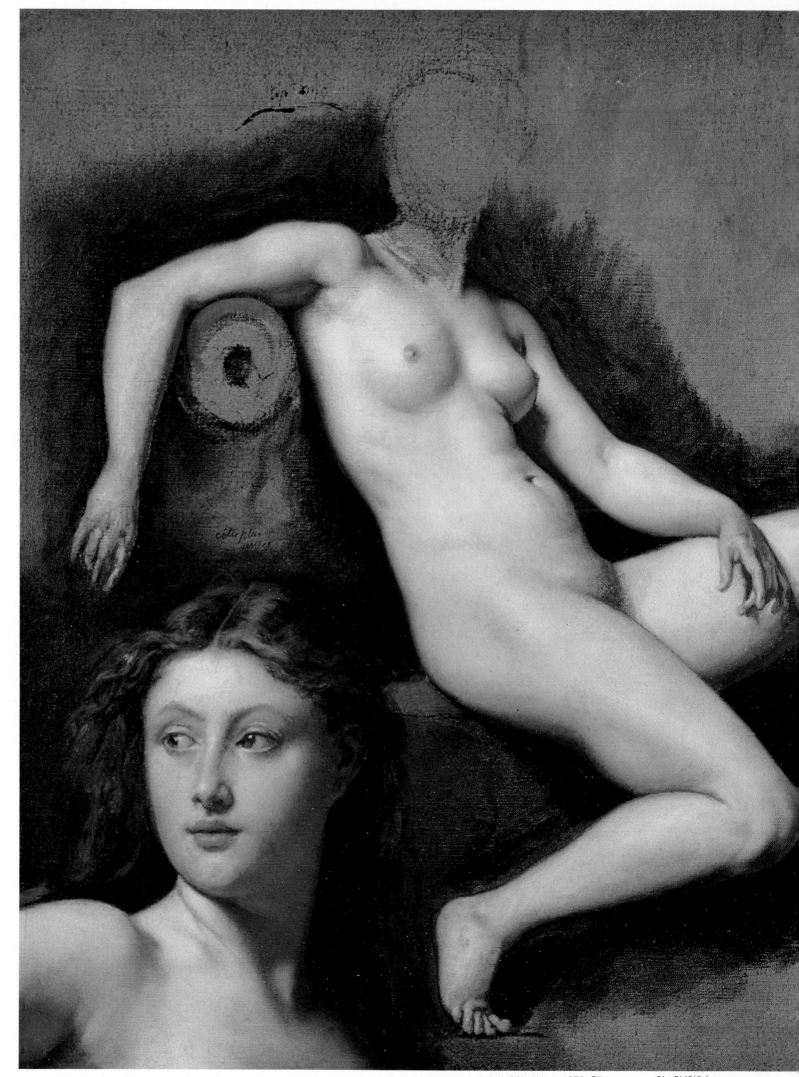

536. Henri Lehmann (1814–82). *Water.* 1870. Oil on canvas, 2′×2′4¾″. Louvre.

## Free as a study, smooth as a picture

Acquired by the Louvre in 1951 with an attribution to Théodore Chassériau and recently reattributed to Henri Lehmann by Jacques Foucart, *Water* (Fig. 536) was made as a study for one of the eight murals (on the themes of Water, Wine, Bread, etc.) intended by the artist to decorate the dining room of his town house in the Rue Balzac. On a warm chestnut ground, the canvas sets forth the figure of a young woman leaning upon an arm rest. The head, although merely suggested above the fully formed body by a few strokes of charcoal, has been much more completely realized, and on a larger scale, in the lower left corner of the canvas. Lehmann was the prototypical academic painter. A scrupulous and finicking heir to his master Ingres, he became director of the Beaux-Arts in 1861 and then professor in 1875. For two years one of his pupils would be Georges Seurat. Even after his death in 1882, Lehmann expressed, through the terms of a legacy meant for the creation of a prize, his abiding hatred of "the degradation encouraged by the nonclassical doctrines of the day." *Water*—and other works of the same type—appeals precisely because of its origin in late 19th-century conservatism. As a direct artistic descendant of Ingres, who gave his sketches for *Saint Symphorian* the status of pictures (Figs. 533–535), Lehmann raised to the level of painting the kind of preparatory drawing that had become a tradition in the ateliers of the Renaissance. He accorded all the prestige of finished, polished work to a trial exercise whose elements, by reason of their incompatible scales, violate the old *convenienza,* the *concinnitas,* the "harmony of the parts" that for Alberti in the 15th century constituted the very foundation of painting. By conjoining on the same surface images that are incommensurable, he replaced composition with agglutination. Whereas an earlier classicist would have ordered the surface by means of a balanced relationship among images, Lehmann simply filled the available zones, "wherever there was room."

Meanwhile, viewers—confronted by an ambiguous work, whose disposition is that of a study but whose facture is that of a finished painting, and invited to consider as a whole images that occupy contradictory spaces—find themselves on unstable ground. Thanks to the picture's polycentric structure, which only modern eyes could read as a picture, we are witnesses to a phase in the accelerating process through which unitary Renaissance space would be destroyed. Here academicism converges, despite itself, with the concerns of the avant-garde.

537. Gustave Moreau (1826–98). *The Suitors*. Begun in 1853. Oil on canvas, 11′5″×12′5½″. Musée Gustave-Moreau, Paris.

## Tiny, lost within the accumulations of an extravagant décor —the hero

Moreau pivoted the axis of his main event some 45 degrees so that the action—the confrontation of the hero and the suitors—occurs not parallel to the painting surface (as, for example, in the friezelike disposition favored by David), but perpendicular to it. Moreover, the staging of the scene required, just as the cinema frequently would, that the motor force of the action (Ulysses) appear not in the foreground—or even in the title—but at considerable remove, there almost absorbed by the architectural setting. (Nor does the position of the "central" character coincide with the center of the perspective, whose lines converge at the foot of the radiant figure of Minerva.) Dislocations of this nature elicit different readings at two separate times. First, we are encouraged to investigate,

wander through, and almost indulge ourselves in the sadistic or fetishistic phantoms that have been spread before us. Finally, on a second reading, we raise our eyes and discover the goddess, who through the intervention of Ulysses, rejects and punishes—but also permits and completes—this race of visionary beings.

Two worlds are in opposition here: that of the decadent suitors; and that of the virile avenger. Also two spaces: the horizontal spread of chaos, which resembles a chessboard strewn with wailing, languid, agonized bodies; and the vertical, rigid dimension formed not only by the architecture but also by the hero who surges up within it. A further conflict derives from two different styles: the careful delineation of everything related to the architecture (columns, paving, décor); and the "Venetian" luminism that melts and modulates the contours of figures. Then, there is the paradox of a distance that affects some forms but not others, for whereas the figures tend to dissolve as they recede into depth, the architecture retains definition all the way to the fluting on the most remote column.

While noting the aesthetic linkage between Delacroix and Moreau (whom a generation separated), Mario Praz, the great Italian historian, also emphasized what makes the two artists irreconcilable: "The first paints gestures, the other attitudes"; the one represents "Romanticism with his fiery, frenetic movement," the other "decadence with his sterile contemplation; their subjects are more or less the same—the exoticism of luxury and blood. But Delacroix lived it from within, and Moreau worshiped it from without. . . ."

538. Gustave Moreau. *The Suitors* (detail of Fig. 537).

# Notes

Introduction
1. This well-known distinction has been borrowed from Michel Foucault.

Chapter I
1. Jacques Foucart.
2. *Ingres* (N.Y., n.d.), p. 68.
3. *Ibid.,* pp. 19–20.
4. Rosenblum, *Ibid.,* p. 164.
5. "Rude Sublime: The Taste for Nature's *Colossi* during the Late 18th and Early 19th Centuries," *Gazette des Beaux-Arts* (April, 1976), pp. 113–126.
6. "Toward Romantic Landscape Perception: Illustrated Travels and the Rise of 'Singularity' as an Aesthetic Category," *The Art Quarterly* (autumn, 1977), p. 108.
7. *Ibid.*
8. *Jean-François Millet* (exh. cat., Paris, 1976), p. 236.

Chapter II
1. Cited by T. Todorov in *Théories du symbole* (Paris, 1977).
2. V. Alleton.
3. Meyer Schapiro, *Modern Art, 19th and 20th Centuries* (N.Y., 1978).
4. Published in France as *Discours des arts plastiques* (1867).
5. *The Fuseli Circle in Rome, Early Romantic Art of the 1770s* (exh. cat., New Haven, Conn., 1979).
6. Hélène Toussaint.
7. Germain Bazin.
8. *French Painting 1774–1830: The Age of Revolutions* (exh. cat., Paris and New York, 1974), p. 167.
9. *Ibid.,* p. 340.
10. *Romantic Art* (London, 1978).

Chapter III
1. As Italian semiologist Umberto Eco uses the term.
2. Quoted by Jean Starobinski.
3. Jean Starobinski.
4. Détienne and Vernant, *Les Ruses de l'intelligence: la métis des Grecs* (Paris, 1976).

Chapter IV
1. *Painting and Sculpture in Europe: 1780–1880* (Harmondsworth, Middlesex, 1960).
2. Maurice Sérullaz.
3. *The European Vision of America* (exh. cat., Wash., D.C., 1976), entry 315.
4. *Turner, Imagination and Reality* (exh. cat., N.Y., 1966), p. 53.
5. Edward Young, "Paraphrase of Job."

Chapter V
1. *English Neoclassical Art: Studies in Inspiration and Taste* (London, 1966).
2. *Piranèse et les piranésiens français* (Paris, 1976).

# Index of Artists and Their Works

The arrangement of this index is alphabetical for artists but serial for their works, with these listed, under the name of each master, by order of appearance in the book. The index also cites photographic sources wherever these are not the same as the collections cited in the legends accompanying the reproductions throughout the book. The index, moreover, identifies the collections owning the works that illustrate the

chapter-opening essays on pages 25–29, 97–101, 173–177, 213–217, and 253–257, where space limitations prevented complete citation. Comparable problems, in addition to the special character of the visual program for the Introduction (pages 4–23), have made it necessary to prepare a separate illustration list, with complete citations, for Figures 1–124. This material can be found at the end of the index.

316

# Full Citations for Figures 1–124

1. Mantoux and Cheyère. *The Romantic.* Satirical lithograph. Bibliothèque Nationale, Paris. Photo Hachette.
2. Ferdinand von Rayski. *Suicide in the Artist's Studio.* c. 1840. Kupferstichkabinett, Staatliche Kunstsammlungen, Dresden.
3. Francisco Goya. *The Idiot.* 1824–28. Photo Office du Livre, Fribourg.
4. Joseph Anton Koch. *The Painter at the Crossroads* (between the Baroque and Neoclassicism). 1791. Graphische Sammlung der Stattsgalerie, Stuttgart.
5. *The Great Battle between the Romantic and the Classic at the Door to the Museum.* 1827. Lithograph. Bibliothèque Nationale, Paris. Photo Hachette.
6. Joseph Vigné. *Romanticism, or the Literary Monster.* 1824. Litograph. Photo Hachette.
7. Horace Vernet. *Joseph Vernet, Lashed to a Mast, Studies the Effects of a Storm at Sea* (detail). 1822. Oil on canvas. Musée Calvet, Avignon.
8. The tranquilizing chair invented c. 1810 by the American physician Benjamin Rush. Engraving by Benjamin Tanner. Photo Snark.
9. Francisco Goya. *The Road to Hell.* 1819. Photo Office du Livre, Fribourg.
10. Francisco Goya. *Courtyard at the Madhouse.* 1794. Oil on canvas. San Fernando Academy, Madrid. Photo Mas.
11. Francisco Goya. *Madness Run Amok.* c. 1815–24.
12. Magician at work under the Empire. Engraving. Musée Carnavalet, Paris. Photo Bulloz.
13. Henry Fuseli. *Screech-Owl on the Body of a Woman.* c. 1820. Chalk and wash. Kupferstichkabinett, Kunstmuseum, Basel.
14. Francisco Goya. *"Who will deliver us?"* 1797–98. Engraving. Photo Office du Livre, Fribourg.
15. Caspar David Friedrich. *Screech-Owl on a Cross over a Grave.* 1836–37. Sepia wash over pencil. Pushkin Museum, Moscow. Photo L. Bogdanov/VAAP.
16. Louis Boulanger. *The Witches' Sabbath.* 1828. Illustration for the *Odes et Ballades* of Victor Hugo. Musée Victor-Hugo, Paris. Photo Bulloz.
17. Gustave Doré. *The Forest of the Damned.* 1861. Illustration for Dante's *Inferno.* Photo Hachette.
18. Victor Hugo. *The Dream.* Pen drawing. Musée Victor-Hugo, Paris. Photo Hachette.
19. Louis Boulanger. *The Phantoms ("Dead at Age Fifteen, Beautiful, Happy, and Adored").* Lithograph by C. Motte. Bibliothèque Nationale, Paris. Photo Hachette.
20. Henry Fuseli. *The Nightmare.* c. 1790. Oil on canvas. Goethe Museum, Frankfurt. Photo Peter Willi/Top.
21. *The Monster of Gévaudon.* c. 1770. Photo Edimages.
22. Henry Fuseli. *Woman Confronting the Laocoön.* 1801–05. Drawing. Kunsthaus, Zurich. Photo Walter Dräyer.
23. James Barry. *Satan, Sin, and Death.* c. 1790. Engraving. British Museum (courtesy of the Trustees), London.
24. Francisco Goya. *The Disasters of War.* c. 1810–11. Etching. Collection Torello, Barcelona. Photo Mas.
25. Victor Hugo. *Laces and Specters.* Drawing. Musée Victor-Hugo, Paris. Photo Bulloz.
26. George Cruikshank. *The Drunkard's Children.* 1848. Engraving. British Museum (courtesy of the Trustees), London.
27. Jacques Gamelin. *The Last Judgment,* from *Nouveau recueil d'ostéologie et de myologie.* 1799. Engraving by Martin.
28. Francisco Goya. *"Nothing. That's what he'll say,"* from the *The Disasters of War.* 1812–20. Etching. Photo Roger-Viollet.
29. Jean-Baptiste Carpeaux. *Guillotined Head* (after Géricault).
30. Project for a flying machine powered by pyroxylin combustion. *Leipzieger Illustrierte,* January 30, 1847. Photo Historisches Bildarchiv.
31. Étienne Louis Boullée. Project for the Newton Cenotaph. c. 1789–99. Lithograph. Bibliothèque Nationale, Paris. Photo Roger-Viollet.
32. Etienne Louis Boullée. Overall view of the interior of the Newton Cenotaph. c. 1789–99. Photo Snark.
33. Karl Friedrich Schinkel. Design for Mozart's *The Magic Flute.* 1815. Gouache. Bibliothèque de l'Opéra, Paris. Photo Snark.
34. Claude Nicolas Ledoux. *Meditation on the Birth of the World,* for the cemetery of the town of Chaux. 1804. Engraving by Bonivet. Photo Bibliothèque Nationale, Paris.
35. John Russell. *The Face of the Moon.* 1795. Pastel. City Museum and Art Gallery, Birmingham.
36. J.J. Grandville. *"He plays with the worlds,"* from *The Mysteries of the Infinite.* 1845. Engraving. Photo Roger-Viollet.
37. *Rouseau Botanizing.* Engraving. Bibliothèque Nationale, Paris. Photo Roger-Viollet.
38. A.Y. Brongniart. Installation plan for the park at Berny. 1786. Photo Musy/CNMHS.
39. James Hall. Reconstruction of a Gothic nave with poles, ash, and willow. 1798.
40. Le Rouge. Ideas for the construction of rocks in "Anglo-Chinese" gardens. 1734. Photo Musy/CNMHS.
41. Marc-Antoine Laugier. *The Primitive Hut* (the origin of the builder's art). Frontispiece to *Traité d'architecture.* 1753. Photo Musy/CNMHS.
42. Sham ruin suitable for habitation in the "Anglo-Chinese" garden of M. de Monville at Retz. 1780–81. Photo Musy/CNMHS.
43. Hubert Robert. *Imaginary View of the Louvre's Grande Galerie in Ruins.* c. 1799. Oil on canvas. Photo Snark.
44. Jacques Louis David. *Marie-Antoinette on Her Way to the Guillotine.* 1793. Drawing. Louvre, Paris.
45. Execution of Marie-Antoinette, October 16, 1793.
46. The Faubourg Saint-Antoine during the revolution of 1830. Lithograph by Villain, after Bodem, Private collection. Photo Snark.
47. Insurrection of February 24, 1848. Lithograph by Collette. Bibliothèque Nationale, Paris. Photo Snark.
48. Francisco Goya. *The Executions of the Third of May, 1808.* Prado, Madrid. Photo Hubert Josse.
49. Anne Louis Girodet. *Napoleon I.* 1812–14. Musée Girodet, Montargis. Photo Bulloz.
50. Jacques-Louis David. *Napoleon Bonaparte Crossing the Alps, May 20, 1800.* Oil on canvas. Musée du Château, Rueil-Malmaison. Photo Hachette.
51. Anne Louis Girodet. *Napoleon at Saint-Cloud.* 1812. Musée Bertrand, Châteauroux.
52. François Rude. *Napoleon Awakening to Immortality.* 1845. Photo Pierre Berenger.
53. William Hogarth. *The Two Apprentices.* 1747. Bibliothèque Nationale, Paris. Photo Lauros/Giraudon.
54. T. Allom. *Printing on Calico.* 1830. Engraving by J. Carter. Photo Edimages.
55. The Queen's crystal factory at Creusot. c. 1785. Engraving. Photo Edimages.
56. View of the old forge for the manufacture of rails at Creusot. c. 1850. Drawing by F. Bonhomme. Photo Roger-Viollet.
57. Thomas Farnolls Pritchard. The Iron Bridge at Coalbrookdale, England. c. 1779.
58. Joseph Paxton. Crystal Palace. 1853. Photo P.H. Delamotte.
59. George and Robert Stephenson. Locomotive. 1829. Photo Roger-Viollet.
60. Cugnot. Steam-powered road vehicle. Conservatoire des artes et métiers. Photo Hachette.
61. J.J. Grandville. *The French Painted by Themselves.* 1840. Musée Balzac, Paris. Photo Hachette.
62. J.J. Grandville. *Money.* c. 1845. Engraving.
63. Children working in the coal mines of Britain. Engraving from the *Magasin pittoresque.* Private collection. Photo Snark.
64. Youth mining coal in Britain. Engraving from the *Magasin pittoresque.* Photo Snark.
65. William Blake. Illustration for John Gabriel Stedman's *Narrative of a Five Year's Expedition against the Negroes of Surinam.* 1793. Engraving. History Department, Public Library, Cleveland.
66. Jean Honoré Fragonard. *The Curious.* c. 1765. Oil on canvas. Louvre, Paris. Photo Réunion de Musées Nationaux.
68. Gavarni. *A Loge at the Italians.* c. 1840. Lithograph by Frey. Photo Hachette.
69. Louis Bouilly. *An Assembly of Thirty-five Expressive heads.* c. 1825. Oil on wood. Musée des Beaux-Arts, Tourcoing.
70. Gavarni. *Behind the Scene.* 1838. Drawing. Bibliothèque Nationale, Paris.
71. William Blake. *The Laocoön.* Collection Sir Geoffrey Keynes.
72. *A Banquet,* illustraton for *La Vie parisienne.* 1853.
73. Benjamin Roubaud. *Caricature of Honoré de Balzac.* 1838.
74. Honoré de Balzac. Printer's proof. Bibliothèque Nationale, Paris. Photo Hachette.
75. Benjamin Roubaud. *Hugo and Paris.* 1841. Bibliothèque Nationale, Paris.
76. Roller coaster ("French mountains") at Beaujon Park. Drawing by L. Garneray, engraving by Lerouze. Photo Bulloz.
77. James Wyatt. Fonthill Abbey. 1796–1806. Bibliothèque Nationale, Paris.
78. Horace Walpole. Stairway at "Strawberry Hill." 1754. Photo Snark.
79. Antonio Canova. *Pauline Borghese as Venus Victrix.* 1804–08. Galleria Borghese, Rome. Photo Scala.
80. Etienne Louis Boullée. Project for a cenotaph in the Egyptian manner. c. 1789–99. Bibliothèque Nationale, Paris. Photo Snark.
81. Karl Friedrich Schinkel. Design for Mozart's *The Magic Flute.* 1815. Gouache. Staatliche Museen, Berlin.
82. Jacques Louis David. *Oath of the Horatii* (detail). 1784. Oil on canvas. Louvre, Paris. Photo Erich Lessing/Magnum.
83. Claude Nicolas Ledoux. Project for the prison at Aix-en-Provence. c. 1785.
84. Jean-Jacques Lequeu. Project for a cowshed. Early 19th century. Photo Roger-Viollet.
85. Jean-Jacques Lequeu. Le Rendez-vous de Bellevue, project for an observatory. Early 19th century. Photo Roger-Viollet.
86. Physionotrace portrait. Engraving by Chrétien, the inventor of physionotrace, after a drawing by Quenedey. Biblithèque Nationale, Paris. Photo Roger-Viollet.
87. G.H. Chrétien. Physionotrace device. Drawing by Quenedey. Bibliothèque Nationale, Paris.
88. Jean-Baptiste Sabatier-Blot. *Mme Sabatier-Blot* (detail). c. 1844 Daguerreotype.
89. Jacques Daguerre. *The Atelier of the Artist.* 1837. Collection Société Française de Photographie.
90. Nicéphore Niepce. *View Through a Window at Grasse.* 1829. Gernsheim Collection, Humanities Research Center, The University of Texas, Austin.
91. Jacques Daguerre. *A Paris Boulevard.* c. 1838. Daguerreotype. Bavarian National Museum, Munich.
92. *Château de Chambord.* September 19, 1843. Daguerreotype. Photo © Archives Photographiques/SPAADEM.
93. Nathaniel Dance. *Fuseli in the Study Hall at the Royal Academy.* British Museum (courtesy of the Trustees), London.
94. J.S. Deville. Plaster mask of the face of William Blake. 1823. National Portrait Gallery, London.
95. Henry Fuseli. *Self-Portrait.* 1780. Dawing. Victoria and Albert Museum, London.
96. Anton Raphael Mengs. *Self-Portrait* (detail). 1774. Uffizi, Florence. Photo Scala.
97. John Flaxman. *Self-Portrait.* 1778–79. Drawing. Collection Hales Owen. Reproduced by permission of the Governors of the Earls High School.
98. Jean-Baptiste Isabey. *Hubert Robert* (detail). Oil on canvas. Musée des Beaux-Arts, Orléans. Photo © Archives Photographiques/SPAADEM.
99. James Barry. *Self-Portrait* (detail). 1767. National Portrait Gallery, London.
100. Antoine Jean Gros. *Self-Portrait* (detail). Musée du Château, Versailles. Photo Roger-Viollet.
101. Anne Louis Girodet. *Self-Portrait* (detail). Drawing. Musée des Beaux-Arts, Orléans. Photo © Archives Photographiques/SPAADEM.
102. J.S. Cless *The Atelier of David.* Photo Roger-Viollet.
103. Jacques Louis David. *Self-Portrait.* 1794. Oil on canvas. Photo Roger-Viollet.
104. J.M. Langolis. *Jacques Louis David.* c. 1825. Drawing. Musée Carnavalet, Paris. Photo Lauros/Giraudon.
105. Fluery-Richard. *Ingres Posing in the Studio of David.* Copy by Flandrin. Musée Ingres, Montauban. Photo Guy Roumagnac.
106. Benjamin Roubaud. *"A la couleur grise, Monsieur le successeur de la maison Raphael, Michel-Ange et Cie."* Cariacture of Ingres. 1842. Lithograph.
107. Francisco Goya. *Self-Portrait.* 1815. Oil on canvas. Prado, Madrid. Photo Anderson-Viollet.
108. Francisco Goya. *Self-Portrait.* 1795. Drawing. Metropolitan Museum of Art, New York.
109. Ary Scheffer. *The Death of Géricault.* 1824. Oil on canvas. Louvre, Paris. Photo Roger-Viollet.
110. Théodore Géricault. The artist's hand sketched on his deathbed. 1824. Cabinet des Dessins, Louvre, Paris. Photo Réunion des Musées Nationalux.
111. Funerary mask of Géricault. Musée Fabre, Montpellier. Photo Claude O'Sughrue.
112. Eugène Delacroix. *Study for the Raft of the Medusa.* c. 1824. Drawing. Musée des Beaux-Arts (donation Granville), Dijon. Photo Bulloz.
113. A.M. Collin. *Delacroix at Age Twenty-six.* Drawing. Musée Carnavalet, Paris. Photo Lauros/Giraudon.
114. *Eugène Delacroix.* Caricature made for *Charivari.* Photo Roger-Viollet.
115. Delacroix in 1842. Daguerreotoype.
116. Cornelius Varley. *J.M.W. Turner.* 1820. Drawing. Graves Art Gallery, Sheffield.
117. T. Fernley. *J.M.W. Turner on Varnishing Day.* 1837. Photo Arts Council of Great Britain.
118. *Turner at Work.* Caricature for *The Almanach of the Month,* June 1846.
119. Ramsay R. Reinagle. *John Constable* (detail). c. 1799. Photo British Council.
120. G. Richmond. *Samuel Palmer.* 1829. National Portrait Gallery, London.
121. Caspar David Friedrich. *Self-Portrait.* c. 1800. Drawing. Statens Museum for Kunst, Copenhagen.
122. Caspar David Friedrich. *Self-Portrait.* 1810. Drawing. Staatliche Museen, Berlin.
123. Philipp Otto Runge. *Self-Portrait* (detail). c. 1802. Hunsthalle, Hamburg.
124. George Friedrich Kersting. *Friedrich in His Studio.* 1811. Oil on canvas. Kunsthalle, Hamburg.

# Acknowledgments

I have incurred many debts of gratitude in the course of preparing this book, and in acknowledging them I want to begin by expressing my warmest thanks to the historian Jean-Pierre Mouilleseaux, whose many suggestions and great generosity were a constant source of help and encouragement. I must also cite Jean Adhémar; Yve-Alain Bois; Allan Braham, the National Gallery, London; David B. Brown, of Oxford's Ashmolean Museum; Jean Cailleux; Jacqueline Christophe; Georges Didi-Huberman; Michael Doran, of the Courtauld Library in London; Jacques Foucart, curator at the Louvre; Pontus Grate, director, Stockholm Museum; Philippe Grunchec, librarian, École des Beaux-Arts; Jean Lacambre, Musée National d'Art Moderne; Monique Mosser; and Arthur Veil-Picard—all of whom have been unstinting in their offer of valued advice. Then, there are the museums and their accommodating curators, both in France and elsewhere, without whose ready cooperation my task would have been impossible. Among these I am especially eager to mention Marie-Pierre Foissy of the Musée Fabre in Montpellier; André Hardy at the Musée de Valenciennes; Catherine Lagrue and Vincent Rousseau in Nantes; Françoise Maison, Arras; Geneviève Monnier and Arlette Serullaz of the Louvre's Cabinet des Dessins; Dominique Recoules, Lyon; Françoise Raynaud, at the Carnavalet in Paris; and Annie Scottez, Musée de Lille.

As the text indicates, I have drawn on many sources. Particularly valuable were: Albert Boime, *The Academy and French Painting* (1971); Lorenz Eitner, *Neoclassicism and Romanticism* (1970); Walter Friedlander, *David to Da Delacroix* (1952); Pontus Grate, *Deux Critiques d'art à l'éopque romantique* (1959); Henri Lemaître, *Le Paysage anglais à l'aquarelle* (1955); Marie-Madeleine Martinent, *Art et nature en Grande-Bretagne au XVIIIe siècle* (1980); Fritz Novotny, *Painting and Sculpture in Europe, 1780–1880* (1960); Robert Rosenblum, *The International Style of 1800* (1956), *Transformations in Late Eighteenth Century Art* (1967), *Modern Painting and the Northern Romantic Tradition* (1975); Jean Starobinski, *1789, Les Emblèmes de la raison* (1973); and William Vaughan, *Romantic Art* (1978). My work has also been considerably enriched by a series of important exhibitions and the published scholarship that accompanied them: *Romantic Art in Britain* (Philadelphia, 1968); *Venise au XVIIe siècle* (Paris, 1971); *The Age of Neoclassicism* (London, 1972); *La Peinture romantique anglaise et les préraphaélites* (Paris, 1972); *Dessins français de 1750 à 1825* (Paris, 1972); *Landscape in Britain* (London, 1973); *De David à Delacroix* (Paris, 1974); *Ossian* (Paris, 1974); *Le Neo-classicisme français: dessins des musées de province* (Paris, 1974); *Füssli* (Paris, 1975); *Éloge de l'ovale* (Paris, 1975); *Millet* (Paris, 1975); *Piranèse et les Français* (Paris, 1976); *The Age of Louis XV* (Chicago, 1976); *La Peinture allemande à l'époque du romantisme* (Paris, 1976); *Jardins 1760–1820* (Paris, 1977); *Courbet* (Paris, 1977); *Greuze* (Dijon, 1977); *Le Spectacle et la fête au temps de Balzac* (Paris, 1978); *French 19th Century Oil Sketches* (Chapel Hill, N.C. 1978); *L'Art européen à la Cour d'Espagne au XVIIIe siècle* (Paris, 1979); *John Flaxman* (London, 1979); *The Fuseli Circle in Rome* (New Haven, Conn., 1979); *Les Arts du théâtre de Watteau à Fragonard* (Bordeaux, 1980).

Finally, the publishers join the author in their appreciation of the kindness shown by collectors in allowing their works to be reproduced here. Sir Edmund Bacon, Bart; Sir Alfred Brett; Lord Clark; Mme Jaeggli-Hahnloser; Sir Geoffrey Keynes; Mr. D. Oppé; the Marquis de Oquendo; the Earl of Plymouth; Mr. David C. Preston; the Marquis de La Romana; Lord Rothermere; the Marquise de Santa Cruz; Mr. Eugene Victor Thaw; Mme Vaudoyer; and the galleries of Jean Cailleux and Joseph Hahn have all been unusually generous to us.